BUREAUCRACY
IN A DEMOCRACY

AMS PRESS
NEW YORK

BUREAUCRACY
IN A
DEMOCRACY

By CHARLES S. HYNEMAN

HARPER & BROTHERS PUBLISHERS NEW YORK

Library of Congress Cataloging in Publication Data

Hyneman, Charles Shang, 1900-
  Bureaucracy in a democracy.

  Reprint of the 1950 ed. published by Harper, New
York.
  Includes bibliographies and index.
  1. Civil service—United States. I. Title.
JK42.H8   1978   353   74-6023
ISBN 0-404-11549-7

MANUFACTURED
IN THE UNITED STATES OF AMERICA

To CHARLES R. DENNY

whose leadership as Chairman of the Federal Communications Commission was the outstanding administrative achievement I observed during five years in the federal service.

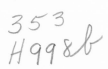

C O N T E N T S

PREFACE   ix

PART I. BUREAUCRACY AND DEMOCRACY: REALITY AND IDEAL

  1. Definition: Bureaucracy and Democracy   3
  2. Challenge: Bureaucratic Power   20
  3. Problem: Direction and Control   38
  4. Solution: Political Supremacy   56

PART II. DIRECTION AND CONTROL BY CONGRESS

  5. Giving the Bureaucracy Its Job   77
  6. Creating the Administrative Organization   94
  7. Providing the Money   119
  8. Fixing Standards of Administrative Conduct   137
  9. Reviewing the Action of the Bureaucracy   158
 10. Choosing Men for Jobs   176

PART III. DIRECTION AND CONTROL BY THE PRESIDENT

 11. What Are the Bureaucrats to Do?   207
 12. How Is the Administrative Branch to Be Organized?   219
 13. Who Gets How Much Money?   234
 14. Making Bureaucrats Behave   252
 15. Hiring and Firing   279
 16. Review and Instruction   299

PART IV. THE CENTRAL STAFF AGENCIES

 17. The Bureau of the Budget   325
 18. The General Accounting Office   355
 19. The Civil Service Commission   383

viii   *Contents*

PART V. DIRECTION AND CONTROL WITHIN THE ADMINISTRATIVE ORGANIZATION

20. The Organization and Its Head   421
21. The Formation and Coordination of Policy   441
22. Organization for Direction and Control   470
23. The Regulatory Commission   498
24. The Problem of Inefficiency and Red Tape   521

PART VI. THE UNIFICATION OF POLITICAL DIRECTION AND CONTROL

25. Congress, President, and Central Council   557

INDEX   581

P R E F A C E

This book is about a problem which is very much on the minds of the American people. What is the place of bureaucracy in the structure of democratic government? Stated another way: What can we do to increase our assurance that the officials and employees who do the day-to-day work of government will actually provide the kind of government the American people want?

I think no reader of this book is likely to question the importance of the problem. If I am condemned for having written a poor book instead of a good one, it will be because my efforts are not worthy of my aim. I may be pardoned, therefore, for saying a few words about the limitations upon my writing.

First, there is no point at which to start and no point at which to stop in an analysis of what we are up against in giving direction to the administrative branch of the government and exercising control over it. Human relationships do not have a starting place and a stopping place. Whatever may be going on today is the continuation of what was going on yesterday and the prelude to what will be going on tomorrow. Everything that is going on at any moment bears some relation, however remote, to a vast range of other things that are going on at the same time. When we subject a sector or segment of human affairs to minute observation, we blind ourselves for the time being to other matters which partially determine the nature of what we observe; when we describe with greatest care what we see, we unavoidably exclude from our description much that is necessary to a full understanding of what we see and describe. Any discussion of the place of bureaucracy in the structure of a democratic society is therefore of necessity only a fragmentary treatment of the problem in its whole implications. My decisions as to what to include and what to exclude in this study are accordingly arbitrary decisions and because of their arbitrary nature are bound to differ from the decisions which many of my readers would have me make.

Second, in writing about the place of bureaucracy in democratic government, I invite dispute with every reader. The American people have an abundance of beliefs about the nature of democratic government and about the nature of bureaucracy and its relation to democratic government. Many of these beliefs are the consequence of wish rather than of inquiry and observation. We see what we want to see. Anything that I say in this book will be set down in the mind of the reader side by side with what he already believes or wants to believe. I cannot discharge the burden of proof which is put upon me by the reader who challenges my statements. For the evidence which I can produce is only a part of the relevant evidence. And my view of the evidence, like that of the reader, is inescapably influenced by my preferences.

The pages of this book are spotted with "this I believe," "this I conclude," "this I propose." In the opening chapter I try to disclose, in so far as I understand it, the nature of my bias in respect to the nature of democratic government and bureaucracy, and the relation of one to the other. I think the reader has a right to know also something about the nature of the experiences upon which my convictions and preferences are based. Therefore the following brief account of my connection with administrative organizations.

Such knowledge as I have of the character of administration in the federal government was acquired mainly during five years in the federal service, from 1942 to 1947. This experience followed approximately fifteen years of teaching courses in American government and politics in three universities. As a faculty member, I was throughout this period a part of an administrative organization. What I observed and experienced as a member of three such organizations prepared me not to expect too much of the federal government and may help to explain why I now feel that administration in the federal government is something in which the nation can take a great deal of pride.

My initial employment in the federal government was in the Division of Administrative Management of the Bureau of the Budget. Perhaps this was as good an introduction to the federal service as I could have had. I was told to observe the way certain administrative organizations were doing their work and to report what I observed to my superiors in the Bureau of the Budget. I soon concluded that my judgment was not worth much on the matters with which I was concerned, but I also concluded that my deficiencies caused no great damage because I saw little evidence that anyone paid much attention to what I reported.

It took me nine months to get out of the Bureau of the Budget and into a job which I felt I was competent to handle. My new duties involved the arrangement of training in universities for military officers assigned to civil affairs in occupied territory. I stayed nearly two years in this position, most of that time with the title, Chief of the Training Branch, Military Government Division, Office of the Provost Marshal General, War Department. This experience involved very little of what we commonly call administrative responsibility. At no time did more than a half-dozen people report to me as their boss, and I was boss of that little group in only a limited sense. I did not hire the few people who worked under me, I could not fire them, and I gave them few instructions which I had not previously talked over with my own boss.

My only experience as the chief of an administrative organization of any size was for a period of thirteen months when I served as Director of the Foreign Broadcast Intelligence Service, a wartime activity of the Federal Communications Commission. I learned more about what is involved in directing a force of officials and employees in the first three months of this job than I had learned during the preceding two years and a half in the Bureau of the Budget and the War Department. In this position I had to find out for myself what I could believe and what I could not believe, learn whom I could trust and whom I could not trust, weigh alternatives, and make decisions. The organization was a small one (approximately 350 employees) and the operations were simple—listening to the radio broadcasts of foreign peoples, translating what was heard, selecting from the welter of words the particular content that any of a dozen federal departments and agencies might want to see, and laying it before them by teleprinter service and mimeographed publications. If a college professor who has never before had administrative responsibilities must be put in charge of other men in time of war, I can imagine no better way to break him in than to give him authority over an organization like the one entrusted to me.

Within a year after I took charge of the Foreign Broadcast Intelligence Service, a member of the Federal Communications Commission called me over to his office and said, "FCC will have to do five times as much work after the war as it did before the war. The place has got to be reorganized and the Commissioners do not have the time to work out a reorganization. Neither have the members of the staff. The members of this staff would not pay any attention to a stranger. They know you and would not be afraid that you are trying to organize them downward so as to organize yourself upward. The Commission wants you to move over to the Chairman's office to work out a new organization." I reassured the Commissioner, who reassured the other Commissioners, that my ambition was to find a lifetime berth in a university and not a lifetime berth in FCC, and a few weeks later I was reintroduced to my associates as Assistant to the Chairman of the Federal Communications Commission. That was in August, 1945.

If I had told the Commissioner everything on my mind at the time of the conversation just related, I would have said that FCC would be reorganized on the basis of hunch and not in accordance with any recommendations I might present. I figured the Commissioner knew this as well as I did, and if he did not mention it, I did not see why I should. I took the job because I thought there were other important things that I could do from the Chairman's office. This proved to be the case. The most crying need of FCC, in my opinion, was to examine everything that was going on, to quit doing things that did not need to be done, and to find better ways of doing the things that it continued to do. The direction of a program of work-review became my principal job. I stayed with it until I left the federal service in January, 1947; then I returned for a three-months period the following summer. Some indication of the nature of the work I engaged in can be found in Chapter 24 of this book. I may add that in this position, I came to have the title of Executive Officer and was given direction of the budget office, the personnel office, and the organization and procedures planning office.

Since so large a part of my education was obtained in FCC, I wish to acknowledge my great debt to the many associates in that organization who tried and tried again to help me understand the problems that are involved in giving direction to a force of officials and employees. I served under three Chairmen and nearly a dozen Commissioners; their toleration of my naïveté and occasional impertinence made it possible for me to stay in a position where I could learn. Undoubtedly I learned most from Charles R. Denny, Commissioner, later Acting Chairman, and finally Chairman; my admiration for his intellectual capacity and will to do is virtually unbounded. Others who contributed greatly to my understanding are: George W. Adams, William H. Irvin, Joseph J. Katsuranis, William B. Robertson, Russel M. Shepperd, George E. Sterling, Robert E. Stromberg, Charles R. Weeks, and Edwin L. White. I trust the many who are not mentioned will not think I have forgotten how patiently they explained things to me.

My debt to Colonel Jesse I. Miller is also great. He was my immediate superior in the War Department and provided me with constant proof that the impediments which adhere in bureaucracy fall away before a man who knows what he wants to do and makes clear to others what he wants them to do.

In the course of writing this book I asked many people for specific bits of information or for criticism of a particular statement which I proposed to make. I will not list them here, but I think the reader may be interested to know to whom I gave parts of my manuscript for careful reading and criticism. I believe that every chapter of this book was read by at least three persons who have had more experience than I in the matters referred to in that chapter. Every one of these people showed me how I could improve my manuscript. I could not make all of the changes which they advised, for many of them gave me contrary advice. No doubt there are many statements in the book which none of them will like. These persons (less one who prefers not to be named because of the nature of her position in the federal government) are: Joseph V. Barile, specialist in job classification, FCC; George Blanksten, formerly in the Office of the Coordinator of Inter-American Affairs and the State Department and now at Northwestern University; Daniel Borth, formerly charged with installation and supervision of accounting systems in the Quartermaster Corps of the Army and now on leave from the University of Illinois to assist in the improvement of accounting practices in the federal government; William C. Burt, attorney in the Civil Aeronautics Board; Paul Cohen, formerly in the Office of Price Administration and now at Northwestern University; David O. Cooper, formerly Budget Officer of FCC; Robert Cox, Budget Officer of FCC; Leon Crutcher, now in the State Department and formerly in three other federal departments and agencies; Robert A. Dahl, formerly in the Department of Agriculture and the War Production Board and now at Yale University; Melvin G. Dakin, formerly in the Securities Exchange Commission and now at Louisiana State University; Charles R. Denny, formerly Chairman of FCC and now Executive Vice President of National Broadcasting Company; James H. Hard, Director of Personnel in the Department of the Treasury and formerly in the Bureau of the Budget; Gilbert H. Hatfield, Director of Personnel, FCC; Walter P. Helwig in the Bureau of the Budget; W. K. Holl, Executive Officer of FCC and formerly in the Bureau of the Budget; Edward F. Kenehan, formerly attorney in FCC; Willmoore Kendall, formerly in the Inter-American Defense Board and Central Intelligence Agency and now at Yale University; Gordon J.

Kent, Finance Officer of FCC; Lynford Lardner of Northwestern University; Michael Liebovitz, Assistant Finance Officer of FCC; Duncan McIntyre of Cornell University; John Brown Mason, formerly in the Board of Economic Warfare and the State Department and now at Oberlin University; Wallace S. Sayre, formerly in the Office of Price Administration and now at Cornell University; Gilbert Steiner of the University of Illinois; Paul Van Riper of Northwestern University; C. Dwight Waldo, formerly in the Office of Price Administration and the Bureau of the Budget and now at the University of California; Herman Walker, now in the State Department and formerly in the Department of Agriculture; and Roland Young, formerly secretary of the Senate Committee on Foreign Relations and now at Northwestern University. I am deeply indebted to every one of the foregoing, but I wish it to be known that I made extraordinary demands upon, and received extraordinary assistance from, Daniel Borth, James H. Hard, W. K. Holl, and Willmoore Kendall.

Four of my students at Northwestern University—Lester B. Ball, Marvin Chaiken, Lawrence Herson, and Sander Vanocur—labored diligently to make this a better book than I could have made it without their help. Dorothy McCreery, Doris Gaston, John L. Robinson, Leonard A. Sawyer, and my daughter, Ruth Anne Hyneman, did far more than they were paid for in helping me put up the manuscript.

Finally I pay tribute to Esther Tager Havrylak. For four years, as my secretary, she guided me through red tape in Washington and saved me from many a disaster which I otherwise would have suffered. She put most of the first draft into readable form (not at government expense) and since I left Washington she has been a faithful observation post, reporting everything she thought I ought to know. One of my principal ambitions is to find another secretary like her.

CHARLES S. HYNEMAN

July, 1949

PART I

BUREAUCRACY AND DEMOCRACY:
REALITY AND IDEAL

CHAPTER 1

DEFINITION:

BUREAUCRACY AND DEMOCRACY

Ours is an age of political power. Everywhere people are turning to government to accomplish purposes that formerly were left to other institutions. The United States has had its New Deal. Great Britain has gone socialist. Government in Russia is both totalitarian and dictatorial.

Bureaucracy is an unavoidable consequence of modern government. The things that government does today cannot be accomplished by the enactment of laws alone. Men and women have to be employed in great numbers to put the policies of government into effect. And men and women, brought together to work in large organizations, constitute bureaucracy.

Bureaucracy as an abstraction is big organization, and any big organization is, specifically, a bureaucracy. When hundreds of men and women are associated together under a common directing authority for carrying on a common enterprise, certain characteristics are bound to emerge. Men and women who make up the organization cannot all be acquainted; consequently they are forced to communicate by paper, even when they would much prefer to talk face to face. One part of the organization does not know and cannot quickly find out what another part is doing. Delays occur in making decisions because it takes time to get the concurrence of the principal individuals who are concerned in the problem at hand.

3

We readily recognize these characteristics as the attributes of bureaucracy. One organization may hold inconvenience, circuitousness, and delay to a minimum, while another is an operating mess. No doubt we may properly speak of one as a "good" bureaucracy and another as a "bad" one. But each is a bureaucracy nonetheless if it is big enough to have characteristics of the kind mentioned above.

Bureaucracy is not limited to government, since large organizations of men and women are not peculiar to government. The concern of this book, however, is with governmental bureaucracy; more specifically with the administrative organizations of the federal government. A good many people in the United States are disturbed about bureaucracy in Washington. With some persons this concern is no more than a sense of uneasiness—a vague feeling of apprehension. With others the concern amounts to a feeling of genuine alarm. Some individuals, indeed, develop something like hysteria on the subject. It is high time, therefore, that we undertake a close examination of our national administrative organizations. A surer knowledge of how they are constructed and how they behave may either assure us that we have no cause for uneasiness or alarm, or show us where danger lies and guide us to corrective measures.

We will not have a dependable understanding of our federal bureaucracy—either what it is like or what it signifies—until many people, looking at it from different vantage points, have reported what they observe. This book, like any other book written by one man, can throw light on only a limited part of the entire area we need to explore. The reader is invited to examine through the pages of this book only those aspects of the bureaucracy that the author chooses to write about. And what the reader thinks he sees as a consequence of reading this book will be greatly affected by the writer's capacity as an observer and reporter—his opportunities to observe, the point of view from which he makes his observations, and his ability to put into words what he has to report. It is important, therefore, that the reader be forewarned, to the extent that the writer can forewarn him, as to the nature of the inspection which is to be undertaken—what aspects of the subject are to be examined, what assumptions underlie the analysis, what bias is likely to influence the author's evaluations.

It has already been said that this book is about the administrative organizations of the federal government. It is not concerned, however, with everything of importance related to those organizations. The primary concern of this book is to consider what can be done to make our federal bureaucracy function as the faithful servant of the American people. There is descriptive material in the book relating to the organization of the administrative branch, the character of its activities, and the nature of its behavior. But the descriptive accounts are limited to what seems necessary for an understanding and evaluation of what we do or might do to keep administrative officials and employees in their place. They are incidental to an analysis of how the bureaucracy is, or can be, given direction and kept in control. This book is not the place to look, therefore, for a comprehensive description of the structure of the administrative branch of the national government, or for a catalog of all the activities in which it engages, or for a systematic examination of the way in which it does its work.

So much for the area of concern. The assumptions which underlie the book and the bias which influences the author cannot be stated so readily or so accurately. Four things, at least, which affect the emphases, the reasoning, and the conclusions of this book must be brought to the attention of the reader. They are: (1) the conviction that bureaucracy must be judged by the way it uses its power, not by its size and what it costs; (2) the assumption that all people who possess authority of government, including those in administrative organizations, ought to exercise their power within limits that are acceptable to the American people as a whole; (3) the conviction that the great power which modern bureaucracy represents can be turned toward ends that are not acceptable to the people as a whole, and may be turned toward such ends if we do not provide proper direction and control for our administrative establishments; and (4) the conviction that elective officials must be our primary reliance for directing and controlling the bureaucracy. The first two of these underlying considerations will be discussed in the remaining pages of this chapter; the other two are examined in succeeding chapters.

The American people are disturbed about bureaucracy in Washington; many of us appear to be alarmed; some of us have developed something like hysteria on the subject. A great deal of what we say about bureaucracy—our questions, expressions of fear, attacks and denunciations—are directed to the size and cost of bureaucracy. Size and cost are significant facts, but we know what their significance is only when we consider size and cost in relation to something else. The great aggregation of land, sea, and air forces which we assembled in World War II was much too big and much too costly, if considered as a force for protecting the nation at a time when no one threatened our security; we thought it not too big or too costly at a time when we were waging war on two continents. So it is with the great administrative force we have built up in our federal government. It is big and it is costly. But is it too big and is it too costly? How do you tell whether the administrative branch of a nation's government is too big and too costly?

The size of our federal bureaucracy depends, ultimately, on two things—the activities we require the federal government to carry on, and the economy of manpower with which those activities are administered. The first of these factors is by far the most important. What do we want the government to do? In respect to our soil resources, do we want government only to protect and preserve our public lands? Or do we want it also to show farmers how to keep their land productive? Or do we want government to go so far as to build dams and reclaim great areas of desert lands? It takes a lot more people to do all of these things than it takes to do only the first of them. We can't move from a system of maximum free enterprise and minimum government control to a system of limited free enterprise and extensive government control without hiring government employees to do a lot of the work that formerly was done by the employees of private concerns. We can't have a New Deal without putting a lot of people on the public payroll.

The size of the bureaucracy does not depend exclusively on the scope of activity in which the government is engaged. If a department of the government is well managed, it will do its work with fewer employees than will be required if the department is not well managed. If the administrative branch as a whole is well managed, the federal bureaucracy will be substantially smaller than will be the case if poor management prevails throughout the federal service. But it must be understood that the size of the federal bureaucracy is far less affected by the quality of administrative management (economy in the use of manpower) than it is by the scope of activity which the administrative branch of the government has to carry out. Fifty years ago, the federal government employed about 200,000 people; today, more than 2,000,000 people (not counting men and women with military status) are working for the federal government. Fifty years ago, the total expenditure of the federal government for compensation of its working force was approximately $100,000,000; the comparable figure for today is about $6,500,000,000. Fifty years ago, the biggest administrative department of the federal government employed little more than 100,000 men and women. Today, the Treasury Department employs nearly 90,000 men and women; the Veterans' Administration employs more than 200,000; the Post Office Department employs more than 500,000; and the National Military Establishment (which combines the former War and Navy Departments) employs nearly 900,000 people over and above those in military service.

The difference in the size of the bureaucracy fifty years ago and today is not explained by difference in the efficiency with which manpower is used in the federal government. There is no reason to believe that the administrative departments of the federal government were better managed fifty years ago than they are today. The great increase in the size of the federal bureaucracy during this period is accounted for almost altogether by the projection of the government into a far greater scope of activities.[1] The total annual cost of the federal government at the beginning of the century was a little more than $600,000,000, and approximately one-sixth of that amount went to compensate people who were working for the government. During 1947–48, the whole cost of the federal government went above $32,000,000,000, and still approximately one-sixth of the whole amount was spent for personal services.

It seems clear enough that if anyone bases his distrust of bureaucracy on its size and its cost, he will have to give serious consideration to the activities which we require the federal government to carry on. Undoubtedly, we can reduce the size of the federal bureaucracy to some extent by effecting more economy in the use of manpower; but there is no reason to believe that the most competent management which the nation could provide would enable the federal government to do all the things we have it doing, without a force of officials and employees somewhere near what we have in the administrative branch of the federal government today. A campaign to reduce the size, and therefore the cost, of the federal bureaucracy to any substantial degree (say more than 15 percent) must be directed toward the withdrawal of the federal government from some of the activities in which it is now engaged.

Such a campaign might attempt to reduce or terminate some of the present activities of the federal government; it might, on

[1] Figures on federal employment are hard to find, and when found, are of doubtful accuracy. The figures given here for employment fifty years ago are taken from *Fifteenth Report of the United States Civil Service Commission, July 1, 1897, to June 30, 1898* (Government Printing Office, 1899), pp. 127–132. The figures for 1949 are taken from a large chart entitled *Organization of Federal Executive Departments and Agencies (data as of January 1, 1949) to Accompany Committee Report No. 5*, U.S. Senate Committee on Expenditures in the Executive Departments (Government Printing Office, 1949).

the other hand, attempt to transfer some of them to state or local governments. In the former case, the importance of bureaucracy in American life would be reduced; in the latter case, the size and cost of federal administrative organizations would be reduced, but the separate and scattered bureaucracies of state and local governments would be enlarged.

This book is not a part of either kind of campaign. The degree to which the American people shall use government—national, state, local—to perform services and regulate their affairs, is a political question. And the distribution of authority between the national government and the governments of lesser divisions is a political question too. Our decisions on these matters are the results of convictions about how governmental authority can and should be used to advance human welfare. In deciding whether to project the federal government into a new undertaking, or to push it farther into an old one, we should take into account the effect of the new undertaking on the size of the federal bureaucracy. And we should also take into account whether, by enlarging the bureaucracy in order to achieve certain values, we create or increase a danger that other things which we value even more will be destroyed. But the effect on the bureaucracy—its size and its portent—is only one of the considerations that must be weighed in making the political decision.

This book is not concerned with these basic political questions. To the extent that current criticism of bureaucracy reflects a dislike for the political decisions that have fixed the scope of governmental activity in the United States, that criticism will find neither support nor rebuttal in this book. There is no argument here about whether government ought to spend money on this or loan money for that, regulate this area of affairs or perform that type of service, move toward collectivism or recede from it. Neither does this book get into the argument as to whether any of the things we want done by government should be located in the national government or in state or local governments. This book is concerned only with a bureaucratic situation that is now in existence. It is based on the conviction that the power which lies in a great bureaucracy can be used for purposes of which the American people, as a whole, do not approve. But it is also based on a companion conviction—that the likelihood that the bureaucracy will use its power for purposes of which we do not approve depends primarily on the way in which it is directed and controlled, not primarily on its size and cost. The greater the number of people who are incorporated in our administrative departments, the more difficult will be the task of directing and controlling them, no doubt. But it is the question of whether we can, and how we can, direct and control bureaucracy—not the size and cost of bureaucracy—which makes it imperative that we subject our administrative arrangements to critical analysis at this time.

This brings us to the second of the considerations listed above as underlying this book and determining its character. Every opinion that is offered in this book rests on the assumption that the power of government, and therefore the power of the bureaucracy, must be exercised within limits that are acceptable to the American people as a whole.[2] That is another way of saying that administrative officials and employees must be put in their proper place and kept in their proper place within the democratic structure of our government.

Democracy and democratic government are terms that enjoy everyday use; but they have not yet acquired precise meaning. We use them to identify the kind of government we now have, and we use them to describe the kind of government we hope

[2] I purposely choose an imprecise phrase. I avoid use of such terms as "majority rule" or "will of the majority" in part because these terms have fixed and different meanings for different people but mainly because I think a great many crucial decisions are made at times and under circumstances when we have no sure way of knowing what most of the people want. I think the next few pages will make clear that I do not want smaller numbers of people to win over larger numbers when matters come to a showdown. For an earnest effort to state with preciseness the nature of the confusion that obtains in literature dealing with concepts in which "majority" is involved, see Willmoore Kendall, *John Locke and the Doctrine of Majority Rule* (Illinois Studies in the Social Sciences, vol. 26, no. 2, Urbana, Ill., 1941), ch. 1.

some day to get. There is a great difference, of course, between what we have and the ideal we look forward to; and there is a great deal of difference between one man's ideal and another man's ideal. It is apparent that misunderstanding is bound to occur in a discussion that makes use of the terms democracy and democratic government, unless the meaning which these terms are given is clearly stated and firmly adhered to.

The essence of democracy, as that word is used in this book, is respect for the individual. The measure of a man's devotion to democracy is determined by the strength of his conviction that men and women should be able to get what they want. The person who believes in democracy accepts the proposition that everybody counts. In a democracy, any man who manages to be born is entitled to consideration. He does not acquire a claim to consideration because he was born into a social class, or because he acquires wealth, or for any other reason that is applicable only to a part of the population; he is entitled to consideration because he is a human being. That is the root idea in democratic theory, as I see it.

It is not enough, however, to say that everybody is entitled to consideration. The next question is, how much consideration? No doubt the least democratic of us is moved by charity. No doubt all of us would have the government which we set up extend its protection to every man, woman, and child within the borders of the country. That is not enough to meet the minimum requirements of democracy, however. Government is our most powerful set of institutions. We turn to government to do things because government has the power to get things done. Government commands the loyalty of more people than any other institution, and it commands so high a loyalty that most of us obey its commands without contemplating resistance. It has the power to take our wealth from us and use it to compel us to do what we do not wish to do. We allow government to maintain men under arms whose sole job is to see that we obey its orders. And if we resist its commands, government may lock us up or take our lives.

A nation that is devoted to the principle that everybody counts must therefore insist that the mass of the people have control of the government. It must insist that the whole people control the government because it dare not let a part of the people do so. If a nation gives the control of the government to only a part of the people, it thereby establishes an incontrovertible fact that some of the people do not count. Government is democratic government only if it is government by the whole people.

The foregoing paragraph is accurate enough as a statement of a general principle. In broad and general terms, it states an ideal. The actual is a long way from the ideal, but we are a lot closer to this ideal than most nations, and there is reason to believe that we are steadily advancing toward our goal. We now have, established and operating, the institutions and ways of doing things that enable the mass of the people to control their government. Our problem from now on is to hold on to what we have, to extend and make stronger the institutions and ways that are essential to popular government. Bureaucracy must find its proper place within this pattern of essential institutions and ways. That is what this book is about—how to relate the federal bureaucracy and the power it possesses to the institutions and ways that are essential to democratic government. Since everything I say in this book is influenced by what I believe these essential institutions and ways to be, they must now be set forth more explicitly. They fall under six headings.

1. *There must be an inclusive electorate.* The right to vote is a license to share in the control of government. If we deny the right to vote to any substantial number of individuals who have a body of important interests not adequately represented by the rest of the electorate, to that extent we limit our democracy. No doubt the most democratic among us will approve the disfranchisement of foreigners who are not yet citizens (they have not been fully admitted to our society), minors (though many would lower the age requirement to eighteen years, as two states have done already), and persons who are in confinement because of

crime or insanity. But if we deny the vote to Negroes or any other sector of the population simply because those of us who have the upper hand at any time do not like them, to that extent we seriously impair our democracy. It is not a democratic government for Negroes in general if large numbers of adult Negroes are not permitted to vote, whether the disfranchisement be effected by force of law, by force of administration, or by force of community prejudice.

2. *There must be ways for the people to be informed.* The right to vote would be a mockery if people did not have ways and means of learning what is going on in the world, of finding what their interests are, of observing where other people stand in relation to their interests. There is no hope for democratic government unless there are facilities for communication which carry fact and opinion throughout the population; which make knowledge and supposition, desires and preferences, beliefs and prejudices, common property of all the nation. This means that there must be a system of education which provides the individual with the tools for learning. There must be agencies for the collection of news and opinion, and agencies for their distribution. There must be press service, newspapers, magazines, books, radio—not all of them, perhaps, but enough of them to give the people knowledge and understanding. And they must be in the hands of men who have both incentive and freedom to pick up and transport the raw materials which make up the mind of a nation. And finally, there must be freedom to talk and to listen, for talk is essential to knowledge and understanding. Talk carries forward in the community what the great channels of communication deliver at the door; talk refines what we think we know and think we believe; talk converts doubt into belief and belief into doubt; talk fixes in our minds what otherwise would soon slip from our grasp. Surely there can be no democracy where there is neither will nor freedom to talk and to listen.

3. *There must be ways for the people to get together.* This is an extension of what has just been said about arrangements for

people to communicate with one another. Common knowledge and common beliefs lay the foundation for common action. But for a nation to reach agreement on courses of action, there must be more than a common body of knowledge and belief. There must be organization for action in respect to matters of public interest. Some people must be in a position to make proposals and observe how other people react to their proposals. Some people must make it their job to bring other people together so that points of agreement and disagreement can be clarified and compromises can be reached. Some people must have opportunity to show their capacity to lead so that other people can be content to follow. All of this is the function of political organization and political activity. Only through political organization and activity can issues be defined so that people can relate their interests to the issues. Only in this way can candidates for office relate themselves to issues, and can the people at large relate their interests to candidates. Only in this way can a group of men stand together in an effort to capture the government, and give the people assurance that they will use their authority toward common ends once they have been given the job of running the government. It may be possible to have democratic government without well-defined political parties; surely there can be no democratic government without comprehensive political organization and vigorous political activity.

4. *There must be ways for recording the will of the people.* This is axiomatic; if the people are to control their government, they must have ways of indicating what they want their government to do. Our scheme of government calls for the people to elect officers who are given authority to run the government for the people. The people indicate their wishes in the choice they make between candidates. We have other ways of indicating our will, and politicians in and out of office keep their ears to the ground to hear what the people are saying. But we speak in unmistakable terms when we choose the men who are to exercise the authority of government; election day is the showdown in

our system of democratic government. This means that we must establish satisfactory ways of determining who is chosen for office —how names get on the ballot, whether a plurality is sufficient for an election, what happens if no one gets a majority where a majority is required. It also means that elections must be administered in a way which makes them an accurate reflection of the will of the people who go to the polls. If voters are deceived or intimidated; if votes are illegally cast, wrongly counted, or dishonestly reported—to the extent that any of these things happens, government by a clique is substituted for government by the people. If a nation cannot provide an honest administration of elections, it has little ground for hope that it can have government according to the will of the governed.

5. *There must be a structure of government which enables the elected officials really to run the government.* This proposition derives from the fact that the people speak authoritatively only in the election of public officials. If the people voted directly on issues, by referendum on legislation for instance, it would be less imperative that the elected officials be in a position really to run the government. But where the only accurate and official registration of what the people want is in the election of officials, then the individuals whom the people select for office must be able to put into effect the things to which they stand committed. This, in turn, requires that the bureaucracy must be under the direction and control of elected officials. If the elected officials cannot direct and control the bureaucracy, who is there to see to it that the bureaucracy provides the kind and quality of government that the people want?

6. *There must be a state of mind that causes people who have governmental authority to exercise it in keeping with their instructions or give up their positions.* Any large organization must operate in large part on faith. It is not possible to police all the individuals who hold important positions in the organization, coercing them to do what otherwise they might not do. Rather, the organization holds together from top to bottom and gets its work

done because men understand what others expect of them and voluntarily do what others expect them to do. This is so in government. The people can choose officials, but they cannot stand over them so closely and observe their work so intimately as to make it impossible for the elected officials to do anything except what they know the people who put them in office want them to do. We do not attempt any such intimate observation of our elected officials. Rather, we assume that they will voluntarily follow essentially the course they indicated they would follow before we put them in office. We assume that the man we elect has a quality of conscience that will cause him to live up to his promises, or that his fear of political punishment and his hope of political reward will cause him to put into effect (when he has the power to do so) the line of action that was popular enough in the campaign to win the election for him.

In like manner, we expect the officials and employees within the administrative departments to be quick to find out what their political superiors expect of them, and to do what is expected of them without waiting for coercion. Only if the host of men and women that make up our government have such attitudes do we stand a ghost of a chance that the people will actually get the kind of government they endorse on election day. And only if such attitudes prevail do we have the assurance that men will give up their authority when the voters have indicated that they have had enough of them. When we have a firm understanding throughout the population that officials and employees must seek to serve the people as the wishes of the people are authoritatively disclosed to them—only when that state of mind is firmly established can we be sure that men who are defeated for office will accept their defeat and not try to hold by force the authority they could not hold by appeal to the voters.

The foregoing paragraphs set forth the concepts of democratic government around which this book is written. Democratic government, as I conceive it, is not something which a nation decrees for itself, or which another nation imposes upon it. It is something that a nation grows into. There is democratic government only when there is vigorous competition for popular approval among men who for one reason or another desire to hold public office and to exercise the authority of government. There is democratic government only when a great number of men make public affairs their business, and in order to stay in business find out what is going on, harangue the public, and organize to put programs of action into practical operation. As I see it, the institutions and ways that I have described above provide just such a system of competition for political power and make government truly answerable to the people. We have advanced a long way toward the realization of that situation in the United States, though we have doubtless not reached what any of us consider to be our goal. Certainly we are challenged to constant vigilance, lest we lose what we believe we have gained. And just as certainly, one of the points to which we must direct persistent attention is the relation of the bureaucracy to those who are in a position to interpret the popular will.

We are now brought up to the third of the four assumptions (listed on pages 5–6) which underlie everything that is said in this book—my conviction that the great power which the bureaucracy possesses can be turned to ends that are not acceptable to the people as a whole, and that it may be turned to such ends if we do not subject the bureaucracy to proper direction and control. This proposition is the subject matter of the next chapter.

BIBLIOGRAPHIC NOTE

We now have in the English language an extensive literature which attempts to explain the nature of democratic government and to describe administrative organizations. We have very little literature, however, which attempts to show, in either comprehensive or incisive manner, the position of administrative organizations (the bureaucracy) in the structure of democratic government. I made a preliminary attempt at analysis in an article entitled "Bureaucracy and the

Democratic System," in *Louisiana Law Review*, vol. 6, pp. 309–349 (1945); I have borrowed freely from that article in this book. Max Weber, who wrote in German, is generally accredited with having made the most imaginative and incisive analysis of the essential characteristics of bureaucracy and of the relation of bureaucracy to the total structure of government. The most significant of Weber's observations are available in English in H. H. Gerth and C. Wright Mills, *From Max Weber: Essays in Sociology* (New York, 1946), pp. 196–244. Two articles which follow Weber's analysis are P. Selznick, "An Approach to a Theory of Bureaucracy," in *American Sociological Review*, vol. 8, pp. 47–54 (1943); and R. Bendix, "Bureaucracy: The Problem and Its Setting," in the same journal, vol. 12, pp. 493–507 (1947).

Carl J. Friedrich and Taylor Cole, in their *Responsible Bureaucracy; a Study of the Swiss Civil Service* (Cambridge, 1932), pp. 8–28, offer an elaborate definition of bureaucracy, but the style of writing discourages rather than invites reading. The essential part of this essay appears in more readable form in Mr. Friedrich's *Constitutional Government and Democracy* (Boston, 1946), chapter 2. Other definitions, descriptions, and explanations of the nature of bureaucracy which are worth examination include the essay "Bureaucracy" by Harold J. Laski in the *Encyclopædia of the Social Sciences*, vol. 3, pp. 70–73; an essay by John A. Vieg (distinguished by its facility of expression) in *Elements of Public Administration*, edited by Fritz Morstein Marx (New York, 1946), pp. 51–71; J. M. Juran, *Bureaucracy: A Challenge to Better Management* (New York, 1944); and a symposium edited by Goodwin Watson which appeared in *Journal of Social Issues*, vol. 1, No. 4 (December, 1945).

A great deal more has been written about democratic government than about bureaucracy, but much of the literature relating to the former subject confuses rather than clarifies our understanding because it mixes up rather than differentiates the ideals of democracy, the conditions of living that facilitate or hinder our advance toward those ideals, and the institutions and ways of doing things that constitute democratic government. One assumes a great risk in selecting some items out of the great mass for listing as best references. The following seem to me to represent some of the more successful attempts to identify, describe, and evaluate the institutions and ways that collectively constitute democratic government: A. D. Lindsay, *Essentials of Democracy* (London, 1935); A. D. Lindsay, *The Modern Democratic State* (vol. 1, New York, 1947); Joseph A. Schumpeter,

Capitalism, Socialism and Democracy (second edition, New York, 1947); C. Delisle Burns, *Democracy* (London, 1935); David Bryn-Jones, *Toward a Democratic New Order* (Minneapolis, 1945); and Alfred M. Bingham, *The Techniques of Democracy* (New York, 1942), particularly chapters 1 to 3.

CHAPTER 2

CHALLENGE:

BUREAUCRATIC POWER

Two million men and women work in the administrative departments of the federal government. Two million men and women, working under common direction, have a vast power over the rest of us. What is the nature of this power? Is it power for good or evil, or only for good? If it is power for evil as well as for good, what evil can these men and women do if directed to evil ends? And what precautions can we take to increase our assurance that the few who direct the many will have ends in view that the nation as a whole finds good?

Many people will regard these questions as evil in themselves, suggesting that officials and employees of the federal government are working against the American people rather than for them. Federal employees, they will say, have not the slightest desire to overthrow our form of government or destroy the liberties of the people. They are not organized for any concerted action to such ends; if a leader tried to direct them to such purposes, they would not follow him. This is undoubtedly true. The officials and employees of the federal government are typical American citizens. They are just as devoted to our ideal of government by the people and just as loyal to our form of government as the farmers of Indiana; they would be as reluctant to leave their homes in the evening and join in a conspiracy against the people as the bankers of Iowa, or the lumbermen of Minnesota.

But just as there are more ways than one of destroying a house, there are more ways than one of defeating the will of the people and destroying the foundations of democratic government. If I hire a man to take care of my house, he may, without any intention whatever of causing me harm, let it fall apart for want of repair, burn it down through carelessness, or leave the door open for my enemy to come in and demolish the entire structure. I may feel less angry toward the caretaker if my loss is due to his incompetence and carelessness rather than to deliberate intention to do me harm, but the injury is the same in either case.

So it is with our federal bureaucracy and its relation to our democratic institutions and ways. It is not enough to know that public officials and employees subscribe to democratic theory and would not intentionally weaken our system of popular government in any way. It is necessary to establish every assurance that they do not inadvertently, through carelessness, ignorance, or incompetence, do things or create situations that defeat the will of the people, destroy faith in popular government, or play into the hands of opponents of our system of government by the people.

The seriousness of any default or misdeed of the bureaucracy will depend, of course, on its character and the circumstances under which it occurs. Bureaucratic behavior that thwarts the will of the people on small things or temporarily, is not as serious as behavior that nullifies a basic program that the people have clearly endorsed. A practice that merely causes impatience and irritation is not as serious a matter as a line of conduct that causes people to conclude that our democracy is a farce. To shake the people's confidence in popular government at a time of general tranquillity is less serious than to excite distrust when the people are torn by antagonisms and uncertainties and when forceful leaders are bidding for power on appeals that deny the validity of democratic assumptions. It makes a difference whether the occurrence is the unintended result of a chain of circumstances, or the directed plan of a leader with power and prestige who is trying to carry out a program regardless of its acceptability to the people.

The possibility and the prospect that two million federal officials and employees may purposely or inadvertently do the nation harm will be affected by the way these men and women are organized. The great federal bureaucracy is many bureaucracies. The two million men and women are, in some measure, bound together as a great working force. They have a degree of loyalty to one another. They are capable of working with some degree of unison toward a common end. But these same men and women are drawn more closely together in segments of the whole. They work in organizations called departments, commissions, agencies, government corporations, and so on. They are likely to be more conscious of loyalty to their respective departments and agencies than to the great composite which we call the federal service. Some of these agencies (the Federal Trade Commission or the Civil Aeronautics Board, for instance) are small enough in number of employees and limited enough in kinds of activity that everyone in the organization knows a great deal about what everyone else is doing. The officials and employees of such an agency may be so closely united in their relations with one another that we say they constitute a tight little bureaucracy; we see the members of such a group maintaining a certain amount of independence from the rest of the great mass of federal officials and employees and protecting their special interests where they appear to clash with the interests of officials and employees who are not in their group.

The great executive department (the Department of Commerce or the Department of Interior, for instance) may seem more like a small edition of the whole federal service than like a large edition of the small agency. The lines of greatest loyalty may be to a division of the department, rather than to the department as a whole. There are so many officials and employees who are engaged in activities so divergent in character that men and women in one sector of the department know little about what those in another sector are doing. The department as a whole may thus be no more than a loose federation of separate and compact bureaucracies, each of which is so concerned about its own interests that its members scarcely recognize an interest in common with the men and women who work in other parts of the department.

The divisive effect of the organization of the federal service into departments and agencies and subdivisions of departments and agencies is enormously augmented by the fact that the great force of federal officials and employees is scattered throughout the United States and its possessions, and, in lesser degree, in foreign countries. Less than 10 percent of the civilian working force of the federal government was located in the national capital in 1948.

The fact that the federal service is sectored and segmented in this way has a great deal to do with the possibility and prospect that the officials and employees of the federal government may be set upon purposes of which the American people as a whole do not approve. The feeble character of the lines of communication and the weakness of the bonds of loyalty between different parts of the public service make it difficult for any leader, or small group of leaders, to change the course of the federal bureaucracy as a whole and move it quickly in any direction to which they may point. We are confronted by the fact that the men and women whom we elect to the political branches of the government will have to overcome resistance in getting their policies put into operation; but we have the comfort of knowing that any group of men who may get into the highest offices of our government against the will of the nation will find our federal bureaucracy an instrument which responds only slowly to the achievement of their purposes.

It follows from the foregoing that popular satisfaction with the performance of the bureaucracy will depend in great part on the character of the leadership under which the bureaucracy does its work. If we conclude that the bureaucracy will much of the time be led by men whose goals are not acceptable to the predominant part of the people, we may decide to preserve and strengthen the arrangements which make for slow response to leadership. If, on the other hand, we feel sure of our ability to provide leadership in which the nation has highest confidence, we may confidently install the arrangements for direction and control which give promise that the bureaucracy will respond more readily to the instructions which are given it.

The selection of the leadership under which the bureaucracy does its work is a function of the political system of the nation. The goal of politics is to control the activities of government; the activities of government are carried on by the bureaucracy; whoever controls the bureaucracy controls the activities of government. The political system of the United States gets its fundamental character from the American concept of democracy. It responds to the institutions and ways which were set forth in the opening chapter of this book as making up the American style of democratic government. By popular election we choose the men and women who compose the political branches of the government—Congress and President. We give the political branches of the government authority to direct and control the bureaucracy.

Our confidence that Congress and the President will have the bureaucracy doing things that the American people want it to do will be in direct proportion to our confidence that the political organization and electoral system of the nation puts into those two branches of government men and women who are eager to provide the kind of government that the people want. If the political organization of the nation is healthy and the electoral system truthfully records what the people say they want, then Congress and President, in the decisions they make and the instructions they give, will reflect with reasonable accuracy what the people want. We are always confronted by the possibility that the Presidency may fall into the hands of a man who is a poor judge of what the people want, or who willfully sets forth to achieve objectives which even he admits do not have the support of most of the people. Congress is less likely to offend in these respects, for the representative assembly consists of many men, chosen by segments of the electorate residing in all parts of the nation. If the President would make the bureaucracy an instrument to achieve his own goals, Congress can stop him, for it has authority in crucial matters which makes it impossible for the bureaucracy to do for more than a short time what the majority of Congress are unwilling to have done.

In considering the possibility and the prospect that the bureaucracy will do us harm, therefore, we are concerned with more than the power which is inherent in two million men and women devoting their energies to programs of government. We are concerned also with the leadership under which they are to work. We are concerned with the evil which the bureaucracy can do because of the slowness or inaccuracy with which it responds to the instructions that come to it from the men and women who have been chosen by the people to give the bureaucracy its orders. But we are also concerned with the evil it can do if the men who give the bureaucracy its orders (because of weakness in our political system) do not reflect with reasonable accuracy what the people want.

The importance of maintaining a system of government which subjects the bureaucracy to elected officials in whom the people have confidence can be fully appreciated only if we have some understanding of the things which the bureaucracy can do to the injury of the people. What are the things—specific acts, standing practices, underlying policies, states of mind—that singly or collectively may defeat the public will and undermine our democratic system of government? Some of them are things which we may think of as spontaneous action of men and women in the lower ranks of the bureaucracy—personal qualities and working habits which result in what we commonly call inefficiency, for instance. Some of them are things into which the great mass of lesser officials and employees may be led by men who occupy the higher offices of the administrative branch. Still others are things which will only come about if the President or other men who occupy high places of political leadership set about using the bureaucracy to further their ends. If the possibilities of abuse which are pointed out in the following pages appear worthy of serious concern, it will be necessary to consider whether they can be avoided by safeguards within the administrative branch, or whether the measures for their prevention must be found in the political system of the country.

I am not aware of any attempt to classify in a systematic fashion the things which the bureaucracy can do, with or without purposeful leadership, to provide a style and quality of government which the people do not want, or to undermine the foundations of our system of popular government. The things that seem to me to be worthy of most serious consideration fall under the following heads: (1) administrative officials and employees may interfere with or prejudice elections; (2) they may misinform the people about the issues that confront the public, about how these issues may be dealt with, and about what is being done to meet them; (3) they may inaugurate and pursue policies of government that are positively contrary to the public will; (4) they may fail to take the initiative and supply the leadership that is required of them in view of their relation to particular sectors of public affairs; and (5) they may, by sheer inefficiency in their operations, destroy popular faith in democratic government.

1. *Prejudicing Elections.* The chief executive and many of our highest administrative officials are leaders of political groups. They got in office by winning elections; they hope to stay in office by winning elections. It is natural that they should seek to win elections by whatever means seem promising, including the use of the governmental authority and power that they may control.

In some countries, the group that gets in power uses the army to break up opposing political parties, to control voting, and to destroy the whole system of free elections. We appear to be safely past that stage in the United States. But the great organizations of civilian public employees can be used to the same end. State and city police forces can break up political meetings, scare people away from the polls, destroy ballot boxes, line up illegal voters, and what not. A state highway department can plaster the telephone poles of the state with posters, coerce voters by putting them on and off the payroll, haul people from precinct to precinct for multiple voting, and do a lot of other things that you and I would consider reprehensible. These things are so familiar to us that illustrations need not be extended.

This sort of thing is not a serious problem in the federal government today. We take it for granted that the FBI will not line up voters for the party in power, and that the employees of the Department of Agriculture will not break up political meetings. The country, by common consent, long ago put a stop to skullduggery of this sort in the federal government. We wrote the latest chapter in that book of reform during the past decade when we enacted the Hatch Act and supplementary legislation making it illegal for federal employees to participate in the activities of political parties. A good many people think we went too far in that particular bit of legislation; it may be that, in our zeal to keep our public officials and employees from exercising an undue influence on the political opinions and actions of others, we denied them a privilege and deprived everybody else of a source of knowledge and understanding that is essential to popular government.

The fact that we have eliminated the more obvious forms of campaign and election-day skullduggery must not lead one to suppose that those who are in control of the federal government find no way of using the power of government to influence elections and make sure their continuance in power. They act in more subtle fashion; the purpose of the act is rarely admitted and frequently hard to identify. Necessary action on legislation is delayed until after elections; contracts are granted or refused; the enforcement of the law grows more lax for some and more rigid for others; important prosecutions are stalled or dropped altogether.

These are things that may be done on the grand scale under the lead of the President, with or without the concurrence of

Congress. They may be the act of a particular administrative department under the lead of a cabinet officer. They may be the program of a bureau chief or the official who heads a local office of a great department. And these are things that may vary only in the slightest degree from the most honest and impartial administration of government. Every popular act of the government is a bid for votes for the party in power, since a program that satisfies the people is the strongest reason for continuing the Administration in power. How are you and I to know when the Administration puts a partisan or dishonest twist on its action for the precise purpose of picking up some votes that wouldn't otherwise be had?

The question of what is proper and what is improper use of governmental power for the purpose of winning elections goes to the very heart of democratic theory. It has not, I believe, been subjected to sharp and comprehensive analysis in studies of government and politics. This book will not attempt to examine the nature and extent of such practices; I hope, however, that it will throw some light on how they may be discouraged or eliminated, insofar as use of administrative organizations is concerned.

2. *Misinforming the Public.* Free elections become a farce if the people do not have sufficient knowledge to support judgments on political questions. Democratic government cannot exist unless the people have access to reliable information on current issues, and are able to participate in the kind of discussion that clarifies their minds and enables them to take intelligent positions on the questions that confront them.

A great part of the information that is relevant to the issues of the day is in the possession of men and women in the administrative branch. They are the ones who know best what the government is actually doing. If they do not also understand better than anyone else what the issues are where policy is undergoing debate, at least they have the fullest information on some aspects of the questions at issue.

It is essential, therefore, that most, if not all, our administrative officials report to the public frequently and fully. And it is most desirable that their reports be truthful and unbiased. But that is much easier to ask for than to get. Public reporting is a part of the politics of the day. The President and his political associates stand on the achievements of the Administration. A good part of the record of achievement consists of the accomplishments of the administrative departments and agencies. High administrative officials who have political sense and political interests (and I presume that most of them do) recognize this and are influenced by it in their reporting. Even a report that is completely honest and unbiased is a political document. If it tells a story of accomplishments that cheers the hearts of the people, it is an argument for continuing the party in power; if it is a record of mistakes and failure, it is a weapon in the hands of the attacking party. But we have not yet found a way of guaranteeing that the administrative official will report truthfully and objectively. If the record is not wholly to his credit, he may sweeten it by omitting this, emphasizing that, and putting a favorable interpretation on something else. If an unavoidable disclosure is bad and cannot be made pleasant, he may time the release for the moment when it is likely to receive the least public attention.

Whatever be the character of the report, it is paid for with your money and mine. It is prepared by public officials and employees; the costs are borne by taxes. You and I thus pay to hear or read the story of what the group in power say they have done or propose to do. Whether it be annual report, press release, or radio address, the report we get is frequently designed not to give the voter the low-down but rather to convince him that those in office should be kept in power.

The relation of public reporting to partisan advantage is now pretty widely appreciated, and a good many people have urged that we do something to limit the influence which those who hold office exert through their reports. So far, we have not made much progress along that line. It is frequently suggested that the volume of public reports should be greatly reduced. The problem is, of course, too complicated for so simple a solution; an undue advantage for the party in power ought not to be remedied by cutting the voter off from the information he needs. Other proposals which have been made to date seem to be equally unsatisfactory.

3. *Pursuing Policies Contrary to the Popular Will.* One of our most treasured maxims is that we have a government of law and not a government of men. The statement has two implications: (a) that all basic policies should be determined by the legislative department; and (b) that administrative officers, in carrying out those policies, should proceed according to announced rules and standards, and not act in an arbitrary or capricious manner. Both these implications of the maxim are sound ideals for democratic government.

The representative lawmaking assembly is an indispensable feature of democratic government. It was by seizing the power first to advise the king on policy, then to veto the king's proposals, and finally to propose and decree public policy by enactment of statutes, that the people of England who were represented in Parliament got control of their government. The failure or inability to establish sturdy and stubborn representative lawmaking bodies is a principal explanation of why the common man has not been able to get a firmer control over government in continental European countries. Even so, the first act of the dictator of our era has been to take over or dissolve the representative assembly, and so remove a primary source of organized opposition to his will.

In our own country, the lawmaking power was firmly lodged in Congress by the federal Constitution. The President shares with Congress the power to enact statutes, and has some power to make law by his own decree. The Constitution, under the construction consistently given it, vests very little authority of the latter kind in the chief executive, however; such power as it gives him to make law by decree arises out of certain specific provisions, the most important of which is the grant of authority to act as commander-in-chief of the armed forces. The situation is different in several of our states. In some states, the governor and other executive officers have virtually no power except that given them by act of the legislature, but in several other states, the Constitution vests directly in the governor and certain other departments of government a very considerable power to make public policy. This practice of removing blocks of governmental authority from the control of the representative assembly has undoubtedly been carried to its extreme in the case of various state commissions that have been given power to make the law on certain matters, interpret it, adjudicate alleged violations, fix penalties, and order punishment. The whole legislative, judicial, and administrative functions are thus combined in one body with no provision for check by any other governmental authority except the power of the legislature to withhold funds and the power of the courts to find the whole arrangement contrary to the United States Constitution.[1]

As a nation, we know better than to do this. Congress is not likely to try to vest such a complete mixture of power in the President or any administrative department of the national government, except possibly for a limited period during war. If it did, the courts would doubtless declare the act unconstitutional. Such combinations of power provide too little assurance that men will have to answer to other men for what they do.

But our concern that administrative departments and agencies get their instructions from the lawmaking body and be required to obey those instructions is by no means due entirely to a fear that administrative officials and employees may try to tyrannize over us. We want the day-to-day business of government to ac-

---

[1] There appears not to be in print an analysis of the exercise of authority by state administrative agencies which have been given these mixtures of power. Several constitutional provisions which vest this amount of power in administrative agencies, and instances of the exercise of extraordinary authority, are cited in Charles S. Hyneman, "Administrative Adjudication: An Analysis," in *Political Science Quarterly*, vol. 51, pp. 383–417, 516–537, at p. 392 (1936), reprinted in *Selected Essays on Constitutional Law* (Chicago, 1938), vol. 4, reference at pp. 497–498.

cord with the standards we have set for it. Legislative supremacy
over administration is a device for making sure that we get the
kind of government we pay for; it is our way of making sure
that we get equal treatment from our public servants.

This does not mean that administrative officials must be so
clamped down by instructions that they have no room for honest
and imaginative exercise of judgment. General expressions of
policy have to be fitted to a great variety of specific situations
and this undoubtedly necessitates extensive delegations of authority to administrative officials. Whether these delegations are
compatible with democratic ideals or not depends on the importance of the affairs to which they relate and the degree of
assurance we have that the administrative official, in the exercise
of his discretion, will have to stay within the bounds of popular
approval.

The ability of an administrative organization to abuse its power
is not measured entirely by the sweep of its grant of discretion.
It may effectively extend its authority by taking preliminary
steps which so prejudice a situation that the legislature has little
choice but to confirm and extend the policy tentatively established by the officials and employees of the bureaucracy. By the
emphasis it gives to administration—vigorous action here, little
attention to that, no action at all in these cases—administrative
officials and employees may convert a carefully worded policy
of the legislature into something the legislature did not intend
and would not approve. And, if it is not adequately directed and
controlled, the administrative organization can nullify almost any
purpose of the legislature by inaction.

4. *Initiative and Leadership.* The emphasis of the discussion
up to this point has been on the possibility that power will be
abused, and upon the necessity of curbing such abuse. Safeguards
against abuse of power can be carried to the point where the administrative official is stripped of the capacity either to plan or to
act. Certainly we want to stop short of that in providing direction and control. Any official who has power can find ways of

abusing it, but we must nonetheless give men the authority necessary to get the work of government done. The administrative official may slant his reports to his own advantage, but we must nonetheless insist that he report on his doings.

We have apparently gotten to the point in America where we turn to government as the way of getting ourselves out of about every bad hole that we fumble our way into. Solutions for difficult problems do not occur to all of us. If someone puts forward a good idea for dealing with a tough problem, we are likely to put him in office and tell him to do the job. We put him there because we want the problem hitched up to his ideas and his energies. If he loses his vision, he loses his greatest usefulness. If he loses his courage, the job will not be done. If he quits telling the people what he thinks they ought to do, the people will not be able to play their part in solving the problem.

The administrative official who is put at the head of an important department of government has need for qualities that most of us do not have. He must be aggressive otherwise, the job will not be done. He must announce his convictions and stand by them; in no other way can the public know whether to support him or tell him to quit. He must have the courage to disregard the demands of individual Congressmen who think they are Congress. He may even have to speak out against Congress itself; for he is often a leader of the political party of the President, and has been given his position in the government with the expectation that he will use it to advance the President's program.

These qualities are essential in the high administrative official if government is to cope with the problems we put upon it. He must be imaginative in conceiving his program; bold in explaining it; ingenious in executing it; and firm in defending it. It is possible that government in America fails to accord with the will of the people fully as much because administrative officials fail to rise to these demands for initiative and leadership as because they overextend the authority that is given them.

But in his eagerness to meet the demands upon him, the administrative official must not deceive the President, Congress, or the people, or so commit them to a program that they cannot repudiate it without disaster. And when the political branches of the government have authoritatively expressed themselves, the official must obey or resign. This is essential to our design of government by the people.

5. *Inefficiency of Government.* Government is created and maintained in order to do things. If it doesn't do these things at all, it has no excuse for being. If it doesn't do them well, it has no claim on the confidence of the people.

The administrative branch carries the principal burden of putting the policies of government into effect. If the administrative organizations do what we expect them to do with dispatch, with due regard for the convenience of the public, and with economy of manpower and materials—in that case, we say the organization is efficient. If the organization offends too badly on any of these points, we say it is inefficient.[2] It makes a lot of difference whether the administrative establishments of the government are efficient or inefficient. If the administrative establishment is inefficient, the people may not get the kind and quality of service they thought they had provided for. As inefficiency mounts, the size of bureaucracy and the cost of government increase. As size of the bureaucracy increases, the difficulties in controlling it become greater. As the cost of government goes up, the possibility of undertaking additional desirable programs is diminished.

Too much inefficiency too long continued may even undermine our entire democratic system. No government will long be tolerated by an intelligent and free people if it consistently fails to do the things the people want it to do. When they get all out of patience with reform movements and repair jobs that still

---

[2] The precise and the popular meanings which are conveyed by the words "efficiency" and "inefficiency," and the risks we run in using them, are discussed below on pp. 521–522.

leave them without the kind of government they want, the people may be induced to turn their government over to someone to run it for them, without assurance that they can take it back.

BIBLIOGRAPHIC NOTE

Since the activities and undertakings of modern government are put into operation primarily by administrative organizations, the authority of administrative officials and employees is virtually coextensive with the whole range of government action. There is no single volume which describes the authority of the administrative branch of the federal government in a systematic and critical fashion. General statements of what the various administrative departments and agencies do can be found in the *United States Government Manual* (Government Printing Office, Washington). New editions of the *Manual* and supplements to it appear frequently. The *Congressional Directory*, which is also published at frequent intervals by the Government Printing Office, indicates very briefly what the major activities of the various departments and agencies are. Over a period of several years, beginning in 1918, the Institute for Government Research (later absorbed in the Brookings Institution, Washington, D.C.) published approximately 70 volumes in a series called Service Monographs of the U.S. Government, each of which was a study of the authority, organization, and activities of one of the administrative establishments (or subdivision of an administrative establishment) of the federal government. Several years later, the Brookings Institution made a much briefer, but perhaps more critical, survey of the authority, organization, and activities of the federal administrative branch (as of about 1937), which was published as Senate Report No. 1275, 75th Congress, 1st session, and entitled *Investigation of Executive Agencies of Government* (Government Printing Office, 1937). The Administrative Procedure Act of 1946 requires each administrative establishment to publish statements which inform the public as to what it does. These are printed from time to time in the *Federal Register*, which appears daily. An unusual number of these statements appear in the issues for September 11, 1946, and immediately thereafter.

The literature cited in the preceding paragraph is primarily descriptive in character, indicating the nature of the activities which are carried on and telling how the various departments and agencies are organized to do their work. None of these items was written to show how much power the bureaucracy has to do good or do harm. Most of the literature which examines the power of administrative organizations from this point of view is admittedly antagonistic to administrative authority. Some of the most vigorous discussions relating especially to· U.S. national government are: James M. Beck, *Our Wonderland of Bureaucracy* (New York, 1932); Ludwig von Mises, *Bureaucracy* (New Haven, 1944); John M. Crider, *The Bureaucrat* (New York, 1944); and Merlo J. Pusey, *Big Government: Can We Control It?* (New York, 1945). A bitter book by an Englishman is Gordon Hewart (Lord Hewart of Bury), *The New Despotism* (London, 1929). An exceedingly systematic, analytical, and critical study of administrative power generally is Ernest Freund, *Administrative Powers Over Persons and Property* (Chicago, 1928). A wealth of information as to how some thirty administrative organizations of the federal government were using their power a decade ago can be found in *Final Report of the Attorney General's Committee on Administrative Procedure,* Senate Document No. 8, 77th Congress, 1st session (Government Printing Office, 1941).

There are scores of books on the handing out of government jobs as means of influencing voters and encouraging people to work for party organizations, but there seems to be not even one comprehensive and systematic study of the way men and women who are already on the government payroll are used to influence voting. Best known of the works on the political importance of patronage is Carl R. Fish, *The Civil Service and the Patronage* (New York, 1905). The principal lines of inquiry in Fish's book are extended to World War II by Paul Van Riper in a doctoral dissertation (MS.) entitled *The Politics of Office-Holding* (1947) and filed in the Library of the University of Chicago.

The provisions of the Hatch Acts and their interpretation are discussed in two publications of the U.S. Civil Service Commission: *Interpretations of the Hatch Act and Regulations of Political Activity* (Government Printing Office, 1940), and *Political Activity and Political Assessments of Federal Office-Holders and Employees* (Government Printing Office, 1944). Perhaps the most critical evaluation of this legislation is by Joseph R. Starr, "The Hatch Act and Academic Freedom," in *Bulletin of the American Association of University Professors,* vol. 27, pp. 61–69 (1941).

The outstanding work on the reporting of what government does is James L. McCamy, *Government Publicity; Its Practice in Federal Administration* (Chicago, 1939). See also the thoughtful article by Harold W. Stoke, "Executive Leadership and the Growth of Propaganda," in *American Political Science Review*, vol. 35, pp. 490–500 (1941); and Bruce Catton, *The War Lords of Washington* (New York, 1948).

PROBLEM:

DIRECTION AND CONTROL

The importance of the federal bureaucracy in American life is clear enough. Government has enormous power over us, and most of the acts of government are put into effect by the men and women who constitute the bureaucracy. It is in the power of these men and women to do us great injury, as it is in their power to advance our well-being. It is essential that they do what we want done, the way we want it done. Our concept of democratic government requires that these men and women be subject to direction and control that compel them to conform to the wishes of the people as a whole whether they wish to do so or not.

Direction and control are key words in this book. Practically everything that is said from here on is related to the direction and control of the administrative branch of the government. It is important, therefore, that there be a clear understanding as to what is meant when these two words are used.

Direction and control are words in common usage. As used in this book, they involve simple, everyday concepts. There is some tendency in the literature dealing with public and business administration to give the words direction and control a narrow meaning. The President has authority to appoint a man to the office of Secretary of State and to remove him from that office later on. We have specific names for these two acts—appointment and removal. But we have not differentiated and given descriptive names to the many different influences to which the Secretary of State is subjected while he is in office. Some writers reserve the words direction and control for these in-between influences. Direction, for these writers, consists of the instructions which a superior gives to his subordinate, and direction shades into control as coercion enters into the instructions.

The words direction and control are given no such narrow meaning in this book. As used here, the phrase direction and control embraces appointment and removal and every other influence to which administrative officials and employees actually respond in any degree. The phrase takes a singular verb throughout the discussion which follows. Direction and control *is* a compound of relationships which determines what the administrative officials and employees of the government shall do and how they shall do it.

When reduced to essentials, direction and control seems to consist of nothing except decisions and instructions. The decisions that are made determine what is to be done, under what circumstances things are to be done, who is to do what, and so on. When a decision has been made, it must be communicated to the proper persons so that they can act in accordance with the decision. The communicating of decisions, with all the explanations of what was decided and all the appeals for individuals to act in accordance with the decisions, are merely instructions intended to put the decisions into effect.

The decisions that enter into direction and control of the bureaucracy include many different kinds of determination. They range from decisions on broad matters of policy controlling action in the future, to decisions on specific items of detail controlling action today. What we think of as a big decision—the determination of a major issue of policy—is pretty certain to be made up of a complex of individual decisions of lesser magnitude. In some cases, the individual decisions—the components of the comprehensive policy—are made first; when the individual decisions have been reached, it becomes apparent that the more comprehensive question has been decided. If we do not like the position on the broad question that we finally reach in this way, we say that we have drifted or stumbled into the policy; if we do like the final result, we say that we have been forced into the policy by the logic of events. In other cases, we make up our minds on the broad question of policy first. When that occurs, we have in effect expressed our faith that answers can later be found for the individual questions which are the component parts of the broad policy. Regardless of which of these two courses we pursue, we are able, sooner or later, to point to broad questions of policy that have been decided. And regardless of how we went about making the decisions that are involved we can usually, if not always, show by analysis that the most comprehensive issues that get decided are only composites of a number of lesser decisions.

The instructions we rely on to put decisions into effect are as varied as the decisions they are supposed to implement. Some of them are addressed to specific individuals, stating in precise language what these individuals are expected to do. Others are general declarations of policy from which thoughtful and conscientious officials and employees derive instructions for themselves. The memorandum for information, the suggestion as to what might be done, the intimation that things could be done better—these are instructions for the official or employee who chooses to respond to them.

There is a tendency, in the literature relating to public administration, to treat the decisions and instructions that make up direction and control of the bureaucracy as falling under one or another of three heads—political, legal, and administrative. To these three heads, some writers add two more—moral and popular. These titles (political, legal, administrative, moral, and popular) suggest that the basis for the classification is the source of direction and control—that the type of direction and control is determined by the point in the governmental system at which the decision is made and the instructions are issued. If the individual official or employee is acting in response to his own convictions, he is responding to moral direction and control. If he is responding to complaints, suggestions, or pressures from individual citizens or organizations outside the government, he is responding to popular direction and control. If the action is in response to decision and instructions originating with Congress or the President or both, then political direction and control has been applied. Legal direction and control originates with the courts and law officers. And administrative direction and control arises out of decisions and instructions originating with administrative officials.

The truth is, however, that neither writers about public administration nor individuals who are caught up in practical situations adhere to any consistent basis in using these terms. Three of these terms at least—political, legal, and administrative—are used to describe the characteristics or the nature of the decisions and instructions that are involved, as well as to indicate where they originate. Any action that involves an important determination of policy, disposing of important considerations affecting many people, is frequently called political, regardless of where the action originates. Any instruction to an administrative official or employee that is based on an interpretation of law is often called legal, regardless of who makes the interpretation and who issues the instruction. And any action which, in the opinion of the person making the comment, ought to be made by an administrative official may be called an exercise of administrative direction and control, no matter whether the action be by Congress, President, court, or anybody else.

The opportunities for confusion and misunderstanding in the use of these terms are almost unlimited. If postmen all over the country are required by statutory provision to deliver mail on holidays, there may be general agreement that the new pattern of conduct in the postal service is in response to political direction and control, because the decision to provide mail service on holidays is an important determination of policy and was made by the political branches of the government. But if the decision were made by the Postmaster General, acting within his discretion, we might say that the change in mail service is in response to political direction and control (because it results from an important determination of policy), or that it is in response to administrative direction and control (because the decision was made by an administrative official). Furthermore, we may at one and the same time say that the postmen who carry the mail are responding to administrative direction and control (because their instructions come from administrative officials), and also say that the Postmaster General, who issued the instructions, is responding to political direction and control (if he acted in compliance with statutory requirement), or is responding to legal direction and control (if he was served with a court order saying he was required by law to issue the order), or is responding to popular direction and control (if he gave the order because of pressures from individual citizens and business firms), or is responding to moral direction and control (if he acted because of religious conviction that there should be no holidays except the Sabbath).

The purpose of the analysis which is undertaken in this book is to try to find out by what means the American people can make sure that the administrative branch of the federal government will conduct itself in accordance with the wishes of the American people as a whole. I do not believe that this inquiry will be satisfactorily advanced by an analysis that treats direction and control under the categories and labels that have just been described—moral, popular, political, legal, administrative. This style of classification holds forth too great an invitation to confusion and misunderstanding. Furthermore, it focuses attention on distinctions that seem to me not to be of significance for the primary objective of this study.

I think we will best understand the relationships that are crucial to the purposes of this study if we organize our analysis about two considerations. One, what are the questions that must be decided and concerning which instructions must be issued in order to give the American people assurance that the bureaucracy will exercise its power in accordance with their wishes? And two, who is to make these crucial decisions and issue the necessary instructions? While one of these considerations is listed ahead of the other, it is neither prior in importance nor prior in order of treatment. The two considerations must be examined in relation to one another throughout the remainder of this book.

As I see it, the questions that are crucial to the direction and control of administrative officials and employees relate to the following matters: determination of the governmental activities in which the administrative departments and agencies shall engage (description or definition of the tasks which the bureaucracy shall perform); setting limits to the scope and intensity of the bureaucracy's effort to carry out different governmental activities (usually accomplished by determining how much money shall be available for carrying on each activity); prescribing the conditions under which and the way in which activities shall be carried on; creating and regulating the organization by which activities are carried on; determining what individuals shall have what authority (by selecting, placing, and removing individuals and transferring authority among them); making clear to individuals what their respective tasks and respective obligations are; investigating the conduct of individuals and organizations; and taking action to make sure that things are done the way they are supposed to be done.

The foregoing enumeration states in general language where the crucial questions are to be found. The various items in the listing will be more precisely defined and more fully elaborated in later chapters of this study. In my opinion, whoever decides (and issues instructions relating to) the more significant questions involved in these matters will effectively determine whether the bureaucracy is going to conform to the expectations of the American people.

The American people are elaborately organized to get decisions made concerning the character and quality of their government and to get instructions issued which will translate their decisions into action. When viewed in its most comprehensive and inclusive terms, the organization of the nation for direction and control of administration embraces all of the institutions, arrangements, and ways of doing things that exert any kind of compulsion upon the men and women who make up the working force of the government. No matter how hard we might try, we cannot hope to identify all these influences, differentiate them, and ascertain their impact upon the behavior of administrative officials and employees. They are the reflection of the complex and changing life of the nation. They express themselves in all the standards of conduct to which men and women in the public service adhere, and in all the pressures to which they respond.

A comprehensive and inclusive study of direction and control might well begin with the moral base of administrative conduct. Some writers have approached the problem in this way. They seek to find out what the public servant believes, what he is committed to, what he is likely to do of his own accord, what appeals and inducements he is likely to respond to, and what appeals and inducements he is likely to resist. Public officials and employees have attitudes about what constitutes a good day's work; convictions about their obligation to find out what superior officers expect of them, and about their obligation to conform to these expectations; habitual reactions which affect the way they treat other people with whom they come in contact. If we bring into the public service only men and women whose attitudes, convictions, and habits are exemplary, and if we put into positions of highest authority those individuals who possess these qualities in highest degree, we simplify our problems of directing and controlling their conduct on the job.

A thorough study of the conditions of American life which determine the quality of men and women who make up the administrative force (which determine the moral base of administration) would require an examination of the entire environment in which they have spent their lives; it would be identical with an exhaustive analysis of American culture. No such undertaking will be entered upon in this book. The analysis of direction and control of administration which is presented here is concerned only with forces which play upon administrative officials and employees, regardless of their personal qualities, after they get into the public service.

The forces which play upon the men and women who make up our administrative organizations are countless and complex. Your attitudes and mine are a part of the welter of influences. If the clerk in the post office tells us to rewrap a package, we tell him not to be too finicky; and if his insistence makes us angry, we tell our Congressman we need a new postmaster. If the representative of the Department of Agriculture cannot answer a question, we ask him if all bureaucrats are as incompetent as he is. If the Bureau of Labor Statistics sends us a questionnaire that we do not readily understand, we purposely fill it out wrongly so as to put the bureaucrats to the trouble of writing a letter. Occasionally we mingle praise and censure. But whether they represent praise or blame, the attitudes of the American people toward their government and the behavior by which they express their attitudes place significant limitations on the conduct of administrative officials and employees. They are a part of the direction and control to which administration responds.

When substantial numbers of us get highly concerned about what the government is doing or not doing, we gang up to put pressure where it is most likely to result in our getting what we want. Usually we act through an organization that was created for other purposes—the National Association of Manufacturers, the American Farm Bureau Federation, the American Medical Association—but sometimes we create a new organization for the special purpose of influencing the conduct of government. We ordinarily think of these organizations as pressure groups putting heat on Congressmen; we call their spokesmen lobbyists because they do much of their work in the lobbies of legislative chambers.

But they work on the administrative branch as well as the legislative. Not much goes on in the Department of Commerce that the National Association of Manufacturers does not know about. If a regulation of the Department of Agriculture displeases a lot of farmers, the officials of the Department will hear from any of a number of agricultural organizations. The Public Health Service will think twice before it does something that the officers of the American Medical Association might find objectionable. The Interstate Commerce Commission listens to what the American Railway Association has to say; members of the Federal Communications Commission sit down to dinner with officers of the National Association of Broadcasters; and high officials of the Bureau of Mines doubtless tremble at their desks when the President of the United Mine Workers bellows forth in his anger.

The influence which is exerted by organizations like those just mentioned is supplemented by what we commonly call political pressure. Government is the politician's business and he works at his business. Many of the politicians are in the public service as officials and employees and are a part of the government which they wish to influence; many more of them are outside the government and therefore are a part of the external forces which put pressure upon government. Much of the time the politician is pressing for favors for his own political organization, as when he demands that members of his organization be put on the payroll. Just as frequently he is trying to get things done for the benefit of the general public because his success in his business depends on his ability to get votes, and his ability to get votes depends in large part on what he does for the community. So the politician works for more housing just as he works for more jobs; and if the housing officials of the national government do not move fast enough to suit him, he does what he can to make them move faster.

The active politicians of a great political party are tied together in an organization that reaches from the community to the national capital. Messages move readily from the politicians in the community to members of Congress, to high officials in the administrative branch of the national government, and sometimes right up to the President himself. This fact is well known to the American people in general, and they make use of the messenger service which the politicians provide. Local businessmen, resolved to get an airport for the community if they can, may go directly to the Civil Aeronautics Administration for advice and assistance, or they may appeal to their Congressman to see what he can do to get CAA interested, or they may dump the problem on the doorstep of local public officials and political leaders who will pursue their own line of communications to get action in Washington.

It is clear enough that an effort to tell the whole story of influence on the administrative branch of the federal government would be an undertaking of enormous magnitude. And it is equally clear that until that story is told, we will not have a full understanding of the direction and control that causes administrative officials and employees of the national government to give the American people the kind of government they want. This book does not attempt to describe and analyze all those relationships. The influences that are examined here arise out of the relationships between people who are a part of the government. This is a book about direction and control which takes place within the structure of the national government. It is concerned with decisions which are made by people who occupy positions in the national government and with the instructions they issue in order to get their decisions put into effect.

If administrative officials and employees are expected to conduct themselves within limits that are acceptable to the American people as a whole, there must be authoritative ways of telling them what the American people want them to do. The authority on these matters, as I have already pointed out, must lie in the political branches of the government—Congress and President. The direction and control which the political branches of the government exercise over the administrative branch is what makes government in operation government according to the will of the people.

The presumption which I have just stated about the necessary relationship of elected officials to the bureaucracy in democratic government underlies everything that follows in this book. This basic presumption is no doubt accepted by all thoughtful observers and students of government. But there is substantial difference of opinion as to how pervasive and how compelling that relationship should be. Some of the recent literature of serious character relating to administration in this country supports a degree of immunity from political direction and control for administrative organizations which seems to me to be incompatible with a sound theory of democratic government. Those writers who argue most effectively for administrative freedom from the political branches rest their case primarily on three lines of reasoning. First, they attach great importance to the obligation of the administrative organization to administer its activities impartially and with devotion to the constitutional mandate that all persons shall enjoy equal protection of the laws; and they believe that political direction and control over administration frequently leads to partiality in administration and unequal protection of the laws. Second, these writers believe that administrative officials in responsible positions (because of professional training, long exposure to the competing pressures which are put on civil servants, and other considerations) can sense more accurately than elected officials what kind of government the American people really want, and are under a great moral compulsion to give them that kind of government. And third, these writers set a high value on the arrangements and facilities which enable people, as individuals and as groups, actually to participate in administration; they believe that the administrator thus obtains, as respects the area of government with which he is concerned, better information than either President or Congressman can get as to what different sectors of the population really want and will insist upon.

There is, of course, a great deal that can be said in support of each of these lines of reasoning. The first point is especially significant. It calls attention to a problem which complicates all of our efforts to give people the kind of government they want. We agree that the American people should be able to use government to accomplish purposes that seem good to most of them; but we also agree that government should not be a tool by which one individual obtains an advantage over other individuals. Where shall we draw the line between governmental action which achieves the public interest at some expense to certain people and governmental action which is admittedly partial and discriminatory? The nation needs more housing and there is a demand that government underwrite housing development. But some people have houses already and do not want to pay taxes to bear a part of the cost of building homes for other people. We take it for granted that this is a legitimate public purpose and all taxpayers have to bear a share of the cost whether they benefit directly from the expenditures or not. But the proposal may be to build houses for city dwellers and not for people who live in rural areas, or houses for people of low income only, or for people who have been in military service and not for anybody else. Some people who will not be eligible to receive the benefits of the new housing (unless they drastically change their status in society) may denounce the housing program as class legislation; but you and I, who think of ourselves as social philosophers, say that the elected representatives of the people as a whole should be allowed to make an estimate of costs and advantages and commit the nation to a housing program that will benefit any substantial sector of the population that the representative assembly believes to have a genuine need. Let Congressmen from the rural areas fight with Congressmen from the cities and get housing for the people they represent if they can; let Congressmen, by their votes, decide whether there will be public housing for people in higher income brackets or for men and women who have not been in military service. This is the proper subject of politics; the decision should be made by the political process.

But what shall we do about selecting families to go into the houses once they have been built? There are not enough houses to go around, even among the people of the restricted class for whom the houses were built. Is the choice among applicants a matter for political decision too? Shall the Congressmen prepare a list of preferred applicants and say that no one else shall have a house until those on the list have been satisfied? Not many people will say yes to this. The Congressmen are likely to make their choices according to considerations that most people think improper. The Congressmen, having future elections in mind, may establish preferences according to political affiliation or contributions to political campaigns or kinship to people whom they know, and these considerations are not relevant to the need we had in mind when we built the houses. Rather, say you and I and the other social philosophers, let us have a rule which is related to need for the benefits which are involved. Let houses go first to people who have longest been out of a house, or people who are now living under worst conditions, or people with the biggest families, or veterans who are disabled or have the most distinguished service record. And if we can't work out a rule which relates benefits to need, then let us have a simple rule of "first to apply, first to be served." Let administration of the law be objective, impartial, free of arbitrary discrimination.

This ideal of objective, impartial, fair administration is what the British people had in mind centuries ago when they began to speak of "the rule of law." The purpose of the law is to lay down standards to guide action in specific situations; if the law is faithfully adhered to, administration is just. Whether we call it rule of law or merely call it fair play in administration, the American people want political considerations excluded when certain kinds of decisions are being made.

The principle is readily understood and generally accepted. But at what point in the process of government does the principle come into operation? The formation and execution of any public policy is a long chain of decisions. Which link in the chain marks the transition from questions that should be decided on the basis of political considerations to questions that should be decided by objective and impartial application of standards laid down in advance? Lawyers have given a lot of thought to this problem. It arises frequently in litigation and calls into consideration such concepts as "equal protection of the law" and "due process of law." Occasionally a statute is held invalid because the judges think it does not make proper provision for objective and impartial decisions in administration of the law; more frequently specific decisions which the administrators have made are set aside by judges because they think the decisions were not actually made in keeping with the standards which the law imposed. But a study of what judges and students of the law have said on this problem reveals that they have not carried their analysis much beyond the point of agreement that decisions must be "fair," "just," "non-discriminatory," "reasonable." Neither have students of government, politics, and philosophy in general given us a battery of tests by which we can pick out the crucial link in any particular chain of decisions and say with confidence, "At this point objective and impartial administration must supplant decision on the basis of political considerations."

I shall not try to provide any tests for identifying the point of transition in this book. As I suggested above, the problem of connecting objective and impartial administration to the decisions of policy which are made by the political branches of the government complicates all of our efforts to give the people the kind of government they want. The question of how this connection shall be made rises to plague us in practically everything we say about political direction and control of administration in this book.

I stated a few paragraphs back that there are three lines of reasoning by which some writers support a greater degree of immunity from political direction and control for administrative organizations than I am willing to agree to. The importance of objective and impartial administration is the first of these; the other two lines of reasoning are based on the supposition that administrative officials have better sources of information than Congressmen and the President as to what the American people want in the particular area of affairs with which the particular administrator is concerned. I think there is a great deal to be said in favor of this, but I think some writers have said entirely too much.

I am sure that the administrative official cannot obtain from the political branches of the government all of the guidance he needs. The directives that come from Congress and President must be supplemented by information, suggestions, concrete propositions which come from individuals who are affected by the government which the administrator provides, either directly or through the various kinds of organization that I discussed above. But this kind of influence must only supplement direction and control by Congress and President, not supplant it. As I see it, there has been a tendency in recent American literature relating to public administration to put the presumption in the wrong place. A number of writers have been concerned, it seems to me, to define an area of autonomy or immunity from political direction and control for the bureaucracy; then having initially determined how much autonomy or immunity the bureaucracy should have, to assign what is left over as the proper area for political direction and control.

The analysis and argument of this book is constructed on the opposite presumption. I think that our assumptions, suppositions, and convictions about democratic government (as set forth in Chapter 1) require us to establish the desirable nature and extent of political direction and control before we reach any conclusions about freedom for the administrator to rely on his own judgment or to seek guidance from other sources. And the reason for taking the position I do, stated generally and briefly, is that the American people have authorized nobody except their elected officials to speak for them. The administrator may have good judgment as to what most of the American people want but he does not know what most of the people want. Those persons, as individuals and as groups, from whom he accepts guidance may speak authoritatively as to what some of the people want but they cannot speak authoritatively for the people as a whole. The elected officials, President and Congress, do not know what most of the people want, either; but they speak authoritatively on that subject because they have been authorized to speak on that subject. If they say the wrong things in their instructions to the administrative branch, they can be got at and repudiated through the procedure set up for popular control of the government—the political campaign and election. That procedure is not available for the direct recall of the administrator who makes decisions which incur widespread public displeasure.

BIBLIOGRAPHIC NOTE

As I indicate in the text of this chapter, an exhaustive account of the direction and control to which administrative officials and employees respond would include all of the conditions of life which make officials and employees the kind of people they are and all of the forces which make an impress upon them as they go about their work. Naturally, no one has attempted to tell that whole story. A number of people have attempted, however, to set down the main features of what they consider to be a proper set of thought-out arrangements for direction and control of bureaucracy. Most of this writing centers on a concept of "administrative responsibility," a phrase that I have purposely avoided in this book because of the different meanings it has for different people. I think the best of the recent general statements of this character are: George A. Graham, "Essentials of Responsibility," in *Elements of Public Administration*, edited by Fritz Morstein Marx (New York, 1946), ch. 22; Carl J. Friedrich, *Constitutional Government and Democracy* (Boston, 1946), ch. 19; John M. Gaus, L. D. White, and M. E. Dimock, *Frontiers of Public Administration* (Chicago, 1936), pp. 26–44, 92–133; Fritz Morstein Marx, *Public Management in the New Democracy* (New York, 1940), pp. 218–251; and David M. Levitan, "Responsibility of Administrative Officials in a Democratic Society," in *Political Science Quarterly*, vol. 61, pp. 562–598 (1946).

Mr. Carl J. Friedrich appears to have written most extensively about what I have called the moral base of administration; he argues with great insistence that administrative officials are subject to a degree of self-limitation which makes unnecessary much if not most of the political direction and control which I say is indispensable if administration is to accord with democratic ideals. In addition to the chapter in his book just cited, see his essay entitled "Responsible Government Service Under the American Constitution," in Commission of Inquiry on Public Service Personnel, *Problems of the American Public Service* (New York, 1935), pp. 3–74; Carl J. Friedrich and Taylor Cole, *Responsible Bureaucracy; A Study of the Swiss Civil Service* (Cambridge, 1932), pp. 60–89; and "Public Policy and the Nature of Administrative Responsibility," in *Public Policy, 1940*, edited by Carl J. Friedrich and E. S. Mason (Cambridge, 1940), pp. 3–24. See also two rebuttals to Friedrich by Herman Finer: "Better Government Personnel," in *Political Science Quarterly*, vol. 51, pp. 580–585 (1936); and "Administrative Responsibility in Democratic Government," in *Public Administration Review*, vol. 1, pp. 335–350 (1941); and a critique of both Friedrich and Finer by V. O. Key entitled "Politics and Administration," in *The Future of Government in the United States*, edited by Leonard D. White (Chicago, 1942), pp. 145–163.

The classic work on the influence exerted by pressure groups on the administrative departments and agencies of the federal government is E. Pendleton Herring, *Public Administration and the Public Interest* (New York, 1936). See also H. Schuyler Foster, "Pressure Groups and Administrative Agencies," in *Annals of the American Academy of Political and Social Science*, pp. 21–28 (May, 1942). Additional writings which deal with special arrangements designed to enable sectors of the public to share in making administrative policies are cited in the Bibliographic Note at the end of Chapter 21.

The lawyers, assisted by political scientists (many of whom seem to be much more interested in law than in politics), have provided an extensive and trustworthy literature relating to direction and control of administration by the judiciary; they have, however, done very little about direction and control through legal advisors who are not sitting in court as judges. Undoubtedly, the best study of book length (comprehensive in concern, exhaustive in inquiry, incisive in analysis) is John Dickinson, *Administrative Justice and the Supremacy of the Law* (Cambridge, 1927). A short list of useful articles will necessarily omit many others that are very good. The following are among the best: John Dickinson, "Judicial Control of Official Discretion," in *American Political Science Review*, vol. 22, pp. 275–300 (1928); E. Blythe Stason, "Methods of Judicial Relief from Administrative Action," in *American Bar Association Journal*, vol. 24, pp. 274–278 (1938); James M. Landis, "Administrative Policies and the Courts," in *Yale Law Journal*, vol. 47, pp. 519–537 (1938); and Harry P. Warner, "An Approach to the Extent of Judicial Supervision over Administrative Agencies," in *Georgetown Law Journal*, vol. 28, pp. 1042–1074 (1940).

CHAPTER 4

SOLUTION:

POLITICAL SUPREMACY

The democratic ideal requires that government in operation be acceptable to the people as a whole. Government in operation is what the administrative departments and agencies make it. We assure ourselves that the administrative branch of the government will respond to the wishes of the people by subjecting it to the elected officials of the government.

The authority of the people, expressed through the ballot, is centered at two points in the federal government—Congress and the Presidency. The people vote directly for Senators and Representatives, indirectly (through the medium of presidential electors) for the President and his potential successor, the Vice President. It is to Congress and the President, therefore, that the people must finally look for the direction and control of administration.

Congressmen and President do not personally do everything that is involved in political direction and control of the administrative branch. Each administrative establishment is organized in a hierarchy of officials and employees with a view to making sure that its work is done in accordance with the instructions that come from the political branches. Administrative officials do not always wait for specific instructions from their political superiors, however. They have their ears to the ground and they anticipate what President and Congress might tell them to do by responding voluntarily to suggestions and pressures from sectors of the population that they think it well to please or placate. Some of the problems of organizing and managing the administrative establishments of the federal government so as to make sure that they will do what the American people want them to do are discussed in Part V of this book.

Congress and President are also assisted in their efforts to direct and control administration by certain specialized organizations that are commonly called central staff agencies. They give advice to Congress and the President, and they advise, assist, and control the many departments and agencies that make up the administrative branch of the federal government. They do not carry on the activities and undertakings which the American people have in mind when they create government and pay for it; their job is to see to it that the establishments which carry on the primary activities and undertakings of government do their work in accordance with the requirements of law and the expectations of Congress and the President. The most important of these central agencies for advice, service, and control (the Bureau of the Budget, the General Accounting Office, and the Civil Service Commission) are described, and their role in administration is discussed, in Part IV of this book.

The courts also participate in direction and control of administration. They may be said to assist Congress and the President, for they see to it that the directives which take the form of law are respected by the men and women who do the work of government. But the courts, while in some important respects under the control of the President and Congress, preserve a high degree of independence from both of them in the interpretation and application of law. They are an integral part of the network of relationships upon which the President and Congress rely to keep administrative officials and employees within the limits set for them, but they are not expected to respond to directives from the President and Congress unless those directives take the form of law. In part because they are not in the main stream of direction and control which stems from the President and Congress, and in part because their role has been so fully explored in other places, the part which the courts play in the direction and control of the bureaucracy is excluded from this study.

In spite of a substantial literature relating to the nature of bureaucracy and the organization of the federal government, we have not advanced very far in analysis and evaluation of the relationships that exist between the highest political authorities and the administrative officials and employees below them. We have not gotten farther because the subject is so complicated. The obstacles to analysis and the hazards that beset any attempt to arrive at conclusions seem to arise out of the following conditions: First, the institutions that are involved (Congress, President, administrative organizations) are exceedingly complex. Second, the relationships between the two political branches (Congress and President) that must provide direction and control for the bureaucracy are numerous, varied in character, and always subject to change. Third, the area of affairs over which the bureaucracy wields power is enormous and the interests of people that are affected by its power vary greatly in significance. And finally, in order for Congress and President to make their direction and control effective, they must be able to resort to many different kinds of measures, and these measures must constantly be adjusted to widely different and changing conditions.

We speak of Congress as the lawmaking body, but that is a loose expression. Actually, Congress and President together constitute the national lawmaking authority. The President must approve the measure in order for a simple majority of the two houses of Congress to enact a bill into law. We do not have anything very firm or solid in mind when we speak of Congress, even when we are clearly differentiating its role from that of the President. The 531 Congressmen are organized into two houses, and the authority of the two houses is not identical. The Senate alone passes on appointments which are proposed by the President and gives or withholds its consent to the final ratification of treaties. The House of Representatives on the other hand must originate bills relating to revenue, and the special provision has been expanded in practice to give the House an extraordinary authority in the determination of amounts of money to be appropriated to the various administrative establishments and governmental activities.

Furthermore, the 531 Congressmen do much of their work through committees and subcommittees. In theory the committee inquires, deliberates, formulates a proposal, and recommends to one or (in case of joint committees) to both houses that the proposal which it has formulated be adopted. In theory all members of the chamber which receives the report consider the merits of the recommendation, discuss it if there is doubt or difference of opinion, and finally vote for or against the proposal, with or without modification, on the basis of individual judgments as to its merits. Actually, of course, many different styles of action take place. The committee's inquiry, deliberation, and report may involve the fullest measure of participation on the part of all members of the committee; they may, on the other hand, represent completely arbitrary action on the part of the chairman or some other forceful member of the committee; or they may represent any degree of common participation and joint effort in between the two extremes. What the members of a legislative chamber do with a committee report when they receive it also varies greatly. It is conceivable that every member may read or listen to it, give it thought, and form a personal judgment on its recommendations. At the opposite extreme, and a more likely occurrence, the report of the committee may receive the attention of not a single member of the chamber other than the members of the committee themselves. What usually happens, of course, is something in between; some members of the chamber give the report some thought and a few members give it very careful thought. Congressmen, like men in other walks of life, have too many things calling for their attention to permit any of them to budget his time as he would like to or as you and I would prefer.

Finally, it must be borne in mind that individual members of Congress carry on their own relations with officials in the administrative departments and agencies. They talk to administrative officials to find out what is going on, so that they can be informed if and when a question about a particular activity of government arises; they tell administrative officials what they think they ought to be doing; they try to get the administrative organization to act quickly or to act in a particular way on some matter in which a constituent of the Congressman is interested; they go to the administrative official with requests for special favors. When the Congressman is acting on his own initiative in such matters, he can cite no official authority to support his mission. But he may be heavily endowed with political power. The administrative official, in dealing with the individual Congressman, must take into account the influence that the Congressman may have with others on occasions when authoritative decisions are being made, and the likelihood that the particular Congressman will use his influence to advance or obstruct the interests of the administrative official.

The President is only one man, but the Presidency, like Congress, is many things. The authority of the President extends far beyond the capacity of the man who occupies the office. The man who is President suffers the limitations inherent in a human being. If he is intelligent, conscientious, and starts with a great deal of experience in public affairs, he can exercise personal judgments in a great many matters relating to the preoccupations and performance of the bureaucracy. But no matter how rich his fund of experience, no matter how well the government may be organized to give him knowledge, no matter how quick and sure he may be in evaluating considerations and reaching a judgment —no matter what the advantages of a particular President may be in these respects, he cannot make personal decisions relating to more than a small proportion of the questions that cry out daily for the attention of someone who can speak authoritatively for the American people. There are too many such questions to permit one man's mind to encompass them.

But while the President, as understander and decider, can operate in respect to only a very limited number of questions, the President as authenticator can operate in respect to a vast number of questions arising throughout a wide range of affairs. The President cannot take time to understand the considerations that are involved and to make a decision on a particular question, but he can decide whose recommendation is to prevail. He can say, "I hope Mr. Kendall and Mr. Kirkpatrick can agree, but if they cannot, I want it to be the way Mr. Kendall says and not the way Mr. Kirkpatrick would like to have it." Much of the President's influence in administration is accomplished by this process of authenticating the decisions of other people. He presumably has men in whom he has confidence at the head of the various administrative establishments that carry on the work of government. He also has the assistance of one or more specialized bureaucracies (notably the Bureau of the Budget) which have nothing much to do but lay proposals before him. He has a substantial number of individuals with or without portfolio who make up a White House coterie. And of course there are lots of other people who have influence with the President. To the extent that the President may be said to direct and control administration, he does it mainly by giving authority to decisions that are worked out by one or more of the individuals that fall in these various groups.

We encounter further complications to our study in the relations between Congress and President. Congress and President, acting separately, exert a great deal of influence on the bureaucracy; they also exert a great deal of influence acting jointly. The President and the two chambers enact legislation which creates the administrative organization, gives it its job, provides it with money to do its work, and regulates its conduct. The President and the Senate, acting jointly, make the appointments which fill the higher posts in the administrative branch. It is clear that the character of the direction and control which the two political branches exercise jointly will depend in large measure on the nature of their working relationships with one another.

The relationships between Congress and President are shaped by many different factors. The majority of members in the two houses of Congress may be of the same political party as the President or they may be of the opposite political party. If the President's party is in control of Congress, the margin of control may be large or small in either or both houses. Some Presidents have opportunities for leadership and qualities of leadership which other Presidents do not have. One President can command support from Congressmen of the opposite party as well as his own; another President cannot even count on the loyalty of a majority of his own party's membership. One President makes a firm statement of what he wants Congress to do and resorts to all kinds of devices to get Congress to do it; another President seems to share leadership with Congressmen; still another reveals neither disposition nor capacity to lead. As a consequence of these and other factors, the relations between Congress and President range from harmonious cooperation to virtual stalemate. And the capacity of Congress and President, jointly or separately, to direct and control the activities of the administrative branch is conditioned accordingly.

These brief paragraphs about Congress and the President should give some notion of what we are up against in our effort to understand the relation of the two political branches to the direction and control of the administrative branch. An examination, equally casual, of the administrative organizations we have set up to carry on the activities of government will make still more evident the difficulties and hazards that are involved in such analysis. The two million men and women who constitute the administrative branch carry on activities that penetrate into almost every phase of human affairs. They are engaged in making policy that regulates our conduct; they adjudicate our differences with one another; they take from us and give back to us in different patterns of distribution; they protect our resources, develop our resources, and convert our resources into useful goods and services; they do scientific study, practice the arts, and carry on business enterprise; they are concerned with our education, care for the sick and wounded, and try to improve our standards of living; they represent us abroad and are the nucleus of our war machine; they are everything that government is in an age of collectivism.

The way in which the administrative branch is organized is determined in part by the nature of the activities to be performed, though the structure of administrative organization is by no means as varied as the activities that are administered or the interests that are affected by these activities. Nonetheless, the differences in the organizations that have been set up for administration are so many, so great, and so significant to the problem of direction and control that a chapter is devoted to the distinctive features of administrative organization at a later point in this book (Chapter 20).

The effectiveness of direction and control is determined, in the final analysis, not by what President and Congress do to make their wishes respected, but by how administrative officials and employees respond to their wishes. If officials and employees are eager to know, adept at figuring out, and conscientious in adapting themselves to the wishes of the political branches, the task of President and Congress is greatly simplified. As one would presume, the readiness with which any sector of the bureaucracy responds to the wishes of President and Congress depends on the way it is organized, the character of its activities, and the nature of the interests that are involved.

Some administrative establishments are headed by individuals who are part of the political leadership of the country. Some of these men sit in the President's cabinet; others who are not in the cabinet are frequently in the White House and are intimate with leaders of Congress. If they do not help President and Congressmen decide what the administrative organizations ought to do, they are at least authoritative in interpreting what President and

Congressmen want these organizations to do. Some establishments are headed by multi-member boards or commissions, the members of which have been chosen to represent different sectors of the population and to reflect different bodies of interest that are affected by the administrative activities that are involved. President and Congressmen may believe that these men are better judges than they as to what the country will find acceptable.

Some administrative establishments are organized to bring spokesmen for different interests into the development of policies and development of plans for putting policies into operation. Arrangements of this sort may facilitate direction and control by Congress, since men who speak for important sectors of the population are able to tell the administrative official directly what they otherwise would have to call upon their political representatives to say for them. On the other hand, direct relations between spokesmen for interest groups and administrative officials can impair rather than facilitate political direction and control. People who represent powerful sectors of the population often act as if particular administrative organizations exist only to serve their various groups rather than to serve the whole of the American people. Their efforts to get what they want for the people they are interested in may complicate and obstruct the efforts of President and Congressmen to make the government serve a broader public interest.

Neither President nor Congressman can know all that he needs to know in order to direct the bureaucracy in the paths he wants it to follow or to keep it there when deliberately or inadvertently it tends to stray. Some things President and Congressmen can find out by personal inquiry. Some things they can find out through institutional channels—the report of an administrative official, the findings of an investigating committee, the inquiry of the specialized bureaucracy that is maintained to assist them. Some things they find out because indignant citizens, men and women of conscience, or spokesmen for special interests make sure that they do find out. Some things, no doubt, persistently escape their attention. In some instances an activity of an administrative division affects no one adversely; administrative officials defend it; the President does not know it exists; Congressmen are too busy to look into it. Many things, it must be remembered, the political leaders do not need to know; if they know this, they can assume that. There are indicators of the state of health in the governmental structure upon which the political leader can rely, as there are indicators of health in the individual upon which the physician can rely. By reading the signs, the President and Congress can determine where to turn for investigation and when to leave well enough alone.

These, as I see it, are the principal facts which complicate our effort to understand and evaluate the arrangements by which President and Congress maintain direction and control over the bureaucracy. They are the facts that must be taken into account in the development of a body of theory as to how our system of political direction and control can be made more to our liking.

A study of the recent literature which is concerned with a more perfect system of direction and control for administration discloses that the writers uniformly recognize and center much of their analysis upon two major issues. Put in question form, they are: first, what are the desirable roles of the President and Congress respectively in the direction and control of the administrative branch; and second, what are the desirable relationships between President and Congress in so far as direction and control of administration are involved? The first question recognizes that political direction and control of administration is not and ought not to be wholly a matter of joint action by President and Congress. It recognizes that President and Congress have separate sets of relationships with the administrative branch which each discharges, if not independently of the other at least not in full cooperation with the other. The second question recognizes that some of the political direction and control of administration is a matter of joint action by the two political branches, and it presumes that it may be desirable to alter the nature of the cooperative action of the two branches or enlarge or contract the range of matters in respect to which joint direction and control shall be applied in the future.

It is obvious from the statement of these two issues of theory that they are closely related to one another. In fact, we cannot get very far in a critical consideration of one without becoming involved in the other. The first question is, however, the primary of the two. We have to see what each of the two political branches does before we can know what both of them do. As we reach conclusions about what each of the two branches can do well or do only poorly, we are in a position to reach conclusions about what might better be done by the two branches jointly. The analysis of direction and control by President and Congress which follows will therefore start with emphasis on what the two branches do (and might do) separately (Chapters 5 to 16) and will close with emphasis on desirable changes in the relationships between the two branches (Chapter 25).

Before we launch upon the detailed examination of direction and control of the bureaucracy by each of the two political branches (which starts with Congress in the next chapter) we ought to have a general view of the issues of theory that divide writers on this subject. No writer or observer can hope, strictly on the basis of objective evidence, to reach his judgments about the capacity of either branch to do any particular thing well. What he concludes after examination of the evidence will be controlled in part by the state of mind with which he starts—his assumptions, convictions, prejudices, preferences. Writers about public administration differ sharply as to what the President can do best and what Congress can do best in the direction and control of administration, and their differences stem largely out of states of mind that are not derived from objective examination and evaluation of evidence.

All writers start with the assumption that many of the crucial decisions relating to administration must be made by the lawmaking process; that the President, as leader of the party in power, ought to take the initiative in proposing legislation relating to administration and ought to feel free to put pressure on Congressmen to enact the legislation which he recommends; and that individual Congressmen ought to exercise a degree of independence in deciding whether to vote for or against such legislation. But to agree on these points is by no means to agree on the respective roles of President and Congress in formulating and enacting legislation relating to administration. What kind of decisions relating to administration ought to be made in legislation, and what kind of decisions ought to be left to the discretion of the President or left to the discretion of the administrative official subject to review by the President? How far should the President go in formulating legislation relating to administration and how much pressure should he feel free to put on Congressmen to induce them to enact what he proposes? How free should the Congressman feel to reject the President's recommendations in favor of his own judgment or the wishes of his constituents where matters relating to administration are involved?

The literature of public administration abounds with differences of opinion on these questions. And the differences of opinion extend to every situation where the authority of President and Congress come together—in the appropriation and allocation of money to administrative organizations, in the appointment and confirmation of administrative officials, in the criticism and review of administrative action, and so on. Practically all of the recent writing which attempts to deal critically with the direction and control of administration sooner or later gets around to this central question—where does and where ought the power of one of the political branches stop and the power of the other begin? At one extreme is the view that Congress and Congressmen tend to meddle in administration and thereby obstruct the orderly efforts of the President to give the administrative branch the direction and control that it needs. At the other extreme is the view that the President could not supply the administrative branch with the political guidance that it needs no matter how hard he might try, and that the bureaucracy would get very little direction and control if Congress and Congressmen did any less to provide it than they do now.

Anyone who has had extended experience in large organizations knows that there is never a line fixed in advance at which the authority of one man stops and that of another begins. Men push their authority as far as seems at the time to be necessary and proper to push it in order to get a thing done: where one man stops depends on where he gets before someone else comes forward to take the job over. How two men fit their authority together depends on the aggressiveness, the persistence, the concern, of each at the time.

It is the same with Congress and President in their relations with administrative organizations. If the President is aggressive in proposing legislation and following up on its execution, Congressmen may be reluctant to pit their influence against his influence. The fact that the President has taken a position on an issue often settles the matter for Congressmen as well as for the administrative official. If, on the other hand, the President has no time for the administrator and his problems, Congressmen will be bolder in their demands; and if they press, the official may feel obliged to yield when he knows he ought not, because he has no one to support him.

It should not be supposed, however, that either Congress or President can be counted on to withdraw because the other has stepped forward. The administrative department and the policies it puts into effect are sometimes the battleground and the spoils of war in a mighty struggle. The President may say, "This is the way I want you to do it, because this is the sensible way to achieve the purposes of the statute." Or the President may say, "This is what I want you to do, because this is what my Administration is pledged to do." But Congressmen in general may disagree with the President as to the purposes of the statute, or leaders of his party in Congress may challenge the President's statement as to what are the pledges of his Administration.

If the President takes a vigorous position in opposition to Congress, the situation becomes one which everybody can understand. It is clearly a political battle. In that case, what can the official do? While a man can (and most of us do) serve two or more masters, he cannot carry out conflicting orders simultaneously. If the official is a part of the executive establishment (as distinguished from an independent regulatory commission) he will ordinarily regard the President as his authoritative superior and comply with the President's wishes when they are made clear. If the President deserts him or Congress makes it impossible for him to stay in office, he is a political casualty. If so, no harm has been done to our concepts of democratic government. This is the way issues are defined for a showdown. This is the way the will of the people is finally made effective.

But often, perhaps most of the time, the President does not get into the controversy between the administrative official and Congressmen. Congress or a committee of Congress or an individual Congressman does not like the action (or inaction) of the administrative official, and says so. The official is certain he is right, in view of the provisions of the law and his obligation to administer the law impartially. The issue is not worthy of the attention of the President, or the administrative official can't get to the President, or the President isn't interested. In any such case shall the administrative official yield to Congress? Congress made the law and (with necessary allowance for Presidential veto) it can change it. If Congress changes the law or by resolution clarifies its intent, the official will yield; if Congress does not express itself in this authoritative way, is the official obliged to enforce the law as he interprets it or as Congressmen tell him they interpret it?

In any of these cases the situation is as confusing to the man in the street as it is embarrassing to the administrative official. If the official resists, is he doing so with the approval of the President, who prefers to keep silent for the moment? Or is the official speaking only for himself, asserting in effect that an administrative officer has a right to tell Congressmen what Congress intends the public policy to be? In the one case he is a part of the political machinery carrying out the democratic processes of government; in the other case is he not an arrogant bureaucrat in rebellion against the representatives of the people? When Congressmen directly or indirectly tell the official what to do, are they clarifying or extending policy which Congress has a right to pronounce? Are they seeking favors for clients which cannot be granted within the limits of equal and impartial application of the law? Are they checking up on administration and supplying the direction that our theory of democratic government says that one or both of the political branches should supply? Or are they merely meddling in administration because they have nothing better to do?

Confusions and embarrassments like these happen with disconcerting frequency. The desire to avoid them has led some students of government to argue that the President should be given a virtual monopoly of the power to see that the laws are faithfully executed. Let Congress (with Presidential approval or over his veto) enact the general policy, by appropriation of funds fix the scope and intensity of the administrative program for carrying the policy into execution, and clarify the policy from time to time by interpretive resolutions or by more definitive enactments. But let the President be the true and the only head of the administrative branch. Let Congress address its recommendations and its complaints about administration to the President. Let the President take them up with administrative subordinates and either insist upon compliance or join an issue with Congress.

Other students of government are unwilling to endorse this proposal. So symmetrical an arrangement for the management of public affairs is attractive, but will it work? Can the President actually exercise an effective direction over the whole of administration? If Congress yields all executive direction to the President, does that not mean that many departments will go undirected? Furthermore Congress must share in fixing at least the basic policies of government. To do that it must go to the administrative official for information. If Congress goes to the official to learn, is it not human nature for Congressmen to praise, to admonish, and to warn? If Congress may act with finality by withholding appropriations or limiting the use of funds, why should Congressmen not do the lesser thing of telling the official how he must shape his conduct to avoid so definitive an action?

Here is the parting of the ways for students of theory of administration. The issue is both one of theory as to where we shall place authority for making public policy and one of theory as to where we shall place authority for directing and controlling administration. The Constitution, in locating certain grants of authority in Congress and in the President, respectively, offers a limited amount of guidance toward the resolution of the issue. But the words of the Constitution are far from conclusive, and the courts have not as yet written any definitive meaning into the document so far as this matter is concerned. The question of how President and Congress should divide between themselves and share together the direction and control of the bureaucracy is therefore an issue in political theory, to be resolved for each man in terms of what kind of direction and control he would like to see made effective upon the bureaucracy and in terms of his supposition that either President or Congress or the two together will most certainly provide that direction and control.

We begin in the next chapter the fuller examination of the considerations, factual and other kind, that are relevant to that issue. The examination starts with Congress.

The things that Congress has done or may be expected to do in the direction and control of administration fall into the following categories: (1) setting the tasks of government (the purposes, the objectives, the things to be done) and specifying the conditions to be observed in achieving them; (2) establishing departments and agencies to carry out these tasks; (3) appropriating money, thereby determining the scope and intensity of the department's program for the accomplishment of the tasks assigned to it; (4) pronouncing rules and standards to govern the way in which the work of government shall be carried on; (5) expressing its approval or disapproval of administrative acts and policies, thereby encouraging or discouraging the administrative official in his program and forewarning him of further possible Congressional action; and finally (6) participating in the selection and removal of officials and employees. The six categories are taken up separately, and in the same order, in the six chapters which follow.

BIBLIOGRAPHIC NOTE

The literature which attempts to explain how the political branches of government in the United States direct and control the administrative branch is fragmentary in character. There is a considerable body of literature that attempts to explain the general character of the direction and control which is effected by the representative assembly in parliamentary systems of government. There is not, however, any extended essay which attempts to treat comprehensively and incisively the whole range of relationships between elected officials (legislature and chief executive) and the appointed administrative officials in this country. We have a few short essays which are concerned with the general problem and a great many more essays (some of book length) which deal with particular aspects of political direction and control. There are several studies, for example, of how the granting and withholding of money is used to determine what the administrative branch shall do and how it shall do whatever it does; there are a few books and several articles on the authority of the chief executive to appoint and remove administrative officials. This particular literature is cited in the Bibliographic Notes which accompany the next several chapters of this book.

A systematic examination of the literature which deals generally with political direction and control of administration in the United States probably should begin with *The Federalist*, Nos. 47–49, 51, 66, 76, 77. What the authors of *The Federalist* papers could say necessarily had to be theoretical, for they were writing about a situation that had not come about yet. And their theorizing about the relation of the political branches to administration was necessarily limited because they expected the national government to be confined to a narrow range of activities and therefore did not expect the administrative branch of the national government to exercise the amount and kind of power that it exercises today. The next examination of the relation of the political branches to administration which has come to be regarded as classic was written by Frank J. Goodnow, entitled *Politics and Administration*, and published in 1900 (New York). In this and later writings, Goodnow differentiated administration from politics, but at the same time argued forcefully that administration must be under the direction and control of the elected officials of the government. Goodnow's analysis and conclusions were eloquently supported by his contemporary, Woodrow Wilson, in his *Congressional Government*, first printed in 1885, and in a short essay entitled "The Study of Administration," which appeared in the *Political Science Quarterly*, vol. 2, pp. 197–222 (1887), and was later reprinted in the same journal, vol. 56, pp. 481–506 (1941).

I think it is fair to say that students of government and politics in the United States have not advanced the literature of this subject much beyond the point to which Wilson and Goodnow delivered it. The textbooks, which might be expected to formulate a succinct and general statement of the relationships between the elected branches of the government and the administrative branch, either scatter their treatment of the subject or ignore it altogether. There are, however, as noted above, a few short essays which attempt to look broadly at the relationships which exist. The best of these, I think, are the following: William F. Willoughby, *Principles of Public Administration* (Washington, 1927), chs. 2 and 3, and *Principles of Legislative Organization and Administration* (Washington, 1934), chs. 10 to 12; John A. Fairlie, "The Legislature and the Administration," in *American Political Science Review*, vol. 30, pp. 241–256, 494–506 (1936); essay by John M. Gaus entitled "The Responsibility of Public Administration," in John M. Gaus, L. D. White, and M. E. Dimock, *The Frontiers of Public Administration* (Chicago, 1936), at pp. 26–44; Arnold Brecht, "Bureaucratic Sabotage," in *Annals of the American Academy of Political and Social Science*, pp. 48–57 (January, 1937); Kenneth C. Cole, "Presidential Influence on Independent Agencies," in the same journal, pp. 72–77 (May, 1942); Harold W. Stoke, "Presidential Coordination of Policy," in the same journal, pp. 101–107 (May, 1942); Herman Finer, "Administrative Responsibility in Democratic Government," in *Public Administration Review*, vol. 1, pp. 335–350 (1941); E. P. Herring, "Executive-Legislative Responsibilities," in *American Political Science Review*, vol. 38, pp. 1153–1165

(1944); four essays by Don K. Price, John A. Vieg, V. O. Key, and George A. Graham in *Elements of Public Administration* edited by Fritz Morstein Marx (New York, 1946), chs. 4, 8, 15, 22; and David M. Levitan, "The Responsibility of Administrative Officials in a Democratic Society," in *Political Science Quarterly*, vol. 61, pp. 562–598 (1946).

For a brief and concise case study of legislative control over one area of administrative activity, see Elias Huzar, "Legislative Control over Administration: Congress and the W. P. A.," in *American Political Science Review*, vol. 36, pp. 51–67 (1942).

PART II

DIRECTION AND CONTROL
BY CONGRESS

CHAPTER 5

GIVING THE BUREAUCRACY ITS JOB

Government exists to do things that people want done. The determination of what the government shall do is the most important decision that we require our political organization to make. The definition of the things that government shall do—the activities to be carried on, the tasks to be performed, the services to be provided, the objectives to be accomplished—ought, in anyone's opinion, to be entrusted to the men and women in whom the nation as a whole has the greatest confidence.

The supreme task which a nation faces in the organization of its government is to provide an institutional arrangement which will bring together the men and women who command greatest confidence and give them maximum opportunity to translate their best judgments into public policy. This institutional arrangement, in our system, is Congress and President. Congressmen and the President translate their judgments into public policy primarily by the enactment of legislation. We call them the lawmaking authority. As lawmaking authority, they decide and announce what activities the government shall engage in.

Lawmaking in the United States is first the business of Congress, which enacts; and second the business of the President, who approves or vetoes. But we give Congress greatest authority in lawmaking, for we allow it, in case of dispute with the President, to maintain its position by overriding the President's veto. Because of its primacy in the enactment of legislation, Congress is referred to in the following pages (as in popular usage) as the lawmaking body.

The determination of what the government shall do involves the definition of the tasks which the bureaucracy shall perform. The definition and assignment of these tasks may be regarded as the most important form of direction and control to which the bureaucracy is subjected. Certainly the legislation which says what the various administrative establishments shall do underlies all other forms of direction and control. The appropriation of money is supplementary to such legislation; it determines the extent to which—how comprehensively and how intensively—the activities which have been assigned to the bureaucracy shall be executed. The investigation of the conduct of an administrative organization, the review and reversal of its action, the punishment of its officials for wrongdoing—all these acts of direction and control are founded on the statutory provisions which state what the organization is expected to do.

No thoughtful person who is devoted to a democratic system of government would propose to take away from the representative lawmaking assembly the power to say what the activities of government and therefore the tasks and undertakings of the administrative branch shall be. But there is room for difference of opinion as to how fully the lawmaking body should control the description of these activities and the definition of these tasks and undertakings. In fact, the literature of public law and political theory in this country reflects a considerable debate on this question. The controversy centers about the concept of delegation of power. In our constitutional-law theory, Congress has the power to describe the things which the government shall do, and therefore to define the tasks of the bureaucracy, in as minute detail as it chooses. But it may, if it chooses, describe and define in general terms and leave the more precise determinations to the President, to the administrative official, or to the administrative official subject to review and approval by the President.

The question of whether Congress may delegate, and of the

extent to which it may delegate, authority to define the tasks of the administrative branch is a question of constitutional law. The question of whether, under what circumstances, and to what extent it appears to be desirable to delegate such authority is a question of political theory. It is with the latter question—the desirability of describing the activities of the government and defining the tasks of the bureaucracy in greater or less detail—than we are concerned here.

The range of choice which Congress has in telling the bureaucracy what it is to do may be illustrated by the legislation which established a public works program in 1935 for relief of the unemployed and stimulation of general economic recovery. The original resolution which was laid before Congress did nothing more than fix a sum of money ($4,880,000,000), state that this sum of money should be spent to accomplish certain very general objectives (e.g., alleviate distress), and list some sample types of projects on which the money might be spent (e.g., slum clearance, rural electrification, grade-crossing elimination). A Senator who certainly did not like the bill in its original form, and who was at least skeptical about the purpose back of the bill, suggested in sarcasm that it be reworded to read: "Section 1. Congress hereby appropriates $4,880,000,000 to the President to use as he pleases. Section 2. Anybody who does not like it is fined $1000."[1]

The scarcastic Senator was not the only Congressman who thought that the legislation which set up a public works program ought to contain some meaningful instructions for the President and the officials of the administrative organization that might be charged with administering it, and some additional instructions were later put into the bill. But how far should Congress go in describing a public works program for relief and recovery? It

[1] The bill (H.J. Res. 117, 74th Congress) appears not to have been printed in the *Congressional Record* in the form of its original introduction. The remarks of the Senator (Arthur H. Vandenberg) are in the *Congressional Record*, p. 2014 (February 15, 1935). There is an account of the drafting and enactment of this legislation in Arthur W. Macmahon, John D. Millett, and Gladys Ogden, *The Administration of Federal Work Relief* (Chicago, 1941), ch. 2.

might try to do no more than state the general and basic features of the works program it wants put into effect. It might state what kind of projects it wants undertaken; how they are to be distributed over the country; what classes of individuals are to be employed on them; whether wages shall be fixed at levels prevailing in private employment, or at a point to provide subsistence only, or in accordance with some other standard. Certainly no one could complain if Congress did write such descriptive provisions into the statute. These are clearly important matters of public policy. These are matters in respect to which Congressmen may be expected to know their own minds. If the legislation did not cover these points, there would be no ground for assurance that the country would get the kind of a public works program Congress hopes to have carried out.

Why should Congress stop with the statement of the general features of the public works program? Why should it not include in the statute a description of every project to be undertaken and list in the statute the name of every person to be employed on a project? It seems pretty clear that Congress could not write these things into the statute without defeating its own purpose. Eight million people were put to work by the Public Works Administration (PWA) during the five years of its existence. Neither Congress nor President nor head of an administrative department can pick out eight million individuals who are in circumstances which Congress wants considered in selecting men and women for employment on works designed for relief. It takes a lot of people to do that job of selection, and to get it done we create an administrative agency—PWA. If Congress called for the findings of the employees in the administrative agency and attempted on the basis of this information to name the individuals to be put to work, it would, from its own point of view, do very badly a job that administrative officials can do much better. Congress would do the job badly because a representative assembly is not organized in a way that would enable it to do such a job well. And while it was doing this particular job, Congress would be neglecting other things that are in much greater need of its attention.

This brief indication of what Congress had before it in enacting public works legislation is illustrative of what Congress has before it in establishing any new governmental program or undertaking. It always has a choice as to how fully it shall describe what it wants done. There is always ground for disagreement between Congressmen, and between Congress and President or Congress and administrative officials, as to how much detail is desirable. While there is no way of finding a "right" answer to the question as to how much detail is desirable, it is possible to identify certain considerations which point to where a satisfactory answer will be found. These considerations, as I see it, are three in number.

First, and fundamental, is the rule that Congress should specify in the statute every guide, every condition, every statement of principle, that it knows in advance it wants to have applied in the situations that are expected to arise. This rule derives from a concept of legislative supremacy. It is based on the conviction that Congress, being the nation's representative assembly, ought to have authority to provide in law for anything that it wants any part of the government to do, so long as it does not violate a prohibition of the Constitution. It is based on a conviction that there is nobody else who has been given authority or who ought to be given authority to gainsay Congress as to what kind of activities should be carried on by the government. If Congress is to have the supreme authority to say what the government is to do, then it must be in a position to describe what it wants done in as much detail as it thinks necessary. If the President thinks Congress has written some requirements into the act that ought not be there, he can veto the bill; if two-thirds of the Congressmen in each house hold to the original position of Congress, they can put the law into effect over the President's veto.

Some students of constitutional law and political science do not agree with the position I take here. They agree that Congress ought to have ample authority to determine what the fundamental features of a program of governmental activity shall be, but they deny that Congress is the repository of best judgment as to what the less-than-fundamental features of the program shall be. Therefore they reject the premise that Congress should be able to write into the controlling legislation every guide, condition, and statement of principle that Congressmen are certain they want respected in the administration of the law. Many of these students would argue, no doubt, that Congress should not be allowed (even though it wished to do so) to name in the law the individuals who are to be employed on the public works and relief program. To support their position, they may cite two limitations in the Constitution: the requirement that governmental action be according to due process of law, which implies a measure of equal protection of the law; and the principle of separation of powers.

The first line of reasoning brings us up against a consideration we discussed at some length in Chapter 3 (pp. 49–51)—the notion that certain kinds of decision ought to be made in such a way that the American people are assured of equal and impartial application of the law. Admittedly, if Congress specifies in the law the standards which administrative officials shall apply in selecting men and women for employment, those standards must be applied in an objective and impartial manner. May Congress avoid this standard for administration by itself naming the persons who are to be employed? I think the rule of constitutional interpretation should be that Congress must meet the same standards for equal protection of the law that we demand of administrative authorities. But I do not think that the imposition of such a standard makes it necessary to conclude that Congress cannot make the decisions which the standard is expected to regulate. The record of Congress for objective and impartial decisions in satisfying claims against the government is said to be very good. If Congress is willing to give the careful consideration to claims for employment on public works that it has in the past given to claims for redress of injuries, I see no reason for holding that the Constitution forbids it to do so.

The second line of reasoning referred to is based on a supposition that the Constitution vests in the President (and administrative officials subordinate to him) exclusive authority to make decisions which are held to be "executive" in nature, and that designations of persons to be employed on public works are decisions of that nature. There is a great deal of support for such a contention in judicial decisions arising under the constitutions of the forty-eight states, and there is some support for such a contention in some things which federal judges have said about the meaning of the United States Constitution. As yet, however, we have not developed any firm rules of constitutional law which limit the kind of descriptive provisions that can be put in a federal statute. There is good reason to believe that the Supreme Court would not allow Congress to name in the statute the person who should be appointed to an administrative position in the organization which administers public works; this limitation on Congress rests on the specific constitutional provision for the President to make appointments to public offices. But there is no specific language in the Constitution which specifically reserves to the President or to anyone else in the executive-administrative branch the authority to define or extend the description of the undertaking which the statute requires to be put into effect. And I understand that the designation of persons to be employed on public works as a means of relief is an extension of the substantive provisions of the law, not an appointment to public office.

I have centered this discussion on legislation providing public works for relief and economic recovery because it shows clearly what my reasoning leads to when I take the position that the Constitution should not be interpreted to limit the ability of the lawmaking authority to control the character of the government which the country is to have. If I have accomplished my purpose, I have made clear my belief that the representative assembly—in our case, Congress—is to be trusted above all other individuals or institutions to determine how much descriptive detail ought to go into the statute in any particular instance.

What I have said is not in the least to argue that the President should be cut out of all influence in determining what the character of governmental activities should be. He was put in the White House by the American people in order to provide a program of government which he espoused in a political campaign and which the people presumably endorsed. He should have ways and means of getting that program into effect. But the ways and means that are proper in a democratic style of government do not allow very much to be done by executive decrees. The President can translate his program into legislative proposals, lay them before Congress, and (since he has received the endorsement of the whole nation) put various kinds of pressure on Congressmen to enact his proposals into law. But he should have to win the approval of a majority of Congress; he should not be able to ignore Congress and put his proposals into effect by executive order. If Congress disagrees with him so far as to put requirements into the law which he finds objectionable, he can veto the bill; if Congress passes it over his veto he should have to live with the fact that he has taken a political licking. These matters of Presidential-Congressional relationships are discussed more fully later on (especially in Chapter 25).

It should also be understood that the reasoning up to this point does not argue that Congress should show no restraint in defining and describing a program of government. If a majority of Congress—two-thirds in case of a veto—know in advance that they want a particular provision in the statute, they should put it there. But they should be sure as to their wishes before they put more than general descriptive statements in the act, for they can easily defeat their own purposes. This brings us to the second and third of the three considerations referred to above as controlling the amount of detail that should go into legislation providing for governmental undertakings and giving the bureaucracy the work it is to do. Congress should not spend so much time trying to find out what it wants done, or trying to reach agreement as to what should be done, that it is kept from giving attention to other matters which in its judgment are more important. And Congress should not define and describe a governmental undertaking in such detail that administrative officials are rendered incapable of achieving the major objectives toward which the legislation is directed.

It is hardly conceivable that Congressmen could know what kind of projects they want undertaken, or what individuals they want employed on projects, when they first conclude that a public works program for relief and recovery ought to be instituted. This is not because of any defect in the character of Congress or because of any shortcoming on the part of individual Congressmen; it is simply a consequence of living outside the Garden of Eden. It is conceivable that Congress could have investigations made and reported to it, on the basis of which it could decide what the first projects ought to be and who ought first to be put to work. But if it took the time to make these decisions, it would thereby cut down the amount of time available for consideration of other matters it counts important. It is a question of priorities. Congress cannot do everything it would like to do. Congress must itself make the comparative evaluation of the many problems that clamor for the attention of the nation's lawmaking assembly. It is unlikely that very many thoughtful Congressmen will believe in a time of major depression that they can best serve the nation's interests by taking time to examine and agree on projects and examine and agree on the claims of individuals for a place on the employment rolls.

Even if Congress did conclude that it ought to specify the first projects and fix the initial list of persons to be employed, its decisions on these points would be of momentary duration only. The nature of a public works program for relief of unemployment and for general economic recovery is such that you must see what happens today in order to decide what to do tomorrow. As projects are completed, others must be devised. Projects which are planned and approved may need to be abandoned because of change in the general economic situation. As opportunities for private employment change, the employment rolls for public works must be revised. If Congress sought to make these day-to-day decisions it would have to renounce responsibility for virtually all other matters which require legislative action.

What was said in the last two paragraphs applies specifically to the second of the three considerations controlling the statutory definition and description of governmental undertakings—the point that Congress ought not spend so much time on one subject of legislation that it is unable to find time for other matters that it considers more important. Much of what has just been said is fully applicable to the third consideration—that Congress should not define and describe a governmental undertaking in such detail that administrative officials are rendered incapable of achieving the major objectives toward which the legislation is directed.

As Congress describes in more detail the character of works projects which shall be undertaken and the classes of people that may be employed, it of necessity limits the discretion of anyone else—the President or administrative officials—to figure out and experiment with types of projects and requirements for employment that did not occur to Congress. Much of our wisest judgment about how to deal with a difficult problem arises out of our experience in trying to deal with it. The administrative official who is actually planning and administering the public works program is bound to acquire knowledge about certain aspects of the program which is superior to that of Congressmen who have not had the opportunities for observation that the administrative official has had. To the extent that the legislation has limited the administrator's freedom of choice in devising projects and certifying people for employment—to that extent the administrator is stopped from putting his best judgment into immediate operation. If he is required to come back to Congress for restatement of his authority every time experience opens up a new avenue for achieving the major objectives toward which the law is directed, not only is Congress diverted from other important matters, but the delay which is incurred may work against the accomplishment of the major purposes which Congress has in mind.

The choice before Congress, in deciding how fully to describe the governmental activity and how fully to define the job of the administrative organization, is not between the one extreme of writing into the act every guide, condition, and statement of principle that Congress believes at the moment ought to be respected in the administration of the program and the other extreme of turning the President and administrative officials loose to do as they please. Congress keeps a hand on the administration of the program by fixing annually (or more frequently if it chooses) the amounts of money that shall be available for financing the program. And it may, if it wishes to do so, require that the administrative officials lay plans and proposals for certain kinds of action before it for approval or disapproval before they are put into effect. These possibilities in direction and control are discussed in succeeding chapters of this book.

The discussion of the authority and capacity of Congress to direct and control administration by defining the tasks of the administrative branch has, up to this point, been developed around a type of governmental activity that is put into operation only under emergency conditions. But what has been said about statutory provisions relating to a program of public works for relief and recovery is fully applicable to what we may call the more normal activities of government. This can be demonstrated sufficiently by a brief examination of one permanent, continuing governmental activity—the regulation of the grading of grain shipped in interstate commerce. Under the Grain Standard Act, the Secretary of Agriculture is "authorized . . . to fix and establish standards of quality and condition for corn (maize), wheat, rye, oats, barley, flaxseed, soybeans, and such other grains as in his judgment the usages of the trade may warrant and permit."[2] Why did Congress not itself determine whether standards of quality and condition

[2] 39 Statutes at Large 482, sec. 2 (1916); U.S. Code, title 7, sec. 74.

should be established for each of the different grain crops instead of merely authorizing the Secretary to do so if he thought it a good idea? And why didn't Congress go even farther than that and describe in the statute the standards of quality and condition that should prevail? Regulations of this sort are important matters of public policy. Are they not therefore proper for inclusion in the law?

The answer, according to my political theory, is that if Congress can make up its mind as to what it wants done in such matters, it ought to incorporate its wishes into law. But it appears that in this case Congress could not decide what it wanted (what grains should be regulated and what standards should be fixed) when the problem first came to its attention. It could not decide these matters because it did not have sufficient information. It could have directed a committee to investigate and make recommendations to Congress, but an administrative department having other duties in the field of agriculture could do that job better. Congress might have directed the Secretary of Agriculture to report his findings to Congress so that it could decide whether to require that standards be fixed for particular grains, and it might even have directed him to report information which would enable Congress to write out those standards itself. But even with the help of the Department of Agriculture it would take a lot of time for Congress to make these decisions; and once made they might soon become unsatisfactory because of a changing situation in the production and marketing of farm crops. Congress could not afford to take the time that would be required to formulate the new policy in detail and make the frequent revisions that would have been necessary during an experimental period.

If, however, the situation becomes stable Congress may some day be able to instruct the Secretary of Agriculture that he must fix standards for certain of these grains, and no others. And if the situation stabilizes still further, Congress may be able to write the standards into the statute. This is the history of a great part of our legislation. In the initial period of regulation, Congress is forced to abdicate to the administrator for the extension of policy beyond the statement of general purposes. As time passes and administrative experience is examined, Congress is able to incorporate into statute the policies formulated and pursued by the administrative department. But for every problem that is mastered to the extent that policy can be defined, there is likely to emerge a number of other problems too novel or too complex to be governed by rule. The policymaking authority of administrative departments is thus generally and unavoidably on the increase. And Congress contributes to the increase by failing to take advantage of such opportunities as it has to transform discretion into statutory prescription.

It is no easy task to make government work out the way we say it ought to when we state our theories. If President and administrative officials do not acknowledge their complete subordination to the lawmaking authority (of which the President is a part) as respects the determination of what government is to do for the people, they can in practice defeat the efforts of the lawmakers to say what the character of government shall be. Something further ought to be said, therefore, about the relation of President and administrative officials to the efforts of Congress to direct and control administration by describing the activities to be carried on and by defining the task of the administrative organization.

The good administrator, according to the reasoning of the past several pages, conscientiously seeks to find out what the lawmaking authority had in mind when the controlling legislation was enacted; when he is confident that he knows what the objectives were, he seeks faithfully to accomplish those ends. He may be put in a quandary if he concludes that statutes clearly require something that the appropriations do not permit, or if he concludes that Congress and President today do not want something which Congress and President wanted when the controlling legislation was passed. We have not worked out any firm body of theory as to what the administrative official should do in either of these instances; but we can conclude that the administrative official ought not take advantage of confusion and uncertainty in the law to institute a program of government activity for which he can find no basis in legislative expression.

What has just been said applies to the administrative official as administrator. But what about the administrative official who is also political leader, serving in the President's cabinet perhaps and speaking frequently in the name of the President or of the party about what the Administration will or will not do? The political-administrative official has a kind of interest in the character of the government that is to be supplied to the people which the official who is administrator only does not have. The political-administrative official may properly oppose the enactment of legislation which he personally considers unwise, and he may speak out against it with all the vigor we expect of politicians. But when Congress and President have overruled him by enactment of the law (or by failure to repeal or revise a law to which he objects), the administrative official who is also political leader, according to my political theory, has neither moral nor legal right further to oppose or sabotage the achievement of the purposes toward which the law is directed. If his conscience forbids him to be a part of a governmental undertaking of which he does not approve, or if he thinks that his further political ambitions will be endangered by staying where he is, he can get out of his spot by resignation.

If this is an acceptable theory as to what administrative officials, both political and non-political, should do in the face of legislative requirements that they do not personally like, then it follows that the President ought not ask administrative officials to do differently in the face of legislative requirements that he does not like. Practice is a long way removed from theory in this respect, however. The President who is unable to secure enactment of a law to which he is pledged sometimes tries to put at least a part of his program into effect by directing administrative officials to proceed under unwarranted interpretations of statutes that are already in effect. If he is unable to secure repeal of a law to which he is opposed, the President sometimes instructs administrative officials to nullify it by inaction. Congressmen know about these things; many of them acquiesce in such practices; sometimes it appears that the political leadership of both parties is in a cabal to put administration at cross-purposes with legislative declaration. A firm declaration in the statutes that trusts shall be busted will please a lot of people; a directive to the Attorney General that trusts should not be busted just yet will please a lot of other people. It may take the first group of people a number of years to find out that trusts are not going to be busted after all.

The administrative official who gets two sets of instructions, both apparently representing the will of the two political branches, may be forgiven if he chooses to ignore the particular instruction which you and I would have him obey. But I do not think that political leaders should be quickly forgiven if they consciously engage in handing out conflicting instruction to the administrative branch. It is such practices that cause people in general to lose confidence in their instruments of government. And it is such practices that encourage men in and out of the government to set the bureaucracy up against the political branches of the government in respect to those matters where the will of the political branches is clear.

BIBLIOGRAPHIC NOTE

The modern literature of government and politics makes no attempt to explain why the lawmaking authority should determine what the activities and undertakings of government are to be. This is probably because there is no difference of opinion on that point; everyone assumes this to be a proper objective of legislation. But it is not so easy to excuse the failure of students of government to develop a body of theory which would guide the lawmakers in deciding how far to go in describing the activities and undertakings which are to be carried on. If there is in print a general examination of the considerations which ought to be taken into account, I am not aware of it. There is, however, an extensive and still growing literature relating to the delegation of authority to administrative officials to extend the provisions of law which they are required to enforce. And there are a few case studies of the formulation and adoption of legislation out of which one may learn a great deal which will contribute to the development of a body of theory.

Most of the literature relating to delegation of discretion to administrative officials is primarily concerned with the constitutionality of delegation or with safeguards against abuse in the exercise of administrative authority. There is a limited amount of literature which discusses the pros and cons of making statutes complete (leaving little to administrative discretion) on the one hand and limiting the provisions of the statute (allowing administrative officials to extend them) on the other. Most of this literature, however, is contentious rather than analytical; the writer is likely to be for or against delegation of authority to administrative officials, and to devote himself fully to the justification of his position. The following are among the best of the works that treat administrative lawmaking power in a general or comparative manner: Frederick F. Blachly and M. E. Oatman, *Administrative Legislation and Adjudication* (Washington, 1934); Cecil T. Carr, *Delegated Legislation* (London, 1921); and James M. Landis, *The Administrative Process* (New Haven, 1938). Some of the most informative studies relate to a single administrative agency or agencies of a particular type. Among the best of these are: Edwin W. Patterson, *The Insurance Commissioner in the United States* (Cambridge, 1927); William C. Van Vleck, *The Administrative Control of Aliens* (New York, 1932); and John B. Andrews, *Administrative Labor Legislation* (New York, 1936). Short articles dealing critically with this subject are: Henry W. Biklé, "Administrative Discretion," in *George Washington Law Review*, vol. 2, pp. 1–12 (1933); and Harold W. Holt, "The Need for Administrative Discretion in the Regulation of the Practice of Medicine," in *Cornell Law Quarterly*, vol. 16, pp. 495–521 (1931); and O. Douglas Weeks, "Legislative Power Versus Delegated Legislative Power," in *Georgetown Law Journal*, vol. 25, pp. 314–337 (1937).

If one wishes to carry his inquiry into original sources of information, he can learn a lot about the advantages and disadvantages of giving administrative officials authority to extend statutory provisions from testimony in hearings before the two houses of Congress. See, as illustrative, *Amendment of Federal Trade Commission Act and Establishment of a Federal Trade Court*, Hearings before Committee on Judiciary, U.S. Senate, 72nd Congress, 1st session (Government Printing Office, 1932); and *Stock Exchange Practices*, Hearings of

Committee on Banking and Currency, U.S. Senate, 73rd Congress, 1st session (Government Printing Office, 1934), part 15.

Our understanding of the matters discussed in this chapter are also advanced by a number of case studies of the formulation and adoption of legislation. The following appear to be most useful: Charles F. Roos, *NRA Economic Planning* (Bloomington, Indiana, 1937), ch. 2; E. E. Schattschneider, *Politics, Pressures and the Tariff* (New York, 1935); and Carl J. Friedrich and E. Sternberg, "Congress and the Control of Radio Broadcasting," in *American Political Science Review*, vol. 37, pp. 797–818, 1014–1026 (1943).

CHAPTER 6

CREATING THE ADMINISTRATIVE ORGANIZATION

The character of the government that the American people get depends finally on the way policies are administered. The men and women who administer a governmental program inevitably have the power to defeat the purposes which Congress had in mind in establishing the program. The likelihood that these men and women will or will not achieve the purposes which Congress had in mind depends on the direction and control to which they are subjected. The first step in effective direction and control is an adequate definition and description of what Congress wants done. The second step is a careful provision for the kind of administrative organization that appears most likely to devote itself to the execution of the program in keeping with the objectives toward which the legislation is directed.

In the preceding chapter, I took the position that Congress should be authoritative as to what the character of the governmental undertaking is to be; that it should put into the statute every guide, condition, and statement of principle that it knows in advance it wants to have respected; but that it should modify its effort to define the job of the bureaucracy by a consideration for other demands on its own time and by a recognition that the administrative official may require some freedom of action in order to achieve the major purposes behind the statute. It seems to me that exactly the same things can be said about the relation of Congress to the creation of the administrative organization that is to administer a governmental undertaking. But I think that the relation between the premise (that Congress should have what it wants) and the modifying considerations (that it ought not spend too much time reaching agreement as to what it wants, and ought not tie too tightly the hands of President and administrative officials) is different in the two cases.

The creation of the administrative organization is secondary in importance to the definition and description of the job that the organization is to do. Congress can afford to neglect a lot of other things in order to clarify minds, reach agreement, and formulate a careful statement of what the governmental activity or undertaking is to be. The determination of the character of the organization that is to administer the activity or undertaking is one of the things it can afford to neglect, simply because the clear definition and description of the government which the people are to get is of more importance than an equally definitive description of the organization that is to provide the government.

This negative consideration (inability to find time for it) is only one reason why Congress should leave many of the decisions concerning administrative organizations to others. There is at least one positive reason for doing so—the chief executive and high officials in the administrative branch can make a case for being allowed to determine the character of the administrative organization themselves. The nature of their interest in the character of the organizations they are to head is different than their interest in the character of the governmental activities that are to be carried out. Their interest in the latter is political only; the President and high administrative officials, being political leaders, will try to influence the enactment of legislation which determines what the government will do for the people. If they suffer a defeat and legislation which they do not like goes on the statute books, they can continue to fight by working for repeal or modification of the statute; they can make no claim for power to undo the legislative decision by the exercise of executive or administrative authority.

If the President is confident that there is more popular support for him than for the Congressmen who outvoted him, he may properly decide that he will put the new governmental activity into operation only to the extent that he is legally obliged to do so, and make his opposition to the new governmental undertaking an issue in the next election. And the administrative official who is obliged to put the new activity into operation can either resign or, like the President, do only the minimum that he feels legally obliged to do and wait for a resolution of the issue in the forthcoming election.

The considerations are different, however, in respect to the organizational arrangements for putting the new activity into operation. Both the President and the administrative official have an obligation to see that the laws are faithfully executed; they can discharge this obligation only if they have an administrative organization which can be relied on to put the law into effect. The President and high administrative officials immediately under him will be blamed if the laws are not faithfully executed. Surely they have good reason for insisting that they have something to say about the organizations upon which they must depend.

The question of how authority over the character of administrative organization should be distributed between Congress, the President, and high administrative officials is the subject of sharp controversy at the present time. Before we attempt an analysis of what is involved in this controversy, we must be clear as to what is involved in the determination of administrative organization. I think it will be sufficient for purposes of this study if we limit our attention to three problems in administrative organization: the distribution of governmental activities among departments and agencies; the character of the office at the top of the department or agency; and the internal organization of the department or agency.

Whoever decides how governmental activities are to be distributed among administrative establishments not only will determine what any administrative establishment is required to do but also will determine how many separate administrative establishments are to make up the administrative branch. The authority to determine the character of the office at the top of a department or agency is authority to say whether the establishment shall be headed by a single official who sits in the cabinet, a single official who does not sit in the cabinet, a commission that makes decisions by majority vote, a board of directors enjoying corporate powers, and so on. The authority to specify the internal organization of the administrative establishment includes the power to create a highly integrated organization, a loose federation of semi-autonomous bureaus, or something in between.

It seems quite clear that the President's Committee on Administrative Management, which reported in 1937, thought that the President should have complete authority over all these matters. Because conditions are constantly changing, the Committee said, "It seems clear that the Executive [i.e., the President] should always be held responsible not alone for the management of the executive departments, but also for the division of work among the major departments. To render the Executive truly responsible for administration and its efficiency, he must be required to accept the responsibility for the continuous administrative reorganization of the Government. The duty of the Congress in reorganization is discharged by the determination of the broad outlines of reorganization, through the creation of the executive departments and the adoption of the general policy that all administrative operating agencies shall be brought within these large executive departments." Furthermore, the Committee said, "Some of the existing independent agencies should be accorded a degree of independence within the department to which they are assigned, instead of being reduced to bureau status. In the assignment of now independent agencies to the departments, those which require a degree of independence from the normal departmental control in any particular because of their nature or stage of development should be accorded a semi-autonomous status within the departments by the terms of the Executive order which establishes their status."[1]

[1] *Report of the President's Committee on Administrative Management* (Government Printing Office, 1937), pp. 33, 35.

It should be noted that the Committee was speaking expressly about reshaping the administrative organization of the federal government, not about the assignment of governmental activities to a department at the time the department is created nor about the assignment of governmental activities to departments at the time the new activities are instituted. I do not find anywhere in its report, however, an indication that the Committee felt that Congress should make the original assignment of activities to departments in either of these contingencies. Its statement of the authority that the President should have to change the pattern of organization includes no intimation that he should leave any governmental activities, even for a limited time, in the particular departments and agencies in which they may have been located by statute. And there is nothing which suggests that the President should follow the advice of the department head as to whether particular organizations which are brought under him should be fully incorporated into the department or accorded a semi-autonomous status.

The Hoover Commission, making its report in 1949, proposed no such authority over administrative organization for the President as the Committee on Administrative Management contemplated. The Hoover Commission did not expressly say where the authority should lie to create new administrative departments and agencies, to assign new governmental activities to departments and agencies, or to determine the character of the office at the top of a department or agency. I think it is clear from the general tenor of its remarks, however, that the members of that body considered all these matters to be proper subjects for legislation. The Commission was of the opinion that the President needs special authority to effectuate reorganizations from time to time as need for changes arise. It recommended the reenactment of legislation that expired in 1948 under which the President could initiate plans for reorganization (reassignment of activities among departments and agencies, consolidation of departments and agencies, etc.), lay his plans before Congress for acceptance or rejection but not for amendment, and put his plans into effect unless both houses voted disapproval. But neither Congress nor the President, the Commission felt, should reach into an administrative establishment to determine the character of its internal organization. That should be the province of the head of the department or agency and of him only. "Each department head," the Commission said, in a formal recommendation, "should receive from the Congress administrative authority to organize his department and to place him in control of its administration." Lest this point not be fully appreciated, it said again, "We recommend that the department head should be given authority to determine the organization within his department." And once more, "Each department head should determine the organization [of his department] and be free to amend it."[2]

I think we may conclude that the head of the administrative department or agency, as administrator, has no rightful claim to a voice in deciding what governmental activities shall be assigned to his organization for administration. His job is to see that the laws which are given him to execute are faithfully executed. If he does not want to take responsibility for executing some of them, he can find another job. If Congress or President propose to put activities in other departments or agencies that he thinks bear a close relation to the activities over which he has charge, he can make clear the advantages of giving them to him for administration. If the decision goes against him, he acquires new obligations to coordinate his activities with those which are placed in another establishment. If the head of the department or agency is a political figure, assuming responsibilities for advising the President and influencing legislation, he has, of course, the interest in the placement of governmental activities within the administrative structure that any person has who considers it his job to save his party from a mistake.

The distribution of governmental activities among the depart-

[2] *General Management of the Executive Branch; A Report to the Congress by the Commission on the Organization of the Executive Branch of the Government, February, 1949* (Government Printing Office, 1949), pp. 37, 41.

ments and agencies which make up the administrative branch is a matter of high concern to the President. He wants his Administration to be a success, and it will not be a success if the activities and undertakings of the government are not actually administered in accordance with the expectations of the American people. I think we may presume that the character and quality of administration will be affected by the way governmental activities are distributed among administrative departments and agencies. And we may therefore conclude that the President will want to be assured that a satisfactory distribution has been made. I do not think it follows, however, that the President must be given authority to say what that distribution must be.

There are two lines of reasoning which may be relied upon to support the proposition that the President should be given authority to assign activities among administrative departments and agencies, thereby determining how many separate administrative establishments there shall be and what activities each of these establishments shall carry on. It may be said, first, that each man who occupies the Presidency has unique qualities, special interests, and ways of working that are peculiar to him; therefore that any man who becomes President may need to change the structure of the administrative branch so as to increase his assurance that he can obtain response to his wishes. There is a second line of reasoning which does not depend upon a presumption that administrative structure needs to be changed with the changing personalities in the White House. It may be argued that if governmental activities are distributed among departments and agencies by legislation, they will not be redistributed (because Congress is slow to change the law) as promptly as changing conditions demand; therefore that the President (who can act promptly) should have the authority to redistribute them.

I think the first line of reasoning must be rejected. It presumes a personal relation of the President to administration which I think most unlikely to come about and which I consider most undesirable if it could be achieved. If the men we put in the White House undertook to work intimately with high administrative officials on a wide range of administrative matters, I think they might find that the pattern of administrative organization which suited one of them would prove frustrating to another. But I think that the President's personal relation to administration of necessity must be (and, for reasons which I give elsewhere, should be) confined to a limited number of issues of outstanding importance. The nature of the administrative structure will greatly affect the ability of any President to get what he wants in administration; but the administrative structure which enables one President to get what he wants will serve another quite as well.

It is the second line of reasoning which appealed to the President's Committee on Administrative Management and led it to recommend that the President be given authority to assign and reassign activities among administrative establishments: ". . . public policy and efficiency require a continual change in the division of work of government. . . . The work of reorganization is a continuing task. . . . It is a task that cannot be done once for all. It will require continuing attention."[3] Admittedly the President can, and if he had the authority doubtless would, change the structure of the administrative branch more frequently than Congress will if changes must be made by enactment of legislation. Why then did the Hoover Commission not recommend that the President be given authority to assign and reassign governmental activities by executive order?

As I said earlier in this discussion, the Hoover Commission appeared to be of the opinion that Congress should determine, at the time it provides for a new governmental activity, where it is to be located in the administrative structure. If it is to go to an existing administrative establishment, the establishment which is to administer it should be named in the law; if a new agency is to be created to administer the activity, the agency should be created by statute. But once the activity has been placed, the President should be able

[3] *Report of the President's Committee on Administrative Management, supra,* p. 33.

to provide for its reassignment in a reorganization plan to be laid before Congress and which shall go into effect without amendment unless rejected by both houses of Congress. Unfortunately for you and me, the Commission did not say why it preferred this arrangement to a grant of complete authority over organization to the President such as the Committee on Administrative Management recommended.

In my own opinion, the position of the Hoover Commission is sounder than that of the Committee on Administrative Management. I arrive at that conclusion because of the basic premise with which I start and which I stated at the beginning of this chapter —that Congress should have what it wants in the way of administrative organization if it can decide what it wants without diverting too much time from other matters which compete for its time, and if it can provide for what it wants without defeating other purposes which it considers more important.

I see no reason to doubt that Congress can find time to inform itself sufficiently to support a judgment as to where any new governmental activity should be located in the administrative structure. Congress is required in our system of government to set forth in the statute the character of the new governmental activity or undertaking which it institutes. Being familiar with and concerned about the public need which calls for action, being preoccupied with the development of a program of governmental activity to meet that need, Congressmen are led to consider what arrangements for administration are most likely to result in the character and quality of administration they desire. For intelligent consideration of that question, they are excellently equipped. As members of appropriations committees and legislative committees before whom administrative officials appear, a substantial number of Congressmen acquire an impressive body of knowledge about the character and quality of administration in different departments and agencies. Their basis for a judgment as to how the new activity would fare if entrusted to any of the existing administrative establishments is doubtless far superior to that of the President, who may know no more than that he does or does not have confidence in the officials who head those establishments.

If the President has a judgment as to where a new activity should be placed in the administrative structure, he is not shut out of influence because the decision will be made by the enactment of a statute. He is a part of the lawmaking process. If he brings in the proposal for the new undertaking, he probably will indicate the arrangements for administration which he prefers. If the bill is prepared by members of Congress, the President will get a chance to say what he thinks it should include. If the measure comes to him with provisions for administration that he does not like, he can veto if his displeasure is great enough to justify so drastic an action.

There was difference of opinion among the men who drafted our present Constitution as to who should decide where to place governmental activities in the administrative branch and therefore decide what new administrative departments and agencies are needed. Some members of the Constitutional Convention thought these decisions (i.e., the distribution of governmental activities among departments and agencies, and the creation of new departments and agencies) should be made by the President as an expression of executive power; others thought they should be made by Congress and the President together as an expression of legislative power. The Constitution as finally adopted contained no positive statement as to where the power to decide these matters should lie, but custom soon fixed the understanding that the decision would be made by the lawmaking body.

The first important departures from this rule occurred in World War II when President Franklin D. Roosevelt was, by statute, given a substantial amount of authority to determine how wartime activities should be administered. Under this grant of power he brought into existence a number of new administrative agencies such as the War Production Board, the Office of Price Administration, and the War Manpower Commission. A few of the agencies established by Presidential order, the Office of Price Administration for instance, were later "re-established" by statute, but most of them carried on their activities and were abolished without ever having received any statutory blessing other than that implied by recognition of their existence in appropriations and other legislative references to their existence.[4]

The grant of authority to the President to decide which administrative agency shall administer a program of government, and to create a special agency for the job if he thinks it desirable, appears to be highly appropriate in time of war. Possibly, there may be occasion for a like grant of authority in other times of emergency, or in ordinary times if the new governmental activity is of minor significance. Clearly, Congress ought not occupy itself in deciding where to put a governmental activity if the majority of Congressmen are of the opinion that they need their time for matters of higher importance.

When a decision is made that a governmental activity shall be administered by a new administrative establishment to be set up for that purpose, it becomes necessary to decide what kind of office shall be placed at the top of that establishment to manage its affairs. This is the second of the three problems in administrative organization listed above (p. 96) for consideration in this discussion. It seems to me that this is a matter which Congress may well insist on deciding itself. For the nature of the office at the top of the establishment will have a significant effect on the character of the administration to be provided. If Congress wants the new activity to be administered with a high concern for the views of the President, it may attempt to get that result by putting a single officer at the top, perhaps specifying that he shall have cabinet rank. If it wants the activity administered without regard for the political policies which may be predominant at any time (as it well may in the case of a regulatory activity), it may decide to put a bi-partisan commission at the top of the establishment and

[4] The principal acts from which President Franklin D. Roosevelt derived his special wartime authority to institute new government activities and set up new administrative agencies are: 54 Statutes at Large, at pp. 676 and 885 (1940); 55 Statutes at Large at pp. 31 and 838 (1941); and 56 Statutes at Large 176 (1942).

insulate the commissioners from easy removal by the President. Or Congress may be of the opinion that still another type of office is called for, as will be the case if it thinks the agency should have the status of a governmental corporation. Certainly these are matters of importance to Congress; I think Congressmen may well consider them important enough to justify the expenditure of time which is necessary to reach judgments about them.

The third of the three problems of administrative organization enumerated above (p. 96) for attention in this chapter relates to the internal organization of the department or agency. When Congress creates a new administrative establishment it is likely to include in the statute provisions which fix its internal organization, specifying the major divisions which shall be set up, naming the activities to be carried on by the different divisions, perhaps even fixing the salaries to be paid to certain officials. In like manner, when it locates a new activity in an existing establishment Congress frequently creates a new bureau, prescribes its general organization, and gives it a special status in the department or agency of which it is to be a part. As I noted above, the President's Committee on Administrative Management appeared to think it proper for the President to do these things, but not for Congress; and the Hoover Commission thought that neither the President nor Congress should make any decisions concerning the internal organization of an administrative department or agency.

It seems to me that Congress can easily defeat its major purposes by excessive regulation of details of administrative organization. What Congress hopes to gain by specifying the internal organization of the department or agency may finally be lost because the official at the top of the establishment is rendered powerless to construct an organization which he can use to administer the laws the way Congress wants them administered. The man who sits at the top of an administrative department or agency is a part of the organization which he heads. The way the organization as a whole does its work will depend in part on the way the remainder of the organization responds to him; and the nature of that response, in turn, will depend in part on the structure of the organization. The objective in devising administrative structure is to make certain that there are open connections for stimulus and response throughout the organization. The official at the top, who is the primary receiver and interpreter of the wishes of the political branches, must have connections with the organization as a whole which assure him that there will be response to the instructions which he issues; and he must have equally adequate connections which bring to him the information and ideas that accumulate and are developed within the organization.

The head of the administrative establishment, as we shall see more fully later on, occupies a crucial position in our system of political direction and control of administration. We can hardly expect to have government in action respond to the wishes of the political branches if the highest officials who connect the administrative force to Congress and President do not have open and easy communications in each direction. I think we are most likely to get that kind of communication, and therefore to get the kind of response we want from the bureaucracy, if the head of the administrative establishment has a substantial amount of freedom to shape the organization to accord with his working habits and his views of how men must be organized to get things done.

It seems to me, however, that the Hoover Commission went much too far if it intended to say (as I understand it did) that Congress should not under any circumstances write into the law provisions which fix the internal organization of the administrative department or agency. It seems to me that there are a number of considerations which may properly lead Congress to put in the statute particular arrangements for administration which the head of the establishment must respect. When Congress provides for a new governmental activity or undertaking, it wants to know that it will fall into the hands of officials who will make an earnest effort to put it in successful operation. If Congress decides to put the new activity in an existing department or agency, must it permit the head of the establishment to scatter the new duties and responsibilities about his organization according to his judgment? I think Congress may properly say, "Set up a special organization [a bureau] in your department to be wholly responsible for this new activity so that it will not fall into the hands of a sector of the bureaucracy that may be antagonistic to the objectives toward which it is directed." Congress may want an accurate reporting on the costs, problems, and accomplishments relating to the new activity. In order to assure a reliable report, I think it may be wise to specify that the activity shall be centered in a special organization.

The same reasoning is applicable to the creation of new departments and agencies. If Congress establishes a single department to administer the many lending activities of the federal government, I think it may have ample reasons for specifying that loans for public housing shall be administered by an organization that is separate from the organization that administers loans for soil improvement and crop production; and that neither of these lending activities shall be mixed up in administration with the lending of money for industrial stability. If Congress creates a Department of Health and Security, it is surely justified in saying (if it considers the point important) that there shall continue to be a Public Health Service. If it decides to bring patents, antitrust law enforcement, and the regulation of trade practices together in a new Department of Industrial and Trade Regulation, Congress may well find that no concern for vigorous or efficient administration outweighs the advantages of preserving in the new department a distinct organization to be known as the Patent Office.

The President's Committee on Administrative Management thought that the President would be wise to create and preserve semi-autonomous bureaus within administrative departments; I think that Congress may properly insist on putting such provisions on the statute books. But I think we may properly ask Congressmen to bear in mind that when such provisions are put in the law, they necessarily limit the ability of the head of the administrative establishment to direct and control the work of the people who are under him. We have many situations, as the Hoover

Commission pointed out, where bureaus within a department have been given, or have achieved, a status which makes them virtually independent of both the head of the department and the President. Surely Congress should contribute to such a situation only after the most careful study.

We may agree that Congressmen are thoroughly competent to decide how activities of government shall be located in the administrative branch when they give that matter careful thought, and at the same time agree that Congress does a poor job of reconsidering their location after these activities have once got going. The same point is applicable to the determination of the character of the office at the head of the establishment and to the determination of features of internal organization. The Congressman is challenged to consider how the activity should be administered at the moment when the necessity for the activity is undergoing debate; he has much less occasion to consider how it ought to be administered when that activity is no longer the subject of controversy. There is a great deal more reason, therefore, for allowing the President to move activities of government about and reshape administrative organization than there is for permitting him to say where new activities shall be located and how new administrative departments and agencies shall be organized.

Congress gave the President his first important power to reorganize the administrative branch in January, 1918, when the Overman Act authorized President Wilson "to make such redistribution of functions among executive agencies as he may deem necessary." If, however, the President concluded that "any bureau should be abolished," he was required to report that fact to Congress, apparently for Congress to make the decision as to whether that bureau should be abolished or kept alive. Under the authority given him in this statute, President Wilson issued a number of orders shifting governmental activities and groups of officials about, and set up new organizations that enjoyed the status of separate administrative agencies. But the authority which the President acquired from this legislation was given him only for the period of the war and six months thereafter, and there was nothing in the law to indicate that he could launch the government into kinds of activity and undertaking that had not previously been authorized by statute.

Experience with the Overman Act and a few other statutes which authorized President Wilson to set up special agencies for special jobs proved to be generally satisfactory, and Congress conferred even greater authority on the President during World War II. President Roosevelt not only had power to shift agencies and functions of government about and to create new agencies; he could determine the necessity of undertaking new activities and could launch the government upon these new undertakings by executive decree. This authority expired at the close of the war.[5]

The necessity for reshaping the administrative structure is especially acute in wartime, but it is by no means confined exclusively to time of war. It is a thing that Congress can do on the advice of the President, but experience shows that Congress is usually slow to respond to his recommendations. The arrangement of administrative offices is of little interest or concern to the people at large; therefore, the judgment of Congressmen as representatives of the people is of limited importance. While many Congressmen personally have a sharp interest in certain departments and maintain a very thorough knowledge of a substantial sector of the administrative branch, most of them are likely to have very slight basis for judging the merits of specific recommendations for change. Where Congressmen are unable to relate a measure to definite considerations of public interest, they are especially susceptible to the pressures of interested parties who lobby for or against the measure under consideration. This has many times been proven to be the case in measures relating to administrative reorganization; it is not the judgment of Congress that prevails, but

[5] The Overman Act is in 40 Statutes at Large 556 (1918). Legislation relating to the conduct of World War I is compiled in *A Source-Book of Military Law and War-Time Legislation*, prepared by the War Department Committee on Education and Special Training (St. Paul, 1919).

the reluctance of Congress to risk an error in the face of organized pressures.

But while Congress, in one sense, has little concern about the structure of administrative departments, it yet has the greatest concern that the administrative organization be adequate to carry on effectively the functions of government which Congress has provided for by law. It may be willing for the President to organize and reorganize administration, but Congress must be assured that this will not be made a device for impairing any activity or undertaking which it wishes to have carried out.

What we need, apparently, is a formula for action whereby the President can shape the administrative branch as he will, so long as Congress finds no ground for positive objection. We appear to have found it.

Faced with the necessity of effecting economies in administration on the one hand and providing for the administration of new governmental undertakings on the other, President Hoover asked Congress to approve a number of organization changes which he recommended and called on Congress to institute a new procedure for dealing with such matters in the future. The procedure which he recommended, and which Congress adopted in 1932, authorized the President to put his proposals for reorganization into the definitive language of an executive order and lay it before Congress; if neither house objected to it, the order would go into effect in sixty days.

This preserved to Congress the full certainty that nothing would be done against its will. It enabled the President to get Congressional action on a proposal drawn up to his own satisfaction. Pressure groups and special interests working through their friends in Congress would have to defeat the measure as a whole; they could not get exceptions for their favored departments or bureaus by injecting amendments into the President's proposal.

The President's new power came too late in his term of office to enable President Hoover to make effective use of it. He submitted eleven separate reorganization plans to Congress in the fall of 1932, but a new President had then been elected and a new party was due to take over the federal government. Congress rejected all of President Hoover's plans and began getting ready for the incoming chief executive who had promised a New Deal. In the spring of 1933 it put on the statute books a new act which greatly enlarged the President's authority, and Franklin D. Roosevelt came into office with a charter of powers over administrative organization that President Wilson had not had in wartime. The President, under the new act, could not only shift administrative units about, he could abolish functions of government and dissolve the agencies charged with executing them. And Congress could neither kill his actions nor alter them.

The authority given President Roosevelt at the beginning of the New Deal was for a two-year period only. Congress has on successive occasions renewed the President's power over administrative organization, each time for a limited period. With the exception of the legislation which was in effect during World War II, none of these statutes gave the President power as comprehensive or as free of Congressional review as that conferred on President Roosevelt in 1933. Each act has given the President authority to redistribute governmental activities among departments and agencies, to abolish agencies that are stripped of their powers, to create new administrative establishments, and to change the internal organization of departments and agencies. Each statute has specified certain governmental activities or administrative establishments which the President may not touch, and each has required that the President's proposed actions be laid before Congress and be found acceptable by either one or both houses. Under the act of 1945 (which expired in the spring of 1948) the President's proposals were to go into effect sixty days after they were submitted to Congress unless during the sixty-day period both houses by majority vote indicated disapproval. President Truman put only a limited amount of reorganization into effect under this act. He presented three plans to Congress in May, 1946, one of which was rejected by both houses. Later he submitted four more plans, two of which were rejected. The Housing and Home Finance Agency was set up by one of the plans which was allowed to go into effect.[6]

The procedure established in the act of 1945 seems to me to provide a highly satisfactory relationship between legislative and executive power over administrative reorganization. To obtain enactment of the laws which he sponsors, the President must win the support of a majority in each house; to make his reorganization plan effective, he needs the support of one house only. And his reorganization proposal cannot be distorted or vitiated by amendments in either chamber. This seems to me an adequate recognition of the President's special interest in the character of administrative organization and a sufficient concession to his capacity for prompt action. I do not think he needs authority to make changes in administration for which he cannot get the support of a majority in either house of Congress. If Congressmen have so little confidence in what he proposes that a majority in both houses refuse to let the President's recommendations go through, is it not best that administrative organization stand as it is for a while longer? If special interests lobbying for a particular agency can induce both houses of Congress to protect their child, is it not too early for the President to defy such a sentiment?

The Hoover Commission considered the Reorganization Act of 1945 so excellent a model that it opened the first of its reports to Congress in 1949 with a plea that it be reenacted. Indeed, it made only one suggestion for change in the law—the elimination of provisions which excepted some departments and agencies from the reach of reorganization plans and limited the nature of the changes which the President could propose. Almost coincident with this recommendation by the Hoover Commission, a bill in keeping with its views was introduced in Congress. After signifi-

[6] The various acts which have authorized the President to lay reorganization plans before Congress are found in: 47 Statutes at Large at p. 413 (1932) and p. 1517 (1933); 53 Statutes at Large 561 (1939); 55 Statutes at Large 838 (1941); 59 Statutes at Large 613 (1945).

cant amendment, it was enacted and on June 20, 1949, went into effect as the Reorganization Act of 1949.[7]

Like previous reorganization acts, the Reorganization Act of 1949 is of limited duration; the last plan to be submitted must get to Congress not later than April 1, 1953. The new act differs from the act of 1945 in three important respects, however.

First, the reach of the President's plans for reorganization may go much farther under the new law than was permitted under the act of 1945. No department or agency is excepted from inclusion in plans for change. The President's plans may propose to move activities away from any department or agency and to attach them to any other department or agency. His plans may alter the internal organization of any administrative establishment (terminate the semi-autonomous status of bureaus, for instance), strip an establishment of all its activities, and abolish it. New administrative establishments may be proposed; even executive departments with secretaries at the top who sit in the cabinet may be brought into existence in this way. And presumably (since there is nothing in the law to indicate otherwise) the plans which the President submits to Congress may alter the nature of the office at the top of any existing establishment.

Second, the plans of the President must go before Congress, where they are subject to study and debate but not to amendment. Either house may kill the plan if a majority of the entire membership vote adversely. This is in sharp contrast to the procedure under the act of 1945 which allowed the plan to go into effect unless both houses acted adversely, and which provided that the decision in either house should be by a majority of the members present and voting.

Third, the Reorganization Act of 1949 provides that the plan which the President lays before Congress may provide for the "abolition of all or any part of the functions of any agency." This is another way of saying that the President may propose

[7] Public Law 109, 81st Congress (Act of June 20, 1949).

the discontinuance of any activity or undertaking of government which has been provided for by law. The effect of this grant of authority is to give the President a special power in respect to the continuance or termination of activities and undertakings comparable to the special power which the right to veto gives him over the institution of activities and undertakings. If the President opposes the institution of an activity or undertaking, he can prevent it unless it is forced upon him by two-thirds of those present and voting in the two houses öf Congress. By including a proposal to do so in a reorganization plan, he can terminate any activity or undertaking unless a majority of all members of one house of Congress vote to keep it going by rejecting his reorganization plan in toto.

It will be seen that the Reorganization Act of 1949 is more than an act to facilitate administrative reorganization. It is an act to provide a ready means for changing administrative organization and terminating governmental activities and undertakings. No doubt the inclusion of the latter of the two purposes in the bill was in large part responsible for the decision of Congress to require the approval of both houses of Congress in order for the President's proposals to go into effect. If so, then Congress is to be applauded for having insisted on the concurrence of both houses, in my opinion. I have said already that I think the President should be able to make changes in administrative organization in any instance where he can win the support of a majority in one house. But I can hardly overstate the strength of my conviction that the President and one house of Congress should not be able to nullify programs of government which the President and two houses of Congress have previously established. I think that the process which the Constitution enjoins for the making of laws is the best process for reaching decisions that the government shall engage in new activities and undertakings; I see no justification for a different process for reaching decisions that the government will no longer engage in those activities and undertakings.

BIBLIOGRAPHIC NOTE

The writing which deals critically with authority to create administrative organization is of recent date, and most of it has as its primary objective to justify the authority given the President to lay reorganization plans before Congress. I have not found in print an extended discussion of the relation of the language of the Constitution to the creation of administrative agencies, or change in their internal structure, but I have had the benefit of a carefully prepared paper by Mr. Lawrence Herson in which he argues most persuasively that the proper interpretation of the Constitution (based on the statements of the framers and their contemporaries and on exegesis of the document) gives the power to create administrative departments and agencies to the President.

The First Congress under the Constitution created three of our present great executive departments: State, Treasury, and War. There was a considerable debate in connection with the creation of these establishments, but it went mainly to the relationship which high officials in these departments should bear to the President on one hand and Congress on the other; very little of significance was said about the authority of Congress and President respectively to create administrative establishments. See: Charles C. Thatch, Jr., *The Creation of the Presidency, 1775–1789* (Baltimore, 1922), ch. 5; Edward S. Corwin, *The President's Removal Power under the Constitution* (New York, 1927), pp. 10 ff.; James Hart, *The American Presidency in Action, 1789* (New York, 1948), ch. 7; and Leonard D. White, *The Federalists* (New York, 1948), chs. 10–12. Corwin's small book is reprinted in *Selected Essays on Constitutional Law* (Chicago, 1938), vol. 4, pp. 1467–1518 (pp. 1474 ff. relevant to debate of 1789).

There are a few books which bring together the principal facts about the creation of the different departments and agencies of the federal government and note the principal changes in their organization which have occurred over the years. There are many more which do this for a particular department or agency. The primary objective in all these writings, however, is to relate what happened; one finds very little to enlighten him about the advantages and disadvantages of legislative control of administrative organization as compared with control by the chief executive or the official at the head of the administrative agency. The most informative of the books which apply to the administrative branch as a whole are: Lloyd M. Short, *Development of National Administrative Organization in the United States* (Baltimore, 1923); and Henry B. Learned, *The President's Cabinet* (New Haven, 1912). Over a period of years, beginning in 1918, the Institute for Government Research published approximately 70 studies of individual administrative organizations (independent agencies and major divisions of departments and agencies), and most, if not all, of these contain a legislative history of the organization. Much fuller accounts of creation and change of particular administrative establishments can be found in the following, however: John M. Gaus and L. O. Wolcott, *Public Administration and the United States Department of Agriculture* (Chicago, 1940); Charles F. Roos, *NRA Economic Planning* (Bloomington, Indiana, 1937); and Gerard Henderson, *The Federal Trade Commission* (New Haven, 1924).

The President's Committee on Administrative Management produced a report of 47 pages under the title of *Administrative Management in the Government of the United States* (Government Printing Office, 1937). The report with nine memoranda which were prepared for the Committee and a brief "Message from the President of the United States" also appeared in a volume of 382 pages under the title *The President's Committee on Administrative Management; Report of the Committee with Studies of Administrative Management in the Federal Government* (Government Printing Office, 1937). Throughout this book, I cite the report as *Report of the President's Committee on Administrative Management;* and I cite the larger volume as *President's Committee on Administrative Management; Report with Special Studies.* These documents are now out of print, but at the time of my writing, a reproduction of the report (not of the special studies) can be obtained from the Public Administration Service, 1313 East 60th Street, Chicago, 37.

The Hoover Commission (official title: The Commission on Organization of the Executive Branch of the Government) made its report in sections which were printed in separate pamphlets by the Government Printing Office during 1949. There are 18 pamphlets which contain findings and recommendations; a 19th pamphlet contains a number of generalizations, summarization of the previous findings and recommendations, and an index of all the pamphlets. This pamphlet is entitled *Concluding Report; A Report to the Congress by the Commission on Organization of the Executive Branch of the Government, May 1949* (Government Printing Office, 1949). The Hoover Commission had a great number of special studies prepared for its use and to date 18 of these have been printed, all by the Government Printing Office during 1949. Each of these is designated on the cover (but not on the title page) as a "Task Force Report" and is given separate identification as an appendix to the reports of the Commission; the first in the series of task force reports is labeled Appendix A, the last Appendix R. *A Digest of Reports of the Commission on Organization of the Executive Branch of the Government* (61 pages in length) appeared as Senate Committee Print, 81st Congress, 1st session (Government Printing Office, 1949) by order of the Senate Committee on Expenditures in the Executive Departments.

The literature relating to the President's authority to lay reorganization plans before Congress is extremely limited. The only careful analysis appears to be: John D. Millett and L. D. Rogers, "The Legislative Veto and the Reorganization Act of 1939," in *Public Administration Review*, vol. 1, pp. 176–189 (1941). One or both houses usually conduct hearings relating to the enactment of legislation providing for the President to submit reorganization plans, and may conduct hearings relating to the plans which he submits. For illustrative hearings, see: *Reorganization Act of 1949;* Hearings before the Committee on Expenditures in the Executive Departments, U.S. Senate, 81st Congress, 1st session on S. 526 (Government Printing Office, 1949); *Reorganization Plans Nos. 1, 2, and 3 of 1946;* Hearings before the Committee on Expenditures in the Executive Departments, House of Representatives, 79th Congress, 2d session on H. Con. Res. 151, H. Con. Res. 154, H. Con. Res. 155 (Government Printing Office, 1946); and *Reorganization Plans Nos. 1 and 2 of 1947;* Hearings before the same committee of the House of Representatives, 80th Congress, 1st session on H. Con. Res. 49, H. Con. Res. 50 (Government Printing Office, 1947).

On the politics of support for and opposition to change in administrative organization, see: E. Pendleton Herring, "Social Forces and the Reorganization of the Federal Bureaucracy," in *Southwestern Social Science Quarterly*, vol. 15, pp. 185–200 (1934); Joseph M. Ray, "The Defeat of the Administration Reorganization Bill," in the same journal, vol. 20, pp. 115–124 (1939); Avery M. Leiserson, "Political Limitations on Executive Reorganization," in *American Political Science Review*, vol. 51, pp. 68–84 (1947); Richard L. Neuberger, "How Much Conservation?," in *Saturday Evening Post* for June 15, 1940; and Leslie A. Miller, "The Battle That Squanders Billions," in the same journal for May 14, 1948. If one wishes to gauge for himself the character of the opposition which comes forth when major changes in administrative organization are proposed, he may find a good deal of the evidence he is looking for in the hearings just cited. See also: *Reorganization of Executive Departments;* Hearing before Joint Committee on the Reorganization of the Administrative Branch of the Government on S. J. Res. 282 of 67th Congress, 68th Congress, 1st session (Government Printing Office, 1924), pp. 415–469; and *National Defense Establishment;* Hearings before Senate Committee on Armed Services on S. 758, 80th Congress, 1st session (Government Printing Office, 1947).

CHAPTER 7

PROVIDING THE MONEY

The lawmaking authority has no more effective means of exercising direction and control over the administrative branch than that of granting and withholding money. As long as money is the medium by which we induce men and women to work and supply the materials that government uses, the amount of money that an administrative organization has to spend will effectively determine what it can do. As we saw in an earlier chapter, the administrative establishment carries on activities which are assigned to it by legislation. While the controlling legislation indicates the nature of the work which the administrative establishment is to do, it rarely, if ever, fixes the "measure" of that work. The annual appropriation, which determines how much money the establishment will have available, regulates the program of activity for the year—how wide a range of activity can be undertaken, how intensively various activities can be pursued, how thorough a job can be done. The controlling legislation fixes objectives and sets limits for the work of the administrative organization; the annual appropriation regulates the measure of its work for the year.

No serious student of government questions the desirability of giving the representative assembly the principal authority to determine how much money the government needs, how it shall be raised, and how it shall be distributed among the various activities and undertakings in which the government is engaged. The history of conflict between autocrats and parliaments is in large part a story of struggle for control of the purse. Wherever parliamentary institutions are dominant, the representative assembly has a substantial authority over the allotment of money to the other branches of the government. We made sure that this would be the case in our own country by writing into the Constitution that "No money shall be drawn from the Treasury, but in consequence of appropriations made by law." State constitutions contain language to the same effect.

But while there is general agreement that appropriations should be fixed by law, and therefore that Congress should have the final say as to how money shall be distributed among the administrative establishments, there is, nevertheless, a great deal of disagreement as to just how much authority Congress should have and as to how it should use it. Do the individual appropriation decisions of Congress add up to an expression of its best judgment concerning the financing of the government as a whole? How much does Congress know about comparative needs for money and prospective uses of money before it appropriates, and how much does it find out about the way money is spent after it appropriates? Do the decisions which are made in appropriating money confirm and support the decisions made in the enactment of the legislation carried out by the administrative branch; or does Congress defeat its major and more carefully thought out objectives by an unsatisfactory appropriation process? Congressmen, bureaucrats, and academic students of government have many different answers for these questions.

It is important to realize, at the beginning of this discussion, that the attitude of Congressmen toward the importance of appropriations has been undergoing change in recent years, and that the appropriation practices of the past, for that reason, cannot be relied on to indicate what the appropriation practices will be in the future.

This point is illustrated by the changing state of mind among Congressmen as to how the total amount of money to be appropriated shall be arrived at. It has long been the custom to handle the appropriations as if they were a number of near-independent problems. For approximately thirty years, the President has annually submitted a budget to Congress in which he has set forth the amounts he would like to have appropriated to each of the administrative departments and agencies. This document has indicated clearly enough the total amount of money that the President thought ought to be made available for all purposes of government. Ever since the executive budget was established (in 1921), Congress has worked from it as a basis for evaluating needs for money and fixing appropriations. But the requests for the several administrative establishments were distributed among a number of different subcommittees of the House Appropriations Committee, and each subcommittee worked on its assignment without much knowledge of what decisions other subcommittees were making. One subcommittee might be operating on a free spending philosophy, while another approached miserliness in its attitude. The same scattering of inquiry, deliberation, and recommendation took place in the Senate when the appropriation bills moved over to that chamber. Some correlation of the recommendations coming in from the subcommittees was effected in the two appropriations committees sitting as a whole (particularly in that of the House), and of course the amounts recommended were subject to debate and alteration on the floor of each chamber. But these integrating influences (including the President's original recommendations) were not sufficient to avoid a net result that the total appropriations for any year were arrived at by adding up a great number of separately considered appropriations. There was not, in either house of Congress, a systematic laying of the proposed appropriations side by side and a thorough going over the whole to make sure that government, in its entirety, was financed according to a body of consistent objectives and evaluations.

The enormous expenditures of the federal government during the depression and World War II, and the prospect of continuing heavy expenditures and high taxes, has forced Congress to face the fact that appropriations must be treated more seriously than heretofore. The expenditures of the federal government are not merely a major item in the national cost of living; they are an important factor in fixing the general price level; they have a significant effect on the availability of money and credit for the nation's non-governmental enterprise. The total of the annual appropriations is more than a calculation of what the nation can afford to spend on the various activities and undertakings of the national government; it is an economic fact of great consequence in itself.

Because it recognized this fact, Congress adopted a self-regulating ordinance in 1946 which provides that each year it shall fix the approximate total cost of the federal government before examining the case for separate appropriations.[1] The amount which the President recommends in his annual budget is, of course, such a figure. If the two houses of Congress are controlled by the President's party and are in complete sympathy with the President's entire program, it may be supposed that they will find his figure reasonably acceptable. The first Congress to act on the budget after the new appropriation practice went into effect was in opposition to the President, however, and in each of its two annual sessions the majority membership in each house took the position that the President's figure was several billion dollars too high. In spite of the fact that each of the two chambers had strong leadership, the majority party membership of Congress as a whole was unable to agree upon a total which should be fixed in advance for the entire annual appropriations. As a consequence, despite the good resolve of 1946, the appropriations for the fiscal years 1947–48 and 1948–49 were made in essentially the same manner as in years past—by fixing appropriations for the several administrative departments one by one, then looking at the final result to see what the total turns out to be. We will not know how the good resolve of 1946 is likely to affect appropriation practice over

[1] This provision is one of several included in the Legislative Reorganization Act of 1946. 60 Statutes at Large 812.

the years until we see what its fate may be at the hands of a Congress which is friendly to the President and in sympathy with his plans for running the country.

Regardless of whether Congress agrees in advance upon a grand total for the annual appropriations, it will have the final say (by passing appropriation bills over the President's veto, if necessary) as to how much money will be made available to carry on the activities of the federal government and meet its outstanding obligations; and it will have the final say as to how this money shall be distributed among the various activities and undertakings of the government and among the administrative organizations that carry on these activities and undertakings.

Not all of the costs of the national government are controlled by annual appropriations. There are a few continuing appropriations and some appropriations for fixed periods which are more than one year in length. The statement can stand as generally true, however, that each year Congress reviews the operations of the national government and establishes for each administrative establishment the measure of its operations for the year—how much it can undertake and how thorough and complete a job it can do in respect to the things that it does undertake.

As noted above, requests for appropriations come to Congress as recommendations of the President, supported by his budget document. The requests (called estimates) are carefully reviewed by a number of small subcommittees that are set up by the House of Representatives to consider the different parts of the budget. Top officials and other spokesmen for the various administrative departments and agencies appear before these subcommittees to explain and defend the amounts that the President has recommended for their respective establishments. Perhaps there is a presumption in the minds of the Congressmen that the recommendations which the President has submitted are carefully and wisely made and should be respected. But it is a presumption that affords the spokesmen for the administrative departments and agencies little comfort. Members of the subcommittees become wise in the ways of the administrative organizations and in certain qualities of the officials who appear before them year after year. They are satisfied, on the basis of past experience, with parts of the administrative operations under consideration; they carve out for extensive discussion those parts of the operations that they do not understand or are skeptical about; they are acute and persistent in the questioning by which they try to determine the relation of the proposed activities to the public interest, as they conceive it.

The recommendations of these subcommittees are reviewed by the entire Appropriations Committee of the House of Representatives, and the recommendations of that body are brought to the floor of the House for approval or modification. The amounts that finally go to the Senate for consideration have thus been arrived at after a considerable inquiry into facts and a thoughtful consideration of the many segments of public policy with which the various departments and agencies are concerned. The Senate, through its Appropriations Committee and subcommittees, may again delve quite fully into the reasons for the amounts requested by the departments and agencies and recommended by the President. For the most part, however, the Senate confines its inquiry to a review of the findings of the House. The administrative official who wishes to protest the determination of the House ordinarily will have a chance to be heard in the Senate; the Senate will itself open up any other part of the House action that it has a reason to question.

The consequence of this process is a searching inquiry into the preoccupations and performance of individual administrative establishments and the relation of what is going on to the public interest, as Congressmen conceive the public interest. When the appropriation for any sector of the administrative branch is made, Congress has announced its determination as to the range and intensity of government activity in which that part of the administrative branch shall engage for the coming year. Whether the decisions of Congress are wise or not, of course, cannot be determined;

who is to say that his judgment is better than that of the representative assembly of the nation?[2]

While we have no standard against which to judge the wisdom of Congress' action in appropriating money, we can make some observations concerning its consistency. Congressmen are among the first persons to admit that the left hand of Congress (the appropriations process) does not always show respect for what the

[2] I feel obliged to note that the literature produced by academic students of government, some of whom have had a great deal of opportunity to observe how Congress does things, is generally in agreement that Congress does poorly what I am convinced it does well. Mr. George B. Galloway, in his *Congress at the Crossroads* (New York, 1946), p. 247, probably speaks for most of them when he evaluates the subcommittee inquiry in these words: "The questions tend to be of a random, impromptu character, picking on this or that item in a spot-check quest for information. Committeemen are faced by departmental experts, schooled in the art of justifying their requests. Burdened with many other duties, committee members are seldom prepared to make a penetrating analysis of the estimates and tend to appropriate blindly."

I forwarded the above statement by Mr. Galloway, with one which reflects my own convictions, to two men whom I consider to be sharp and thoughtful observers. Both have long been engaged in the preparation of estimates of appropriation requirements and in defending them before Congress. One wrote in reply: "My own observation is that for the most part the inquiry of Congress into appropriation requests is very superficial. How can it be otherwise? A few Congressmen, pressed for time by the many general bills before the Congress and by the deadlines for the appropriation bills, can give only a few hours, or at most a few days, to any one agency. The small staffs of the appropriation committees can give little more time to an agency. A large part of the time that can be devoted to an agency by the committee members is frequently spent upon inconsequential matters because of a special interest of some member or because of a lack of understanding about what are the important facts. The result is that reductions and increases are made with what seems to me to be astonishingly little knowledge." The other official (now deceased) wrote: "I am glad to say that my observation and experience checks with yours as to the evaluation of the effective manner in which the appropriations committees of Congress do their job. While undoubtedly there are episodes of the type described I think the impression that is apt to be gained from the paragraph you quote from Dr. Galloway's book is one that very much underrates the capacity of these subcommittees to get at the basic considerations involved in the multitude of matters that come before them. Over the years I have come to have very great respect indeed for their ability to examine programs, isolate issues, and formulate judgments. If it is correct, as Dr. Galloway points out, that 'they are seldom prepared to make a penetrating analysis,' then the effective work they do, and which you also state you have observed, is all the more remarkable because it is done in spite of that."

right hand (the legislative process) is trying to do. At the same time or at any time after Congress (acting on the recommendation of legislative committees) lays out a program of activity to be carried on by an administrative department, Congress (acting on the advice of appropriations committees) may make it impossible for the same administrative department to meet the unavoidable costs of doing what it has been ordered to do.

Some of the gap between the legislation which gives the department its job and the appropriations which determine how much of the job can be done is intentional. Congress might reasonably (in the authorizing legislation) tell the Coast Guard that it is to proceed as rapidly as possible with the construction of lighthouses where needed; then, when the country goes to war, tell it, by making no appropriation for that purpose, that it shall construct no lighthouses for the duration of the war. There can be no objection to this, if the appropriation act makes clear to administrative officials what part of the department's activities are to be cut down and gives them a guide as to how Congress wants the appropriation spread over the activities that are to be carried on. This it does not always do. The result is that administrative officials, having instructions to do many things but not enough money to do all of them, use their own judgment and not that of Congress as to what shall be done and what shall not be done.

The legislation providing for regulation of packers and stockyards, for instance, makes it mandatory for the Department of Agriculture to post in each public stockyard information pertaining to charges which may lawfully be made for various services and uses of stockyard facilities, and pertaining to certain other conditions of doing business in stockyards. The officials of the department frequently, if not ordinarily, find that the appropriation which is provided for this purpose is insufficient to enable them to make these postings as required by law. The administrative officials, not Congress, then decide whether to make adequate postings in some places or to pursue inadequate postings everywhere. An official with a substantial amount of experience in two or three administrative departments of the federal government, speaking of this situation generally (not with reference to the regulation of packers and stockyards), tells me that he thinks direction and control by Congress is frequently weakened, if not totally destroyed, right where it is most needed, by the inconsistency of legislative requirements and appropriation provisions.

It must not be supposed that all appropriations are indefinite, leaving the administrative officials highly uncertain as to what Congress wants done with the money which it provides. Many appropriations acts contain sharp and precise statements as to how money shall be used and how money may not be used. Some of the limitations are specific prohibitions, others are allocations of specific amounts for clearly defined purposes. The Department of the Navy, for instance, may be told that none of its appropriation shall be used to make time and motion studies relating to civilian personnel; the Department of Agriculture may be forbidden to use any of its money in an effort to determine whether sprays that kill bugs are harmful to man.

More frequently, however, the limitation is in the form of an itemization of purposes with an indication of the specific amounts that may be spent for each. The appropriation is likely, for example, to state the maximum number of automobiles that may be purchased and the maximum amount of money that may be spent for them; in this way, Congress both honors and puts teeth in the general dislike of the American people to see bureaucrats riding around in public-owned cars. It has been the custom for several years to segregate and definitely limit the amount of money that may be spent for printing and binding; by this device, Congress hopes to prevent an abuse (too much publicity) that it believes to be an occupational disease among bureaucrats. Congress is skeptical about that group of activities that falls generally under the heading of research and planning. If it thinks that a government department is being turned into a laboratory for the delight and support of college professors, or is engaged in inquiries that will be used by administrative officials or others to force the hand of

Congress in establishing public policy—in either event, Congress is likely to demand that all of the department's activities of this sort be brought together in one appropriation estimate. This makes it easier for Congress to see just what is going on and enables it to put a ceiling on such activities by fixing a maximum amount which may be spent on them.

Limitations on expenditures vary widely. Some of them reflect Congress' distrust of the officials who will be charged with spending the money; some of them represent nothing more than the continuance of a practice that got started long ago; some of them are favored, if not requested, by the officials of the administrative establishment. The appropriations to the Federal Communications Commission are regularly in two sums, a small amount for printing and binding, and a lump sum for all other purposes. Limitations are imposed, however, on the amount that may be expended for certain purposes. Of $6,240,000 allowed to FCC for the year 1947–48, not more than $3,612,500 could be spent to pay the salaries and wages of employees in Washington, D.C.; separate ceilings were fixed for a few other items (e.g., $122,500 for motor vehicles and travel expenses), but the total of the latter kind of limitation amounted to less than $200,000.

I am not acquainted with any analysis of appropriation practice which indicates how far the experience of FCC deviates from the typical, if there is a typical experience. Veterans' Administration, during recent years, has been given more than a billion dollars in a lump sum for salaries and expenses. The Interstate Commerce Commission, on the other hand, gets a total appropriation about twice the size of that for FCC in four separate sums; no part of the money appropriated for one block of activities can be devoted to any of the activities which are provided for in another sum. And the Hoover Commission reported that the Bureau of Indian Affairs in the Department of Interior received its money for 1947–48 in approximately 100 separate appropriations ranging in amount from $114.53 to more than 11 million dollars.

The Hoover Commission deplored the lack of uniformity in

the breakdown of appropriations and stated that present practice causes administrative departments and agencies to employ more people than they would employ if their appropriations had less the effect of a strait jacket. Since it proposed a different kind of budget from that which is now submitted to Congress by the President, the Hoover Commission did not feel obliged to indicate what would constitute a proper breakdown of appropriations based on the present type of budget.[3] If anyone else has developed a systematic body of theory concerning the practical consequences of breaking down appropriations in different degrees of detail, I am not aware of it.

Regardless of what one thinks of the restrictions which Congress imposes on administration in the appropriation act, it in no sense approaches the hands-tieing practice of many state legislatures that single out individual employees and minor officials and fix specific salaries for them. A friend of mine, while teaching in a southern state university, was accosted by a fellow faculty member with the remark, "Come on down to the State House with me and see the legislature raise my salary." I once sat in a meeting of the Appropriations Committee of the Illinois House of Representatives and heard a member of the committee make the following remark: "Mr. Chairman, I have an amendment here to raise that salary item from $1500 to $1800. That fellow is up in my

[3] The proposal for a new type of budget and appropriation practice is in *Budgeting and Accounting; A Report to the Congress by the Commission on Organization of the Executive Branch of the Government, February 1949* (Government Printing Office, 1949). The statement concerning the breakdown of appropriations for the Bureau of Indian Affairs is on page 7 of that document. The statement that present practice in breaking down appropriations leads to unnecessary employment appears on page 33 of *General Management of the Executive Branch; A Report to the Congress by the Commission on Organization of the Executive Branch of the Government, February 1949* (Government Printing Office, 1949). The findings and recommendations of the Commission's research and advisory staff concerning budgeting and appropriations are in *Fiscal, Budgeting and Accounting Systems of Federal Government; A Report with Recommendations Prepared for the Commission on Organization of the Executive Branch of the Government [Appendix E]* (Government Printing Office, 1949).

district, employed as a plumber's assistant in the state institution there. He's had a lot of sickness in his family during the past year. I know him and his family and I think we ought to help him out."

Nothing like that goes on in the appropriating action of Congress. Congress has its pork barrel and it has its patronage. It may try to make a river out of a creek by ordering it dredged. It may save a fellow Congressman's political hide by authorizing a new post office building where the teetering Congressman admits that none is needed. But Congress does not tie the hands of administrative officials with detailed specifications in the appropriations act in a degree comparable with what regularly occurs in many of our states.

The appropriation acts of Congress are enactments of law; being law, they must be obeyed. They are, however, subject to different interpretations. The task of interpreting appropriation language falls first upon the department or agency to whom the act of appropriation applies. The officials of the department or agency must determine what Congress meant to authorize and what it did not mean to authorize before they can proceed to spend the money. The General Accounting Office shares the task of interpreting the appropriations act, for it is a central accounting office having authority to decide whether money is legally or illegally paid out of the treasury. Finally, Congress may itself, in subsequent actions, restate or explain more fully what was its intent in particular acts of appropriation. Rarely do questions as to the meaning of appropriation language go to the courts for decision.

Under these circumstances, it is certainly natural and surely quite proper for the various individuals concerned to check their judgments with one another. Officials in the administrative departments and agencies frequently discuss with officials of the General Accounting Office the intent of Congress and the legal effect of appropriation language. The determinations of the Comptroller General are published and constitute a body of case law for the guidance of administrative officials. In the same manner, administrative officials seek the advice of Congress as to what it intended in particular appropriation language, and what it would like in instances where its instructions are not clear.

There are many signs indicating the intention of Congress, in addition to the plain meaning of plain words, which the administrative official may examine and heed. The appropriations committee, or its subcommittee, may include in its printed report statements which give some indication of what those particular members of Congress expect the administrative establishment to do with the money given it. While such statements do not have the force of law, they are carefully studied by administrative officials; and many, if not virtually all, officials who have been a long time in the federal service regard these statements as binding instructions. Individual members of the committee, or other members of Congress speaking on the floor, may indicate understandings as to the limitations implied in the appropriation act; if there is reason to believe that these expressions represent the general understanding of Congress, they will be respected by administrative officials.

Especially binding are the commitments made by officials of the administrative establishment in explaining the activities and needs of their organization to the subcommittee. The recommendations for the administrative establishment in the President's budget constitute at least the skeleton of a plan for operations. They show the amounts that will be needed to carry on particular activities or phases of the agency's program. The presentation which the officials of the agency make in explanation and support of the President's recommendations set forth their plans for the year's operations even more fully and create a presumption that the money which Congress allows will be spent in accordance with the plans that are set forth. There may be statements by the committee members that the agency ought not, or statements by administrative officials that the agency will not, spend money for this or for that. Such statements reinforce the understanding that Congress is appropriating money for particular purposes and in particular amounts.

Qualifying and interpretative language does not have the force of law unless it is incorporated in the appropriation act or elsewhere expressed in formal enactment. Nevertheless, an agency that treats lightly clear indications of Congressional intent is pretty certain to encounter the wrath of Congress sooner or later; and the administrative officials who offend in this respect get little sympathy from their fellow bureaucrats around Washington. Consequently, administrative officials take out insurance against reprimand or punishment by consulting with Congress before making a departure in spending that might later be construed as inconsistent with understandings previously arrived at.

Congress, as a whole, is not a body to which one can carry specific questions. It has not set up an office or committee to receive and give authoritative answers to specific questions. Administrative officials, therefore, lay their doubts before the chairmen of the appropriations committees of the two houses or of the subcommittees before which they appeared. Some of these communications inquire about the intent of the language in the appropriation act. More frequently, perhaps, they are simply informative statements, telling Congress of action taken or about to be taken that might occasion surprise if not adverse criticism. If the chairmen of the committees concerned have been advised that a novel step is about to be taken, and no objection is made, the administrative official has taken out insurance against reprimand at a later date.

This practice of seeking the advice and courting the approval of Congressional committees for particular acts contemplated by the administrative establishment has been adversely criticized by some students of government. A judicial court, faced with a difficult question as to the meaning of a statute, does not write to the Congressional committee that reported out the bill; the judge makes his own interpretation and enforces it. If Congress does not like the interpretation, it can change the language of the law. Appropriation acts are law; should not the administrative official make his own reading of the act and stand on it? So some have argued.

The principal objection to the communications between Congress and administrative officials relating to the activities of administrative departments and agencies does not rest, however, on an analogy to the position of the courts in law interpretation and enforcement. The objection is that the advice which Congressmen and Congressional committees give obstructs the efforts of the President to direct and control administration. If administrative officials may go to Congress for advice, Congressmen may go to administrative officials with recommendations. Congressmen may originate instructions as readily as administrators may originate inquiries. If Congressmen can tell an administrator what they meant by statutory language, or what they intended by remarks made in a hearing, they can tell him what they probably would have said if they had thought of it. If Congressmen can tell an administrator what he is legally obligated to do, they can also tell him what he would be politically wise to do.

The consequences of Congressional intervention in administration, and the considerations that must be weighed in deciding what we should do about it, are given considerable attention at later points in this book, and they need not be further discussed at this moment. Regardless of how one feels about the present practices of Congressmen in checking up on administrative activities, there is general agreement that Congress ought to have some systematic and dependable means of finding out whether its intentions are respected and its instructions are obeyed by the several departments of government. If the representative assembly is really to control the purse, it must be able to do more than specify the purposes for which the money may be spent; it must know, before making more money available, that what it has provided to date has been used for the purposes specified.

It is generally conceded that Congress does not now have any dependable source of information on this matter.

The President, as the highest official in the administrative branch, might be required to make an annual report showing just how the year's appropriations were spent. Probably no one would consider this an adequate accounting. Congress may distrust the reporting of the President, as it distrusts the reporting of the various administrative departments themselves. The representative assembly is justified in refusing to depend upon the executive branch for the sole report on the money given it.

Most Congressmen (but certainly not all of them) apparently believed they were setting up an instrumentality that would provide independent scrutiny of spending and unbiased reporting of findings, when the General Accounting Office was established in 1921. The GAO, as we shall see more fully later on (Chapter 18), was given extensive authority to inquire into the financial transactions of the administrative departments and agencies. Special pains were taken to protect the GAO against intimidation and coercion by the President and administrative officials under the President. The head of the GAO, the Comptroller General, was made removable from office only by act of the two houses of Congress. He was declared in the act to be "independent of the executive departments," and at least one later statute stated that the GAO is "a part of the legislative branch of the Government."[4]

In spite of the fullness of its authority and the completeness of its immunity from executive influence, there has been widespread dissatisfaction with the performance of GAO as an auditing agency. It has not, in fact, subjected very much of the national bureaucratic domain to searching scrutiny. A good many critics of the GAO—and some Congressmen are in this group—think that the shortcomings of GAO derive in large part from the fact that the controlling legislation requires it to carry out incompatible functions. Others think that its shortcomings have been due to the character of leadership supplied by the Comptroller General, and many persons who fall into this group believe that GAO has lately begun to demonstrate that it can and will give Congress the kind

[4] The General Accounting Office was created and given its principal authority in the Budget and Accounting Act of 1921, 42 Statutes at Large 20; U.S. Code, title 31, secs. 41 ff. The act which stated that the GAO is in the legislative branch of the government is in 59 Statutes at Large 616 (1945).

of service that it presumably wants. And finally, there are some persons, Congressmen among them, who think that the defaults of GAO to date can be charged mainly against Congress—that Congress has not been organized in a way that would enable it either to advise GAO as to what studies it would like to have made or to give the consideration to the reports that would make it worth while to have them prepared. These matters are discussed further in Chapter 18.

Whatever be the explanation of the failure of Congress to get conclusive information concerning the way the executive branch uses the money which is appropriated to it, there is reason to believe that the deficiency is now being corrected. The GAO is making more audits than in times past and probably has improved the quality of its audits. And Congress, in keeping with a pledge made in the Legislative Reorganization Act of 1946, has created for each house a committee on expenditures in the executive departments and given these committees authority to receive reports from the GAO and recommend action by Congress. These and other evidences of a growing determination of Congress to know how administrative departments and agencies use the money that it makes available, give us increasing assurance that direction and control of bureaucracy through appropriations will be far more effective in the future than in the past.

BIBLIOGRAPHIC NOTE

The principal work dealing with the relation of Congress to the financing of the national government is Lucius Wilmerding, Jr., *The Spending-Power; a History of the Efforts of Congress to Control Expenditures* (New Haven, 1943). Mr. Wilmerding searched through a wide range of materials, apparently in a painstaking manner, and brought together and examined critically a great deal of information about the evolution of attitudes and practices in Congress, of relations between Congress and the chief executive and administrative departments and agencies, and of arrangements for making sure that money is actually used in ways that Congress intended. Less comprehensive than Wilmerding's book, but also highly informative, is an article by Arthur Macmahon, "Congressional Oversight of Administration: The Power of the Purse," in *Political Science Quarterly*, vol. 58, pp. 161–190, 380–414 (1943). These two authors have not told us all that we need to know about the authority and influence of Congress in monetary matters, but they certainly have shown us how to go about finding out what we need to know.

The studies of Wilmerding and Macmahon are by all odds the best we have, judged by the range of matters covered and the incisiveness with which matters are examined. There are many general statements of the nature of the authority and influence of Congress in monetary matters in textbooks on government and public finance, books about Congress, etc. Among the best of these general statements are: Roland Young, *This is Congress* (New York, 1943), ch. 7; and Daniel T. Selko, *The Federal Financial System* (Washington, 1940), ch. 7.

There is also a great deal to be learned about the part Congress plays in the financing of government in the letters, memoirs, and other writings of members of Congress and other persons who have participated in making decisions. I am not aware of any effort to run down and list the more significant of these odds and ends of revealing information. Wilmerding and Macmahon cite the Congressional materials for many of the incidents of greatest significance—debates in the Congressional Record and its predecessor publications, committee and subcommittee hearings, committee and subcommittee reports, etc.

There appears to be very little in print concerning the way the President and administrative officials respond or fail to respond to the evidences of Congressional intent in monetary matters. There are a few informative paragraphs on this in a discussion of budgeting in the Department of Agriculture, prepared by Verne B. Lewis and printed in John M. Gaus and L. O. Wolcott, *Public Administration and the United States Department of Agriculture* (Chicago, 1940), pp. 403–460.

CHAPTER 8

FIXING STANDARDS OF
ADMINISTRATIVE CONDUCT

We have seen, in the last three chapters, how the administrative organization is created and given a job to do by legislation, and how the measure of what it is expected to do is restated each year by appropriation of money. If Congress and President, as lawmaking authority, do these things well, the nation will have a high degree of assurance that government will be administered within limits that are acceptable to the people as a whole. But these three means of supplying direction and control to the administrative branch are not all that we expect of the lawmaking authority. The lawmakers must also establish standards and lay down rules which guide administrative officials and employees in the performance of their work. We need a body of law which conscientious administrative officials can turn to for their own guidance, which higher officers can stand upon in giving instructions to their subordinates, which the citizen can appeal to in asserting his rights against men and women who exercise power over him, and which the courts can read and cite in their effort to give us a government of men regulated by law.

The need for legislation which regulates the conduct of administration is not an American discovery. The people of England knew about this long before Columbus came to the Western Hemisphere. Perhaps the British people came to appreciate earlier than they otherwise would the importance of having a body of law which the courts could enforce objectively and impartially upon administrative officers because they did not have a political system through which the great mass of the people could effectively determine what their governing officials would do. Perhaps the development of a theory of supremacy of law, judicially enforced, over administrative officials was a part of the process of learning how to create a political system that would give the people control over their government. Whatever the facts be as to these matters, even after the British people had developed a political system which gave elected officials the power to direct and control the government as a whole they found it desirable to extend and improve the arrangements whereby the judicial branch could exert restraint over the bureaucracy. The courts and other agencies of law enforcement are always at hand. If the law states clearly what administrative officials and employees are permitted to do, what they are required to do, and what they are forbidden to do; if the law makes clear under what circumstances they are to do things and how they are to do things—in that case there is ready at hand effective machinery for making government in operation conform to the expectations of the lawmaking authority.

In large part through the rulings of their judges, but perhaps mainly through the acts of Parliament, the English people made clear at an early date that the king's ministers, subordinate officials, and all other people who carry a badge of public authority can only do what the law authorizes them to do and can only do it in a way that the law permits. The authority to kill a horse afflicted with glanders is not authority to kill a horse that appears to be afflicted with glanders but actually isn't. And the authority to destroy a piece of property which is found after a hearing to be a nuisance is not authority to destroy it without a hearing, no matter how much evidence there is that it is a nuisance in fact. The man who is injured by a show of public authority has his day in court to determine whether there was really authority to do what was done. This is a theory about the proper nature of government which the American people initially acquired from England, but it is as much an American theory today as it is British. No doubt the men and women who make and interpret law governing administrative conduct in Britain today rely as much on American experience as we do on British experience.

When the area of governmental activity is small and government is concerned mainly with matters we all understand it is possible to write down in some detail the limitations that will safeguard us from arbitrary or reprehensible action. But legal controls are doubtless of least importance under such circumstances because we understand what is happening to us and have other ways of dealing with the situation. It is when government becomes a great bureaucracy and deals with problems so big that none of us can see clear across them that we need to develop legal controls to their fullest extent. And it is under such circumstances that it is most difficult to fix the limitations that will keep the public official and employee within proper bounds. There is a possibility that, in our effort to keep administrative officials and employees from doing what we do not want them to do, we may tie their hands so that they cannot do what we do want them to do or cannot do things the way we want them done. If an official must be given broad discretion to deal with a problem that is not yet fully understood, it is no easy job to fix restraints that will keep him from abusing his authority.

Congress has put on the statute books a great amount of legislation which is intended to fix standards and provide rules to guide administrative officials·and employees in the performance of their work. Congress has undoubtedly done a much better job of this than has any of our state legislatures. Even so, our national legislation is far from adequate. Some of the laws were written for times long gone by and are ineffective if not inoperative today. Some provisions of the legislation are so ill-fitted to modern government that they cause officials and employees to do things that are silly by any test. Some of the legislation, I have no doubt, gives rise to evils that are greater than the evils it is supposed to prevent.

And without question there are many areas of conduct for which general statutory regulation would be appropriate, but in respect to which Congress has not yet enacted any provisions.

The law in the statute books is supplemented first by the case law that is developed in court decisions, and second by the regulations and rulings of certain agencies that have been created to advise, assist, and control the rest of the administrative branch, notably the Bureau of the Budget, the General Accounting Office, and the Civil Service Commission. This great body of law and approved practice has never been brought together in a handy reference work. It has not even been classified or summarized in any one place. As a consequence, the significance of much of this controlling law escapes many of the bureaucrats because they do not even know that it exists. Blessed is the department head who has not only competent legal counsel but also experienced fiscal, property, and personnel officers to tell him what he may and may not do.

It will be readily seen, therefore, that anyone who has not lived officially for many years under this body of law runs a great risk of describing it wrongly or misstating its significance. For that reason, I have not undertaken to summarize it here; rather, I attempt by means of illustration to indicate its principal purposes and general nature. The illustrations are drawn from the legislation which is directed at four points where misuse and abuse of administrative authority is most likely to occur and, when it occurs, most likely to prove especially offensive. These four problem areas are: employment, property, finance, and relations with the public.

Congress has enacted a great body of legislation intended to regulate federal employment.[1] Some of this legislation dates from the very founding of the national government. In 1883, Congress enacted our greatest landmark in federal employment legislation, the Pendleton Act, which established the Civil Service Commis-

---

[1] The main body of legislation relating to federal employment is brought together in U.S. Code, title 5, chs. 12–18.

sion that sits at the head of the federal employment system today. In this act and many other statutes enacted since that time are found the basic regulations governing federal employment. The structure of a merit system is set forth and the President is authorized to bring additional blocks of employees under it from time to time. Provision is made for the selection of employees— impartial examinations, appointments from among those at the top of the list, apportionment of appointments among the states with some regard for population, etc. The pay of employees is regulated in great detail. Standards for fixing the grade of work (difficulty and responsibility of duties) are included in the law, all jobs under the merit system must be classified accordingly, and the classification given the job determines the pay it will receive. Other provisions in varying degrees of detail relate to hours of work, vacation and sick leave, grounds for discharge, retirement benefits, compensation for injuries, and a great many other matters.

Employment legislation has four basic objectives: to give everybody a chance to get a job in the federal government, to fix standards of fair treatment for employees, to increase the quantity and improve the quality of work, and to keep the great force of public employees from being used for political advantage. The first two of these objectives are worthy enough but not highly important to the fundamental concern of this book. The third and fourth objectives relate directly to the prospect that the administrative branch will actually give us the kind of government we want and will not use its power to prejudice the decisions of the electorate as to whom shall be given the job of running the country.

It was argued at the beginning of this book that public confidence in our form of government depends in good part on a widespread conviction that our administrative force will adequately carry out the activities and undertakings that are assigned to it. Incompetence on the part of public employees, making a racket out of federal jobs, and all other practices and conditions that collectively constitute what we commonly call inefficiency in government can destroy public confidence that democratic institutions meet the needs of the time. Legislation cannot give the nation an efficient public service, but it can lay the basis for it. A first great forward step was accomplished in the Pendleton Act, in establishing the principles that employees should be chosen on a basis of merit and should not be fired for reasons which are irrelevant to their ability and willingness to meet the obligations of their employment. Other enactments of law have attempted to secure these principles more firmly. Against some of this legislation we may lodge the protest that it misses or defeats its purpose. As we shall see at later points in this book, some of our legislation supports procedures for the selection of employees that seem designed to hinder rather than to facilitate the selection of employees according to promise of competence. It is generally acknowledged that the legislation which is intended to assure comparable pay for comparable work has put unnecessary limitations on the ability of administrative officials to organize employees and assign work with a view to getting best results.

It must be recognized that some of the specific provisions of law which limit or vitiate the effectiveness of the whole body of law, so far as securing a competent public service is concerned, were put there for reasons which bear little or no relation to considerations of competence. Devotees of the merit system frequently complain about the requirement that consideration be given to state of residence in filling jobs. Congressmen are doubtless fully aware that this may cause some jobs to go to less able individuals living far away from Washington instead of to more able individuals living in states nearby; the requirement may be justified by a number of values, unrelated to personal ability, which lie in bringing persons from all parts of the nation into the federal service. Veterans, like mothers injured in childbirth, are entitled to the nation's gratitude; and the legislation that gives them preference in federal employment is an effort to pay a debt, not an attempt to advance efficiency in the public service. This is not enough to condemn the law. It is entirely proper for Congress to say whether and to what extent an obligation to those who fought its wars, or the importance of promising future employment advantage to those who contemplate military service, justifies a departure from the objectives incorporated in the merit principle. But we may properly ask that Congressmen inquire whether objectives that are unrelated to competence in the public service may not be achieved more satisfactorily in other ways. The nation cannot afford to let any considerations, no matter how worthy or pressing, lower the quality of the public service to a point which causes the American people to lose faith that democratic government is competent for any task that confronts it.

What has just been said in description and evaluation of federal legislation relating to public employment is concerned with its effect on the competence of the public service. It is important also to understand what this legislation has to say about the use of public employees for political purposes. Promises of public employment can be used to advantage by both those who are in power and those who are out and trying to get in. But the greatest advantage is to those who are already in control of offices, for a promise to let a man keep what he has sounds more convincing than a promise to give him something that isn't yet in hand. The purchase of a man's vote with a job has an important bearing on the freedom of elections, but of much greater significance is the influence that public employees can have on the votes of other people if they go into the campaign to work for the candidates of the party in power. Their salaries are paid from taxes and therefore are paid in part by the very people they are working against. The election is not a fair contest for the endorsement of the electorate if the public pays the campaign expenses of one side and leaves the other to shift for itself. No one recognizes this any better than Congressmen who have been up against it as a practical problem throughout their political experience.

The Pendleton Act (1883) was an important step toward the goal of removing federal employees from politics, since it made merit instead of politics the determining factor in hiring men and women and fixing their status in the federal service. Other legislation reinforced this basic law to some extent, but it was not until the enormous expenditures of the New Deal showed how influential the federal payroll could really be in campaigns and elections that Congress enacted a thorough body of restrictive legislation. The institution of a generous program of employment on public works as a means of providing relief put millions of people on the federal payroll who were not, in the customary sense, federal employees. The fact that a pay check was made available was enough to cause many victims of the depression to favor the party in power; it takes little imagination to see what the administration of relief employment could do for the party that does the administering if the millions of relief employees are converted into party workers. There is a sharp difference of opinion as to how much political use was made of relief employees during the depression, and Congress did little to forbid or restrict it until well after the peak of such employment had passed. Then, in two acts sponsored by Senator Hatch, Congress adopted a body of regulations in 1939 and 1940 which are generally recognized as definitive and severe, and which are considered by many persons who are deeply concerned about free elections to be unnecessarily drastic. These acts attempt to distinguish between those people in the public service who have a political status and are entitled to wage a political campaign and those who are merely public employees and ought to preserve neutrality. Individuals in either group are forbidden to use their power of office ("use his official authority") to influence elections, but the great body of non-political civil servants are forbidden even to "take any active part in political management or in political campaigns." And the prohibition of political activity is carried clear down to employees of state and local governments financed in whole or in part by grants or loans of federal money.

The Hatch Acts have been sharply attacked, both as unsound in principle and unworkable in practice. It may be that they went too far. Public employees are an important sector of the electorate, both in number and articulate interest; to limit their political activity is to remove from the political arena a lot of the best information on the consequences of alternative political policies. Society is elaborately organized to prejudice opinions and intimidate the voter; to take the public employee out of the fight is to increase the advantage of other centers of power. And finally, the consequences of enforced neutrality are especially serious in time of depression when millions of the lowest income group are being paid in whole or in part by the federal government. To remove so many individuals of one economic class from political activity may effectively handicap any political party that stands on proposals which appeal especially to the part of the population that is down and out.

Legislation which is intended to safeguard public property rarely attracts the attention of the general public. It is nevertheless of great importance as a limitation on misuse and abuse of authority by the bureaucracy. The federal government owns an enormous amount of property, both real and movable. Its real property includes public buildings, monuments and parks in Washington, post offices and courthouses throughout the country and its possessions, office buildings in most large cities, military reservations and defense establishments everywhere, and great stretches of territory embraced in national parks, forests, and other reservations. Its holdings in movable property are scarcely less imposing. The Hoover Commission reported in 1949 that the federal government had in storage in continental United States military and civilian inventories valued at 27 billion dollars and that it was spending more than 6 billion dollars a year for new materials, supplies, and equipment. "No one knows accurately the total worth of Government personal property currently being used," the Commission stated, "but its million or more motor vehicles, for example, have a value of at least 2 billion dollars."[2]

[2] *The Organization and Management of Federal Supply Activities; a Report to the Congress by the Commission on Organization of the Executive Branch of the Government, February 1949* (Government Printing Office, 1949), p. 23. This report is bound in the same pamphlet with a report entitled *Office of General Services.*

These few facts should be enough to make clear that the federal government needs carefully planned laws governing the acquisition of property, requiring its safe custody, safeguarding its use, and fixing the conditions under which it may be disposed of. The law governing the letting of contracts alone covers more than ten pages in the United States Code, and the law of public buildings, property, and works occupies well over fifty.[3] The Hoover Commission found that "Disposition of surplus property is governed by over 369 separate statutes."[4] Generally speaking, the legislative enactments on this subject appear to be emphatic enough in their statement that federal property may not be maliciously damaged or destroyed, carelessly lost or allowed to deteriorate, given away, stolen, or otherwise converted to private use. The penalties are there, and arrangements for apprehension and punishment are provided.

But the effectiveness of legislation like this lies at least one-half in the property records that are maintained. One cannot tell whether property is safe if he does not know where it is; one cannot tell who is responsible for its loss if he does not know who last had it in his control. It may be that responsibility for preparing and maintaining such records is amply expressed or implied in the law. Many people in the federal service believe, and the Hoover Commission agreed, that records are not generally maintained in accordance with the highest standards of the accounting and appraisal professions. We have inadequate assurance, it appears, that property does not pass over the line from public to private to the advantage of the individuals who arrange its transfer. The responsibility for this situation, if it exists, must be shared by Congress, the various administrative establishments of the federal government, and the central agencies that are expected to police the administrative departments and agencies that carry on the work of government.

[3] The main body of legislation of this character is brought together in U.S. Code, titles 40 and 41.

[4] *The Organization and Management of Federal Supply Activities,* cited *supra,* note 2, at p. 37.

Regulations governing transactions in money are especially important because money that is wrongfully obtained has no special identity and it changes hands with a maximum of ease. The financial transactions that occur daily in the federal government are truly stupendous. The American people now turn approximately one-fifth of the national income over to the federal government, and the most hopeful conservative among us scarcely hopes to see the day when federal expenditures will drop to 25 billion dollars a year.

We therefore need a body of legislation that is designed to make sure that federal money is devoted to the purposes for which Congress makes it available. Congress has recognized this since the very founding of our present system of government, and we now have an extensive body of law that thoroughly regulates the handling of money. Offenses are clearly defined, and the consequences of violation are severe.[5]

But the enforcement of honesty in financial matters, like the safeguarding of property, may be largely defeated if the records which are maintained do not fully and correctly reveal what goes on. We seem to have done much better in accounting for money than we have in accounting for property. Money moves almost exclusively on paper. The department or agency that receives the appropriation from Congress may not see a dime of cash. It may have a credit in the Treasury and pay its bills by issuing paper. It may have authority to write checks; it may, on the other hand, only issue an instruction asking the Treasury to write the checks. In either event, the department, by appointing one or more responsible persons to sign and countersign the paper, can make sure that each transaction undergoes responsible inspection.

The Treasury maintains one or more accounts for most administrative establishments having an appropriation, and will call a halt on spending when the accounts are exhausted. For many administrative establishments, the General Accounting Office examines

[5] A large part of the legislation relating to financial transactions is brought together in U.S. Code, titles 31 and 37.

vouchers before or after they are paid and will stop the payment or call for redress when it detects an illegal action. Since it is the high court that sits in judgment over them in matters of spending, administrative officials go to GAO for advice when they are uncertain whether they may lawfully incur an obligation. And finally, most if not all administrative establishments are subject to investigation of their financial affairs—organization, procedures, records, and specifications—as frequently and as thoroughly as GAO considers advisable and is able to carry out.

These arrangements are highly effective in safeguarding money when they are fully in operation. They doubtless break down under the avalanche of contract writing, unprecedented purchasing, underwriting of production, and other extraordinary transactions that take place in time of war. But it is extremely unlikely that there is much embezzlement or other illegal use of federal funds in time of peace. Indeed, the more common complaint is that we have carried some of our safeguards to unnecessary lengths. Usually, it takes a lot of time and a lot of paper to complete a financial transaction. Some businessmen, for that reason, are unwilling to sell to the federal government or perform work for it. Estimates of the cost of verifying and executing an order for payment of even the least-questionable items strike the layman as nothing short of fantastic. The Hoover Commission found in 1948 that the work involved in paying a bill cost more than the amount of the bill to be paid in the case of nearly one-half of all purchase orders; i.e., nearly one-half of all purchase orders involve payments of amounts up to $10, and the work involved in making the payment (verifying the bill, making records, writing the check) costs the federal government approximately $10 per bill paid.[6]

The fantastic becomes ridiculous when the federal government is paying itself for things it sells to itself. The payment of post-office box rent makes a good illustration. Suppose the Soil Conservation Service has a local office in Red Wing, Minnesota, and

[6] *The Organization and Management of Federal Supply Activities*, cited *supra*, note 2, at pp. 26–27.

rents a post-office box in the Red Wing post office. Until the end of World War II, the Red Wing post office billed the local office of Soil Conservation Service monthly for this rental (perhaps 90 cents), and each month the Soil Conservation Service issued an order for payment. But a careful study made during the war led to the conclusion that the total costs chargeable to sending out and paying such a bill amounted to more than $20. At that rate, it was costing the federal government something like $240 a year to pay itself about $10. Today the cost of paying for this $10 worth of service is down to something like $20, for the local post offices now send out one bill for the whole year's box rental and the whole year's rental is paid in one transaction. Perhaps the time will come when, by a single transaction in Washington, the Department of Agriculture will turn over to the Post Office Department whatever amount it ought to have for all kinds of service rendered by post offices all over the country to all divisions of the Department of Agriculture.[7]

If safeguards relating to the custody and use of federal money are not what they ought to be, the responsibility for shortcomings can be traced to many different people. Officials in the various administrative establishments that incur obligations and payments of money have authority to alter many of the practices which are followed within their respective organizations. The Treasury Department and the General Accounting Office also have authority to institute many changes in procedure, both within their own organizations and throughout the administrative branch. Some of the things which competent critics find objectionable are required

[7] I received conflicting statements as to the situation in respect to post-office box rent, and decided to accept the following from a former employee of the Bureau of the Budget who participated in a project to simplify the arrangements. He writes: "Your illustration of postoffice box rental before the war is correct. That has now been altered to some extent. Post-office box rent can now be paid annually in advance. We undertook to get agreement from the Post Office Department that all box rent could be paid by one voucher, with a supporting schedule listing the locations, but the Post Office Department registered violent protest. Their only reason was that some postmasters were paid on a fee basis and this would make the revenue of such a postoffice more difficult to determine."

by statutory provisions. Congress and President are finally responsible for these defects (if they are defects), but they are not always responsible in the first instance. If administrative officials in central agencies and operating departments of the government do not make clear to the political branches just what the deficiencies are, how they are supported by legislation, and how new legislation can effectively correct them, neither President nor Congressmen can be expected to enact the corrective legislation.

A fourth type of legislation by which Congress attempts to keep the bureaucracy from misusing and abusing its authority is that which regulates relations between the administrative branch of the government and the people with whom it does business. Most of this legislation is applicable to a particular administrative establishment, but an increasing amount of it is addressed to administrative departments and agencies in general. A great deal of the law which governs the relations of a particular administrative establishment with the people for whom it provides government must necessarily be addressed specifically to that organization. Every administrative establishment has its own particular activities and undertakings to carry out, and the nature of its relationships with the public is determined in large part by the peculiar character of those activities and undertakings. If the Comptroller of the Currency is the only administrative agency of the federal government that has occasion to examine the records of banks, then there must be some legislation governing the way bank records are to be examined which is applicable to the Comptroller of the Currency only. If, however, the Federal Reserve Board and the Federal Deposit Insurance Corporation are also given authority to examine bank records, it may be possible to enact statutory provisions which regulate the relations of all three agencies with banking institutions.

A good time to determine how an administrative establishment shall do business with the public is right at the time when it is created and given a job to do. This is fully appreciated by Congress. When Congress passes a law providing for a new governmental activity or undertaking and creating an organization to administer it, it is pretty certain to set forth procedures that shall be followed, announce standards that shall be adhered to, and in other ways indicate how the organization shall go about doing its work.

It will readily be appreciated that these legislative procedures differ too widely to permit a summarization of their contents. Some of these provisions date from the beginning of government under the Constitution; it is not unlikely that some remnant of legislation enacted by every Congress convened since that time survives in the law which is in effect today. As a consequence, these regulations in the mass reflect the many different theories or points of view that have predominated in Congress over a period now more than a century and a half.

Confronted by the multiplicity and variety of these provisions and the administrative-made regulations that interpret and extend them, the businessman long ago surrendered himself to the lawyer. Washington is now the seat of a great aggregation of men, trained in the law and familiar with administrative practice, who guide the businessman and others doing business with the government through the procedural maze that admits them into and leads them back out of a government department. While Washington lawyers in general profit from the complexities of the situation and many of them doubtless seek to make it worse, a number of lawyers in Washington have been leaders in an insistent demand that the conditions of doing business with government departments and agencies be made more nearly uniform. In 1941, after more than a year's study, a committee appointed by the Attorney General made a very thorough and critical report which described what went on in more than thirty administrative establishments of different types. The committee brought its work to a close with recommendations for legislation that it thought would remove some of the more important objections to existing procedures and introduce the first steps toward more nearly uniform administrative practices. The recommendations of the Attorney Gen-

eral's committee were generally supported by associations of lawyers and businessmen, though some of them urged Congress to
adopt legislation that would have gone much farther in regulating
the practices of the departments than the Attorney General's committee thought wise.[8]

The outcome of all this interest, study, and agitation was the
Administrative Procedure Act of 1946.[9] This act applies to all
the administrative departments and agencies of the federal government, except to the extent that requirements of secrecy may make
the provisions of the act inappropriate. Special provisions in the
law relating to particular administrative establishments, no matter
how ancient and how sacred to that sector of the bureaucracy, go
by the board where they conflict with the new law.

While this act does not make the practices and procedures of
all departments and agencies uniform in all their ramifications, it
moves in that direction by three principal routes: (1) Each department or agency of the federal government is required to publish all the information of importance that the public needs to
know in order to do business with it—how the agency is organized; who within it has authority to act; where those officials
can be found; the procedures for doing business with them; and
the rules, regulations, and rulings (decisions) they have issued
which reveal the many policies of the organization. (2) The act
invites interested parties to participate in the making of administrative rules and regulations. Notice must be given that rules are
to be made; interested parties must be given an opportunity to be
heard; and administrative officials must give weight to the recommendations that are made. (3) And the procedure by which the
administrative agency makes individual decisions which affect people outside the government is put on a basis much more like a
court than has generally been the case to date. The investigatory

---

[8] The report of the Attorney General's Committee was published as U.S.
Senate Document No. 8, 77th Congress, 1st session, under the title *Ad-
ministrative Procedure in Government Agencies* (Government Printing
Office, 1941).

[9] 60 Statutes at Large 237; U.S. Code, title 5, secs. 1001–1011.

and enforcement activities of the agency must be separated from the judicial function. In order that the individual who conducts a hearing may be as free from prejudice as possible, he must be kept free from other activities which might tend to prejudice him. The report of findings which he makes and the recommended decision which he prepares must be based on the record compiled in the case; the great body of understandings, convictions, and prejudices that are built up by the staff of an administrative department or agency are not permitted to enter into the decision of the case at this point. The Act of 1946 does not give the hearing officer authority to make the final decision, however. The final decision by which any department or agency makes government effective upon the citizen will be made by the head of the agency or by such other official as may have been designated in the law which is applicable to that particular administrative establishment. This official, like a court, may take judicial notice of certain facts and considerations that may not have impressed the hearing officer, and he is entitled to his own independent judgment as to what conclusion is warranted by the evidence and the arguments that appear in the record.

The relation of the Administrative Procedure Act of 1946 to the way administrative departments and agencies subject the citizen to their authority is discussed more fully in Chapter 21.

The power of Congress to regulate the conduct of administrative officers and employees in their official duties is as complete as Congress wishes to make it. This discussion has centered upon four points of conduct where misuse and abuse of authority are most likely to prove serious—employment, property, finance, and relations with the public. No doubt most of the existing legislation regulating administrative behavior falls in these areas. But Congress has authority to extend its regulation to other areas of conduct whenever it thinks it desirable. And there is not at present any significant body of constitutional law, superior to statutory enactments, which limits the degree of restrictiveness to which Congress may go in its regulation. If Congress does not forbid a practice that you and I think ought to be stopped, it is because it disagrees with us or neglects to take action; its failure to act is not due to any lack of authority to deal with the problem.

As noted at more than one point in the foregoing discussion, some of the legislation regulating administrative conduct seems to have been carried to undesirable lengths. Statutory provisions intended to limit or prevent abuse in some cases constitute serious handicaps for the conscientious official who wants to do well what Congress has told him to do. This consequence cannot be avoided altogether. The law must be written to cover unforeseen occurrences. If Congress knew which officials were to be trusted today, it would not know which ones could be trusted tomorrow.

There are two things that administrative officials can do to keep excessive restrictions at a minimum. The first, which has already been pointed out, is to keep Congress informed as to what the questionable restrictions are and how they can be removed without impairing the effectiveness of the law for achieving the purposes which Congress has in mind. The second is for administrative officials to quit doing things which invite excessive restrictions. Congressmen can get mad just like other people, and when they are angry they do things they would not do in more sober moments, just as other people do. And a good many of the legislative restraints that conscientious administrative officials complain about were put in the law at a time when Congressmen were over-fed-up with something that was going on in one or another part of the bureaucracy. As we shall see in a later chapter, we had a narrow escape during the late war from a statute which would have required Senate confirmation of all officials appointed to jobs paying $4500 or more per year. While this bill was sponsored by Senators whose principal aim was undoubtedly to get control of patronage, the measure got support from a lot of other Senators and Representatives who were looking for some means of correcting what they believed to be an indefensible laxity in picking men for important positions.

The creation of the House and Senate committees on expenditures in the executive departments gives reason for believing that legislation regulating administrative conduct may be steadily improved in the future. These committees have authority to conduct inquiries and make recommendations concerning any aspect of administrative conduct at any and all points in the administrative branch. The central administrative agencies that are supposed to advise Congress on such matters—notably the Bureau of the Budget, the General Accounting Office, and the Civil Service Commission—have been conservative rather than aggressive in advising Congress on need for legislative action up to this time. If they have been discouraged from aggressiveness because of doubt that Congress was prepared to hear and ponder their suggestions, the existence of the two new committees may challenge them to a new conscience and a new vigor.

BIBLIOGRAPHIC NOTE

As stated in the text of this chapter, the great mass of laws and regulations which regulate the conduct of federal administrative officials and employees has never been brought together in a handy reference work. The statute law is in its proper place in the United States Code of Laws, but the scheme of organization according to which the laws are arranged tends to scatter rather than bring together the legislation of this character. A great many of these statutes will be found in Title 5 (Executive Departments and Government Officers and Employees); Title 18 (Criminal Code and Criminal Procedure); Title 31 (Money and Finance); Title 37 (Pay and Allowances); Title 40 (Public Buildings, Property, and Works); and Title 41 (Public Contracts).

The most important statutes of general application relating to federal employment, together with executive orders and regulations of the Civil Service Commission on that subject, are printed in a systematic arrangement in the *Federal Personnel Manual,* a loose-leaf publication of the Government Printing Office which is kept up to date by the frequent appearance of new materials. The whole body of legislation relating to employment will not be found in this collection, however, for it will omit many acts which are applicable only to a particular administrative department or agency. It is stated in one of the documents of the Hoover Commission that there are 199 laws which affect personnel management in the Department of Agriculture; many of these will apply only to that department. The best general discussion of the nature of the law and regulations relating to federal employment is in William E. Mosher and J. Donald Kingsley, *Public Personnel Administration* (New York, 1936). The most informative items relating to the Hatch Acts are cited in the note at the end of Chapter 2. Other items relating to federal employment are cited in the note at the end of Chapter 19.

There is not any compilation of the laws and regulations relating to the acquisition, custody, use, and disposition of federal property which is comparable to the *Federal Personnel Manual*. Neither is there a comparable compilation of the laws and regulations governing financial transactions in the federal government. Perhaps the best introduction to the problems which are involved in control of property is a document prepared for the Hoover Commission entitled *The Federal Supply System; A Report with Recommendations Prepared for the Commission on Organization of the Executive Branch of the Government [Appendix B]* (Government Printing Office, 1949). There is a more extensive literature relating to financial administration. Study of this literature may well begin with Daniel T. Selko, *The Federal Financial System* (Washington, 1940), and Edward F. Bartelt, *Accounting Procedures of the United States Government* (Chicago, 1940). Other items are cited in the note at the end of Chapter 18. For one who wishes to know how the law and regulations governing financial transactions are made effective in practical situations, the best place to go is the compilation of *Decisions of the Comptroller General of the United States*, published by the Government Printing Office.

The problems and conditions of administration that create the need for such legislation as was recommended by the Attorney General's Committee on Administrative Procedure, and went on the statute books as the Administrative Procedure Act of 1946, is discussed by Louis L. Jaffe in "The Reform of Federal Administrative Procedure," in *Public Administrative Review*, vol. 2, pp. 141–158 (1942). The report of the Attorney General's Committee on Administrative Procedure was published as U.S. Senate Document No. 8, 77th Congress, 1st Session, under the title *Administrative Procedure in Government Agencies* (Government Printing Office, 1941). The general report was supplemented by a number of small publications relating to the different departments and agencies which the Committee studied, and these are printed as *Senate Document No. 186*, 76th Congress, 3rd session (Government Printing Office, 1940).

The Administrative Procedure Act of 1946 is in 60 Statutes at Large 237; U.S. Code, title 5, secs. 1001–1011. The act is reprinted with full explanation, legislative history, and other related matter in Senate Document No. 248, 79th Congress, 2nd session, under title of *Administrative Procedure Act: Legislative History* (Government Printing Office, 1946). Some of the most important commentary on the act is listed in the note at the end of Chapter 21.

CHAPTER 9

REVIEWING THE ACTION OF THE BUREAUCRACY

We commonly refer to Congress as a lawmaking body. The picture that most of the American people have in their minds, no doubt, is that of an assembly debating and voting on legislative measures or sitting in committees to consider alternative legislative measures. We have this picture because that is the part of the work of Congress that we hear most about. The most important acts of Congress take the form of statutes—enactments having the force of law which receive the approval of a majority in each house and are printed in statute books. The most spectacular determinations of Congress go to broad issues of policy; new activities of government are authorized, established governmental undertakings are revised or terminated, the President is supported or overruled in his request for money to finance government on a scale which some of us approve and others disapprove.

But Congress is more than a lawmaking body, as we have already observed in this book. It participates in day-to-day direction and control of the bureaucracy. It supplies direction and control to the administrative branch by enacting laws; but it also gives direction and control in ways that do not involve the enactment of laws. Some of the things that Congress does differ in no significant way from acts of the President that we commonly call executive or administrative direction and control. The framers of the Constitution clearly intended this to be the case, for they provided that the President should secure the Senate's approval in appointing men to high offices and they gave the two houses authority to remove men from administrative positions by the process of impeachment.

Members of Congress, however, have resorted to ways of exerting influence over administration that are not mentioned in the Constitution and probably were not contemplated by the men who drew up that document. Regardless of what the framers of our system might have provided for if they had foreseen what was likely to come about, members of Congress have developed an amount and style of direction and control over administration which many students of government today consider to be both objectionable on its merits and a usurpation of the executive power given to the President in the Constitution.

The fact is that many administrative officials now receive a great deal more day-to-day guidance from Congressmen than they get from the President. Congressmen are not content only to enact laws which lay down the general policy that shall guide the administrative official in his work. They like to tell him what to do in specific instances. They ask him why he did this; they complain because he did that; they suggest that he proceed in this way; they bawl him out if he proceeds in that way.

It must be taken for granted that Congressmen will be interested in and express themselves on administrative matters; some of it is not only unavoidable, but highly desirable. The branch of the government that is responsible for saying what the government is to do must be in a position to observe what the government is already doing. Congressmen cannot decide whether further legislation is necessary until they have discussed with the administrator what he is doing under his present authority. The Congressman is under pressure from people who want government to do certain things; if the administrator cannot or will not do the things that people demand, the Congressman must consider the desirability of further legislation. Is it not entirely proper for him first to urge the administrator to make every effort to meet the demands of the public within the provisions of the law already on the statute books?

This relationship between Congressman and administrator is by no means entirely a one-way affair. The Congressman puts pressure on the administrator, but the administrator also goes to the Congressman for counsel. Where can he get better advice as to what the people want him to do with the authority that is given him? The administrator has his direct contacts with various sectors of the American people, but they are likely to be groups with a special interest. The public that the administrator deals with rarely represents the interests of the whole people. The Congressman may be his best source of information as to what the general public wishes or will approve of.

If the relations between Congressman and administrator were confined to what is suggested in the last two paragraphs, students of government would have little ground for objection. But Congressmen go much farther than this. The advice they give the administrator and the complaints they address to him are not always concerned with matters of general policy, nor are they always compatible with anyone's conception of the general public interest. The trouble lies in the fact that the Congressman is more than a representative of the general public; he is a representative of his particular constituency and all the special interests within it. He not only speaks for groups of people who have a common interest; he is Washington agent for individuals and business firms located in his constituency and having business to transact with the federal government.

The American people appear to want it this way. While they respect the authority of government as a matter of general theory, they establish few presumptions in favor of government in specific instances. They view bureaucracy and the officials who sit at the top of bureaucracy with suspicion. They contest the administrative official at every point where his authority obstructs their purposes. And they regard their Congressman as their special agent located in Washington to defend or advance their interests with the bureaucracy as the situation may demand.

The administrative official accordingly sees the individual Congressman operating in at least three different capacities. First, the Congressman tells the administrator what he understands the law to permit, require, and forbid; this is a valuable service, for some of the Congressmen may have helped to make the law and many of them may have good judgment as. to what Congress intended to provide. Second, the Congressman tells the administrator what he thinks the American people want in the way of governmental service; on this point, also, he is entitled to great respect, for the Congressman gets to be Congressman and remains a Congressman only if he is sensitive to the convictions and the whims of the people. In the third place, the Congressman appears before the administrative official as special agent for his constituents; in this role he must be viewed with suspicion if not positive mistrust.

When the Congressman tells the administrator what his constituents want, he is performing a useful service. When he urges the administrator to satisfy these wants, he may be asking for an unequal and unlawful administration of the law. If the Congressman, pressing for legislation which his constituents want, loses his fight by the refusal of the majority of Congress to enact that legislation, he and his constituents should have to take their licking just like everybody else. The individual Congressman ought not to be able to gain what the majority of Congress denied him by inducing the administrator to treat the people of his constituency differently from the rest of the country.

It is rare, if indeed it ever happens, that any Congressman asks an administrative official to apply the law (either statute or administrative-made regulation) in such a way that his constituency as a whole enjoys a treatment that cannot be accorded to the rest of the country; but he may ask that concessions be made to his constituents in particular instances. The Congressman will not ask that all radio broadcasters who live or do business in his district be given preferential treatment over all other broadcasters in the nation; but he may ask that the petition of one of his constituents for a more satisfactory wave-length be taken up for consideration before the petitions of other applicants which have been waiting longer. The Congressman will not ask that he be given the privilege of approving and disapproving the applications from all broadcasters who reside or do business in his district; but he may let loose a blast against administrative officials if they grant a license that the Congressman would like to see denied or deny one that the Congressman would like to see granted. The two letters in the footnote at the bottom of the page represent a frankness in asking for special consideration that is not often encountered. The seriousness of such a challenge to orderliness and impartiality in administration is made more apparent when it is understood that one of the two Senators was then chairman of the Senate committee on appropriations.[1]

[1] The following letters, each addressed to Mr. Charles R. Denny, Acting Chairman of the Federal Communications Commission, are taken from *Broadcasting* (a trade journal of the radio industry), issue of November 11, 1946, at p. 17.

"Dear Mr. Denny:
  "I have just received your notice that you had granted the application of the Capital Broadcasting Company, owned by A. G. Beaman and T. B. Baker, Jr., at Nashville, Tennessee.
  "I want to protest against this.
  "Senator Stewart recommended to you that you grant a station to the Tennessee Broadcasters owned by Mr. E. E. Murrey, Frank Hobbs and others, and to the Tennessee Radio Corporation owned by Mr. W. D. Hudson and his three sons. Mr. Hudson was in World War I and also in World War II.
  "We recall that in talking to your predecessor about it he said he did not see how he could turn down a family of four soldiers with the splendid records they had, but you have turned them down. I think you have made a great mistake. Is it too late to mend?
  "Where the other station that you granted to Mr. A. G. Beaman and T. B. Baker, Jr., will finally go I do not know. It seems to me that you could not have made a worse choice.
  "There was another application before you—that of Mr. J. W. Birdwell whom we recommended. It seems that your office takes pleasure in turning down our recommendations. Senator Stewart and I were together in all of these recommendations. Of course, you know all about Tennessee and We know nothing. Very frankly, Mr. Denny, I resent very much your action in the matter.
                              Very sincerely yours,
August 8, 1946   /s/ Kenneth McKellar"

There can be no question that much of the pressure which individual Congressmen put on the administrative branch is unworthy of men who occupy so high a position in public life and have an obligation to represent the nation as a whole as well as their own constituents. And there can be no question that administrative officials have an obligation to resist this pressure when it calls for them to depart from the impartial administration of the law which they are pledged to provide. But there is something to be said in defense of many of the demands which originate with Congressmen looking out for the interests of their constituents.

The discomfort which the administrator suffers at the hands of the Congressman is not unique in his experience; he is subjected to a like embarrassment from many other sources. The American people are elaborately organized to tell the public official what he ought to do and to punish him if he does not comply with their wishes. Both directly and through their various associations, they bombard him constantly. And these spokesmen for individuals and groups play as many roles as the Congressman does. They tell the official what he can and cannot do; and their advice is frequently good because they pay able lawyers to give them memo-

---

"Dear Mr. Chairman:

"I have a copy of 96808 concerning application of the various corporations at Nashville, Tennessee.

"I suppose it will do no good to protest this matter now, but I would like for you and the other members of your Commission to know that this is about the most contemptible (sic) deal I have ever had perpetrated on me since I have been in Washington. It was nothing more than an effort to embarrass my good friend and colleague, Senator McKellar, since the award you made was to a man who had assisted in the fight to defeat Senator McKellar in his campaign for renomination to the United States Senate. I suppose it will be your policy in the future to always penalize our friends.

"I have read the reasons you have assigned for making the award and I think they are about the most absurd excuses I have ever heard. You certainly could not have called them reasonable. In my judgment they lack anything that approaches reason.

"The applicants in which Senator McKellar and I were particularly interested both had sons overseas, but you seem to take a delight in discriminating against overseas men.

Yours very truly,

/s/ Tom Stewart"

August 12, 1946

randa. They tell him what the general public wants, at least when it is favorable to their cause; and their advice on this may be good, too, for they have ways of finding out where people stand. But they, like the Congressman, can also forget, distort, or even deny the existence of a general public opinion or interest when it is contrary to their special interests. It is a wise administrator that knows to whom he is talking when it is the voice of Jacob but the hand of Esau.

Some people regard the Congressman's interference in administration as especially objectionable because he has the power to punish the administrator if his advice or demands are not accepted. He can support legislation that will cripple the administrative program and he can oppose the appropriations that are necessary to its success. But this is only power to try to punish the administrative official. The individual Congressman cannot decree the legislation that he would like to enact; his power is only as great as his influence with other Congressmen. In this respect, most Congressmen (perhaps nearly all of them) are much less powerful than many other individuals who represent organized groups that bring pressure to bear on the administrative official. Any number of associations representing businessmen and people in other walks of life, through their power to influence voters, the President, and members of Congress, can visit a punishment on the administrator that few individual Congressmen can approach.

It will be seen that the pressure which Congressmen put on administrative officials is only one factor in a highly competitive system of pressures. If we ask Congressmen to quit pushing the claims of their constituents upon administrative departments, we do not do so with the expectation that the administrator will be set free to act according to his own estimate of the public interest. Rather, we ask Congressmen to surrender the field to others who will continue unabated their effort to get what they can out of government. To ask the Congressman from the South to lessen his effort to influence action in the Department of Agriculture is to propose that he stand aside and watch the agricultural policy of the country drift more steadily to the advantage of the corn and hog farmers who, if not better organized, are more numerous and have more money to spend than the cotton farmers. Who is in a position to say that the general interest of the nation will be better served by the new resolution of forces that will result when the Congressman is removed from the pattern of influence that now prevails? Does the Congressman not have something of a moral obligation to continue his pressure on administration until he is assured that other pressures will recede when his own is withdrawn?

The individual Congressman who goes to the administrative official seeking special treatment for his constituents goes without support of authority. The administrative official knows this and takes it into account in deciding what to do about the Congressman's request. The official may be far from certain, however, as to the weight of authority that supports a suggestion by a House or Senate committee. Committees of Congress are generous in giving advice to administrative officials, and occasionally they speak as if they were giving commands. It is rare that a Congressional committee is given authority to tell officials in the administrative branch what Congress expects them to do. But since each house of Congress relies so heavily on committees to formulate proposals for legislative action, the advice which the committee gives the administrator today may turn up as law tomorrow. Not everything that is said in the name of the committee represents the will of the committee's members, however. The committee ordinarily speaks through its chairman; there is always a possibility that the chairman is speaking for himself only when he says that he is speaking for his colleagues.[2]

---

[2] After reading what I have said in the past few pages, an attorney with approximately ten years of service in a federal regulatory agency wrote as follows: "I think you make a gross oversimplification when you say that the Congressman who tells the administrator what he understands the law to permit or require is providing a valuable service because he may have helped to make the law. Most Congressmen who were present when the basic act under which my agency operates was written, are not in Congress now. Most Congressmen who were there when the act was adopted merely

The relation of the appropriations committees and their sub-committees to the day-to-day conduct of administration has already been discussed. The standing committees which report on legislative measures also confer with administrative officials concerning the administration of the law in their respective areas of concern. When any sector of the administrative branch is under searching investigation by either standing or select committee, it may be told in detail and emphatically what it is required to do under provisions of law and what it ought to do in the exercise of its discretion. The committee may make a report to one or both houses in which it repeats what it has already said to the administrative official, and the report may be confirmed by action that is taken on the floor of one or both houses. But committees will also give suggestions to the administrator and make demands of him which are neither presented to the whole Congress nor endorsed by either house.

The direction and control which the administrative branch receives from Congress through its committees is spasmodic and uncoordinated. What one committee suggests may be in conflict with what another committee has demanded, and what each committee calls for may actually be contrary to what the majority of Congressmen would want if they knew what was going on. Such inconsistency and conflict is, of course, undesirable.

Congress could greatly improve the situation for both itself and the administrator if it would clarify the responsibility of the

---

accepted a committee report and had no personal judgment concerning the act. I think it would be far more reasonable to say that in 999 out of 1000 cases where a Congressman tells an administrative agency what an act means, he is not stating what his intent was when the act was passed. He is presenting an argument on behalf of a constituent. We hear a great deal about what our act means from Senator _____. We hear that because he has been educated by the railroads. We hear a great deal about what Congress intended from Senators _____ and _____. They obtain their information from the same business firm, which is one of the most powerful that is affected by our regulatory actions. We also hear a great deal from Congressmen who want us to do something which affects one or more cities in their districts. These Congressmen are not interpreters of the intent of Congress; they are advocates of a particular view which coincides with the interests of one or more of their constituents."

Congressional committees for advising administrative officials. Under the internal revenue laws, the Commissioner of Internal Revenue is required, in the case of certain taxes, to submit to a joint committee representing both houses of Congress all proposed refunds amounting to more than $75,000. The refund cannot lawfully be made until the committee has had thirty days in which to study it. While the committee has no authority to cancel the proposed refund, it is clearly invited to express its opinion on the validity and propriety of the proposed action, and does so. As a result, the Commissioner of Internal Revenue has on numerous occasions reconsidered and revised his calculations as to the amount to be repaid the taxpayer. Where the administrative official bows to a Congressional committee under a statutory provision such as this, he does so knowing that the committee cannot escape sharing responsibility for the final action; he has an answer if it is charged that he is yielding to the pressure of Congressmen who are trying to save the skin of a client.[3]

The question as to whether committees of Congress should be authorized to speak officially for Congress in day-to-day direction and control of administrative departments and agencies is secondary in importance. The primary question is, should Congress be engaged at all in such continuing direction and control—should Congress, acting through any channels of communication, tell the administrative official how he is to interpret the law which

[3] The statutory provision is in 45 Statutes at Large 882 (1928); U.S. Code, title 26, sec. 3777. For an incident illustrating the nature of relations between the Congressional committee and the Bureau of Internal Revenue, see Congressional Record, vol. 93, Appendix, pp. A4319–4325 (August 15, 1947). In January, 1933, Congress sent to the President a measure which provided that all proposed refunds in excess of $20,000 should be laid before the Joint Committee on Internal Revenue Taxation, that the Committee should pass upon and fix the amount to be paid, and that the Commissioner of Internal Revenue should not make any refund in excess of $20,000 "without the approval of said committee." The Attorney General advised the President that the measure was in violation of the Constitution (he gave two reasons), the President vetoed the measure, and the measure failed in the House of Representatives to get the two-thirds vote necessary for repassage. The opinion of the Attorney General is in *Official Opinions of the Attorneys General of the U.S.*, vol. 37, p. 56 (1932–34).

he administers or how he should use the discretion which has been vested in him by law?

There has been a marked tendency in recent writing on this subject to take the position that Congress should not attempt to exercise a continuing direction and control over administration, but rather should content itself with the enactment of legislation and the voting of appropriations. The reasons for taking this position are not often carefully stated; it seems likely, however, that most of these writers are influenced by one or more of three considerations. First, they may be attracted by the argument that the Constitution, in declaring the President chief executive and giving him certain powers of direction and control, intended to vest in him exclusively all of the authority that is requisite for acting as chief of administration. Second, they may set a high value on consistency in the instructions that go to the various administrative establishments, and be of the opinion that the amount of consistency which they desire is more likely to be achieved if the President has a monopoly on day-to-day direction and control of administration. And finally, they may recognize merit in continuing direction and control by the whole of Congress (acting by majority vote), but be of the opinion that the direction and control which actually emanates from Congressmen is something other than the will of the whole Congress.

I find none of these considerations, nor any others that I have been able to think of, sufficient to bring me to the same conclusion. There is very little indeed to support the point of constitutional theory. The framers of the Constitution certainly did not make it explicit that Congress was to refrain from addressing instructions to the heads of administrative establishments. The Supreme Court has not, as yet, written any such interpretation into the Constitution. And the history of the relations between the two political branches and the administrative branch is replete with instances of Congressional action which had the effect of telling individual administrative officers what they should and should not do in particular situations.

The second support for the position which these writers take—that direction and control by the President exclusively will result in more consistent instructions to administrative establishments—seems to me to lose its strength when subjected to careful analysis. It must be admitted that there is a great inconsistency in the instructions that emanate from Congress, particularly if one includes all of the suggestions and demands that individual Congressmen impose on the administrative branch. There is little question that pressure from different Congressional committees results in a good deal of working at cross-purposes on the part of different administrative organizations. There is reason to believe that the relations between Congressmen and bureau chiefs often hinder the efforts of the department head to direct the affairs of his department. No doubt, the demands which Congressmen put on administrative officials are frequently counter to the wishes of the President.

If we assume, for purposes of analysis, that all these consequences of Congressional direction and control are bad, we are not thereby forced to a conclusion that Congress should be stripped of a continuing direction and control of administration. A fire escape may be rickety and lead to many broken legs, but it does not follow that the fire escape should be destroyed; it may be possible to repair it. The values in continuing direction and control by Congress may be so great that we ought to continue it with all its faults; and there is surely the possibility that by reordering its relations with the administrative branch, Congress can eliminate the worse of the evils. Neither does it follow, because Congress does a faulty job of direction and control, that the President will do a better job. There is evidence to the effect that Presidents frequently give conflicting instructions, set administrative organizations to working at cross-purposes, and go over the heads of high officials to do business with their subordinates.

The third ground for concluding that Congress should give up its continuing direction and control—that what Congressmen do does not reflect the will of the whole Congress—seems to me the least convincing of all. If Congressmen believe that things are now being done in the name of Congress which do not have its approval, the remedy is for Congress so to regulate its relations with administration that the will of the whole Congress will be ascertained and expressed. If it be said that Congress is unable to control the relations of individual members and committees with administrative officers, then it follows that Congress cannot prevent those relationships. How can we argue that Congress should withdraw from a kind of direction and control which we find objectionable if we conclude that Congress cannot withdraw—i.e., if we conclude that Congress does not have power to regulate or prevent the particular occurrences which constitute that direction and control?

Not only do I not find convincing the considerations which appear to have convinced other writers, I see great advantages to be gained from the continuation of day-to-day direction and control by Congress. The withdrawal of continuing direction and control by Congress, it seems to me, will have the almost certain result of reducing the amount of political direction and control to which the administrative branch is subjected, rather than of substituting a more systematic and thorough political direction and control on the part of the President. It must be remembered that political direction and control, as the term is used in this book, means direction and control by men who have been chosen by the people and can be thrown out of office by the people. The direction and control which Congress supplies is political direction and control in this sense because it represents the personal decisions of men and women who have been elected by the people. The instructions that go to the administrative branch in the name of the President are not instruments of political direction and control, as that term is used here, unless the decisions upon which those instructions are based represent the personal judgment of the President.

What the President can do personally and what others do in his name is the subject of considerable discussion in later chapters of this book. I may anticipate that discussion by saying here that I do not believe the President can personally consider and decide anything like all the questions that are involved in giving the administrative departments and agencies the political direction and control which they require. There are too many things of high political importance which require his attention for the President to be able to turn over in his mind some of the lesser things which are still important enough to be pondered by an official who is directly answerable to the people. To give the President a monopoly on the issuance of instructions to the administrative branch, as I see it, is to free administrative officials to follow their own will (respond to other pressures) where they are today required to bow to the will of Congressmen. To give the President the whole job of direction and control is to acknowledge that for many affairs of high importance and in respect to which we want political direction and control, the President will either be silent or will do no more than authenticate instructions that reflect the mind of someone else.

It may well be that we can achieve a high degree of consistency in the instructions that go to the administrative departments and agencies in the name of the President. It may be that we can greatly reduce working at cross-purposes on the part of different administrative establishments and channel instructions from the White House to the heads of administrative organizations rather than to men below them in authority. But it must be understood (assuming my argument is sound) that if we ask Congress to give up its day-to-day direction and control of administration so that these results can be achieved, we do not propose to substitute direction and control by one elected official for direction and control by an elected representative assembly. Rather, we substitute for the instructions that represent the wishes of men who won their office by election, instructions for which we may be able to say no more than that an elected official (the President) did not know enough about them to be either for or against them.

If Congress continues to maintain day-to-day direction and

control over the various administrative establishments, it will surely be wise to consider carefully in what manner that direction and control is to be exercised. Undoubtedly, a great many things are done in the name of Congress which do not reflect the will of the majority of Congress. It may be that Congress ought to do something to curb the activities of individual members who set themselves up as one-man authorities to tell administrative officials what to do. If it seems desirable to let committees speak officially for Congress in the review of administrative action, it may be desirable to clarify the authority of the committee by resolution or statute, as was done in the case of the joint committee which reviews tax refunds ordered by the Commissioner of Internal Revenue.

No doubt, a great deal of administrative action that Congress does not like arises out of the indefiniteness or inconsistency of the statutory provisions under which the administrative establishment carries on its activities. If so, a consistent effort to make the statutes say what Congressmen have in their minds may be one of the most effective ways of keeping the administrative branch in subjection to the political branches.

Finally, a great deal of Congressional dissatisfaction with specific administrative acts can be traced to the wide range of discretion which so much of our legislation entrusts to administrative officials. For this, there appear to be three remedies, each of which can be accomplished by majority vote of Congress. When Congress observes that administrative officials are proceeding in a direction which is not in keeping with its wishes, it may be possible, by joint or concurrent resolution, to state more precisely how Congress wants the statute interpreted. This is a remedy for imprecise legislation that has seldom been used in this country.[4]

[4] Perhaps the best known instance is the Hoch-Smith resolution passed in January, 1925, telling the Interstate Commerce Commission what Congress considered to be the "true policy" to be pursued in fixing railroad rates, and instructing the ICC to make necessary investigations and take necessary action to put the true policy into effect, 43 Statutes at Large 801, U.S. Code, title 49, sec. 55. Another instance is the Joint Resolution of July 12, 1932, telling the Tariff Commission "the true intent and meaning" of certain

Second, as experience in administration develops a body of policy supplementary to the statute, Congress may be able to incorporate some or all of it into the statute, thereby reducing the likelihood that administrative officials in the future may be able to upset expectations which those who are governed have come to depend upon.

A third measure which Congress may adopt to limit the exercise of discretion which it has granted in the statute would require that the crucial decisions made under that delegation of authority be submitted to it for approval or disapproval. This is a procedure that is extensively used in Great Britain and some other countries. Under various statutes in force in Great Britain, administrative acts of major significance (e.g., a departmental regulation fixing standards of wages in an industry) must be laid before Parliament for review. Certain types of administrative acts become law if Parliament does not veto them within a specified period; others fail automatically if Parliament does not vote its approval. Either procedure guarantees that the administrative department will not consistently thwart the will of Parliament on matters of great importance.

This is in substance the pattern we have established for acting on proposals for the reorganization of the administrative branch which are submitted by the President. As noted in Chapter 6, the President may draw up an order which reorganizes the administrative branch to his full satisfaction; he then lays it before Congress, which can keep it from becoming effective by an adverse vote in either house within a period of sixty days.

Congress has not made any systematic application of this procedure to the acts of administrative departments and agencies, though it has instituted such a procedure in respect to certain matters about which Congressmen have become especially concerned. For instance, the Attorney General is required to lay be-

language in the Tariff Act of 1930, 47 Statutes at Large 657, U.S. Code, title 19, sec. 1503 a. The Supreme Court construed the Hoch-Smith resolution narrowly, and perhaps effectively nullified it, in *Ann Arbor RR. Co. v. U.S.*, 281 U.S. 658 (1930).

fore Congress the names of aliens (with relevant facts about the case) who have been found liable for deportation but who have not actually been deported within a period of six months after the finding. This moves authority in the particular case out of the hands of the Attorney General. The controlling statute says that if Congress by concurrent resolution orders deportation, the Attorney General shall deport at once. If Congress passes no such resolution within a specified time, the deportation proceeding shall be canceled.[5]

Provisions for review of administrative action by Congress comparable to that provided for the deportation orders of the Attorney General are exceedingly rare. Many persons have urged the extension of this method of congressional review to other situations. I have never seen a good argument against it. Surely, it promises a type of political direction and control that we badly need in areas where administrative discretion must be broad because basic policies are necessarily uncertain.

BIBLIOGRAPHIC NOTE

No one has yet made a study of the day-to-day or continuing direction and control of administration by Congress comparable in scope and incisiveness to Wilmerding's study of direction and control through the provision of money. The best account and analysis that we have at present is a short essay by V. O. Key entitled "Legislative Control," in *Elements of Public Administration*, edited by Fritz Morstein Marx (New York, 1946), ch. 15. In general, Key views day-to-day direction and control by Congress with much less favor than I do. Taking essentially the same position as Key is a thoughtful essay by Pendleton Herring, "Executive-legislative Responsibilities," in *American Political Science Review*, vol. 38, pp. 1153–1165 (1944). See further, for different points of view, Robert D. Leigh, "Politicians vs. Bureaucrats," in *Harper's Magazine*, pp. 97–105 (January, 1945); and testimony in *Organization of Congress;* Hearings before Joint Committee on the Organization of Congress, 79th Congress, 1st session, on H. Con. Res. 18 (Government Printing Office, 1945), par-

[5] U.S. Code, title 8, sec. 155.

ticularly by William A. Jump (Part 3, pp. 685–697), by Walton Hamilton (Part 3, pp. 699–719), and by Chester Bowles (Part 4, pp. 727–742).

For the British practice of laying administrative orders before Parliament for approval or disapproval, see Cecil T. Carr, *Delegated Legislation* (Cambridge, 1921); and John A. Fairlie, *Administrative Procedure in Connection with Statutory Rules and Orders in Great Britain* (Urbana, Illinois, 1927). The feasibility of adopting this practice in our own national government is discussed by Roland Young, *This Is Congress* (New York, 1943), pp. 209–218; and James M. Landis, *The Administrative Process* (New Haven, 1939), pp. 77–80. Harvey C. Mansfield examines our experience under one of the few laws which most nearly resemble the British practice in "The Legislative Veto and the Deportation of Aliens," in *Public Administration Review*, vol. 1, pp. 281–286 (1941).

CHAPTER 10

CHOOSING MEN FOR JOBS

The framers of the Constitution expected Congress to share in the direction and control of administration. There is positive evidence of this in the provisions of the Constitution for appointment and removal of officials of the national government. The article which establishes the office of President and gives the President his principal powers states that he "shall nominate, and by and with the advice and consent of the Senate, shall appoint" all public officials of the United States except those which are elected (Vice President and members of Congress) and such "inferior officers" as may be excepted from this process by legislation providing for another method of appointment. The same article of the Constitution provides that all civil officers of the national government may be removed from office by a process of impeachment, and the article which creates the two houses of Congress and gives them their principal powers states that the House of Representatives shall have the sole power to bring charges of impeachment and the Senate shall have the sole power to try the case.

The language of the Constitution which provides for removal from office by process of impeachment makes it clear that a formal proceeding comparable to a judicial trial is expected. The grounds which will support removal (treason, bribery, or other high crimes and misdemeanors) involve legal concepts normally interpreted and applied by judges; the impeachment charges are "tried"; a "judgment" shall be reached and if the judgment is adversed to the officer impeached, the officer stands "convicted."

This is clearly language appropriate to a judicial proceeding. We may conclude, therefore, that the role which the framers of the Constitution expected the two houses of Congress to play in removal of men from public office is of a judicial nature; the House is a special and temporary prosecuting authority and the Senate is a special and temporary court, reaching its decisions by a two-thirds vote of the Senators present.

It is unnecessary to determine why the framers did not provide for the case to be tried before the Supreme Court if they wanted a judicial trial where the grounds for removal are treason, bribery, or other high crimes and misdemeanors. Possibly they believed that political considerations were bound to intrude in a proceeding that they wanted to move primarily on considerations of objective evidence and legal concepts; possibly they thought that political considerations were likely to be so prominent in removal cases that the Supreme Court would be drawn too far into politics if it undertook to render judgments resulting in removals. Regardless of why they did so, the framers gave Congress authority to remove men from public office on certain specified grounds, and subsequent events proved that political considerations would be prominent in the determination to remove or not remove.

Removal by process of impeachment must therefore be considered as one of the devices for political direction and control of administrative officials. It has not proved to date to be of importance as a means of congressional direction and control of administration, however, and there is no evidence that it is likely to be of more importance in the future. Since the Constitution went into effect the Senate has tried only twelve cases of impeachment, and only one of the twelve (Secretary of War William W. Belknap in 1876) was an officer in the administrative branch. Of the remaining eleven, one was a President (Andrew Johnson), one was a member of Congress, and nine were judges. Four of the judges were removed from office; in all the other cases, including that of Belknap, there was not a sufficient vote to convict and remove. Because removal by impeachment has not been of importance to date, it is given no further consideration in this analysis of direction and control of administration.

Except in the case of treason, bribery, and other high crimes and misdemeanors where removal by impeachment process is provided for, the Constitution is silent as to how administrative officials may be removed from office. By force of custom and the rulings and remarks of judges, however, we have made a great deal of progress toward a set of rules governing the authority to remove. It now seems fairly clear that the President may remove at pleasure any official or employee in the administrative branch unless his power to do so has been limited by law; that the nature of the limitations which may be imposed by law on the President's power to remove will depend on the character of the office involved; that there may be some offices in respect to which the President's removal power cannot be limited in any way; and finally, that the consent of the whole Congress, or of either house, cannot be made a condition for removal by the President. It has been provided by statute that the Comptroller General and Assistant Comptroller General, who are the highest officials in the General Accounting Office, may be removed only by joint action of the two houses of Congress; but the GAO is generally thought of as subject to direction and control by Congress rather than the President, and at least one statute of temporary duration has stated that the GAO is a part of the legislative branch of the government. No court has yet ruled on the validity of the statutory provision for removal of the Comptroller General and Assistant Comptroller General, and it seems clear that the validity of the removal provision can be upheld without vitiating any of the rules governing the removal power which are stated above.

This brief account of the constitutional basis for the power to remove indicates that Congress has little share in it. It will be seen later on, however, that what they cannot do directly, Congressmen are sometimes able to accomplish indirectly; there are a number of instances where Congress by legislative action has been able to force men out of office.

There is nothing in the language of the Constitution relating to appointments which suggests that the role of the Senate in filling public offices was, like its role in removals, expected to be judicial in nature. Rather, the language (the President "shall nominate, and by and with the advice and consent of the Senate, shall appoint") seems to indicate that the President was expected to take the initiative in appointments, but also was expected to consult fully and informally with the Senators so as to find men for public office who would prove most satisfactory to President and Senators alike. Apparently the Senators, like the President, were expected to be guided in their action by any considerations which seemed to them to be relevant and significant. There is no provision in the Constitution, as there is in the case of conviction on impeachment charges and concurrence in treaties, that the Senate is to act by a formal vote. It is reasonable to suppose that if the framers had intended to limit the Senate to something less than a full participation in the political process of choosing men for public office, they would have put language in the Constitution to make that intention clear. If they had wanted such a procedure they might, for instance, have provided that the President should submit to the Senate the name of the person whom he preferred for any office, and that the Senate should approve or reject the nomination by formal vote.

In this case, as in the case of removal by impeachment, it is unnecessary to reach a conclusion as to why the framers chose the particular language which they put in the Constitution. Practice has established two general procedures for filling public offices by action of the President and the Senate. In the case of an office located within one of the forty-eight states, one or both of the Senators from the state in which the office is located will inform the President of one or more men whom they (or one of them) prefer; when the President has been given the name of a man who is acceptable to him, he will submit a nomination to the Senate; and the Senators, by majority vote, will approve or disapprove the nomination, ordinarily acceding to the wishes of the Senators of the majority party from the state where the office is located. In the case of offices that do not fall within this practice of "Senatorial courtesy," the President will get his advice where he pleases; the President will nominate the man whom (presumably) he personally prefers; and the Senators will approve or disapprove by majority vote, their inclination to let the President have whom he wants ordinarily being determined by the nature of the office in question and the friendliness of the majority of the Senators toward the President and his program.

The President is given authority to make temporary appointments when the Senate is not in session, and these appointments are sometimes renewed for a considerable period of time before a permanent appointment is accomplished by the process described above.

How shall we view these provisions for Senate participation in the appointment of officials as they apply to the selection of men for positions in the administrative branch of the government? Is the President required to share with the Senate an authority over the administrative branch that we would be better satisfied to have exercised by the President alone? Does the authority of the Senate in respect to appointments provide a necessary check on power that the President might otherwise abuse and increase the likelihood that men who go into high administrative posts will faithfully administer governmental activities and undertakings in keeping with the instructions given them by the political branches of the government? Does the constitutional provision for Senate advice and consent represent a mistake of a past generation that we must put up with only until we can take it out of the Constitution? Or does it provide a wise and effective arrangement for assuring responsiveness of administration to the will of the people as expressed by the men and women whom the people have chosen to run their government?

It seems impossible to avoid the conclusion that the President should have the major influence in the selection of officials who are to have highest authority in the various administrative establishments. Such a conclusion is forced by our conception of the fundamental nature of our form of government and the President's position in it. The entire construction of his office as founded in the Constitution and shaped by experience presumes that the President will answer directly to the people for what the administrative branch of the government does. The American people will punish Congressmen as well as the President if they do not like the conduct of administration, but the President's name and office will appear more prominently in the criticism than the names of Congressmen and the institution that we call Congress. The President's name and office may be most prominent in popular expressions of dissatisfaction with legislation also, though we do not expect him to have the major influence in the enactment of law; but the American people have shown that they are able to differentiate the roles of President and Congress in legislation and to support the President at the very moment when they are condemning Congress. It is extremely unlikely, their assumptions about administration being what they are, that the American people will consistently excuse the President for what they believe to be serious misconduct in administration, even though the President might truthfully say that he had not the power to correct the administrative deficiency. Because the quality of administration, measured in terms of what the people like and dislike, is largely determined by the character of the men who head the various administrative establishments, the President therefore needs to enjoy a primary influence in selecting those men.

The quality of administration as a whole program of national government in operation also depends in large part on the way in which the activities of one administrative organization are related to the activities of other administrative organizations. The Presidency (the President personally, the White House functionaries, and the specialized bureaucracies that respond primarily to the President's wishes) is an effective institution for coordinating the activities of different administrative organizations. The ability of the Presidency to effect this coordination will be determined in great measure by the degree of loyalty to the President which the highest officials throughout the administrative branch display. And the degree of loyalty to the President will, in general, be much greater if these men are selected by a process in which the President has the principal influence.

Does the fact that the President must obtain Senate confirmation of his appointments to high administrative posts unduly hamper him in his efforts to provide the kind of administrative program that the American people expect? The power of the Senate to approve or disapprove a proposed appointment is not the power to tell the President whom he must appoint. Where the office to be filled is located in one of the states, the Senators from that state will exercise a most important influence on the choice of a person to fill it. The President will have to name someone who is satisfactory to those Senators (or one of them); otherwise, the Senate as a whole will not approve his nomination. And the President may find that very few individuals are acceptable to the Senators concerned. But with few exceptions indeed, these positions are not crucial to the success of the President's administrative program.

As to the higher positions at the seat of government and outside continental United States, it is usually said that the President has essentially a free hand in making his selections. Certainly few of his nominations are rejected by the Senate. It must be assumed, however, that the necessity of getting Senate approval causes him to pass over some men whom he would otherwise appoint. How shall we view this limitation on the President's power to appoint the men he wants? If the proposed appointment is objectionable to a majority of the Senators, would it not be objectionable to the country as a whole? If the person in question cannot satisfy the Senate that he is the man for the job, could he ever win in either house the legislative support that is necessary to carry forward a program of government?

It is true that the Senate may reject a nomination for reasons that in no sense reflect a judgment concerning the nominee's ability and intention to perform the duties of the office in keeping with Senators' notions as to how those duties ought to be performed. This is not likely to happen if the President and the majority of the Senate are of the same political party and enjoy a mutual feeling of confidence. If the President and the leadership of his party in the Senate have broken, the necessity of getting the approval of the latter for the President's nominations may be an effective stay on chaos in government that would otherwise develop. Certainly the appointment of high officials who are acceptable to both factions is more likely to heal the breach within the party and give the nation a responsible government than for the President to fill these high places with persons who are unacceptable to the wing of the party that opposes him.

The President must be advised by someone in making his appointments. He does not know personally a number of the men and women who must be given consideration in making his choices for the many positions which he must fill. President Woodrow Wilson met Franklin K. Lane for the first time when the latter entered the White House and introduced himself with the statement, "Mr. President, I am your Secretary of Interior." The constitutional requirement of confirmation undoubtedly causes the President to seek the advice of Senators of his party long before the Senate is called upon to approve his final selections. Where could he turn for advice in which he could place greater confidence? The Senators come from different parts of the country. They know, or know about, the leading men of the nation. They are acquainted with the President's plans for government. In respect to matters of government and politics, they enjoy the confidence of the people who put the President in office.

If the party to which the President belongs is not in control of the Senate, he will encounter greater difficulty in getting approval for his appointments. But government at such a time is more than ever the joint enterprise of two parties. What less can one ask in a time of coalition government than that both parties be satisfied with the men who head the administrative departments and agencies?

In addition to the considerations which have been discussed, and which seem to me to support overwhelmingly the requirement of Senate confirmation, there is one further consequence of the requirement which should be noted. The processes of the executive are likely to be secret. The people may know nothing of the considerations that lead the President to pass over a hundred men and select another. But a contest over the approval of an appointment brings many things into the open. The Senators in opposition make sure that the issue is known to the people. A fight at the top level of the government commands public interest. This is the way the nation gets its political education. A sharp debate over the qualifications of a man for high office may give the people more understanding of the functions of an administrative department and more appreciation of what government might do for them than they would acquire in a lifetime from less sensational disclosures.

The considerations which are set forth in the past few paragraphs are no more a support for confirmation of appointments by the Senate than they are for confirmation by Congress as a whole. Every advantage credited to Senatorial confirmation in this discussion would be equally realized if appointments had to be approved by a majority vote in each house of Congress. There is a further consideration which makes confirmation by the whole of Congress seem preferable to confirmation by one house only. Congress as a whole passes the laws that describe the activities and undertakings which the administrative departments and agencies are expected to administer. The likelihood that the objectives which Congressmen in both houses have in mind will be realized in administration depends on the way administrative officials interpret their legislative instructions and exercise the discretion delegated to them. The concern about the character and quality of government that leads Congressmen to enact the legislation which an administrative establishment enforces impels Congressmen in both houses to demand that the officials who direct that establishment be in sympathy with the objectives back of the legislation. The opportunity to reject the President's nominations for these high offices is a means of enforcing that demand.

The extension of the requirement of confirmation to both houses of Congress has not been considered as a practical proposal so far as I know, and I have no intention of recommending here that we take such a step. The framers of the Constitution, if we understand them correctly, did not intend to subject the chief executive and the administrative organizations under him to the degree of legislative supremacy which we have long understood to obtain in parliamentary systems of government. Confirmation by the Senate was apparently intended to give the President benefit of an advisory council, not to subject him to legislative domination. As long as we think of the confirmation process as an arrangement which permits a group of elected men and women to tell the President when he is too far offside in his proposed appointments, confirmation by one house of Congress is undoubtedly sufficient. But we may well reconsider the matter if it becomes evident that, in the general character of our government, we are moving toward a greater resemblance of the parliamentary system. As we shall see later, a number of people have seriously recommended that the President be given the power to dissolve Congress and force a general election in which the issue which leads to dissolution is presumably resolved by the people. If we make so great a departure from our present arrangements for separation of powers, it will be timely to consider whether we ought not require both houses of Congress to approve appointments to the highest administrative positions so as to make sure that the new system of government will be one of legislative rather than executive supremacy.

There is no reason to suppose that all the considerations which have a bearing on the process of filling high administrative positions support the case for confirmation, either by one or by both houses of Congress. None which I have been able to identify as challenging the case for confirmation seem to me to match in weight those which I have set forth in this discussion as standing in its support. The most important objection to confirmation of which I am aware is that it causes men whom the President and the majority of the confirming body would like to put in office to reject an offer of appointment. The consideration of the President's nominee for an important post provides the legislators who are in opposition to the President with an opportunity to attack the President, his party, and everything which the President and his party stand for. The nominee becomes for the moment the prime recipient of this attack. All the supposed sins of the President and his party may be made to appear the willful machinations of the individual who is under consideration for appointment. This is by no means what usually takes place in the hearing of the committee or in the debate on the floor where the qualities, qualifications, and probable future conduct of the nominee are discussed. It does, however, occur from time to time, and the person under consideration is sometimes made most uncomfortable due to no faults and no shortcomings of his own. And it may well be that some persons whom the President and the majority of the confirming body would like to put in office are unwilling to risk the abuse which they fear might be visited upon them.

I have not seen convincing evidence that many persons have been eliminated from nomination for office by the President because of fear of embarrassment or abuse, and I personally doubt that this aspect of the confirmation proceeding has a significant effect on the availability of men for public office. Even if the field from which the President can pick is substantially reduced for this reason, I think that this consideration adverse to the requirement of confirmation is greatly outweighed by those which support it. And I may say in addition that, in my opinion, it is not a matter to be seriously objected to if there is a considerable amount of discomfort and embarrassment connected with confirmation for appointment to high office in the administrative branch of the government. It is, as pointed out above, through the attack upon and the defense of the candidate for appointment that the American people get a great deal of their education about what their government is doing and how it is run. Men and women who rise so high in the affairs of their party or in public estimation as to be considered for important administrative positions may properly be asked to lend themselves to the process by which that public knowledge and understanding is accomplished.

What has been said up to this point about the process of selecting men for public office has been directed to the filling of administrative positions of major importance. But the authority of the Senate in the appointment of administrative officials is by no means limited to the highest positions in the administrative branch. By far the greater number of appointments to which the Senate must consent (more than 90 percent during the decade 1933 to 1942) involve the commissioning of officers in the armed services and the appointment to first-, second-, and third-class postmasterships. The authority of both the President and the Senate is greatly limited as respects these postmasterships, however. Applicants for these positions are required to pass a civil service examination and the three persons who are rated highest become eligible for appointment. The President submits one of the three names to the Senate for confirmation, and the practice of Senatorial courtesy which was described above obtains. The Senate is not likely to approve the name submitted by the President if the Senators (provided they are of the majority party) from the state where the post office is located hold out for one of the other two eligible candidates.

The case that can be made for the requirement of confirmation of high administrative officials has little application to officials in the lower levels of the administrative organization. The considerations set forth above in support of confirmation acquire whatever relevance and validity they have from the fact that the officials who are subject to confirmation will be able to exercise great influence over the character and quality of administration. Military officers in the lower grades, postmasters, collectors of the customs, and other officials of lower rank which the Senate now confirms have collectively an enormous influence over the character and quality of administration, and individually, at least some influence. There should be rigid standards for the qualification of men who go into these positions and the qualities of men and women who are considered for these positions should be carefully studied. But there is surely a better way for the legislative body to make certain that men in these lower ranks will possess the qualities that are desired than to require members of either or both houses to review the qualifications of the thousands of men who each year go into positions of that character. The members of neither house (nor of the two houses if they divided the job between them) can afford to give the time which would be necessary for a careful consideration of the influence which these men and women would probably exert on the character and quality of administration.

I have not seen any thoughtful analysis of the authority and influence of administrative officials in the federal government which supports a confident judgment as to where the requirement of confirmation ought to stop. The Constitution states that "inferior officers" may be removed from the requirement of Senate confirmation; but it seems necessary to conclude that what is an inferior officer will be determined by the desirability of confirmation, not that an established concept of what constitutes an inferior officer will control the requirement of confirmation. Surely there is nothing in the nature of his authority or the dignity of his office to lead Congressmen to think of the Director of the Bureau of the Budget as an inferior officer. Rather, Congressmen thought that the relations between the President and that official would be such that the President ought not to have to yield to the wishes or judgment of anybody else in picking him. Therefore, they construed the office to be "inferior" and provided that the President could fill the position without submitting a nomination to the Senate.

In the enactment of legislation creating administrative offices, however, Congress has not been guided by any consistent theory as to where the authority to appoint should be located. What it provides (i.e., whether or not it requires confirmation) when it creates a new administrative organization seems to depend on one or more of four considerations or principles. Each of the four is defensible; at least two are such that Congress might properly make either of them its sole or controlling guide in deciding whether or not to require confirmation of such offices as it creates from now on.

The first consideration which guides Congress in deciding whether or not to require confirmation is that of "position in the hierarchy." Congress might provide in all legislation enacted hereafter that only the head of the administrative establishment will be appointed by the President with the advice and consent of the Senate; or that the head and a small group of officers with general authority in the organization (Under Secretary and Assistant Secretaries) will be selected in that way; or that officers in the foregoing categories and the chiefs of the largest operating divisions (bureau chiefs) will be subject to confirmation; and so on. Such a principle, if made the exclusive guide in determining when confirmation will be required, would be easy to apply. And it can be justified in reason. The statute which creates the administrative establishment can give the official or officials who fall within the confirmation class the kind and amount of authority which will enable them effectively to direct and control the force of officials and employees below them. Congress would be assured that the men and women whom the President and Senate pick for these highest jobs have it in their power to determine the character and quality of government which the administrative branch provides.

A second consideration to which Congress gives weight in deciding how administrative officials shall be chosen is that of "authority over policy." Many Congressmen have said, and some have argued most earnestly, that the requirement of confirmation should be restricted to "policy-determining" officers. Authority over policy, unlike position in the hierarchy, is not an easy standard to apply. Administrative officials do not fall into two classes—those who determine policy and those who do not. Every official and every employee of the government who makes a decision or takes an action which effectively determines what government is going to be like in any respect is engaged in determining policy. The men and women who are in the highest positions of an administrative organization, we hope, will have a great deal more influence on the character of governmental policies than the men and women in the lower ranks. But the difference in amount of policy-determining which one official does and the amount which is done by the officials below him is ordinarily only a matter of degree.

When Congress sets up a new administrative organization, it may be able to put language in the statute which increases the assurance that the officials who are at the top of the organization will have adequate authority to review and approve or disapprove the policies which are made by the officials and employees below them. If Congress succeeds in giving the highest officials effective control over the policies which are made at any point within the organization, it may be able to honor the standard of authority over policy without extending the requirement of confirmation to a large number of officials; if such is the case, the standard of authority over policy becomes for all practical purposes identical with that of position in the hierarchy.

The Hoover Commission appears to view such a result as desirable if it can be achieved. It would, in all cases, have the President submit to the Senate the names of those persons whom he proposes to put at the head of the various administrative establishments and into the positions of general authority immediately under the head of an establishment (Under Secretary and Assistant Secretaries); it would only in exceptional cases have him submit the names of persons proposed for the position of bureau chief. "These officials [head of the establishment, Under Secretary, and Assistant Secretaries] being of policy rank, should be appointed by the President and confirmed by the Senate." On the other hand, "the staff officials and, as a rule, bureau chiefs should be appointed by the department heads."[1]

The language used in reference to bureau chiefs reveals a doubt on the part of the Commission that the relation between position in the hierarchy and authority over policy is the same in all sectors of the administrative branch. I feel quite certain that the relationship is far from constant. I do not believe that the test of position in the hierarchy and the test of authority over policy will usually point to the same stopping place for the requirement of Senatorial confirmation unless we greatly reduce the range of activities and undertakings that are to be administered by a single administrative establishment. As I point out in a later chapter (Chapter 21), I think a great deal of our government consists of policies (call them regulatory policies for the moment) that will be satisfactory to the American people only if they are made by officials who have close contact with the individuals and groups of individuals who are most significantly affected by those policies; and I think further that the determinations of policy that are made by these officials ought not be subject to review and reversal by superior administrative officials. If Senate confirmation is to be required for officials who effectively determine this kind of policy, then, so long as we keep our present pattern of administrative organization, confirmation will have to extend far below the level of bureau chief in many instances; there may be cases where certain officials are appointed by the action of the President and Senate, while the bureau chief and other officials above them in the administrative hierarchy are appointed by the head of the department or agency. Only if we take these regulatory matters out of the great administrative departments and set them up in separate agencies, it seems to me, can we expect the many officials

[1] *General Management of the Executive Branch; A Report to the Congress by the Commission on Organization of the Executive Branch of the Government, February 1949* (Government Printing Office, 1949), pp. 37–39; *Departmental Management in Federal Administration; A Report with Recommendations Prepared for the Commission on Organization of the Executive Branch of the Government* [*Appendix E*] (Government Printing Office, 1949), pp. 8–10, 31–32.

who effectively determine policy to occupy like positions in the administrative hierarchy.

A third consideration which Congress weighs in deciding whether or not to require confirmation is that of "congressional elimination of undesirables." The political party which is trying to run the government can be greatly embarrassed if a few prominent officials make fools of themselves in the eyes of the people. Congressmen may be punished individually when they come up for re-election if a great many people have been offended by the conduct of certain administrative officials. Members of Congress know that the President cannot personally screen the many thousand appointments that are made annually in the administrative branch. To date, they have not been willing to trust the screening entirely to administrative officials in the various departments and agencies, even when assisted and regulated by civil service legislation and the Civil Service Commission. Some Congressmen in both houses prefer that the Senators have an opportunity to examine long lists of persons proposed for certain offices so that they can eliminate those who appear most objectionable, even though only an occasional person fails of confirmation. This is undoubtedly the principal explanation of why Congress continues to require that the advice and consent of the Senate be obtained for the commissioning of officers in the armed services; most of the commissions are for officers at the bottom of the hierarchy, few officers have any important authority over policy, and patronage (the fourth consideration which supports confirmation) is certainly not involved.

A general agreement among Congressmen that the Senate should be in a position to keep undesirables from getting into the federal service offers little help in deciding when to require and when not to require confirmation, unless it is agreed that the Senate should have a chance to scrutinize every appointment to a federal job. The most lowly employee can bring the federal service into disrepute; there is no dividing line which separates government positions according to likelihood that the party in power or individual Congressmen will be embarrassed by unfortunate appointments. If it be said that Senators will keep our post offices from falling into the wrong hands ("The people of Savonburg will not tolerate a Brooklyn accent."), what may we say about the men who deliver mail to our homes? How are we to be saved from postmen who might insult our wives, spread leprosy through the community, and break all the tricycles that are left on the sidewalks? Must Senators save us from all prospect of displeasure with our public servants?

The third standard, elimination of undesirables, is regularly advanced, of course, when the real reason for requiring confirmation is to give individual Congressmen a chance to name for office the men and women whom they personally prefer. We may say, therefore, that Congress is governed by a fourth consideration in deciding which offices should be filled with the advice and consent of the Senate—"the desirability of congressional patronage." Senators get the patronage in the first instance, of course, since their power to turn down appointments enables them to bargain for the nomination of men and women in whom they are interested. But the Senator, in turn, needs advice in filling positions scattered over his state, and much of his patronage becomes patronage for the Representatives of his party who can be counted on to support the Senator in future elections.

The academic students of government and politics (the political scientists) rarely have a good word to say for the efforts of Congressmen to hold on to patronage through the power of the Senate to approve or reject appointments. The political scientists would like for the Congressman to stand or fall in a contest for reelection solely on the basis of what he has done or promises to do in the form of legislation; they do not like for him to secure votes through his power to decide who is and who is not to be put on the federal payroll. The political scientists are deeply attached to the principle that federal jobs ought to go to the men and women most likely to do their jobs well and prove their competence for more responsible positions in the public service; they recognize that the Congressman is primarily concerned with making appointments which will have a favorable effect on voting when the next election comes around.

There is more at stake in the use of patronage to influence elections than is mentioned in the foregoing paragraph, and I think that Congressmen generally have been more fully aware of it than the political scientists. Up to now at least, the American people have not been deeply enough concerned about programs of government to permit issues of policy to dominate their interest in elections. Large numbers of votes have been turned by the efforts of active party workers, and the efforts of party workers have been paid for in the main by places on public payrolls. We have not put our states, cities, counties, and other units of government on a merit system of employment. State and local jobs have been available to finance party activity. If virtually all party activity, over the years, had been financed by state and local government jobs, I think we may assume that Congressmen would have been much more in bondage to state and local political leaders than they have been.

It is generally believed that the United States Senate won a great degree of freedom from state political leaders when we took the power to select Senators away from state legislatures and gave it to the people. And the freedom which the Senate won in this way has generally been hailed as a reform of great merit. In less spectacular manner we gave the members of both houses of Congress a measure of freedom from state and local political leaders when we made it possible for individual Congressmen to strengthen their positions in the party organization by control of certain federal appointments. By giving the Congressman control over federal patronage, we did not divorce federal politics from state and local politics; but we did give the Congressman a way of defending himself and what he stood for against other politicians who drew their strength from state and local patronage. In using his power over federal employment to influence voting in national elections, the Congressman increased the likelihood that we would elect someone who had not been hand-picked by the local political machine.

This brief analysis of the practical consequences of the patronage which the Senators and Representatives share suggests only a few of the benefits which the nation may have derived. If Congressmen had not been able, through the power of the Senate over appointments, to control so much of the federal patronage, would the President and the heads of administrative departments have had a freer hand to build up political machines to keep themselves in office? Or would the election of the President, in the absence of Senatorial confirmation, have fallen more fully than it did under the influence of state and local political organizations?

It is clear that much can be said in favor of applying a standard of desirability of congressional patronage when Congress has to decide whether or not to subject certain offices to confirmation by the Senate. It must also be said that many of the reasons which could be cited for giving patronage to Congressmen in the past may be entitled to less weight or no weight in the future. The American people, in recent years, have advanced a long way in appreciation of what their national government means to them. It may be that their understanding of and concern about what the national government does and might do for them will sustain such an active interest in national elections that congressional control of federal patronage is no longer needed as a bulwark against state and local political machines, or as a safeguard against the construction of political organizations by the President and federal administrative officers.

We may suppose that these four considerations are usually mixed up together in the minds of Congressmen when they are deciding whether or not to require Senate confirmation of a particular office or of a class of offices. This is illustrated by the bill introduced by Senator Kenneth McKellar of Tennessee in 1943 to provide by law that no person should be appointed to a position in the administrative branch of the federal government paying $4500 or more unless the Senate had first given its advice and consent to that appointment. As introduced by Senator McKellar, the bill fixed a four-year tenure for the positions that fell within its terms, and confirmation by the Senate would have been necessary for reappointment to any such job or for transfer or promotion from one such job to another.

Senator McKellar's great reputation as a patronage-getter makes it difficult to believe that a desire for personal control of appointments was not a major consideration in his decision to introduce and support the bill, even though he specifically stated that he had no wish to extend his control over patronage. It may also be supposed that other Senators and Representatives gave support to the bill because they hoped that the requirement of confirmation would enlarge their personal influence in appointments. But the desirability of patronage for Congressmen was by no means the sole consideration that weighed with Senators and Representatives when they argued and voted for and against the McKellar bill. Each of the other three considerations which were discussed above as standards to be applied in deciding whether or not to require confirmation figured in the action of the two houses. The bill, by its terms, paid tribute to the principle that the requirement of confirmation should relate to position in the hierarchy, for we have no measure applicable throughout the administrative branch which serves better than salary to indicate the relative importance of different administrative positions. Some members of Congress attacked the bill on the ground that the requirement of confirmation should be confined to positions that carry authority over policy; others defended the bill on the ground that positions paying $4500 or more usually, if not always, give the incumbent the power to make important determinations of policy.

But it was the third of the four considerations discussed above, congressional elimination of undesirables, that figured most prominently in the debate. Both Senators and Representatives made it clear that they had little confidence in the appointment practices which were being pursued in the administrative branch. They had heard too much about some of the men that were going into high-salaried jobs. Too many nincompoops, dead beats, and damned fools from back home were getting on the payroll and the people were letting their Congressmen know what they thought of it. Men were going up the salary scale too fast; strolling through Washington with a pay increase at every step had to be stopped. There were too many high-salaried jobs in proportion to the little ones anyway; if the executive authorities wouldn't do anything about it, the Senators would, by withholding confirmation. The Congressmen had passed civil service laws which had cut themselves out of the patronage; what the Congressmen had given up had fallen into the laps of others who were putting their men into all the strategic positions.

The strongest supporter of executive authority and merit system legislation can feel a great deal of sympathy for Congressmen who propose drastic remedies for some of the abuses of the hiring process which occur in wartime. But screening by the Senate is not the proper remedy for these abuses if a better remedy can be found. If the Senate did a thorough job of checking on a great mass of appointments, it would do little else; if it did a cursory job of screening, it would probably correct few abuses and it might do a lot of positive harm to administration. Surely, the best way for Congressmen to prevent abuses in filling federal jobs is to lay down controlling regulations and establish authority to enforce them. We have laws, as pointed out in Chapter 8, which fix salary scales, relate them to the quality of the job, and regulate promotions. If these laws were inadequate for the wartime situation, then improved legislation was needed. If the enforcing authority was too weak or incompetent, then better administrative machinery could have been established. This the lower house of Congress seems to have considered the proper way to achieve reform, for it voted down the legislation which Senator McKellar sponsored.[2]

[2] Senator McKellar's bill and the issues which it raised are carefully examined by Arthur W. Macmahon in his article "Senatorial Confirmation," in

Much of the reasoning which supports congressional participation in filling administrative positions is equally applicable to congressional participation in removing men from administrative positions. If, for instance, Senatorial screening of appointments is a good way of keeping undesirable people out of the government service, then an occasional examination of the employment lists by one or both houses should be a good way of throwing out the undesirable individuals who slipped by in the appointment process. Both houses of Congress, acting separately or jointly, are almost constantly doing something which enables them to locate men and women in the government service who, in the judgment of some of the Congressmen, ought not be where they are. Sometimes one or both houses resorts to drastic action to get some of these people out of their jobs or out of the federal service altogether. Members of the appropriations committees scrutinize closely the grade and salary distributions of the various departments and agencies. They call for lists of employees and officials who have had unusually rapid promotions; if the promotion policy of a department or one of its divisions seems unduly liberal, then the committee or a subcommittee may call for a special report on the promotion history of everybody in the organization. Similarly, if the general salary level of a department or one of its divisions appears to be unreasonably high, the proper appropriations subcommittee may call for a report on the training and experience of every official and employee.

Out of such inquiries, Congress gets information which enables it to pass laws to keep the more offensive appointment and promotion practices from taking place in the future. Frequently, however, Congressmen are not content to pass laws of general application; they may decide instead to punish the administrative

Public Administration Review, vol. 3, pp. 281–296 (1943). The principal sources for testimony and argument concerning the bill are *Congressional Record*, vol. 89, parts 3 and 4 (78th Congress, 1st session); and *Senate Confirmation of Officers and Employees*, Hearing before a Subcommittee of the Committee on Judiciary of the U.S. Senate, 78th Congress, 1st session on S. 575 (Government Printing Office, 1943).

officials who are responsible for the offensive practice and to apply corrective legislation to the particular administrative organization that is out of line. This seems fair enough in theory, but experience shows that the results of such an effort are likely to prove unsatisfactory to members of Congress and everybody else. Congress may, by law or appropriation act, cut the salary of one or more top officials; this does not do much good if the officials refuse to admit guilt and view themselves as martyrs or victims of a political maneuver. Congress may reduce the appropriation which is available to finance the administrative establishment, but that may have no effect except to reduce the amount and quality of the service which the administrative organization provides for the American people. Congress may impose limitations on rate of promotion or on the number of positions in the higher grades, but this penalizes employees who earn what they get and are entitled to go ahead at a faster rate than the crowd.

Most Congressmen appreciate better than you and I how crude these remedies are in their application. As a consequence, there is frequently a demand in one or both houses that a particular official or employee be dealt with directly. We had a dramatic instance of this only recently. Early in World War II, an investigating committee of the House of Representatives named several employees of the federal government, each of whom it charged with disloyalty to the United States. A number of voices, including those of many Congressmen, called for those men to resign from the service. Many, if not all of them, refused to quit, and they were not fired. Finally, in 1943, Congress named three of these individuals (William E. Dodd, Jr., Goodwin Watson, and Robert Morss Lovett) in an appropriation bill and specified that the money appropriated should not be used to pay any part of their salaries.

The validity of this action under the Constitution was a nice question. Congress could define loyalty and disloyalty, and no doubt could bar from federal employment all individuals who could not meet the test of loyalty that it set up. But could it bar individuals from employment without a trial to prove they failed to meet the test of loyalty? And could Congress itself conduct the trial if it wanted them to have one?

These questions bothered Congressmen who wanted those men off the payroll. A test of loyalty had been applied to the three men but it wasn't a very definitive one and it was adopted by a committee only, not by Congress as an enactment of law. The men were interviewed by a committee of the House, but the occasion bore slight resemblance to a trial. And if it was intended to be a trial, why was a committee of the House conducting it? The Constitution describes a procedure whereby Congress may remove men from the federal payroll; it calls for impeachment by one house and a trial by both houses, one prosecuting and the other sitting as judge and jury.

The legal effect of the appropriation act which carried the proscription of Dodd, Lovett, and Watson was questioned by the top officials of the two administrative agencies in which the three men were employed. They were not discharged but were permitted to work beyond the period for which the appropriation legislation permitted them to be paid. Then they sued for pay, standing on the ground that the action of Congress which denied them pay was illegal. So the Supreme Court decided in 1946 (*United States v. Lovett*, 328 U.S. 303), a majority of the justices holding that the limitation in the appropriation act constituted a bill of attainder. The three men finally drew pay for the period of their work, but the court decision did not order them to be taken back into federal employment.[3]

Aside from the illegality of its action, what Congress did to force Dodd, Lovett, and Watson out of the service was surely a poor way to deal with disloyalty. If these three men were disloyal, there were doubtless a great many more who were equally dis-

[3] The fullest treatment of this incident appears to be by Robert E. Cushman in his article, "The Purge of Federal Employees Accused of Disloyalty," in *Public Administration Review*, vol. 3, pp. 297–316 (1943). The debate is scattered through volumes 88 and 89 of the *Congressional Record* (77th Congress, 2nd session, and 78th Congress, 1st session).

loyal. The Congressmen who voted for the restriction in the appropriation bill did not believe they were cleaning up federal employment; they understood that they were getting three men and missing a whole lot more. If the offense with which these men were charged was serious enough to warrant their removal, then it was time to pass a law defining that offense and setting up a machinery to get all the officials and employees who had committed that offense. In the time that Congress spent getting at these three men, it could have devised a law that would provide a way for getting all officials and employees who could not meet the test it proclaimed.

The lesson to be drawn from this incident is not that Congress has no legitimate concern in the character of the men and women who work for the federal government. In my opinion, Congress is entitled to have the highest concern about the quality of the federal service, and it should be able to enforce its standards for employment upon the chief executive and the administrative branch. The lesson to be drawn from the Dodd-Lovett-Watson affair is that there are effective and ineffective ways of enforcing the will of Congress, and legislation which applies generally to the government service may usually, if not always, prove to be the most effective way of enforcing the will of Congress.

As I see it, Congress should constantly inquire into the employment, placement, and promotion practices in the administrative branch, and it should satisfy itself that it is not getting the wool pulled over its eyes. Where Congressmen see practices that offend them and find individuals that they believe unworthy of their posts, they should tell the responsible administrative officials what they object to orally or in writing through their committee chairmen and more formally through resolutions of the whole Congress. If administrative officials cannot justify what they have done and will not correct what Congress objects to, Congress may be able to get the President to straighten the matter out. If the President will not act, and Congress (acting by a majority in each house) is certain of its mind, then Congress ought itself to pursue the corrective action which promises to put a stop to the offense with least damage to the objectives which caused the administrative organization to be established and given a job to do.

If legislation of a general character will not remedy a situation in a particular administrative establishment, then Congress may have to give its action a specific application. If, for instance, it is determined to force a particular individual out of the government service (as I think it may properly do under certain circumstances), then Congress might address a resolution to the proper administrative official or the President, announcing its lack of confidence in the administration of a particular sector of the administration and indicating the possibility that appropriations will for that reason be reduced in the future. The President and other high administrative officials may, if they wish, stand on their constitutional rights to determine (short of impeachment) who shall and who shall not be removed from administrative office; they can hardly deny that Congressmen have a right to regulate their appropriation of money by the degree of confidence which they have in the men who will spend that money.

BIBLIOGRAPHIC NOTE

On the relation of Congress to the selection of administrative officials, as on many other interrelationships of politics and administration, we are indebted to Arthur W. Macmahon for our most informative and critical study, "Senatorial Confirmation," in *Public Administrative Review*, vol. 3, pp. 281–296 (1943). This analysis is focused especially on the attempt of Senator McKellar to extend the requirement of confirmation to all positions paying more than a certain amount of money (discussed in the text of this chapter), but its significance is not limited to the facts and implications of that incident. This article is ably supplemented by Dorothy G. Fowler, "Congressional Dictation of Local Appointments," in *Journal of Politics*, vol. 7, pp. 25–57 (1945). For discussion which goes beyond these articles, either in accounts of what has occurred or analysis of implications, one must be content with bits here and there. There is something to be learned from the literature relating to patronage and civil service reform, books on Congress and the President, and memoirs and other papers of men who have, in one way or another, been involved in the process of Presidential nomination and Senatorial confirmation. See the note at the end of Chapter 15 for some references.

The leading work on removal of federal officials by impeachment seems to be Alex Simpson, *A Treatise on Federal Impeachments* (Philadelphia, 1916). See also Leon R. Yankwich, "Impeachment of Civil Officers Under the Constitution," in *Georgetown Law Journal*, vol. 26, pp. 849–867 (1938). I have seen only one account of efforts of Congress to force officials or employees out of the federal service by methods other than impeachment, Robert E. Cushman, "The Purge of Federal Employees Accused of Disloyalty," in *Public Administration Review*, vol. 3, pp. 297–316 (1943).

PART III

DIRECTION AND CONTROL
BY THE PRESIDENT

CHAPTER 11

WHAT ARE THE BUREAUCRATS TO DO?

Congress and President share responsibility for political direction and control of administration. The most significant issues we face in our efforts to make political direction and control more effective relate to the distribution of authority and influence between Congress and the President. We have examined the role of Congress; we have now to examine the role of the President. In order to bring the issues relating to distribution of authority and influence into sharpest focus, the discussion of Presidential direction and control which follows (except for minor changes in the order of treatment) is organized in the same pattern as the discussion of congressional direction and control which has already been presented. The first area of concern is the part which the President plays in describing and defining the governmental activities and undertakings which the administrative establishment is to carry out.

What the activities and undertakings of the government shall be is pre-eminently a question to be decided by the lawmaking process. This point was developed at some length in Chapter 5, and need not be labored further.

The President contributes to decisions as to what the government shall do, for he participates in the making of laws. No generation* of Americans has had a better opportunity than this one to understand what the President's contribution can be. For the New Deal was one of the most important and one of the most sensational shiftings of course that American government has undergone since the present Constitution was adopted. If the New Deal was not the idea of Franklin D. Roosevelt, its aims and its methods were authoritatively announced by him. The legislative measures that were drawn up to put into effect the objectives which he announced showed the marks of his personal convictions and predilictions. And the strategy, if not the tactics, that won the country to his support and induced Congressmen to put his proposals into law were in large part the product of Mr. Roosevelt's own mind.

For the President to play such a role in the enactment of legislation is in keeping with our theory of government. The Presidency is our highest honor, and the President is our highest official. We elect the President not merely to direct the administration of laws already on the statute books; we elect him to direct the whole power of government toward the objectives that he has espoused. Government is never altogether what we want it to be; the President is the man we think most likely to point out and drive toward the improvements which accord with our momentary desires.

But we do not elect the President to be a dictator. We do not authorize him to decree the laws. From the forty-eight states and more than four hundred districts, we elect Senators and Representatives to check his judgment. The President is the central figure in the group that assumes the power of government. He is the individual about whom many leaders rally. It is his job to find bases of agreement among them. And it is their job collectively to set the government toward the purposes that have won their common approval.

This is sound in theory and workable in practice. If the President is not sufficiently a leader to bring the majority party in Congress to a common program, it is no solution to give him arbitrary power. If he personally lacks the powers of leadership necessary to win Congressmen to his cause, then he will probably soon lose the confidence of the people as a whole. If the nation sets up President of one party and Congress of another to run the country it is especially a time for talking and the clearing of minds; it is not yet time for precipitate departure on new programs of government. If the vagaries of death and mid-term elections turn Congress over to the party opposing the President and give us a style of government we do not like, the remedy lies in correcting our electoral system, not in endowing the President with authority to do the things that he cannot induce the representative assembly to do.

But there are circumstances in which we think it proper to delegate lawmaking authority—even authority to say what the activities and undertakings of government shall be. The considerations which presumably guide Congress and President (who enact the statutes) in deciding what to put in the statute and what to leave to the judgment of someone else were discussed at some length in Chapter 5. Most delegations of authority to fill out or extend statutes are made to high administrative officials in the administrative establishment that is charged with carrying out the statute. But Congress has, in a number of enactments, put the authority in the President. This is undoubtedly the more desirable arrangement where the matters involved go beyond the concern of any one administrative establishment. The necessity of giving the President some authority of this nature was revealed at the very beginning of our present system of government. The first major crisis that confronted President Washington fell upon him with the outbreak of war in Europe in 1791. The Constitution provides that Congress (the President having the power to veto) shall have the power to declare war. Therefore, said Attorney General Edmund Randolph, only Congress (again subject to Presidential veto) can declare that there shall not be war; the President has no authority, by his sole determination, to decide that there shall be a state of neutrality. This was not as foolish an argument as it may appear today, because the United States had entered into treaties which some people thought made it mandatory for us to fight on the side of France. Whatever the legal or moral obligation of the United States to go to war, President Washington decided that the United States should be neutral and he so announced, without consulting Congress, in his now famous neutrality proclamation of 1793.

Whether or not this announcement of neutrality was (as Randolph believed) a usurpation of legislative authority, what the President did to make it effective certainly involved decisions of a kind usually made by legislative enactment. The proclamation raised a great number of questions of highest importance. Could war vessels of the fighting countries put into American ports for food and other supplies? Could they repair the damage done to them in storm or battle? Could they sell the prize goods they had captured from the enemy? Could the belligerent nations contract with American shipbuilders to construct war vessels for their use? Could they set up recruiting offices in America, hire American citizens for service in their armed forces, and train them on American soil?

These and many other questions had to be answered and answered at once. Congress was not in session, and it could not be convened within a few weeks in those days. So the President assumed lawmaking authority himself and decreed the rules which should govern American citizens and foreigners within our gates. War vessels of belligerent nations, forced into American ports by distress, could "refresh, victual, repair, etc." But none of the vessels of the nations at war could take on equipment "of a nature solely adapted to war." Neither could American citizens fit out privateers in American ports or accept commissions to sail as privateers; and the remedies and penalties would include stripping the offending vessel of its arms, freeing any prizes taken, and prosecuting persons contributing to the offense. Other decisions of the President, announced in relation to a specific case or incorporated in general regulations, related to recruitment of American citizens and aliens within the United States for service in the armed forces of a nation at war, sale of prizes in American ports, trade in contraband of war, and a wide range of other matters relevant to the neutral position of the United States.

These decisions were announced, both to the people who were

expected to obey them and to the officials who were expected to enforce them, over the signatures of the Secretaries of State, Treasury, and War; but in all cases they were in fact the personal decisions of the President.

Whether instructions and commands prove to be law or merely a bluff by the official who issues them depends on what finally happens when an attempt is made to enforce them. The neutrality regulations were enforced. Under the authority conferred by their provisions, and without the support of any statutes or treaties to authorize them, property was taken from A and given to B. And some of the measures for enforcement were reviewed and approved in state and federal courts.[1]

Whether any action by the President is within the authority given him by the Constitution depends on what the United States Supreme Court says the last time it speaks on the subject. The highest court did not express itself on the legality of the neutrality regulations. It is extremely doubtful that a President, without statutory authority to back him up, could get away with such action today.

Even where Congress wants to give the President authority to make law, the courts may hold it invalid. No doubt the most familiar, as well as the most sensational, instance of statutory grant of authority in time of peace was the National Industrial Recovery Act of 1933 which authorized the President to promulgate codes of law regulating the nation's industry. The codes were drafted by representatives of industry in collaboration with federal officials. But the result of their work became law only when it received the approval of the President and, on his order, was promulgated as law. For the codes were intended to be the law, carrying penalties for violation. The codes that were issued ran to nearly

---

[1] The principal body of regulations for the enforcement of neutrality is in *American State Papers, Foreign Relations*, vol. 1, p. 141 (Washington, 1833). The principal court decision which gave the President's policies standing in judicial proceedings was *Glass v. Sloop Betsey*, 3 Dallas 6 (1794). This incident in our history is generally discussed in Charles S. Hyneman, *The First American Neutrality* (Urbana, Illinois, 1934).

1000. Collectively, they constituted a major sector of the regulatory program of the New Deal. And they received no review from Congress before they went into effect.[2]

These codes had the force of law for as long as they were in effect. But they were not in effect for long. In 1935, two years after it was enacted, the NIRA was a dead letter by order of the Supreme Court. The act was unconstitutional, said the Court, because it put lawmaking power in the hands of the President that could not be delegated to him. It is "delegation running riot," said Justice Cardozo. With the fall of the statute, down went all the codes that had been promulgated by the President.

This decision (*A. L. A. Schechter Poultry Corp., v. United States*, 295 U.S. 495), together with other decisions of the United States Supreme Court, makes it clear that there are limits to the amount of power that can be given to the President (at least in time of peace) to extend the area of governmental activity or change the character of the rules that apply, even where Congress and President agree by statutory enactment that he ought to have the power. The actual limits to the power that he may have will remain unknown except as the courts may say in decisions from time to time.

This much can be said with assurance, however. Neither the President nor any administrative officials of the national government will, in time of peace, be given the sweep of authority regularly exercised by certain governmental bodies in a number of our states. The practice of removing blocks of governmental authority from the control of the customary lawmaking process has been carried to its greatest extent in the case of a number of commissions (notably in the field of public-utility regulation) that have been created by state constitutions and given the power to make the law on certain matters, interpret it, adjudicate alleged violations, fix the amount of the penalty that should apply, and

[2] The National Industrial Recovery Act is in 48 Statutes at Large 195 (1933). For a discussion of the nature of the codes, how they were formulated, and experience in enforcing them, see Leverett Lyon and others, *The National Recovery Administration* (Washington, 1935).

order punishment. The whole legislative, judicial, and administrative functions are thus combined in one body with no provision for check by any other governmental authority except the power of the legislature and governor to withhold funds, and the power of the courts to find the whole business contrary to the United States Constitution—which they are quite likely to do one of these days.[3]

We have learned, in more than a century and a half of experience under our Constitution, that it is sometimes wise to let its meaning be governed by the needs of the occasion. So the power of the President may be greater in time of war than in time of peace, though there be nothing in the Constitution to indicate why this should be so. The lawmaking power of the President undoubtedly rose to its greatest height in World War II. Under the First and Second War Powers Acts, and under many statutes relating to specific subjects, the authority of the President was extended to matters over which he had no control in time of peace. But even so, a study of these statutes and the executive orders issued by the President to carry them out, reveals that the basic law giving the President his authority indicated limits within which that authority should be exercised.[4]

Even in time of war, deliberation is needed, and Congress, it seems to me, is the best body to do the deliberating and make the final decisions on the issues of the most fundamental importance. The people of the nation continue to have opinions, prejudices, doubts, and fears in time of war as they have in peace. The war cannot be won unless the people win it. And Congress is surely the best judge as to the terms on which the people can be mobilized and organized for victory. But decisions must be made more quickly in time of war than in time of peace, and the nation cannot afford in war the inconsistencies and contradictions that it puts

---

[3] See footnote on page 31 for references.

[4] These statutes are cited in footnote on page 104. The authority of the President in time of war is carefully examined by Professor Edward S. Corwin in his *The President: Office and Powers* (3rd ed., New York, 1948), ch. 6.

up with in time of peace. This makes it important for the men and women who determine the most important policies to be closely associated with the men and women who must carry them out. We effect this closer relation of policy making with policy enforcement by delegating to the President and to other military and civilian officials a far greater authority than they have in time of peace to fill out the policies made by Congress, to extend them, and to modify them.

But the principles which should govern the delegation of law-making authority to the President, it seems to me, should be the same in time of war as in time of peace. Congress should continue to determine what the nature of the activities and undertakings of the government shall be. And it should carry its determinations as far in the direction of detail as it can go with full assurance that it knows what it wants and is providing for what it wants. It is time to delegate authority to somebody when Congress cannot foresee what will happen and cannot say what it wants done, or when Congress (because it has more important things to do) cannot take the time to reach agreement as to what shall be done, or when Congress concludes that a fuller statement of its wishes would lessen the ability of administrative officials to accomplish the most important objectives which Congress has in mind. This point, where legislative prescription should stop and delegation of authority to make policies should begin, is arrived at more quickly in time of war than in time of peace. The nation has turned over more of its affairs to government, new programs of governmental activity must be set going and old ones must be revised, and the fortunes of war force drastic changes in governmental policies on short notice. Congress has more things among which it must distribute its time; the life expectancy of governmental policies (the period for which any policy can stand unchanged) goes down; and ability to evaluate the merits of alternative courses of action moves toward the men and women who are directing the execution of governmental policies.

The facts of life in wartime force Congress to recede from its customary position in respect to the formation of policy; they do not, however, require that the formation of governmental policies be dispersed among the multitude of officials who are charged with executing the activities and undertakings of government. At the very time when there is greatest need for giving military and civilian officials maximum freedom to choose between courses of action, there is maximum need for coordination of the activities and undertakings of government. New agencies of coordination, therefore, come into existence and those which are already in existence get new grants of authority. A War Production Board and a War Manpower Commission are established, and the Joint Chiefs of Staff makes decisions that were previously made by someone else. A great part of this job of coordination falls upon the President. And, because the coordination of activities and undertakings is accomplished by deciding what shall be done, and when and how it shall be done, the President must be given a great amount of authority to say what the activities and undertakings of government shall actually be.

It is of highest importance, in my opinion, that Congress and not the President set the limits to the President's authority to determine what the activities and undertakings of the government shall be in time of war. There is a strong contention to the contrary among people who have given serious thought to the problems of conducting a war, and there is a great deal of support for their point of view in the literature relating to American government. It is frequently, if not usually, said in the literature of this subject that the provisions of the Constitution which make the President chief executive, which give him special authority in respect to foreign relations, and which declare him to be commander-in-chief of the Army and Navy make it necessary to conclude that the framers of the Constitution intended the President to assume practically any authority which he thinks he ought to exercise in order to make sure that the nation will win its war.

I do not reach any such conclusion. It would have been easy for the framers to say in the Constitution that the distribution of authority between President and Congress should be different in time of war than in time of peace, if they wanted that to be understood; I think some significance may be attached to the fact that they did not say so. I do not think that the prior position which is given to the President in respect to the direction and control of our relations with foreign nations makes it necessary for him to say how the nation shall go about maximizing its strength when it has decided to use force to achieve or maintain its position in respect to other nations. If the framers had provided that the President, by and with the advice and consent of the Senate, should appoint a commander-in-chief of the Army and Navy, it is most unlikely that there would be much support for the proposition that that official should make the most important decisions as to how the nation as a whole should conduct itself and use its resources-in-general to put the full strength of the nation into the prosecution of the war. And finally, there are many expressions in the Constitution which make it clear that the President is not even to have a full authority to direct and control the forces that are under arms—e.g., Congress shall have power to make rules governing captures on land and water; to make rules for the government and regulation of the land and naval forces; to "exercise like authority [apparently "to exercise exclusive legislation in all cases whatsoever"] over all places purchased by consent of the legislature of the State in which the same shall be, for the erection of forts, magazines, arsenals, dockyards, and other needful buildings."[5]

I am most sympathetic with the contention that the Constitution should not be interpreted primarily to achieve the intentions and expectations of the framers but rather to increase the certainty that the American people will get the kind of government they want. It is because I have this view of the Constitution that I urge the interpretation which gives Congress rather than the President the authority to determine what matters the President may decide in time of war. It is my strong conviction that the

---

[5] See the careful analysis by Professor Corwin, *ibid.*

American people are most likely to win their wars with dispatch and in a decisive manner, and at the same time be certain that government after the conclusion of the war will still be government according to the will of the people, if their representative assembly insists on making the major decisions as to how the war shall be conducted. If there is widespread and serious doubt that Congress can make the major decisions—including the decision as to what authority the President shall have—in a way that the American people as a whole will find acceptable, then we had better get busy with the improvement of our political organization, our electoral system, and the organization of Congress so that the grounds for such doubt will be removed.

BIBLIOGRAPHIC NOTE

The literature which discusses the authority and influence of the President is not organized according to the pattern which I pursue in this and the next five chapters. What the President can do and has done to determine the activities and undertakings of government is consequently not differentiated for separate treatment; what other authors have to say on this point can usually be found only by a general examination of their writings.

A good deal of attention has been given to the part which the President plays in the enactment of legislation. Two recent books which deal broadly as well as acutely with this subject are: Wilfred E. Binkley, *President and Congress* (New York, 1947); and Lawrence H. Chamberlain, *The President, Congress and Legislation* (New York, 1946). E. E. Schattschneider, *Politics, Pressures and the Tariff* (New York, 1935), is an excellent study of a special application of the President's influence. The leading work on the President's power to make law in his own right (by issuing proclamations, executive orders, etc.) is James Hart, *The Ordinance Making Powers of the President* (Baltimore, 1925).

The leading book which deals generally with the authority and influence of the President is Edward S. Corwin, *The President: Office and Powers* (3rd ed., New York, 1948); chapter 4 is most relevant to my discussion. The special authority and influence which the President exercises in time of war and other major crises has especially attracted the attention of American students. See on this: Clarence A. Berdahl, *War Powers of the Executive in the United States* (Urbana, Illinois, 1921); Edward S. Corwin, *Total War and the Constitution* (New York, 1947); James G. Randall, *Constitutional Problems Under Lincoln* (New York, 1926); Louis W. Koenig, *The Presidency and the Crisis* (New York, 1944); Clinton L. Rossiter, *Constitutional Dictatorship* (Princeton, New Jersey, 1948), chs. 14–18; Albert L. Sturm, "Emergencies and the Presidency," in *Journal of Politics*, vol. 11, pp. 121–144 (1949); and Charles Fairman, "The President as Commander-in-Chief," in *Journal of Politics*, vol. 11, pp. 145–170 (1949).

CHAPTER 12

HOW IS THE ADMINISTRATIVE BRANCH TO BE ORGANIZED?

The President answers to the people for broad policies of government. He satisfies the people, or fails to satisfy them, largely by his successes and his failures in getting legislation enacted. But some of the important policies of government in which the people have an active interest are determined in the course of administration. Most of our talk in campaign time is about the legislation that the country needs or does not need. But the nation's satisfaction or dissatisfaction with what has happened in the administration of governmental programs may be important enough to constitute a decisive factor in the election. It is in this way that the President is actually held accountable for his constitutional charge to "take care that the laws be faithfully executed."

If the President must answer to the people for the way the laws are executed, he ought to have enough authority to assure himself that the laws will be properly executed. This calls up the ancient maxim, Authority must be commensurate with responsibility. Stated in more familiar terms, if a man is to be blamed for the way things are done, he ought to have enough authority to see that they are done in such a way that he will not be blamed. Whichever way you state it, this is a sound rule. We recognize that we do a man injustice if we blame him for something he could not possibly have kept from happening. But while this is a sound rule, it is not one that is easily applied. How do you know when a man has enough authority to protect himself against adverse criticism? How do you know when his authority is commensurate with his responsibility?

The quality of administration we get will depend in part on the way the administrative branch is organized. Today, the basic structure of the administrative branch is determined mainly by law. Can we safely presume that the President can induce the administrative branch, organized the way it is, to give us a quality of administration which the people will find acceptable? Or must we suppose that the President will not be able, with the machinery available for him, to get the quality of administration which the people will hold him accountable for at election time? And if the answer to the last question is yes—the President cannot be sure of satisfying the people with the administrative machinery that is available to him—does it follow that the President should have the authority to change the machinery to suit himself?

These questions cannot be answered with statements of fact because we have not yet isolated all the considerations which are involved so that we know what facts are necessary to answer the questions. For the present, we can only set forth best guesses and convictions which are based on general observation and speculation.

The case for legislative control of administrative structure was set forth at some length in Chapter 6. Legislative provisions fixing administrative organization give stability to the administrative structure because legislative provisions are not easily changed. And stability in administrative structure is desirable. There must be stability in the organization of government just as there must be continuity in the activities of government. We will never construct and maintain a dependable system of national defense if we jump around from a basic strategy founded on a big surface Navy to a strategy assuming all air power and no fleet to one that makes no use of either fleet or air power. Neither will we construct and maintain an effective national defense if we build independent organizations for land, sea, and air forces; then unify them in a single organization; and again, before we have fairly tried out that arrangement, tear them apart for some new type of organization. The great body of individuals who collectively provide our national defense by laying plans for future action, directing others toward established objectives, and pursuing their individual assignments can do none of these things if they are never able to settle down into an organization where they learn their several tasks and their relations with one another. The work that is done after the rattle of finding out who is to do it has subsided represents the activity that accomplishes the purposes for which the organization was set up.

There is another reason for insisting upon stability in governmental organization. The confidence of the American people that they understand what their government is doing is closely related to their familiarity with the organization that does the work. It takes time to acquire this familiarity. If the administrative departments are constantly being torn down, rebuilt, and renamed; if functions of government are repeatedly moved from one department to another—then the continuous building up of knowledge and understanding in the minds of the citizens that is necessary to democratic government will be cut short.

This is the case for stability in administrative structure. And stability is most certain when administrative organization is fixed by statute. But there is a case for flexibility also. And flexibility is provided when the chief executive is given authority to change the structure of administration and shift the activities and undertakings of government from one department or agency to another.

The need for flexibility in administrative organization is greatest when the activities and undertakings of government are rapidly changing and increasing. This is the situation at the beginning of a war. The government plunges into production activities and into controls over the non-governmental activities of the nation that had no counterpart before preparation for war began. Normal or peacetime activities of government may be reduced or terminated. The executive skill of the nation is too limited to satisfy the military, industrial, and other needs, so organizations have to be built around those individuals of rare ability who are available.

This is a time for Congress to recede from its ordinary control over administrative organization. The whole attention of Congress is needed for the consideration of matters having a greater bearing on the successful conduct of the war—how to allocate the manpower and material resources of the nation, how to ration consumers' goods, how to apportion the cost of paying for the war. Congress cannot afford to take time for thinking about best administrative arrangements. If it did set up the administrative agencies for carrying on the war, it would constantly be doing the job over. Congressmen do not know enough about organizing the nation for war to set up an administrative structure that would prove satisfactory for very long. They do not know enough for the same reason that no one else knows enough. In time of war we set up, try out, rearrange, and try out again. The lawmaking process is not a good one for making quick changes and readjustments.

This is a time for the President to control administrative organization—not because he is wiser than Congressmen or can devote more time to thinking about problems of administration—the job falls upon the President for the same reason that nearly everything else falls on the President. The nature of the executive branch (i.e., the character of the relationships between people who make up the executive branch) lends itself to quick decisions and change of pace; and the American people have come to expect that the White House will be the center of activity in planning for war and putting plans into effect. The construction of administrative organization must go hand in hand with decisions as to what men are to do. Since so many of the decisions of the latter type have been turned over to the President, the control of administrative organization must go to him too.

This is not to say that the President will personally determine the shape of the administrative structure. Others in the executive branch may do it in his name. One President will find time for a good deal of thought about organization; another may find virtually none. The President, in time of a major war, will be able to think about only a small proportion of the things that pass through his hands; which ones pass through his mind, as well as his hands, will depend on his personality and that of his advisors.

We can get our affairs into such a mess in time of peace that it takes emergency legislation comparable to that of wartime to straighten them out. We were confronted by such a situation in 1933 when we launched the New Deal. Congress had its hands full deciding what the government ought to do. The administrative organization to put these activities and undertakings into effect should have been developed experimentally. But we hadn't yet come around to the idea that the President ought to build the organization, and we hadn't yet given him the special facilities he would need for doing the job anyway. So Congress, acting on the recommendation of the President, set up the new agencies by statute and, on the whole, probably didn't do a very good job of it.

We have since made an effort to give the President the facilities that would enable him to set up a provisional administrative structure. In 1939, Congress approved a reorganization plan of the President which brought into existence the Executive Office of the President. This office serves (among other purposes) as a basin in which new functions of government can rest until we find or construct a permanent place to put them. The President is the head of the Executive Office of the President. Over it and all the activities within it, he has the authority of a department head. Officials who are lodged within the Executive Office of the President and charged with carrying out a new activity of government are subject to the President's fullest command; he does not have to maneuver for a result if he prefers to order it.

To assist him in supervising new activities, the President can now turn to the Bureau of the Budget, a bureaucracy of substantial size that is also located in the Executive Office of the President. While the officials who have been charged with executing the new program of government are giving all their time to questions of what they are going to do right now and how they are going to do it, the Bureau of the Budget can be figuring out what kind of an organization will be needed to carry on the activity when it really gets going. The Bureau can do things like this with some success because it is made up of people who have nothing to do with the time they are paid for except figure out how the things that other people are doing could be done better.

The time comes when the head of the new activity has conquered the worst of his problems and finds that his most pressing need is to improve the character of his organization. As soon as it is clear that he is sufficiently in control of the situation to run his agency like any other going concern, it is time to move his organization out of the Executive Office of the President and set it up in its proper place in the administrative branch. From then on, the head of the new department will deal with the President according to the relationships of a department head with the chief executive of the United States; not, as heretofore, as a bureau or division chief reporting to a department head who is so busy being President of the United States that he has no time whatever to be a department head.

What we have been talking about occurs in exceptional times. Under normal circumstances, the need for a new administrative organization arises from time to time as new activities of government are launched. As Congress makes up its mind that it wants a new activity undertaken (e.g., control of production and distribution of atomic energy) it considers what kind of organization should be established and where it should be placed in the total administrative structure. But the President should make up his mind about this first. He will be required to take a position on the provisions of the law when it comes to him to sign or veto; he has the strongest invitation, therefore, to make his opinions known to Congress as soon as he has opinions. Because he has the greatest interest in the character of the administrative organization upon which he must depend for the faithful execution of the laws, he should certainly have no hesitancy in telling Congress what kind of agency he wants created to carry on the new activity. If the President enjoys the prestige among Congressmen that we hope he will have, he will ordinarily get what he wants. If Congress ignores his recommendation, he suffers a political setback which he can accept or resist as he sees fit. He can fight it out by use of the veto power if he wishes to do so; he wins or loses as the veto is sustained or overruled. If the President is defeated, it is a temporary defeat only. Once the new department has been set up and tried out, he can recommend a different arrangement. If he makes a proposal concerning its further disposition in a general plan for administrative reorganization, it will take a majority of members in one house to kill it. What he loses a second time, he can try a third.

As I see it, this is the way it should be. If the issue is important enough for Congress to defy the President, it is important enough to be settled by the lawmaking process. If the President cannot prevail by power of persuasion or show of political force, then the considerations against his recommendation are strong indeed. If the President thinks the majority of the people are back of him and considers the issue to be important enough, he can carry it to the people in the next election. It is no solution for the problems that excite great political interest to remove them from solution by the most representative procedure that we have.

While I have argued that it is quite proper to set up new administrative departments and agencies by legislative enactment, I feel quite differently about legislative determination of the internal structure of particular departments and agencies. The relationships that obtain within an administrative establishment are of the greatest concern to the administrator at the top of it. He does not need to be a czar in order to execute his program. But he cannot discharge his obligation to carry on government in keeping with the instructions that come to him from the political branches if the great number of men and women who work under him are not organized so that they readily respond to his instructions.

Many department heads in the federal government are confronted by just such a situation. It has been the custom since the beginning of our present form of government for the statute which creates an administrative establishment to specify the major subdivisions among which the work of the department shall be divided. These provisions are not temporary, intended to govern only until the new establishment is a going concern; they control the internal structure of the establishment until they are altered or repealed by another act of legislation. Sometimes (as pointed out in Chapter 6) Congressmen know what they want in respect to the internal organization of an administrative department or agency and can give good reasons for requiring the particular structure which they specify. But also, as pointed out before, the considerations which make a particular structure desirable when the new establishment is created may have no application whatever within a few years after the new organization gets going. And frequently the developments that make the original structure no longer necessary in the eyes of Congress make it positively objectionable to the man who is charged with directing the organization.

Legislation which merely freezes the structure of an administrative establishment after the reasons for requiring that particular style of organization have passed is bad enough; but legislation which gives the component parts of the establishment autonomous status are far more objectionable. More than one of our highest administrative officials sit at the top of establishments which they have little chance of controlling. Statutory provisions have given particular divisions a status which makes them in effect islands of power fortified against invasion by the head of the department in which they are placed. Many of these autonomous situations are the result of a poor job of consolidating agencies together; frequently, the statute that transfers a service fails to incorporate it fully into the structure of the department to which it is moved. The unfortunate consequences of such situations are effectively pointed out in the reports and supporting studies of the Hoover Commission.[1]

For the features of administrative organization which the President does not like, he now has an effective remedy. Under the provisions of the Administrative Reorganization Act of 1949 (discussed on pp. 113–114), the President can lay before Congress the reorganization of the administrative branch which he considers ideal; it will go into effect unless a majority of the members of one house of Congress overrule him. But while the President's reorganization power appears to be a sufficient remedy for correction of the things which the President does not like, may we consider it sufficient for correction of the things that the head of an administrative department does not like? The President can include in his reorganization plan changes in administrative structure which are purely internal to a particular department or agency. If the head of the administrative agency enjoys the confidence of the President, he will presumably be able to get his recommendations for change incorporated in the plans which the President lays before Congress. Is this not sufficient for his needs? The Hoover Commission did not think so and recommended that "Each department head should receive from the Congress administrative authority to organize his department and to place him in control of its organization."[2]

The position of the Hoover Commission in respect to the reorganization of administrative departments and agencies is explained in part by the apparent conviction of that body that it is never proper to fix the internal structure of an administrative establishment by statute. If Congress is never again going to tell the head of an administrative department or agency (going concern or newly created) how his establishment shall be organized, then it

[1] *General Management of the Executive Branch; A Report to the Congress by the Commission on Organization of the Executive Branch of the Government, February 1949* (Government Printing Office, 1949), p. 4; *Departmental Management; A Report with Recommendations Prepared for the Commission on Organization of the Executive Branch of the Government* [*Appendix E*] (Government Printing Office, 1949), pp. 27–29, 33–34.

[2] P. 37 of first report cited in note 1, above.

makes sense to give all the present heads of administrative departments and agencies the authority to reorganize their establishments to suit themselves. If, on the other hand, one concludes, as I have argued in an earlier chapter (pages 106–107), that there can be sufficient reason for putting certain requirements concerning internal structure of an agency into the law, then we face the question of best arrangements for getting those requirements out of the law when the reasons for putting them there have disappeared.

It seems to me that if Congress has interest enough in the organization of an administrative establishment to specify some of the features of its internal organization when it creates that establishment, it has interest enough to be given a chance to say how long those features of its organization shall continue in effect. It seems to me that we do not put too much of a handicap on the administrative official if we require him to convince the President that the things which the official finds objectionable should be corrected in the President's reorganization plan. It seems to me also that the interest of Congress in preserving the organization which it once set up would be sufficiently protected if an adverse vote by both houses were required in order to reject the President's proposals. This was the arrangement for effecting reorganizations which was provided in the Reorganization Act of 1945. The statute now in force, however, allows one house to reject the President's plans, provided a majority of all members (not merely a majority of those present and voting) vote to reject.

To require the administrative official to submit to the President his proposals to throw off statutory restrictions concerning the organization of his establishment is to require him to get the approval of another sector of the bureaucracy, the Bureau of the Budget. For the President will ordinarily not have the slightest interest in the problem himself. If the President is from Oklahoma, he may know his mind on the place and authority of the office that is charged with Indian Affairs, but this is because of personal associations. If a big block of his electoral votes come from the water-hungry states of the West, the President will be interested in the organization that is concerned with water supply and irrigation, no matter where he came from himself; but this is because there are political implications.

If there are no personal or political implications in the proposal for change in a department's structure, the President probably will not and certainly ought not give it his personal attention. To ask that he endorse the proposal and send it to Congress for acceptance is to ask that it be approved by the Bureau of the Budget. For the Bureau of the Budget is the piece of bureaucracy that speaks the mind of the President on these matters when the President has no mind.

It is noteworthy that the Hoover Commission did not express itself on the desirability of obtaining the approval of the President for major changes in the organization of departments and agencies, including those that do not involve the throwing off of statutory restrictions. It may be that the Commission assumed that the heads of administrative departments will always consult the President and find out whether he has objections before proceeding with any reorganization that might excite public protest or political opposition; it may be, on the other hand, that the Commission felt the President could have no interest in the internal organization of an agency which the head of that agency could not express better than anyone else.

My own inclination is to hold that there should not be a blanket requirement that the heads of administrative establishments must get the approval of the President for changes in the organizations over which they preside. If the head of the establishment has reason to think that the President will be interested, he should be free to lay his plans before the President; if the President hears of reorganization plans that he wants to know more about, he should be free to ask that the plans be laid before him. This, it seems to me, should give the President adequate assurance that he will not be embarrassed by overly impetuous or too drastic action, or by failure to act firmly enough on the part of a department head who looks at his segment of the bureaucracy in too narrow perspective.

If, however, we ask that all plans for major changes in the internal structure of administrative departments and agencies be approved by the President, we provide that the plans be reviewed (and ordinarily rejected by the President if not approved) by one or both of two groups—a specialized bureaucracy (presumably the Bureau of the Budget) and the coterie of political advisors who are quartered in the White House. If central review of reorganization plans meant only that the President would have his attention called to possible important political implications, and that the head of the establishment proposing the reorganization would have his attention called to things that might have escaped his attention, I should think there could be no objection to a standing requirement that all such plans be submitted to the President. But I think that a great deal more than this would result from the requirement. The specialized bureaucracy most likely would come to believe that it has a special *expertise* in respect to the relation of administrative organization to the achievement of policy and performance of work, and the political contingent in the White House would come to believe that it has superior knowledge of the relation of administrative structure to the fortunes of the President and the party which he heads. I think that neither supposition should be nurtured.

In my opinion, the greatest wisdom in respect to administrative organization is obtained by living with a particular problem; and so far as the needs of a particular administrative establishment are concerned, this wisdom is most likely to be possessed by the men and women who have lived and worked in that establishment. If they are baffled by their problems and feel the need of consulting men who have read books or have had significant experience in other administrative situations, we may suppose that they will prove their good sense by going of their own accord to the Bureau of the Budget or elsewhere for counsel. If they are required to listen to advice which they do not want, I think they are likely to be worried into decisions which their own judgment warns them against and which, for that reason if no other, are likely to prove unsatisfactory when put into effect.

My feelings are much the same concerning the advice which would be proffered by the politicos who inhabit the White House. As the White House advisors are given excuse to press their political views upon the head of the administrative establishment with expectation that he will bow to their judgment, the head of the administrative establishment is invited to assume less obligation to make up his own mind concerning the political implications of his actions. If this is what actually comes about, we will advance farther along a course that I think we have traveled too far along already. There has been a marked tendency in recent years to fill our highest administrative positions (including those of Cabinet status) with men who are certainly not leaders of the party in power, and who apparently feel no great obligation to make decisions with a view to their effect on the fortunes of the political party which is charged with running the government. As I say at greater length elsewhere in this book, I think we are most likely to get government which operates within limits that are acceptable to the American people as a whole if the most important decisions are made by leaders of a political party who understand that they will be thrown out of office when they transcend the limits of acceptability. And I think that the important decisions are most likely to represent the judgment of the leaders of a political party if the officials who head the major administrative departments and agencies have had long and intimate acquaintance with the men and women scattered about the country who best know what the people who make up that party want in the way of government. Proposals to require Presidential approval of changes in the structure of administrative departments and agencies, as I see it, should therefore be judged primarily according to the likelihood that they will strengthen rather than weaken the conviction of high administrative officials that they have an obligation to consider political implications in making decisions concerning the arrangement of the organizations which they head.

BIBLIOGRAPHIC NOTE

I know of no single work which provides a comprehensive statement of the authority and influence of the President over administrative organization. All books which deal generally with the office of the President have something to say on the subject. Of these, the fullest discussion is in Edward S. Corwin, *The President: Office and Powers* (3rd ed., New York, 1948), ch. 3. See also Caleb P. Patterson, *Presidential Government in the United States: The Unwritten Constitution* (Chapel Hill, N.C., 1947), ch. 8; essay by James Hart, "The President and Federal Administration," in *Essays on the Law and Practice of Governmental Administration*, edited by Charles G. Haines and M. E. Dimock (Baltimore, 1935), pp. 47–93; and essay by John A. Vieg, "The Chief Executive," in *Elements of Public Administration*, edited by Fritz Morstein Marx (New York, 1946), pp. 158–183.

The entire *Report of the President's Committee on Administrative Management* (Government Printing Office, 1937) was centered on the office of the President and the arrangements needed to increase the President's authority and influence over administration. Pages 31–47 deal especially with the relation of the President to administrative organization. The Hoover Commission had a broader charge than the Committee on Administrative Management, and 'it put less faith in the ability of the President to give personal direction to administration. No one of its reports deals pointedly with the relation of the President to administrative organization. Most relevant to this subject is *General Management of the Executive Branch; A Report to the Congress by the Commission on Organization of the Executive Branch of the Government, February 1949* (Government Printing Office, 1949).

For description and comment on the Executive Office of the President, see: Louis Brownlow, and others, "The Executive Office of the President," in *Public Administration Review*, vol. 1, pp. 101–140 (1941).

I know of only one thorough analysis of the President's power to reorganize administration under legislation which authorizes him to submit proposed changes to Congress for approval or rejection: John D. Millett and Lindsay D. Rogers, "The Legislative Veto and the Reorganization Act of 1939," in *Public Administration Review*, vol. 1, pp. 176–189. The plans which the President submits to Congress can be found in the *Congressional Record* at the time of submission; if (not rejected by Congress) they go into effect, they are printed in the *Statutes at Large* and the *U.S. Code.* Illustrative hearings of House and Senate Committees relating to statutes authorizing reorganization by the President and plans which he submits are cited in the note at the end of Chapter 6.

CHAPTER 13

WHO GETS HOW MUCH MONEY?

The control of money is a prime feature of any effective arrangement for the direction and control of administration. The President would have little power to influence the character and quality of government if he could not influence the distribution of money by which the activities of government are financed. The provision of money determines what the government will undertake to do and fixes the measure (regulates the scope and intensity) of each undertaking. Whatever the government undertakes to do costs money; for public undertakings like private enterprise are a joining of human effort and material goods, and both must be paid for whether they are joined under public or private authority. Yet the costs involved in setting two million men and women busy doing things represent only a minor part of the total significance of money in our national government today. For the role of the national government in our time is largely one of collecting money from the American people and handing it back to them and to other people in different patterns of distribution—paying out social security benefits, paying money to farmers, satisfying claims of veterans, purchasing supplies for Europe, paying for dams which are built by private contractors, and so on far into the billions.

The appropriation of money accordingly joins the formation of public policy right up to administration. If the President could not share in the appropriation process, he would suffer a double loss of power. He would be stripped of much of his power in fixing the basic program of his Administration, and he would lose a great deal of his power over the subsequent execution of that program. The appropriation of money provides the flexibility that makes government in operation as nearly as possible what the American people want it to be. The laws that set the ends of government and describe the particular activities and undertakings by which those ends are to be achieved cannot readily be changed. Once we have fought through the pressures to a compromise enactment, we find it wise to let the statute which formulates the compromise stand for an indefinite period. But appropriations are voted every year (there are some exceptional appropriations that stand from year to year). We do not change the provisions of the underlying legislation, but we revise the measure (restate the scope and intensity) of the effort that is to go into the fulfillment of the objectives stated in the underlying legislation. The competing interests are still there, of course, though probably not to contest so bitterly since the fight is now about the operations for the coming year and not about a law that will stand for a generation or longer.

It is consequently through the fixing of the appropriations that the group of men who are currently in power usually make their principal impression upon the policies of government. Sometimes the significance of the appropriations is pushed into the background by a dramatic new program of legislation, as in the first days of the New Deal. But generally speaking, the contest between Democrats and Republicans, conservatives and liberals, contenders for this and contenders for that, is fought out mainly in fixing the financial support that will be given to various activities and undertakings of government.

Just as the provision of money determines the scope and intensity of government activity, so also it restrains and disciplines administrative officials and employees. If the head of an administrative establishment acts in defiance of the wishes of Congress or the people, his fire can be reduced to smoke and ashes in the next appropriation act. If any sector of the bureaucracy starts building up an empire that Congress will not tolerate, Congress can tear it down by cutting off its financial income. If bureaucracy as a whole, or any part of it, is insolent or inefficient or just plain too big, it can be jerked back into line by a judicious distribution of money.

The President, as participant in planning the general program of government which his Administration will provide, is interested in the amount of money to be allotted to the various activities and undertakings. As the official head of the administrative branch, he is interested in the amount appropriated for each administrative establishment. We have given a good deal of thought to the relation of the President to the financing of government over the years and have given him a number of specific powers by which he can make his wishes respected.

There are four principal ways in which the President shares in providing money for the departments and agencies of government. First, through his capacity to influence the actions of Congress (including exercise and threat to exercise the veto) he shares in the enactment of appropriation acts as he shares in the enactment of all other legislation; second, he directs a study of the monetary needs for the many governmental activities and the many administrative establishments that put these activities into operation and submits his findings to Congress in an annual budget; third, he has a limited power to control the expenditure of the money which has been appropriated; and fourth, he has a fund made available to him alone which, within certain limits, he may use at his discretion to advance any activity or undertaking that he thinks not adequately financed.

The first of the four ways in which the President influences the financing of government—his general authority to participate in the enactment of legislation—requires little comment. In his regular message at the beginning of a session of Congress, and in special messages, he may call upon the legislative branch to provide money for this purpose or that. He watches the progress of appropriation acts through the two houses and intervenes to advance or retard them as he does in the case of any other legislation which is vital to the success of his administration. If he does not like an appropriation measure he can veto it, though he rarely does so.

The President does not have the authority, enjoyed by the governors of more than half of our states, to single out individual items in appropriation acts and veto them; he must either allow the measure which comes to him from Congress to go into effect without change or he must veto everything that is in it. The more inclusive the appropriation act is, therefore, the more reluctant the President will be to use his veto power. Virtually the whole of the appropriations for the federal government are now included in about a dozen separate appropriation measures. Usually they get to the White House for approval or disapproval only a short time before the new fiscal year begins. A veto, under these circumstances, is likely to result in no money for federal employees on one or more paydays after the new fiscal year starts. This is a consequence which the President does not relish, and he usually permits the appropriation act to become law, no matter how strongly he objected to particular amounts when Congress had them under consideration. The likelihood of the President's ever using his veto power in respect to appropriations will be even further diminished if Congress, as some people earnestly recommend, accumulates all of its appropriation decisions in one omnibus measure.

Even if the President had authority to make his veto applicable to particular items in appropriation measures, it is questionable whether he would be able to make effective use of it. Many state legislatures itemize appropriations in considerable detail. The governor who has the item veto is thus enabled to disapprove specific amounts for specific purposes, with no adverse effect on the amounts provided for other purposes. Congress, on the other hand, rarely breaks the appropriation down into small enough items to enable the President to pick out and kill what he does not like without also killing many other things that he wants to keep alive. In view of the great concern in recent literature relating to administration to increase the President's ability to get what he wants, it is surprising that there has not been any serious suggestion, first, that the President be given an item veto, and second, that Congress put up the appropriation measures in a degree of detail that would enable him to make effective use of the item veto. The proponents of greater executive authority in administration have generally taken the opposite position, so far as the form of the appropriation act is concerned; they want the appropriations to be made in fewer and more inclusive amounts rather than in a greater number of less inclusive amounts. This suggests that they see no hope of amending the Constitution to give the President the item veto; they may, therefore, begin to argue that all or a major part of the appropriations should be made to the President, giving him authority to distribute funds among the several governmental activities and administrative organizations according to his own wishes.

The second way in which the President shares in financing government consists of preparing annually a comprehensive proposal for appropriations—the budget of the United States Government. Presidents have always advised Congress, and some have lectured it, as to the amount of money required to carry on the work of the Government. President Taft found this not enough. In the face of a clear statement by Congress that it did not want him to do so, he prepared a comprehensive statement of the financial needs of the government during the last year of his administration and submitted it to the House of Representatives with the suggestion that this document serve as the basis for the appropriation of money for the next fiscal year. His "budget" was summarily laid on the shelf as he doubtless foresaw that it would be. Nonetheless President Taft had a good idea, and he lived to see it in effect. In 1921, Congress enacted the Budget and Accounting Act which set up standards for better accounting in the federal government, created the General Accounting Office headed by the Comptroller General to maintain certain safeguards over expenditures, and provided that the President should annually submit a plan for financing the cost of government during the approaching fiscal year.

The Act of 1921 placed the responsibility for preparing this financial plan (subject to the President's direction) in a Bureau of the Budget which was set up in the Treasury Department. There was some suspicion (and no doubt some evidence to support it) on the part of other Cabinet officers that the Secretary of the Treasury exercised an influence over the preparation of the amounts recommended for their departments which was not compatible with their co-equal status in the government. Stated conversely, there was reason to think that the Director of the Budget was not completely free to make the figures reflect what he sensed to be the President's wishes. Consequently, during the second term of President Franklin D. Roosevelt the Executive Office of the President was established, the Bureau of the Budget under a Director of the Budget (hereafter called Budget Bureau and Budget Director) was put in it, and a new Director having no previous connection with the Treasury Department was brought in to direct the preparation of the annual plan of expenditures.

Since the appropriation of money for the purposes of government is so vital to the political program of the President and his party, the President will personally play a part in the preparation of the estimates of appropriation. How big a part he plays will depend upon the interests and the aptitudes of the man who happens to be President at the time and upon the pressure of other demands for his attention. Some of the questions relating to the financial plan are of such a nature that no one else can take the responsibility of answering them for him. There are other questions that a department head or the Budget Director can answer for him because they know his mind; how many of these questions go to the President for personal consideration depends on how accessible he is. But the great body of decisions necessary to the preparation of the estimates that go before Congress in his name must be made without the President having the slightest notion of what they are; the chief executive of this nation has far too many other demands on his time to permit him to be his own budget officer.

Some idea of the kind of decision that must be made at the top can be drawn from the letter that goes out each year to the heads of departments and agencies calling on them to submit statements showing the amounts they will need to carry on their activities during the next fiscal year. In the call for estimates in the summer of 1946, the Budget Director wrote, "The President has given me the general instructions that for fiscal year 1948 [i.e., the year ending June 30, 1948] we must plan not only for a balanced budget, but for a substantial surplus to be used in the reduction of the national debt . . . strict economy must be exercised in Government expenditure programs and high taxes must be retained."

There is no reason to question the truth of this statement that the President had issued the general instruction. The war was over, and we had a national debt of a size that we would have considered disastrous a few years earlier. No matter how busy the President was with affairs in Europe, Asia, or anywhere else, his obligation to the American people required him to turn over in his own mind the alternatives of reducing taxes or reducing the national debt. Presumably he talked this issue over with many people in addition to the Budget Director—casually and intermittently but also in serious and searching conversations. Conceivably he never did arrive at a conviction as to what position he really ought to take on the subject. But nobody else could decide it for him, and if he was reluctant, nevertheless the time came when he had to say, "This is it."

"Estimates for authorized civilian public construction and improvement programs," the letter went on, "should be limited to those for which the public need is so great, both from the standpoint of economic return and social benefit, that it is not in the national interest to postpone them. All other projects, especially those which would impede the flow of materials and manpower to the emergency housing program, should be deferred until a later year." This instruction also sounds as if it came direct from the mouth of the President. The housing situation being what it was, the President could not escape having a policy concerning housing. Housing was one of the problems he had looked into personally and talked about in speeches. He had a basis for knowing whether he wanted housing to take precedence over other kinds of construction in which the government was engaged.

But the preparation of a budget does not stop with the announcement of a few broad policies like these. The estimates that go up to Congress in the name of the President constitute a printed book of around 1500 pages. This volume is a series of statements of what the departments and agencies propose to do and how much money it will take to do those things, with comparative figures showing what they had for those purposes in previous years. How much of this compilation can represent the personal convictions of the President?

It seems reasonable to expect him to review the grand total that is proposed for submission to Congress. He should have time to be told:

Mr. President, the estimates for maintaining occupation forces in Europe and Japan are running much higher than we anticipated. Cost of housing, veterans' hospitals, irrigation dams, and other public improvement projects are running far above calculations because prices keep shooting up. When we add to these factors your wish to increase the benefits for veterans, it becomes clear that we are going to have a total estimate at least 17 percent above the amount submitted to Congress last year. I know this is flatly contrary to your wishes. I have gone back over this several times and I do not see how I can escape asking your judgment as to where we had better start cutting down.

I do not know how they do these things but I should think that the President would be given a small table breaking the total estimates down under a few headings such as national defense, veterans' services and benefits, agriculture and agricultural resources, interest and retirement of the public debt, and half a dozen more.

Surely the President can be expected to study this. Unless he is a peculiar man I should think that he would have his closest political associates in, jointly to beat their heads, curse the day they went into politics, and finally tell the Budget Director where to start cutting down on the estimates. Possibly some Presidents would present the issue for discussion in cabinet meetings. From what I can learn, however, most of our Presidents either did not trust the cabinet enough or did not value cabinet recommendations enough to submit such a matter to cabinet discussion.

I think the President can, and probably most of them do, go even farther than this in stating their wishes in respect to the appropriation estimates. I think the President may say to the Budget Director, "I hate to see that item for housing so high. But I told Sandy Herson that he was to have what it took to get housing back under way. He came in on those terms because he wouldn't come on any other. I have to give him a green light on this figure." And the President can say, "I imagine you know the Secretary of Interior was over here yesterday. I'm afraid it puts you in a bad spot to find the savings somewhere else, but I told him I would ask you to put his figure back up by the amount he gives here in this memorandum. We went over the matter very carefully and I guess he is right in saying there will be plenty to pay out in the West if we don't go ahead with construction on those dams. I hope you can pick up that amount somewhere else. I'm glad I don't have your job."

I do not see how the President can afford to go much below this level of importance and difficulty in settling questions relating to the amount of money needed to run the government. Unless times are a great deal more serene than we have known for many years, there are too many other things to occupy his attention. We charge him with personal responsibility in international affairs, expecting him to choose between the major alternatives that are open to us. This means that the principal considerations that govern a choice between alternatives must pass through his mind. The President's preoccupation with foreign affairs alone is sufficiently exacting to limit drastically the time he can have available for questions of domestic character.

If the President cannot make the plan for expenditures, then someone else must do it for him. This job falls on the Budget Director, who is located within the Executive Office of the President, who reports directly to the President, and who is frequently said to be the President's right-hand man. If the Budget Director is as close to the President as he ought to be, he will know with virtual certainty how the President would answer many of the questions that arise if he had time to think them through. And if the Budget Director is the kind of man he ought to be, he will decide them in exactly that way. Where the Budget Director is uncertain as to what the President would consider to be for the best interest of the country and the party in power, he will undoubtedly seek out the best political advice he can get. Presumably that will come from the same individuals that the President customarily relies upon when he has a question of such a character.

It would be a great mistake, therefore, to suppose that the President's influence on the preparation of the appropriation estimates stops at the point where he drops out of the talking. His will is projected by what he says on a multitude of things and by the actions that he takes in a multitude of different situations. Other men read his mind, because it is their business to read his mind. And this is true, of course, not merely in making a budget, but in all other matters that are supposed to be carried on in keeping with the President's wishes.

The President directs the administrative branch of the government by fluid drive most of the time; only rarely is there a direct meshing of gears.

The control which the President exerts over his plan for expenditures depends, therefore, on the ability of his Budget Director to reflect in his own judgment the will of the President. The job of the Budget Director is primarily a political one, to decide what the President would have him do, to make that understood by the many officials who have an interest in what goes into the estimates, and to interpret it to the members of his own staff who do for him the job of compiling the budget document. It is at this point that our arrangements reveal a great deficiency, in my opinion. As I will point out in greater detail at a later point, I do not think that the Budget Director has available to assist him men of the political stature that is required to make the President's policies understood and accepted so that they can be incorporated into the document that goes to Congress.

The discussion to this point accounts for two of the four ways (listed above, page 236) in which the President shares in providing money for the administrative branch—his general authority in the enactment of legislation and his special authority to lay before Congress a plan for national expenditures. The two remaining methods of participation are of far less significance than the first two.

The third of these methods, as listed above, arises out of the President's power to apportion the money that has been appropriated. The Budget and Accounting Act of 1921 has been interpreted to give the President authority to say when and in what amounts the money that is appropriated to a department or agency shall become available to it. At the beginning of the fiscal year, when the new appropriation becomes effective, the several departments and agencies that have received an appropriation lay before the Budget Bureau a set of figures showing how they propose to spread the money over the twelve-months period. Not until the Budget Bureau approves the expenditure plan will any of the money become available.

At the present time, the allocation of money is made by quarterly periods. If its work spreads out evenly over the year, the administrative establishment will ordinarily propose to spend its appropriation in approximately equal quarterly amounts, and ordinarily the Budget Bureau will approve the plan. Thereafter the department or agency may spend the money, committing in any quarter the amount allowed for that quarter in the plan approved by the Budget Bureau.

This power to apportion appropriations is used primarily to induce departments and agencies to set up reserves. If the work of the department is seasonal, the Budget Bureau can check any inclination on the part of administrative officials to use the money up before the time when it is most needed. If the money was appropriated with a view to a future contingency that may not arise (e.g., for the operation of industrial plants that may have to be taken over by the government), the Budget Bureau can make sure that the money will be on hand if and when the contingency does arise. If there is evidence that drastic price rises are impending, the Bureau can make sure that provision is made for the higher costs in the later quarters of the year.

If the Bureau can put money into reserve for future expenditure by the department, then it can order it held in reserve with a view to returning it to the Treasury. If the expected future contingency which occasioned the appropriation does not occur at all, the money ought to revert to the general funds, and everyone will recognize the propriety of some central review to make sure that it will do so. But suppose prices break downward after the appropriation is made; shall the Budget Bureau impound the difference between estimated and actual cost (e.g., in the case of a great irrigation dam) and force it back into the treasury? Or suppose that the top officials of any agency, or of a bureau within an agency, suddenly reveal that they have no plans and no prospects for improvisation which would enable them to carry out a particular part of their operations with anything approaching efficiency; should the President, or a central reviewing agency, be in a position to impound for the remainder of the year and then return to the treasury the part of the appropriation that they are certain will not be spent to good purpose?

Congress has been very reluctant to concede this authority, either to the President directly, or to the Budget Bureau for exercise in the President's name. An appropriation to an administrative department or agency is a declaration that Congress wants that amount of money spent for the specific activities that that department has been charged to carry on. Sometimes these appropriations are made in opposition to the President's recommendations. There is a possibility that he would use his power to impound money to win back a point that he lost in the original act of appropriation. At least a great many Congressmen seem to have some fear of this.

The reluctance of Congressmen to give President or Budget Bureau a broad power to capture money and return it to the Treasury is undoubtedly due in part to their belief that the Bureau has already extended its authority beyond the contemplation of the law, and that the President has condoned transfers of money that defeated the will of Congress. As stated above, the present practice of making quarterly apportionments and putting money into reserves is based on an interpretation of the Budget and Accounting Act. I have read that act carefully and I have heard spokesmen for the Budget Bureau explain the Bureau's interpretation at some length, but I have never been able to see how the language of the statute supports the conclusion that either the President or the Bureau has authority to withhold from an administrative establishment the money that is declared available to it in the appropriation act.

I can readily appreciate, therefore, why Congressmen hesitate to give the Bureau still greater power. Congressmen have been offended even more, however, by action which was taken by heads of departments and agencies (undoubtedly with the knowledge and approval of the President) under relief and public works appropriations during the recent depression. New agencies that were set up to expend money for relief and recovery quite naturally turned to the established departments and agencies of the government to direct and supervise projects which would put unemployed people to work and at the same time result in a valuable public asset. But to turn money over to the Federal Communications Commission to build a thousand Adcock direction finders for subsequent use by FCC (a fictitious instance) is to give it money for a purpose that Congress could very well have provided for in the appropriation direct to FCC. And it may be that the transfer of funds from the public works authority to FCC will actually enable the latter agency to do something that Congress specifically considered and turned down. If transfers of money appropriated for relief and public works were not actually used to finance undertakings that Congress had refused to authorize, something so close to that did happen that many Congressmen have been sour on the impounding and transfer of money ever since.

It seems clear enough that someone who is not immediately connected with the departments and agencies that carry on the work of government ought to be given authority to capture a part of their money under certain circumstances and force that money back into the general treasury. That agency might be a committee of Congress; it might be the President personally; it might be a central administrative agency (Budget Bureau) acting on its own authority or acting in the name of the President. The Hoover Commission was of the opinion that the authority should be vested in the President: "We recommend . . . that the President should have authority to reduce expenditures under appropriations, if the purposes intended by the Congress are still carried out." There seems little doubt that the Commission presumed that the Budget Bureau would make most of the decisions for the President.[1]

Only in the face of spectacular events could the President make the decisions personally. If Alaska suddenly sinks beneath the sea, he can tell the Department of Interior not to build any more nurseries for bears in Alaska. If discussions with Russia take a certain turn, he can tell the Atomic Energy Commission what that implies for their current plans for production. But the job of reviewing appropriations and the operating plans of administrative departments with a view to capturing money under the circumstances discussed above is something that must go on clear through

---

[1] *Budgeting and Accounting; A Report to the Congress by the Commission on Organization of the Executive Branch of the Government, February 1949* (Government Printing Office, 1949), p. 17.

the calendar if not around the clock. The setting up of reserves and the release of money is something that is worked out, not something that is decreed on inspiration. The action that is taken reflects the state of the argument when one side gets tired of trying to talk the other out of or into something. The final result of the argument can be laid before the President for his signature. But why should it? He will see only a stack of papers with the bottom half-inch of each projecting like the steps on a stairway. He will start at the top and work his way to the bottom by writing his name on each step. And all he will know about what he is doing is that his secretary will say, "These are Budget Bureau orders returning money to the treasury. Mr. Ralph Claggett put them together, and he says that they are all ready for your signature." Let us not inquire whether Mr. Claggett knows any more about what is in them than does the President.

The case for the President signing documents, however, does not turn on the question of whether he will know what he is signing. The movement of the paper from the Budget Bureau to the White House creates an opportunity for one more appeal. Review of plans for expenditures can only be successful if it is accomplished by a process of negotiation. Ordinarily, the officials who are trying to seize the money and the officials who are trying to hold on to it will come to agreement as to what is the fair thing to do. But there will come a time when the reviewing agency will say, "Either we mean business when we start looking at a department's plans, or we don't. If we mean business, this is the time to crack down." And the head of the department that is being cracked down on may say, "This is something I would like to hear the President say himself." Should the reviewing agency be final or should the President hear the dispute?

We have never settled, by making consistent provisions in the laws, what should go to the President and what should stop off at some lower place of authority. Neither have the students of government worked the matter out in theory. My own answer at this moment would be that any man who thinks he is big enough to carry such an issue to the President should be in a position to try it. If he is really big, he will get through the little bureaucracy that guards the President's time and sensibilities; let us hope that the President will make it clear that he had better not come back with such a question again unless it really has a high political significance.

We can provide Presidential review of this kind without subjecting the President to the danger of writer's cramp. We can surely have an understanding (and I am sure we do) that the Budget Bureau will not impound the money of an agency without full knowledge on the part of top officials in that agency that it proposes to do so. And we can have the further understanding that top officials in that agency can discuss the matter with the top officials in the Budget Bureau before the latter commits itself. If the Bureau hasn't got enough men of genuine political stature to do all the talking that will be necessary (and I doubt that it has), then let its staff be increased in top levels. If these responsible officials agree that an issue of high political significance is involved and they can't agree on an answer, then they may be able to agree that the case is important enough to be laid before the President. And if they can't agree on that, then let the order stand in abeyance until the official who does not like the *status quo* finds out whether he is big enough to get through the doors of the White House.

Since the appropriation was made by act of law, it may be that only Congress should decide whether any part of it should revert to the Treasury. We want Congress to keep its hands on the money; on the other hand, we want the President to keep his hands on the officials that spend the money. The President has no time to decide any issues in dispute except those of very high political significance; but he has close working relations with and direction over the administrative force that will do the work of detailed review. Congress has no staff of its own for such an inquiry and has shown little inclination to use the Budget Bureau for its purposes; but the members of a congressional committee can spare far more time for determination of the hard cases than the President can. If final authority is to rest in the President, the Budget Bureau will have a very great determining power. If the final authority is to rest in Congress, the Bureau or some other agency will study and recommend, but any of its recommendations that are opposed will get a pretty thorough examination at the hands of one or more committee members.

What I have said concerning review of appropriations and capture of surplus money would have little application if all money were appropriated to the President, who then distributed it to the several departments and agencies in accord with his own best judgment. We do something like this in some of our states, where money for supplies and equipment is appropriated to a central agency that either buys for other departments or releases money to them as it thinks they are entitled to have it. The British carry this practice of centralized appropriations much farther; most of the money provided by Parliament is held to the account of the Treasury and will not be released to a department except as it satisfies the Treasury with its plans for expenditure.

Our practice, so far as the federal government is concerned, has been uniformly and consistently in favor of appropriating specific amounts of money to the various departments and agencies that are charged with putting governmental activities and undertakings into operation. We make one minor departure from this rule, however—the last of the four ways (listed at the beginning of this chapter) by which the President shares in providing money for the departments and agencies that make up the administrative branch. Each year the President is given a certain sum of money to use according to his own judgment. For the year 1947–48, this free appropriation amounted to only $500,000; for 1948–49, it was reduced to $200,000. Ordinarily the only important restriction on the President's disposition of this money is that he may not use it "to finance a function or project" that Congress itself considered and turned down. During World War II, however, the amount was far greater (amounting to about $100 million during one fiscal year) and there were few if any restrictions as to how the President could spend it. Since the President had so much money which he could put where he thought it was needed, it was possible to reduce the amounts for unforeseen contingencies in the appropriations to the various administrative departments and agencies. As money for needs that might not actually arise was eliminated from the appropriations to administrative departments and agencies, there was less occasion for later review of these appropriations to capture and return excess amounts to the treasury.

BIBLIOGRAPHIC NOTE

I am forced to conclude that no one has put in print an informative account of the relation of the President to the financing of administration. What there is on this subject is scattered in the biographies of Presidents, their memoirs, and the books written by men who were in a position to observe what one or more Presidents did. I have not systematically examined this literature and will not cite particular works which contain bits of information. Books which deal with the appropriations process generally throw some light on the role of the President. This literature is cited in the note at the end of Chapter 7. The same can be said for the literature dealing with the Bureau of the Budget, which is cited at the end of Chapter 17.

C H A P T E R 14

MAKING BUREAUCRATS BEHAVE

The President plays a dual role in the direction and control of administration. He is the chief executive of the national government and serves as the principal connecting link between Congress and the administrative branch. In order to provide an effective connection between Congress and the administrative branch, he must be a part of each. Thus it is that he serves in two roles so far as administration is concerned. In one role, he is political leader and participant in the enactment of the legislation which the administrative branch must put into effect. In the other role, he is chief administrative official and shares with other administrative officials and employees the authority and obligation to put the laws into effect.

These two roles are by no means entirely separate; rather, they are the two ends of the authority and influence which the President exercises in government. As he participates in the formulation of broad policies of government and does what he can to get them enacted into law, the role of the President as political leader and participant in legislation is emphasized. As he participates in making the decisions which are necessary for putting the law into effect and does what he can to see that the objectives of the law are made effective in actual government, the role of the President as chief administrative official is emphasized.

In the discussion of direction and control of administration up to this point, we have dealt primarily with the President in the first of these roles. In deciding what the activities and undertakings of government shall be, the President functions almost entirely as political leader and as a part of the lawmaking authority. The same is almost equally true of his relation to the creation of administrative departments and agencies, the alteration of administrative structure, and the shifting of governmental activities from place to place in the administrative branch. Under certain circumstances, the President may be permitted to do these things on his own authority; ordinarily, however, he gets what he wants only if Congress approves. Finally, as respects the provision of money for governmental activities and administrative organizations, the President exerts his greatest influence by participating in the lawmaking process. He has a limited power to control the spending of money after Congress has made the appropriation, but what he does at this point has far less effect on the character and quality of administration than what he did earlier in preparing a financial plan for the government (the annual budget) and pushing it through Congress.

We now come to a point, in considering the President's capacity for giving direction and control to administration, where the relative importance of his two roles begins to change. Three areas of the President's authority and influence over administration remain to be examined: regulation of the conduct of administrative officials and employees (discussed in this chapter), appointment and removal of administrative officials and employees (Chapter 15), and review and coordination of administrative operations (Chapter 16). The President makes an impress on the standards and regulations which govern the conduct of administrative officials and employees by participating in the enactment of legislation which fixes such standards and regulations (discussed in Chapter 8); but he makes perhaps as great an impress through the decisions which he makes and puts into effect on his own authority. There is no such equality in the importance of his two roles, as respects the selection and removal of officials and employees and reviewing and coordinating administrative operations. In respect to these matters (discussed in the next two chapters), the President influences administration primarily through his authority as chief official in the administrative branch; what he does in his role as political leader and participant in the enactment of legislation has far less impact on the character and quality of administration.

The distinction between the two roles of the President which has been made in the past few paragraphs is of more than academic importance. It is helpful in, if not essential to, the evaluation of recent proposals for general reconstruction of the executive-administrative branch of the national government—both the recommendations of the President's Committee on Administrative Management in 1937 and the recommendations of the Hoover Commission on Organization of the Executive Branch in 1949.[1]

It seems to me most unfortunate that both the President's Committee on Administrative Management and the Hoover Commission found it unnecessary to provide a carefully reasoned statement of the more important beliefs and convictions which underlie their respective proposals for change. The method of the President's Committee consisted essentially of announcing certain assumptions and presumptions about the way government ought to be organized, formulating proposals for change which would bring the actual arrangements into conformity with the announced assumptions and presumptions, and exhorting all who had authority and influence in the matter to take whatever action might be necessary to put the recommended changes into effect. The report of the Hoover Commission seems to me to be much less doctrinaire and less given to exhortation, but I think it does little if any more than the report of the President's Committee to show what are likely to be the consequences (direct and indirect, immediate and long run) of alternative arrangements at the top of our government.

The objective in each case, but especially in the case of the President's Committee, is to bring the administrative branch as a

---

[1] The documents produced by the President's Committee on Administrative Management and by the Commission on Organization of the Executive Branch of the Government are described in the note at the end of Chapter 6.

whole more fully under the direction and control of the President by increasing the authority of the President over administration, by enlarging the establishment in and around the White House which is most useful for effecting central direction and control, by reducing the number of separate departments and agencies, and by cutting off some of the relationships which run directly from the administrative departments and agencies to Congress. But there is not in either report, or in the documents which support the reports, even a fragmentary discussion of what the President is likely personally to take an interest in or have time to think about if he is interested; of what kind of issues are likely to be resolved finally in the name of the President but actually by the contingent of politicos and specialized bureaucracies that dwell in or revolve in an orbit about the White House; or of what effect the proposed changes would probably have on the relations between the President and the heads of the reduced number of administrative departments and agencies individually or collectively as a cabinet.

Because of the failure of the two bodies to supply anything approaching a full statement of the basic theories of government underlying the two reports, one can only speculate as to what either body contemplated would be the personal relation of the President to administration under the new order which it hoped to see established. "It is our recommendation," said the chairman of the President's Committee in testimony before a committee of Congress, "that the Congress give the broad power of management of the organization to the President. . . . We believe that the Chief Executive should be given more authority over the management of the Executive branch in order to make that authority more commensurate with his responsibility. . . . "[2] The Committee was called a Committee on Administrative Management, and the phrase "administrative management" is prominent in the

[2] Testimony of Mr. Louis Brownlow in *Reorganization of the Executive Departments;* Hearings before the Joint Committee on Government Organization, 75th Congress, 1st session (Government Printing Office, 1937), pp. 8, 12.

report of the Committee, in the supporting "studies" which the Committee had printed, and in the testimony of the members of the Committee before Congress. This has led one or more persons who have studied these documents, and who are doubtless well acquainted with one or more members of the Committee, to say that the President's Committee viewed the President as a "glorified factory superintendent," interested in acquiring and able to maintain a high degree of knowledge of what is going on throughout the administrative branch and capable of making personal judgments which he thinks better than those of the heads of administrative departments and agencies as to how the affairs of their respective establishments shall be conducted.[3]

The character of the recommendations made by the Hoover Commission, and the nature of the language which it used to explain and justify its recommendations, indicate that that body expected the President to give much less personal attention to "management" of the administrative branch than the President's Committee contemplated. Even so, the Hoover Commission (if I read the right meaning into its reports) was primarily concerned to increase the ability of the President to direct and control administration rather than to relieve him of the necessity for doing so.

It seems to me that these are times when we most need to have the President free from involvement in administration so that he

[3] A thoughtful student of government who has served in at least two federal administrative agencies and contributed several incisive essays on administrative relationships wrote me that he thought it "highly unrealistic to think of a President as actually 'managing' the Executive Branch. I think the origins of public administration in private management and municipal government predispose the reformers to come at the presidency in the wrong way: to think of him as a sort of glorified factory superintendent. I don't think Presidents have time for institutional management (I know it for a fact that Roosevelt was profoundly uninterested in any personnel problem that did not have a highly personal angle) or that they should take time. I think it is a fact of the greatest significance that the three men who were the President's Committee on Administrative Management, though, of course, highly able men, were men whose roots and experience were in municipal government. I think they utterly failed to see some significant differences between the job of city manager or mayor and the presidency—differences quantitative and qualitative."

can devote himself most fully to political leadership in affairs of greatest current importance to the nation. The concern of the President to exert an influence on what the government of the United States actually does in respect to these affairs of greatest importance undoubtedly requires that he exercise a substantial amount of direction and control over administrative departments and agencies. But that same concern equally requires that he not be diverted from those affairs which are of greatest importance by a preoccupation with problems of administration that are of less importance.

Any critical evaluation of the recommendations of the President's Committee and the Hoover Commission, it seems to me, must turn in large part on their relation to these basic considerations. Do the recommendations of either or both of these bodies contemplate that less important matters will win over matters of greater importance in competition for the time and energy of a chief executive who does not have enough time and energy for all of them? If the arrangements which either body proposes would put obligations on the President which he cannot discharge, or will not undertake to discharge, what persons (individuals or organizations) may be expected to assume those obligations, making decisions and issuing instructions in his name? If there is a high degree of probability that the authority which either or both of these plans proposes for the President will in fact be exercised by someone else, would the nation not be happier if all or a part of that authority were exercised by Congress instead? These questions must be kept prominently in mind in the discussion which follows in this and the next two chapters.

In discussing the relation of Congress to standards and regulations governing the conduct of administrative officials and employees (Chapter 8), attention was centered on four areas of activity where misuse and abuse of authority are most likely to occur: employment, property, finance, and relations with the public. In each of these four problem areas the President and Congress jointly exercise a substantial amount of direction and control by the enactment of legislation. What does the President do, and what might he do, in respect to these matters through his authority as head of the administrative branch?

At present, the authority and influence of the President (except as he participates in legislation) is confined almost exclusively to the first of these four areas: employment. Apparently, he has little knowledge of, and gives little attention to, the arrangements which determine how property and money will be handled and accounted for; and if he takes an active interest in the practices and procedures which determine how administrative departments and agencies will do business with the public, he apparently finds it unnecessary to do much about them.

As for the property of the federal government, the President doubtless decides what kind of lead pencils will be kept on his desk and raps people's knuckles if they reach for his fountain pen. But except for what is in and around the White House, he has little to do with the acquisition, custody, safeguarding, and disposition of the property of the national government. Surely no one would ask that he occupy himself with such matters except when a new problem of major importance arises (such as the disposition of surplus holdings at the end of a war) or when he is confronted by a scandal of major proportions (such as the burning of the *Normandie*). The Hoover Commission found the administration of property to be extremely unsatisfactory, on the whole, and proposed that an Office of General Services be set up immediately under the President, with authority to provide the direction and control necessary for securing a better administration of property and the records relating to property. But the Commission proposed that this new office report directly to the President only because it could find no other place to put it. "Obviously," said the Commission, "the President cannot personally exercise this responsibility except in the most unusual circumstances."[4]

[4] *Office of General Services; A Report to the Congress by the Commission on Organization of the Executive Branch of the Government, February 1949* (Government Printing Office, 1949), p. 1.

The President personally displays great interest in the way money is distributed among governmental activities and administrative organizations. What ought to be his relation to the arrangements which are set up to make sure that money is spent in keeping with the provisions of the appropriation acts which he helps to put on the statute books? Does it make any difference to him what kind of bookkeeping systems are maintained, so long as he has reason to believe that they are good systems? Does he need to know anything about the quality of the people who handle the money and keep the financial records, other than that the arrangements for selecting them and providing for their direction and control are said to be satisfactory? Does he need any reports concerning the status of funds and the use that is being made of money which he can only get if he has some personal authority over the people who keep the financial records?

As matters now stand, the President has little indeed to do with financial administration. The maintenance of the primary or foundation records relating to the expenditure of money is scattered over the administrative branch among the departments and agencies that do the work of government and incur the costs of government. The money that is paid into the federal government flows to the Treasury Department for custody, and the Treasury Department pays out most of the money and keeps the records showing the status of the funds. The General Accounting Office, which acknowledges scarcely any allegiance at all to the President, serves as a general policeman in matters relating to money, passing on the propriety of individual financial transactions, ordering departments and agencies to improve their records and procedures, and reporting to Congress what it thinks Congress ought to know about the use that is made of the money which it appropriates. In all of this elaborate system there is nothing which is designed to give the President an effective influence on the administration of financial affairs after the money has been made available to the administrative establishment.

While there may be general agreement that the President does

not need to know or do much about the administration of property, there is, on the other hand, a widespread conviction if not
general agreement that the President does need to know and
ought to be able to do something about the handling of money and
the administration of records relating to money. But the area of
general agreement does not extend very far beyond the statement
of the general principle. Perhaps no issue relating to the proper
authority of the President over administration has been argued
more vigorously by students of government in recent years than
that of where to draw the line between Presidential and Congressional authority in respect to the character of bookkeeping systems, control of expenditures, reporting of costs and status of
funds, and audit of financial records and practices. Because this
issue is so sharply argued and is so intimately connected with the
character and role of the General Accounting Office, discussion of
the relation of the President to financial administration is reserved
for the chapter which deals with the General Accounting Office
(Chapter 18).

It is surprising that a literature which is so predominantly concerned to enlarge the authority and influence of the President over
administration makes scarcely a passing reference to his authority
or lack of authority to prescribe the conditions under which the
American people do business with their government. The arrangements (procedures, practices, attitudes) which govern the contacts between administrative officials and employees on the one
hand and the public for whom they supply government on the
other have a most important effect on the character and quality
of government in operation and largely determine the satisfaction
we get out of our government. Surely a President who is concerned to give the people the kind of government they want
and who hopes that we will think well enough of his Administration to keep his party in power will wish to be sure that we have
a minimum of cause to complain about the nature of our contacts
with the administrative branch.

What authority over the relations between the public and the administrative branch can the President effectively exercise? He participates in the enactment of legislation of the character discussed in Chapter 8 (see particularly pp. 150–153). Through his general power to give direction and control to administration, he can influence these aspects of administration. Is that enough? If the President needs special authority to regulate financial administration or to regulate the conditions of employment as indicated in the pages which follow, does he not need special authority to regulate the conditions under which the American people do business with the administrative departments and agencies? By enacting the Administrative Procedure Act of 1946, Congress and President sought to force upon the administrative branch arrangements for doing business with the American people which administrative officials had not voluntarily adopted. The requirements of this statute must be supplemented by policies adopted within the administrative branch. Should the authority to formulate and pronounce these supplementary policies be vested exclusively in the several departments and agencies or should the President have authority to promulgate the supplementary policies that he personally prefers? No doubt he can induce high officials in many of the departments and agencies to promulgate what he recommends, particularly where he can support his recommendations by removing men from office. But ought the President to be relieved of the necessity for persuasion and coercion by a grant of authority to issue the regulations over his own signature?

Neither the President's Committee on Administrative Management nor the Hoover Commission thought this matter of sufficient significance to merit consideration in their reports, and (as noted above) it has not received attention in the general literature relating to American government. The extent of the President's present authority in this respect, if indeed he has any authority, is most uncertain. The Budget and Accounting Act of 1921 provides that the Bureau of the Budget, when so directed by the President, shall "make a detailed study of the departments and establishments for the purpose of enabling the President to determine what changes (with a view of securing greater economy and efficiency in the conduct of the public service) should be made" in the organization, activities, and methods of business pursued in those departments and establishments. "The results of such study," the act continued, "shall be embodied in a report or reports to the President, who may transmit to Congress such report or reports or any part thereof with his recommendations on the matters covered thereby."[5]

The phrase "economy and efficiency" can be construed to include studies which have as their objective the improvement of working relations between administrative organizations and the public, though it is doubtful that many Congressmen had that objective in mind when they considered the language of the act. The stipulation that the President "may transmit" the results of studies to Congress with his recommendations on the matters which they cover is not an express declaration that he may not act upon those matters himself, but it certainly lends no support to a supposition that Congress, when it adopted the act, expected the President to take such action on his own authority. If the President has any authority to put into effect by his own signature the orders which change the arrangements and procedures under which the American people do business with their government, that authority must be derived from other statutes or from the constitutional grant of authority to see that the laws are faithfully executed. I have not been able to find any statute which confers such authority, and I am not aware of any authoritative declaration that such power is vested in the President by the Constitution. Certainly it may be argued with force that the only authority which the President enjoys in this respect is the authority to induce the proper officials of the various departments and agencies to issue the orders which he wishes to see in effect, backing up his recommendations with such coercive measures (including

[5] 42 Statutes at Large 22, sec. 209 (1921); U.S. Code, title 31, sec. 18.

removal from office) as may be available to him and as he may care to invoke.

My convictions concerning what the President can and cannot do personally, and my uncertainty concerning the consequences of having decisions made in his name by the political retinue and the specialized bureaucracies that surround him, make me reluctant to recommend the enlargement of the President's authority in respect to administrative matters. Nevertheless, I think that the conditions under which the American people do business with the administrative departments and agencies have so great a bearing on the ability of the President to convince the American people that he or his party ought to be kept in power that I am inclined to recommend that he be given opportunity to influence these conditions by issuing regulations on his own authority. In any event, it is high time for people who know more about the actual conditions of doing business with the government than I do to explore the pros and cons of enlarging the authority of the President in this respect.

The relationship of the President to the administration of the employment policies and practices of the national government is rooted in our basic civil service legislation. The original civil service law of 1883 (the Pendleton Act) recognized the need for a central administrative agency to direct the administration of employment policies. But the statute did not bring the agency into existence. It described the organization that might be established (a Civil Service Commission of three members) and left it to the President to decide whether to call it into life. President Arthur promptly did so and we have had a Civil Service Commission ever since. The long history of its continuous existence, together with subsequent statutory references to it, suggest that the courts might now hold that the President has a legal obligation to keep the Commission in existence.[6]

---

[6] The Pendleton Act is in 22 Statutes at Large 403 (1883); U.S. Code, title 5, chapter 12.

The principal substantive feature of the Pendleton Act was a body of provisions to govern the selection of federal employees and to regulate in some degree the conditions of their employment following their entry into the service. But again that statute fell a long way short of bringing the provisions of the law fully into operation. The President was authorized to designate the groups of employees or segments of the public service to which these regulations should become applicable. The President, to put it in other words, was authorized to extend the classified service as he saw fit. While the statute did not say that the President should consult the Civil Service Commission before taking action, it became the practice to do so. The Civil Service Commission has, in fact, become the President's principal adviser on the practicability, if not the desirability, of extending the classified service in any direction.

The relationship between the President and the Civil Service Commission in the issuance of rules and regulations relating to the federal service is very confusing to the casual observer. The Pendleton Act stated that the Commission may, "subject to the rules that may be made by the President, make regulations" relating to certain phases of employment policy. On later occasions, Congress set up additional personnel agencies (e.g., Bureau of Efficiency and Personnel Classification Board) and gave them rule-making power. These were abolished shortly after 1930, and a part of their functions and authority was transferred to the Civil Service Commission. The Commission thus acquired (particularly from the Classification Board) new legal authority for issuance of rules, and the necessity of going to the President for confirmation of the Commission's regulations on certain matters was thrown into question. Whatever be the proper interpretation of the statutes, however, the Civil Service Commission today lays most of its rules and regulations before the President for promulgation. Unlike other agencies of the government that draw up regulations according to their own judgment and give them force of law by their own acts the Civil Service Commission relies on the President to make most of its regulations effective.

The President thus has two important sources of authority over the Civil Service Commission. He may, as he sees fit, extend or contract the area of public employment over which the Commission has jurisdiction. And he may review most of its rules and regulations before putting them into effect. To make sure that the working relations between the Civil Service Commission and the White House will be smooth and friendly, President Roosevelt's plan for an Executive Office of the President (effective in 1939) included an Assistant to the President to serve as Liaison Officer for Personnel Management. The nature of that connection was described by the first Liaison Officer some two years after his appointment in the following words: "The President has delegated to the Liaison Officer for Personnel Management authority to decide, on his behalf, those problems which the Officer considers of concern to the Chief Executive. . . . The Liaison Officer, of course, subsequently reports to and discusses with the President the matters that have thus been considered."[7]

Is this a sound working relationship? Authority over certain questions of greatest political significance (extension and contraction of the classified service) vested directly in the President; the remaining authority vested in a Commission, except that some of its acts (certain rules and regulations) must be approved by the President before they go into effect; and a Liaison Officer running between with authority to make up and speak the President's mind. If we must assume that the President will delegate to another man all of the authority that is vested in him, why do we vest that authority in the President in the first place? If the President is not personally going to review the Civil Service Commission's rules, why do we not authorize the Commission to issue the rules itself without sending them to the White House for ap-

[7] William H. McReynolds, "The Liaison Office for Personnel Management," in *Public Administration Review*, vol. 1, pp. 121–126, at p. 125 (1941).

proval? If the Commission cannot be trusted to decide what is a good rule but the Liaison Officer can, why do we not make the Liaison Officer the actual head of the civil service agency?

I think the answer is that this is not a sound working arrangement. If so, then why did we create it and why do we persist in it? The explanation is the same as for most of the anomalous situations in our government. The arrangements were built up bit by bit, not systematically planned. Each addition to the structure was the result of compromise, not what anybody considered ideal. We are not happy with what we have; but we have not been unhappy enough to go to the trouble of fixing up something better.

We are plagued in our administrative arrangements and policies relating to federal employment by the conflict between two important considerations. We want the arrangements and policies relating to employment to give high officials in the administrative branch assurance that they can control the character and quality of administration; but we also want to be sure that the great mass of positions in the federal service will not be filled by men and women who are selected, placed, and retained because of their personal political affiliations. The first of these considerations argues that the President and high administrative officials should have considerable authority over employment policy and employment administration; the second consideration argues that employment policy and administration should be largely under the authority of a nonpartisan or bi-partisan board. The Pendleton Act of 1883 represented our first important compromise of these conflicting considerations. The creation of the Liaison Officer for Personnel Management represents one of the most recent. The Hoover Commission proposed still another.

The purpose in establishing the Liaison Officer for Personnel Management was to enlarge the President's influence in employment policy and administration. The Liaison Officer was a substitute for a whole new central personnel organization recommended by the President's Committee on Administrative Management in 1937, but which could not be put through Congress.

The President's Committee proposed that the Civil Service Commission be abolished and its authority divided between a Civil Service Administrator and a Civil Service Board. The Administrator was to head the central personnel agency, to "act as the direct adviser to the President upon all personnel matters," to lay before the President the employment policies which he thought the President ought to approve and promulgate, and (within the limits of the law) to see that the President's wishes concerning personnel matters were put into practical operation. The Civil Service Administrator and the organization which he was to head were expected to enlarge the President's influence in respect to federal employment. The Civil Service Board was expected to see to it that the President's influence was not enlarged enough to cross over the boundaries set for it in the civil service legislation; its primary function would be "to act as watch dog of the merit system and to represent the public interest in the improvement of personnel administration in the Federal service."

A reading of the entire report of the President's Committee leaves little room for doubt that the Committee believed the President ought personally to exercise a great deal of influence on employment policies and employment administration; in creating the Civil Service Administrator and a central personnel agency under him the Committee hoped to give the President assistance in matters relating to employment, not to remove these matters from his area of interest and preoccupation. "Personnel administration," the Committee said, "lies at the very core of administrative management." Again, "Personnel management is an essential element of executive management." To these broad statements which appear in the Committee's report may be added the following from a special study prepared under the Committee's direction: "A specialized personnel agency at the highest level of administration is necessary for the same reasons that specialized personnel agencies are necessary at all major levels of administration. General administrators can seldom equip themselves with the technical knowledge and skill now available for concentration upon the personnel function, and cannot devote the personal attention required by the importance of the problems. The President, as a general administrator, is no exception to this general rule."[8]

Additional light is shed on the Committee's concept of the President's interest in employment policies and employment administration by an examination of the arrangements which it proposed for the selection of the Civil Service Administrator. The Administrator, said the Committee, "should possess a broad knowledge of personnel administration, and should be a qualified and experienced executive. He should be appointed by the President, with the advice and consent of the Senate, on the basis of an open competitive examination conducted by a special board of examiners appointed by the Civil Service Board." Surely everyone will acknowledge that this is a strange way to pick a man who is expected to help the President decide the matters relating to employment which have the greatest political implication. The President must personally name the men who are to go into the highest positions in the administrative branch. He needs help in this, for (as noted in the next chapter) the President cannot know personally all the people who ought to be considered for these positions. Similarly, the President needs someone to help him make up his mind as to whether this high official or that one is discharging the duties of his office in keeping with the President's expectations. He needs help in working out plans to shift men about in the high positions of the administrative branch. The President may conclude that the Secretary of Commerce ought to go to London as ambassador, but be unwilling to act until he knows whether so-and-so will come into the government as Secretary of Commerce. And the President may be unwilling to tell either man what he is thinking about until he has a pretty good notion as to how each

[8] The foregoing and later quotations from the *Report of the President's Committee on Administrative Management* will be found between pages 7 and 14 of that document. The quotation from the special study is in *Report of the President's Committee on Administrative Management with Special Studies* (Government Printing Office, 1937), pp. 95–96.

will react; someone else must make the soundings for him.

If these are the kinds of problems that the President wants his principal personnel adviser to help him with, the President will surely not be willing to appoint one of the three men turned up for him in an open competitive examination conducted by a Civil Service Board. We would have to charge the President's Committee with being ridiculous if we supposed that it expected the Civil Service Administrator to serve the President in this manner. It seems necessary to conclude that the Committee expected the President to display an interest in the kind of affairs which the Civil Service Commission is now concerned with. The Committee wished to make it possible for him to impress his will easily and firmly upon those affairs, and to accomplish that result it proposed as a substitute for the present bi-partisan Commission a single official immediately accountable to the President but whom the President could not freely choose.

The Hoover Commission was less explicit than the President's Committee as to its general conception of what the relation of the President to administration ought to be. And it was little if any more explicit as to what it conceived to be the nature of the President's interest in matters relating to employment. Like the President's Committee, the Hoover Commission did not concern itself with the President's need for help in making decisions of high political significance; its recommendations are limited to policies, procedures, and organization for handling the kind of affairs with which the Civil Service Commission is now charged. The Hoover Commission was of the opinion that the President ought to have a very close relation to the agency and the officials at the top of the agency which has authority relating to employment throughout the federal government. The most significant feature of the Commission's proposals concerning employment was the recommendation that the authority and influence of the central agency be greatly reduced so that the departments and agencies that carry on the work of government could have a freer hand in managing their own employment problems.

A necessary consequence of such a decentralization of authority over employment policies and employment administration would be to restrict the President's authority and influence to a much lesser scope than the President's Committee thought it desirable for him to have.

The Hoover Commission was not at all specific as to what connection the President ought to have with employment policies and administration. The federal government, it said, is faced with "more complex and difficult problems in the personnel field than any other employer in the Nation today," and "programs for strengthening the management side of Government will be worthless" unless these personnel problems are solved effectively. The President "is in the final analysis, responsible for seeing to it that these problems are solved," and if he "is to discharge this responsibility in an effective manner, he should receive continuous staff advice and assistance from someone who is in close touch with the civilian career service of the Government." Therefore, the Commission stated, there should be an Office of Personnel within the President's Office, and the head of the Office of Personnel

should function as the principal staff adviser to the President in connection with problems related to the career civilian service of the Federal Government. He should, for example, be responsible for keeping in close touch with the work of the various offices of personnel within the departments and agencies. Also, the director [the head of the Office of Personnel] should advise the President on ways and means of identifying exceptional talent within the Federal Civil Service in professional, scientific, and executive posts, and of making sure that this talent is being utilized in the most effective possible manner. Furthermore, the director of personnel should be in such close touch with the conditions surrounding employment in the Federal service that he will always be in a position to advise the President as to the steps which need to be taken to put the Government in a position where it will be looked upon as one of the most progressive employers in the Nation.[9]

[9] *General Management of the Executive Branch; A Report to the Congress by the Commission on Organization of the Executive Branch of the Government, February 1949* (Government Printing Office, 1949), pp. 23–25.

In addition to giving the President the advice and assistance that he needs, the Hoover Commission found four other functions for the central personnel agency: to fix government-wide standards for employment; to stimulate and assist the administrative establishments of the government in the improvement of employment policies and practices; to perform certain services relating to employment where central administration is better and cheaper (e.g., recruiting and examining activities for lower grade positions); and to police the various departments and agencies in order to make sure that they adhere to the standards which have been set up to govern them.

I think we may conclude that the Hoover Commission considered the four functions just enumerated to be more important than the function of giving advice and assistance to the President, for it proposed that the central personnel agency be headed by a bi-partisan Civil Service Commission in the future as at present. It recommended, however, that the chairman of the Civil Service Commission should be the head of the Office of Personnel to be established immediately under the President. Perhaps the Hoover Commission assumed that the Chairman would have, to assist him as Director of Personnel, a small staff that would not be a part of the organization under the Civil Service Commission; if so, it did not so state.

Mr. James K. Pollock, a member of the Hoover Commission, dissented from the recommendations which have just been described, primarily on the ground that there is not enough to be done by a central personnel agency to justify the continuance of a Commission. Mr. Pollock was of the opinion that the day has passed when there is need for a central agency, kept out of politics by a bi-partisan commission, to police the employment system to make sure that it is not used for the special advantage of the party in power. "It is my conviction," wrote Mr. Pollock, "that a statute outlawing political favoritism in the appointment of Federal employees, coupled with enlightened agency management is sufficient to provide adequate protection [against spoils]."

Experience with the Tennessee Valley Authority, he thought, proved that we can accomplish this happy combination of statutory prohibition and enlightened agency management; if anyone is skeptical, he thought that "a part-time advisory board of distinguished citizens" could do all the policing that would be required. In the judgment of Mr. Pollock there are two important roles for the central agency concerned with employment. First, it should "become a real staff arm to the President. It would serve him both as advisor on personnel policy and in cultivating a modern approach to personnel management within the departments and agencies of the executive branch." And second, it "would act principally as consultants to the departments," advising them in the improvement of their employment policies and practices, helping them solve problems, encouraging them to innovate and experiment, devising means for evaluating the success of departments and agencies in respect to matters of employment, and passing from one administrative establishment to another the fruits of successful experience.[10]

It will be seen that there are three major roles for a central agency concerned with matters of employment. It may furnish advice and assistance to the President, it may advise and assist administrative departments and agencies, and it may police the administrative departments and agencies. We will be concerned for the remainder of this chapter with the first of these three roles only; the other two roles will be further considered in the chapter relating to the Civil Service Commission (Chapter 19).

It is noteworthy that none of the documents which have just been examined (the report of the President's Committee on Administrative Management, the special study prepared under its direction, the reports of the Hoover Commission, and the dissenting remarks of Commissioner Pollock) offered more than a few hints as to what the President needs to know about federal employment,

[10] Mr. Pollock's dissent is in *Personnel Management; A Report to the Congress by the Commission on Organization of the Executive Branch of the Government, February 1949* (Government Printing Office, 1949), pp. 47–59.

or knowing, would want to do about it. I am sure that the documents of the President's Committtee were not more explicit because the men who prepared them believed it to be evident from the general nature of government and administration that the President should maintain an intimate connection with the kind of employment policies and problems that a central personnel agency should be concerned with. I suspect that the majority of the Hoover Commission and the dissenting Mr. Pollock said as little as they did on this subject because they were uncertain as to what the connection of the President with those matters ought to be.

I share the uncertainty which I attribute to the members of the Hoover Commission, but I find my position prejudiced by a strong presumption that the President should have very little connection indeed with the kind of affairs for which a central personnel agency could provide useful advice and assistance. There are a great many things relating to federal employment that we want done the same way, or done within certain limits, throughout the federal service. We will get those things done uniformly, or within fixed limits, only if there is a central agency with some authority over the employment policies and practices of the departments and agencies that do the work of government. All departments and agencies want the same kind of people for certain kinds of work (e.g., clerical, stenographic); consequently a central testing service may prove economical and convenient. Employees should be able to move from one administrative establishment to another; therefore rules governing transfers and some supervision of transfers may be desirable. A new law alters the rights of individual employees to retain their jobs when the total force of employees must be reduced; someone must prepare the supplementary rules and regulations that are necessary to give the law full effect.

These are things that every President will want done and want done well. Therefore, he will want to know that there is a central personnel agency which can be counted on to do these things well.

But will any President who is concerned to devote his time and energy to matters of greater rather than lesser importance ever want to participate in such affairs or be consulted about them? Will the President not usually be most satisfied with the central personnel agency when he is unconscious that it exists?

There come times, however, when the President acquires a very active interest in federal employment. He wants to be sure that disabled veterans get a certain kind of treatment in the federal service and he may take a hand in the formulation of policies that govern their treatment. Congressmen may be worked up because employees have been promoted too fast and may threaten to require that great categories of jobs be filled only by Senatorial confirmation; the President may counter by ordering a thorough survey of promotion practices and he may personally study the findings. If the President is pledged to reduce the size of bureaucracy and cut the cost of government, he may wish a number of conversations with the man who can tell him where the payrolls are biggest. In a time of manpower shortage, recruitment for the public service may for a time become a major personal concern of the President. And, of course, at any time the President may want a search made for positions to which faithful party men can be appointed.

All of these except the last one are thoroughly proper interests for the President; and the last one is proper too, if kept within proper limits. We want the President to have his way about these things. But to say that the President ought to have his way is not to say that the President's signature must authenticate all the decisions and instructions which put his wishes into effect. It seems to me that the President is now required to promulgate by means of his own signature many regulations relating to employment that might better be authenticated and promulgated by the Civil Service Commission. I suspect that the necessity of getting the President's signature has many times been made an excuse for inaction or delay in action by the Civil Service Commission in respect to matters concerning which the President has no personal judgment one way or another. And I doubt that the process of getting the President's signature on matters of employment in which he has no personal judgment results in calling the attention of the Commission to considerations which it has not taken into account, or results in the improvement of the Commission's recommended action because those who determine what the President will sign have a judgment that is superior to that of the Commission on employment matters.

A conclusion that the President ought to be able to get what he wants in certain matters not only leaves unsettled the question of what documents he should sign; it also leaves unsettled the question of what organizational arrangement is most likely to assure that he will get what he wants with minimum drain on his time and energy. There is good reason to believe that the President will get what he wants in respect to employment policies and employment administration only if there is a central personnel agency which possesses two qualities or capacities. The officials at the top of that agency must be willing, even eager, to serve the President's needs, and the head of that agency must be able to get immediate response from the force of officials and employees that comprise the central personnel agency.

Both of these objectives are most easily and most surely achieved by putting the central administration of personnel or employment policies under a single administrative official. It is easier for the President to explain his wishes to one man than to a commission of three such as we have at present. It is easier for the President to get rid of one man than to dispose of three when he thinks that his wishes are being nullified or sabotaged. And the single administrator can speak to his staff with a force and an emphasis that is often watered down in an organization that is divided in the leadership at the top.

If the only objective we had to consider were that of making sure that the President would get what he wants in respect to employment, I think all people might agree with the President's Committee and Mr. Pollock of the Hoover Commission that the central personnel agency ought to be headed by a single official who recognizes the President as his only boss. It seems to me, however, that we must continue to compromise between the interest of the President in a certain amount of influence over employment and the concern of the nation that the President's influence not extend to the coercion or bribery of voters in elections. I do not share Commissioner Pollock's confidence that we can establish a combination of statutory prohibition and enlightened agency management which will allow us to dispense with a bi-partisan commission for the policing of employment policies and employment administration.

If we continue to believe that compromise is necessary, then we face the practical problem of devising a central organization for personnel administration which will respond to the President's wishes on some matters and resist his wishes on others. It seems to me that the matters relating to employment which require government-wide administration are of such a character that the job of administering those matters ought not be divided between two organizations. I see little, therefore, to recommend the arrangement which the President's Committee on Administrative Management proposed—a Civil Service Administrator (with a large force of officials and employees under his direction) to advise and assist the President and to see that employment policies and employment practices throughout the administrative branch are in keeping with the President's wishes, and a Civil Service Board with authority (and at least a staff of temporary employees) to see that the Civil Service Administrator and his organization are not able to accomplish everything that one President or another may happen to wish.

The arrangement proposed by the Hoover Commission seems to me more likely to effect a satisfactory compromise of the conflicting considerations. Under this plan, we would continue with the present three-member, bi-partisan Civil Service Commission, and the Civil Service Commission would retain all the authority which it now has to police the administrative departments and agencies with a view to assuring compliance with the requirements of the laws and regulations which are intended to give us a merit system. The Civil Service Commission would, however, withdraw from much of the central administration of federal employment which it now engages in, depending on investigation and audit of what the administrative departments and agencies do for its assurance that the objectives of the merit system are attained. The Chairman of the Civil Service Commission would be given authority to direct the activities of the force of officials and employees who make up the central personnel agency, it being his obligation, of course, to see to it that this force of men and women are doing what the three members of the Civil Service Commission think they ought to be doing. Finally, the Chairman of the Civil Service Commission would be a special agent of the President, serving ex officio as head of an Office of Personnel under the President and replacing the present Liaison Officer for Personnel Management in this capacity.

The superiority of this arrangement over what we now have (if it proves to be superior) rests on the prospect that the central personnel agency will respond more readily and more fully than heretofore to the wishes of the President in respect to matters of employment, so long as the wishes of the President do not contravene the principles of the merit system. The arguments against the proposed arrangement, beginning with the dissent of Commissioner Pollock, are likely to stand on the supposition that the Civil Service Commission will not respond readily enough and fully enough to the wishes of the President, and that the force of officials and employees under the Civil Service Commission will not respond readily enough and fully enough to the determinations which are made by the Commission.

We have, of course, no experience with a central personnel organization of this character to guide our speculation as to what is likely to come about if we set one up. Even if it results in the President's having no greater influence over employment policy than he has at present, I think it is unlikely that the nation will suffer greatly because of that fact. I have been told by some of its severest critics that the alacrity with which the members of the present Civil Service Commission (even though bi-partisan and lacking a chairman with a desk in the White House) respond to the voice of the President is fully the equal of that which marks the response of many cabinet officials. And I suspect that the specialized bureaucracy which the three commissioners now command (even though the chairman has no special authority to supply that command) is only slightly more of a trackless jungle, cut off from communication with its headquarters, than many another of comparable population and geographic extent under the direction of a single bureau chief.

BIBLIOGRAPHIC NOTE

I am unable to provide references on the relation of the President to control of the property of the federal government or on his relation to the conditions under which the American people do business with their government. References to the relation of the President to financial administration are included in the note at the end of Chapter 17; and references to his relation to federal employment policies and practices are in the note at the end of Chapter 19.

CHAPTER 15

HIRING AND FIRING

No one is in a better position to exert an effective influence on the character and quality of administration than the officials who head the various administrative establishments. In the case of many departments and agencies all of the authority of the organization is legally vested in the head. Where this is not so, the close association of the top official with other officials who share the authority of the organization gives the former ample opportunity to make his wishes known and a substantial amount of power to make his wishes effective.

The selection of the individuals who shall head the various administrative departments and agencies is therefore one of our most dependable devices for making sure that the great force of subordinate officials and employees will give us the kind of government we want. If our highest administrative officials are fully informed of and in sympathy with the objectives and the policies of the group or party that has been charged with running the government, we have good reason to expect that the administrative force as a whole will respond to the top political direction. This assurance is at its maximum, of course, if the top administrative officials are themselves political leaders who share in the formulation of the most important policies of the government of the day.

It is of greatest importance, therefore, that we find a way of selecting these high officials which will guarantee that one of two situations will obtain—either the highest administrative officials must be a part of the political leadership that has been chosen by the people and can be turned out of office by the people, or they must recognize an obligation and display an eagerness to respond promptly and fully to the wishes of those individuals who constitute the elected political leadership. The American people are fully cognizant of the soundness of this principle and have been for a long time. This is what our forefathers had in mind when they formulated the proposition, "When annual elections end, tyranny begins." This is what Andrew Jackson and his associates had in mind when they stood fast for short terms of office and rotation of officeholders. They were seeking assurances that the individuals in places of power would be in sympathy with the current wishes of the people.

One way of providing for this connection between political leadership and administrative leadership is to let the people choose the top administrative officials at the polls. This does not work to our complete satisfaction in local affairs; it would undoubtedly prove far less satisfactory if we tried to elect the principal administrative officials of the national government. When officials are chosen in a nationwide election, the most that the people can do is to make a choice between lists of candidates that have been submitted to them for approval or rejection. Whoever prepares the slates of nominees will inevitably have enormous influence on the final determination as to who will get into office. The voters when they go to the polls can only make their choice within limits imposed upon them by those persons who prepared the slates of nominees.

While the nominating process has been subjected to frequent and severe adverse criticism, I think we may conclude that it has not been a serious limitation on the popular choice of a chief executive for the nation. The office of President is so important in the public mind that the members of the national conventions are under a strong compulsion to nominate candidates for President who have already developed great public followings. But the questionable character of some of our nominations for Vice President indicates on what a precarious base we stand when we try to apply popular selection to an office that does not command the highest public interest. There is every reason to believe that the nominating arrangements which we have tried out to date would be even less likely to provide the voter with satisfactory alternatives for his election-day choice if extended to officials of less importance in the public mind than those of President and Vice President.

A further difficulty would also trip us up if we attempted popular election of the principal officials in the administrative branch. It is not enough that our high administrative officials, as individuals, be acceptable to the people. It is essential that they stand on common ground in respect to the things that the government is to do. The various administrative departments and agencies must work toward certain common objectives. The effort of one department to accomplish an important purpose, say to encourage production of certain farm products, must not be allowed to impair or nullify the effort of another department to accomplish an equally important purpose, such as the curbing of inflation.

I do not see how we could devise a nominating process that would pick out from the various parts of the nation a group of men who, if elected to office, would prove to be a working team in running the government. If we could occasionally accomplish this for the party that is already in power, we would fail miserably for the leading party that is out of power and for the various parties of lesser strength. We have trouble enough selecting slates of candidates that will work together in harmony when they get into office in our cities and other local governments where the political leaders live close enough together to know one another personally.

If we are to fill our top administrative offices with men who will pull together and give us the kind of government to which the victorious party is pledged, we must permit those men to be selected by the principal leader or a nuclear group of leaders of that party. In our system of government the man who has been elected President is the man to whom we look for the discharge of this responsibility. To what extent the President should act on the basis of his personal judgment and to what extent depend on the judgment of others is a debatable question and one that will be resolved differently by different Presidents. Under the constitutional provisions that have been in force for more than a century and a half, he shares the formal act of appointment with the Senate. How this works out in practice, and the desirability of continuing this arrangement, was given consideration in Chapter 10.

We have not developed a consistent policy concerning how far down the line among the important offices of a department or agency we should carry this process of political appointment. Where the top official possesses the entire legal authority of the organization, it may be argued that only he need be selected with consideration for loyalty to the policies of the party in power. If subordinate officials do not respond to the instructions of the head of the organization, he can fire them and replace them with others who will carry out the instructions that are given them. I do not think that, in practice, government can be made to work satisfactorily in that way. The business of carrying on government is not accomplished, ordinarily, by giving orders and firing men who do not respond to them. The head of a great department of government cannot find the time to tell the principal officials under him everything or anyway near everything that he wants them to do and to check up to see whether they do those things. Indeed, he will usually not know enough about the activities of his organization to give such instructions; he is as dependent on the advice they give him as his subordinates are on the instructions that he gives to them. The head of the administrative establishment must be able to proceed on faith that lesser officials know his mind and will respond to it.

The things that the highest official can do to make sure that his principal subordinates will know his mind are discussed at some length in Chapter 22. It is sufficient to say here that the head of the administrative establishment will have his greatest assurance that his principal subordinates will devote themselves loyally to the objectives of the government of the day if those subordinates are themselves a part of the political leadership that has taken on the job of running the government. A wide distribution throughout the public service of men who, by their political activity to date, have proven their loyalty to the party that is in charge of the government is the best assurance that the various sectors of the government will proceed in accordance with the policies of the leadership at the top.

The Hoover Commission, as pointed out earlier (pages 190–191), would restrict appointment by the President and Senate to the head of the administrative establishment and the few officials of general authority immediately under the head (Under Secretary and Assistant Secretaries); other officials would be appointed by the head of the establishment. The Hoover Commission offered no comment on the desirability and undesirability of considering political prominence and political loyalty when the head of the establishment makes his selection of men for the most important positions (including chiefs of bureaus) which he can fill on his own authority. The literature produced by the academic students of government is overwhelmingly in support of the proposition that the job of bureau chief should virtually always go to a man who has worked his way up from a long way down in the administrative organization, and that political convictions and evidence of loyalty to the party in power should not be a consideration in selecting among competitors for these positions of great authority and influence. My own supposition is that the nation would gain rather than lose if many of these positions were filled with men having a high loyalty to the party that is charged with running the government.

The recommendation of the Hoover Commission that the President appoint with Senate confirmation the officials with general authority at the top of the various departments and agencies (head, Under Secretary, and Assistant Secretaries) seems to me to be entirely sound. I think it may be desirable also for the President to have a good deal to say about the selection of men for some of the positions below that level. The officials who effectively determine what the government is going to do and how it is going to do what it does should be more than a force of men who help plan and direct the undertakings of the government; they should be also a connecting link between the highest political leaders in the capital and the leaders of the party throughout the nation who are not employed in the government. It is not enough that the men who go into secondary administrative posts be devoted to the welfare of the party and the success of its program; some of them must contribute to the government of the day not only their own loyalty but the confidence and loyalty of different sectors of the population. In many instances the primary reason for picking a man for a post may well be to bring to the support of the party in power a body of voters who have hitherto counted themselves a part of the opposing party.

The President cannot delegate completely to others the selection of such a political-administrative group. Neither can he select it all by himself. He does not know enough people as individuals, and he does not know enough about the people in mass. The choice of political leaders for the second level of administrative posts, like the choice of those above them, is a task for group judgment.

In this group judgment, the heads of the various departments and agencies must play a major role. Ordinarily the head of the administrative establishment has a greater concern than anyone else that wise choices be made for the positions in his agency. In every instance he wants to be sure that his subordinate officials will be loyal to him personally and sympathetic with the policies he stands for. And if the department or agency head is also a pillar of the party in power, devoted to its continuing success, he will be a trustworthy adviser as to the political advantage that would accrue from the appointment of any of the various men who are under consideration.

What has been said down to this point is based on the presumption that we want the highest places in the administrative branch, like the White House and the majority of seats in the two houses of Congress, to be occupied by men who have established themselves as leaders of a political party. From this presumption I would personally withdraw one important group of administrative officials—the members of those commissions and the chiefs of those bureaus that are predominantly concerned with the administration of governmental activities in respect to which we want political considerations held to a minimum or excluded altogether. I argued in the preceding chapter that the President, even though he be the choice of the people by an overwhelming vote, ought to be limited in his influence over the selection, placement, and retention of men and women in the lower levels of the government service. This is to say that there are some standards for administration which we incorporate in law and which we want the President to respect like everybody else, unless he has sufficient influence (and goes to the trouble of exerting that influence sufficiently) to get the law changed. There are a great many areas of governmental activity where we encounter this difficult situation —impartial application of the law is exceedingly important and most difficult to achieve; and the leaders of the party in power may have a strong inclination to have this law administered for the special advantage of the party in power. I think it is quite proper, as I indicate more fully later in this book (especially Chapters 21 and 23), for Congress and President, by enactment of legislation, to remove these activities from easy political interference. This may be done by giving the officials who are charged with administering these activities a special status in the administrative structure; for instance, by creating non-partisan or bi-partisan boards, by limiting the power of removal, and by other devices. In such cases the President and other leaders of the party that is running the government can resort to legislation to remedy the conditions they do not like.

It is necessary to point out that our practice to date has not been in close conformity with the presumptions underlying my reasoning in the past several pages. The men who head the administrative departments and agencies (even those who sit in the President's cabinet) are not always, perhaps not even usually, men who have achieved prominence in the affairs of the party in command of the government. During recent years it has been the practice to fill many of these top administrative posts with men who have not been active in politics but whose position in industry or other sector of American life and affairs is such that their appointment will bring to the support of those in charge of the government parts of the population that otherwise might be in opposition. This is undoubtedly the consequence of the failure of the American people to develop their political institutions as rapidly as they have enlarged governmental authority. Our predominant attitudes toward active participation in politics are still in large part the attitudes of a period when government appeared to be not of great importance in our affairs. Men and women of extraordinary capacity for achievement who are ambitious for places of high prestige generally seek paths to prestige that lie outside the area of active party politics. A large proportion of the population views with suspicion men and women who have become identified as active party leaders, and suppose that capacity to handle affairs of importance is held almost exclusively by men and women who have occupied themselves mainly if not entirely with affairs outside the realm of politics. This is a condition of American life which, we may be sure, will change as the American people come to a full realization that their government has a far greater effect on their livelihood than was formerly the case.

As the situation now stands, a President is confronted by a fact of two-fold implication—the men and women who have proven their attachment to the things which the party in power is pledged to do (as the President understands its pledges) may not have proven their capacity to direct the extensive and complicated affairs of great administrative departments; and substantial sectors of the population that have, by their votes, given the leaders of the party a charge to run the government may yet not have confidence in the ability of those leaders to run the government. The consequence of this unhappy situation is that most if not all Presidents feel obliged to put in many of the highest administrative positions (including cabinet positions) individuals who neither have strong convictions as to what the people want their government to do nor feel an obligation to find out what other high officials and political leaders think the people want their government to do.

The President may put at the head of an administrative establishment a man who has demonstrated neither party loyalty nor party leadership, but at the same time be unwilling to have the second-level positions in that department filled by the same kind of men. This will be especially true where the President, for the purpose of achieving some measure of coalition government, puts a person of the opposite party at the head of an important administrative establishment. In any such case the President may insist that men of his own choice go into second-level positions (including positions of bureau chief) which he would ordinarily permit the head of the organization to fill according to his own judgment. I do not see why this should be considered either an injustice to the head of the administrative establishment or an infringement of any known principles of sound administrative relationships. The part that the head of the establishment plays in the selection of his principal subordinates, and whether he has anything to say about it at all, will presumably be determined in the original understanding that brought him into the government. If the man under consideration for the top position insists that he must be allowed to staff his organization on his own terms, the President can decide whether he wants him at that price; if the President insists that he must fill the subordinate positions with men of his own choice, the prospective department head can make up his mind whether he is willing to take the place on those terms.

There will be a further limitation on the freedom of top administrative officials to select their principal subordinates, even where these officials are influential members of the President's party and enjoy the highest confidence of the President. The balancing of interests among sections of the nation and sectors of the party may require that some of the secondary posts be filled by certain men who are not looked upon with favor by any of the top officials to whose agency they might be assigned. This also seems to me not to be a serious problem. If the President has filled a number of his highest positions with men who are devoted to the success of the President's program and are wise in the ways of politics as we play it, one or more of those men will acknowledge the necessities of the situation and welcome the forlorn adventurers into the fold.

The discussion so far has been concerned with the considerations that enter into the selection of men for important administrative positions. The question of who shall perform the act of appointment is of much less significance. This is a matter which Congress and the President determine by the enactment of legislation, subject to a minor restriction in the Constitution. Justices of the Supreme Court and the principal officials who represent us abroad ("ambassadors, other public ministers and consuls") must be appointed by the President with the advice and consent of the Senate; "but the Congress may by law vest the appointment of such inferior officers, as they think proper, in the President alone, in the courts of law [in the case of officers of the judicial branch presumably], or in the heads of departments." The courts have not as yet made any authoritative statement as to what may be treated as an inferior office. It is commonly said that any office is inferior if the controlling statute provides that it shall be filled by some method other than Presidential nomination and Senate confirmation. To this general statement there probably should be added one limitation—if the office in question is the principal one in an establishment which the judges consider to be a "department" within the meaning of the language of the Constitution quoted above, they are not unlikely to rule that the Constitution requires that the office be filled by Presidential nomination and Senate confirmation.

I see little reason for giving the President authority to appoint subordinate officials within an administrative department or

agency whose responsibilities are not thought to be of such an order that the names of persons who are considered for appointment
should go to the Senate for confirmation. If the position is not of
sufficient importance that a majority of the Senators should agree
as to who shall fill it, then it seems to me that the appointment
should be executed by the head of the administrative establishment
in which the position is located. If, for any reasons sufficient to
them, other political leaders feel obliged to interpose in the filling
of an inferior office, they can make their representations to the
head of the department or agency concerned. If he will not yield
to their recommendations, they can call upon the President to in-
tercede. If the department head or agency is still not disposed to
capitulate, the principals to the disagreement can fight it out as
any other battle is fought out among the political leaders at the
top of the government. It is better, it seems to me, that the President urge occasional appointments to inferior offices upon the
heads of departments and agencies than that those officials lay all
their recommendations before the President for official appointment. There is far more likelihood that the President will misunderstand the wishes of the heads of administrative establishments, or will be misled by others as to what those officials desire,
than that those officials will misunderstand the wishes of the President. This appears to be the view which Congress has generally
taken of the matter; for a task force of the Hoover Commission
reported that of 73 bureaus concerning which it inquired, 41 were
headed by men appointed by the head of the department or
agency, 29 by men appointed by the President with the consent
of the Senate, and only 3 by men who were appointed by the
President alone.[1]

The Constitution is completely silent concerning the removal of
administrative officials from office, save in those circumstances
where removal by process of impeachment is proper. The silence

[1] *Departmental Management in Federal Administration; A Report with
Recommendations Prepared for the Commission on Organization of the
Executive Branch of the Government* (Government Printing Office, 1949),
pp. 9, 31–32.

of the Constitution on this point, plus the fact that men who are removed from office have more ground to support a grievance than men who fail to win appointment, has led to a great deal more litigation concerning authority to remove than has arisen in connection with authority to appoint. The absence of guidance from the framers of the Constitution has been a standing invitation for the judges of federal courts to create constitutional doctrine on the subject. This they have attempted to do on several occasions but with results that seem to me, on the whole, to create and compound confusion rather than to clarify understanding. About all that is established with sufficient clearness to preclude difference of opinion is that legislation may impose greater limitations on the authority of the President to remove some officers (or have them removed) than it may impose on his authority to remove others (or have them removed). The nature of the rulings and reasoning of Supreme Court and lower federal judges with respect to the President's authority in respect to removal has been so fully discussed by men who make exegesis of the Constitution their principal business that no more need be said here than what is necessary to indicate the general effect of the constitutional interpretation on the capacity of the President to give effective direction and control to administration.

The present understanding as to what the Constitution requires, permits, and forbids in respect to the authority of the President to effect the removal of administrative officials from office is derived mainly from two cases which came before the Supreme Court within the past twenty-five years—*Myers v. United States* (272 U.S. 52), and *Humphrey's Executor v. United States* (295 U.S. 602), decided in 1926 and 1935. The first case required a decision as to whether the Postmaster General, acting on instructions from the President, could remove from office a first-class postmaster (in Portland, Oregon) in view of the fact that a statute stated that such a postmaster should hold his office "for four years unless sooner removed or suspended according to law," and that such a postmaster "shall be appointed and may be removed by the

President by and with the advice and consent of the Senate." In this case the postmaster (Myers) had not completed a four-year term of office; he was ordered to vacate the office by the Postmaster General and not by a document signed by the President; and the Senate did not render advice or give consent to the order of removal. The Supreme Court, some justices dissenting, held that the removal was valid and the office was vacated.

Four different opinions were written and approved by one or more of the nine justices who sat in the Myers case and shared in its decision. Collectively, the members of the court found many different meanings in the Constitution which they applied to the question before them. The decision and opinions of the justices have since been the subject of highly critical examination and extensive commentary by a great number of students of constitutional law and administrative practice. These critics and commentators have found in the Constitution meanings which the justices did not find, or if they found them, did not point out; they have read out of the Constitution meanings which one or more of the justices claimed to have found in it; and they have no doubt read into the opinions of the justices meanings which the justices themselves did not recognize that they had fathered. In view of this competition among meanings, I think it is best if we attribute to the decision and the reasoning in the Myers case only what the justices of the Supreme Court (some of whom participated in the Myers case) later attributed to it in the Humphrey case.

The Humphrey case required a decision as to whether the President had legally removed Humphrey from his position as a member of the Federal Trade Commission. The controlling statute (the Federal Trade Commission Act) stated that the seven members of the Federal Trade Commission should be appointed by the President with the advice and consent of the Senate for a term of seven years, that not more than three should be members of the same political party, and that "Any commissioner may be removed by the President for inefficiency, neglect of duty, or malfeasance in office." President Franklin D. Roosevelt twice asked

Humphrey to resign his office; and when Humphrey finally announced his refusal to do so, the President wrote him, ". . . you are hereby removed from the office of Commissioner of the Federal Trade Commission." There was nothing in the removal order which made any reference to the grounds for removal that were specified in the statute; and the language of the President's two earlier letters asking for resignation made it clear enough that the considerations which persuaded him that Humphrey ought to vacate his office were not of a character which lawyers understand to be implied by any of the three terms specified in the statute. The Supreme Court ruled that the restrictions on the removal of the members of the Federal Trade Commission which were stated in the Federal Trade Commission Act were not forbidden by the Constitution, and therefore that the President was required to respect those restrictions in his efforts to remove members of that Commission.

The opinion by which the Supreme Court supported its decision in the Humphrey case makes it clear that the members of the court did not intend to reverse the decision in the Myers case. Rather they sought to narrow the implications of the decision and principal opinion in the Myers case and to point out differences between the facts in the two situations which would justify holding the removal of the postmaster to have been accomplished in a proper manner, and the removal of the Federal Trade Commissioner to have been accomplished in an improper manner. The differences in the two situations which the court found controlling were differences in the character of the two offices. The justice who wrote the principal opinion in the Humphrey case summarized the principal part of his remarks in the following statement: "The result of what we now have said is this: Whether the power of the President to remove an officer shall prevail over the authority of Congress to condition the power by fixing a definite term and precluding a removal except for cause will depend upon the character of the office; the Myers decision, affirming the power of the President alone to make the removal, is confined to purely executive officers. And as to officers of the kind here under consideration [a member of the Federal Trade Commission], we hold that no removal can be made during the prescribed term for which the officer is appointed, except for one or more of the causes named in the applicable statute."

A postmaster, it seems, at least one who is in charge of a first-class post office, is a "purely executive officer"; a member of the Federal Trade Commission is something different. A postmaster, said the justice elsewhere in his opinion, is "restricted to the performance of executive functions"; he is "merely one of the units in the executive department." The Federal Trade Commission, on the other hand, "is an administrative body created by Congress to carry into effect legislative policies embodied in the statute, in accordance with the legislative standard therein prescribed, and to perform other specified duties as a legislative or as a judicial aid. Such a body cannot in any proper sense be characterized as an arm or an eye of the executive. Its duties are performed without executive leave and, in the contemplation of the statute, must be free from executive control."

As to officers who, like a first-class postmaster, are "purely executive officers," are "restricted to the performance of executive functions," and are merely "units in the executive department," the President's power of removal is "exclusive and illimitable" and "unrestrictable," if I correctly understand the Humphrey opinion. But in the case of a member of the Federal Trade Commission, the opinion expressly stated, "illimitable power of removal is not possessed by the President."

What are the facts about an official in charge of a first-class post office which bring that official under the exclusive, illimitable, and unrestrictable power of the President to remove? Is the controlling factor one or all or a combination of these—the kind of office which he occupies, his place in the structure of the administrative branch, the nature of the affairs over which he has authority, the nature of his authority over those affairs? Is the President's power to remove the postmaster complete because the postmaster is a single official and not a board or commission? Or because he is under the Postmaster General and the Postmaster General sits in the cabinet? Or because the collection and distribution of mail and the other things that are done in a post office bear some special relation to the authority which the Constitution vests in the President? Or because, in the discharge of his duties, the postmaster has no opportunity to do anything which would cause great injury to American citizens? If the Federal Trade Commission were replaced by a single official having the same affairs to regulate and the same authority in respect to those affairs, would the President's removal power become complete? Would the President acquire complete authority to remove the Commissioners if a statute moved the Federal Trade Commission lock, stock, and barrel into the Department of Commerce or the Department of Justice? Or can Congress continue the limitations on the President's power to remove, regardless of change in the type of agency or its location in the general structure of the administrative branch, so long as the agency continues to have the same kind of functions and authority that the Federal Trade Commission had at the time Roosevelt removed Humphrey?

It is frequently said that the Federal Trade Commission carries on quasi-legislative and quasi-judicial functions and the postmaster does not, and that this is the difference between the two offices which determines whether or not legislation can restrict the authority of the President to remove. This is much too simple an explanation. The Postmaster General has authority over the welfare of individuals (e.g., through his power to exclude certain things from the mails) which we expect him to exercise by making rules and regulations (quasi-legislative) and by hearing evidence and argument and judiciously applying the law (quasi-judicial); I am informed that a first-class postmaster also has power of the same character. It may be said that the authority of the Postmaster General and the postmasters under him is only to deny people a right to make use of a service which the federal government provides, whereas the Federal Trade Commission limits the ability of people to use their own property. But there are, if not in the Post Office Department, in practically every other department and agency of the government (including the Cabinet departments) officials and employees who are making rules and regulations and sitting like courts to determine what men and women can do with their own property, their own time, and their own energy.

What may we suppose to be the status of these officers so far as the removal power is concerned? In the Department of Commerce is a Patent Office under a Commissioner of Patents who is appointed by the President with the advice and consent of the Senate. The Patent Office (legally the Commissioner of Patents) issues patents "under the direction of the Secretary of Commerce" and prescribes rules and regulations relating to patents "subject to the approval of the Secretary of Commerce." Under present legislation the Secretary of Commerce has no authority to review the decisions of the Commissioner of Patents and modify them or set them aside; if any party to a patent case wants to appeal from the Commissioner of Patents, he must carry his case to the Court of Patent Appeals. Can Congress and President, by the enactment of legislation, limit the authority of the President to remove the Commissioner of Patents, for instance by specifying that the Commissioner can only be removed for "inefficiency, neglect of duty, or malfeasance in office?" Or does the fact that the Patent Office is in one of the great executive departments, headed by a Cabinet officer who is a member of the President's official family, create an implication that the Constitution will allow no restraint on the power of the President to get rid of the Commissioner of Patents?

The decisions and opinions of the Supreme Court justices in the Myers and Humphrey cases do not provide us with a body of understandings as to how far the courts will allow the legislative body to go in restricting the authority of the President to remove (or cause to be removed) administrative officials; they only establish two bench marks from which the charting will still go forward. The uncertain state of our fundamental law on this subject is but one of a multitude of illustrations which prove the point that it takes a nation a long time to arrive at firm understandings as to how authority ought to be distributed among officials at the top of its government.

The job of the Supreme Court, so far as the removal of administrative officers is concerned, is only to decide (by reading meaning into the Constitution) what authority is reserved to the President, and therefore in what manner and to what extent his authority can be restricted by legislation. It is the job of Congress and President who share the task of enacting legislation to decide whether any restrictions (within the limits set for them by the Constitution) shall be imposed, and if so what the nature of the restrictions ought to be. The determination of whether any restrictions ought to be put on the President's removal power, and if so what they ought to be, calls for an examination and weighing of the experience of the past (especially the not-long-past and the right-up-to-now), speculation concerning the probable events of the future, and the relating of the two. Legislative action, in other words, must follow an excursion into political theory relevant to this matter and represent the acceptance of that theory as a basis of action. The development of the theory which will supply a basis for legislation must be a joint enterprise of men of practical affairs and academic students of government. The knowledge which is requisite for the development of useful and usable theory is possessed mainly by the President (at least after he has struggled for a while with his office), Congressmen, and men and women who have held important positions in the administrative branch. Some one must examine the bits of knowledge which these people contribute, select and discard, weigh the items that are retained as relevant and important and label each according to its relative importance, assemble them into a pattern, and glue the whole thing together with speculation.

There are many men and women in the public service (President, Congressmen, administrative officials) who have the capacity for constructing the political theory that we need to support decisions relating to the removal power of the President. They are not likely to do so, however; not many of them are interested in doing the job thoroughly, and their other preoccupations prevent their doing it if they are interested. The job is not likely to be done, therefore, unless the academic students of government, the political scientists, take it on.

To date, the political scientists have not made much progress on the job. As I see it, the political scientists, like the lawyers, have done a good job of criticizing the rhetoric and the logic of the judicial decisions relating to the power to remove. I do not think, however, that they have made much of an effort to identify and evaluate the probable consequences of the determinations that have been made up to this date in either legislation or court decisions. And they have done even less to identify, evaluate, and put together the considerations that Congress and President should take into account and weigh when the time comes to make the next decision. Surely this is a deficiency that the profession should try to correct at once.

BIBLIOGRAPHIC NOTE

This chapter closed with an adverse criticism of the political scientists. The point of my remarks is that the profession as a whole has not done what the country has a right to expect it to have done before now; my remarks must not be understood to contend that none of the political scientists have done laudable work on this subject. I wish especially to pay high tribute to the contributions of Professors Edward S. Corwin and James Hart, who have searched indefatigably into the evidences of past experience, related what they found to present and anticipated problems, and pointed out significances which only men who have made investigations comparable to theirs could have pointed out. They have been ably supplemented at one point or another by a number of other men. Professor Corwin's outstanding work, referred to in several of these bibliographic notes, is *The President: Office and Powers* (3rd ed., New York, 1948); pages 82 to 136 are especially relevant to the subject of this chapter. He supplies a more extended treatment in *The President's Removal Power Under the Constitution* (New York, 1927), reprinted in *Selected Essays On Constitutional Law* (Chicago, 1938), vol. 4, pp. 1467–1518. Professor Hart's principal work on this subject is *Tenure of Office Under the Constitution* (Baltimore, 1930). Other studies of the President's removal power worthy of noting here are: Charles E. Morganston, *The Appointing and Removal Power of the President of the United States*, Senate Document No. 172, 70th Congress, 2nd session (Government Printing Office, 1929); Howard L. McBain, "Consequences of the President's Unlimited Power of Removal," in *Political Science Quarterly*, vol. 41, pp. 596–603 (1926); and William J. Donovan and R. R. Irvine, "The President's Power to Remove Members of Administrative Agencies," in *Cornell Law Quarterly*, vol. 21, pp. 215–248 (1936), reprinted in *Selected Essays on Constitutional Law*, vol. 4, pp. 1519–1549.

The authority and influence of the President in appointing to office has not been studied in a measure comparable to what has been done on the removal power. The only extensive examination of this subject that I know of is Lucy M. Salmon, *History of the Appointing Power of the President*, printed in American Historical Society, *Papers*, 1, No. 5 (New York, 1886). Discussion of the subject is also scattered throughout Carl R. Fish, *The Civil Service and the Patronage* (New York, 1905).

If one is willing to search the writings of people who have occupied high positions in the federal government, he can pick up items here and there which throw a good deal of light on what particular Presidents did in respect to the selection and removal of their subordinates. Former President William Howard Taft contributed some pleasant gossip but not much else on this subject in his *Our Chief Magistrate and his Powers* (New York, 1916), ch. 3. For other interesting stories, see: *The Intimate Papers of Colonel [Edward M.] House*, vol. 1 (London, 1926), ch. 4; Herbert S. Duffy, *William Howard Taft* (New York, 1930), ch. 23; and Harold L. Ickes, "My Twelve Years with F. D. R.," in *Saturday Evening Post* for June 26, 1948.

CHAPTER 16

REVIEW AND INSTRUCTION

We measure the quality of our Presidents by what they stand for and what they accomplish. Generally speaking, we have been most impressed by those Presidents who left behind a legacy in new and forward-looking legislation. All of our "great" Presidents were able to put significant legislative programs through Congress. But stimulating and giving shape to legislation is not the whole job of the President. Whatever the special interests and aptitudes of the President may be, he must give some direction to the officials who are in charge of the administrative organizations that carry on the work of government.

Presidential direction of administration takes on a multitude of forms. No uniform style of relationship between the President and the heads of administrative departments and agencies exists or can be expected to exist. Many factors contribute to the diversity in relationship, the more significant of which appear to be the following: the character of the man who is President; the character of the administrative official who is involved; the legal status of the administrative establishment and the legal provisions which govern its relation to the President; and the presumptions and expectations that prevail as to what the relationship between the particular administrative official and the President "ought" to be.

Each man who becomes President is different from all other men who become President. Each of these men makes the Presidency a different thing than it has been before. One President tries to find time for the problems of all of his administrative family;

299

another is occupied almost wholly with foreign relations or national defense or something else. A Woodrow Wilson or a Franklin D. Roosevelt may start out with a deep interest in domestic affairs, only to put those matters all but completely out of mind later on because of an absorbing concern to find a solution for the problem of war.

As Presidents differ in their interests and preoccupations, so they also differ in the methods or devices they rely upon for the direction of administration. One President may depend heavily on personal conversations with individual administrative officials. Another may make a greater use of the cabinet for conference and instruction. Still another may build up a White House secretariat or kitchen cabinet to serve as liaison between President and the various administrative officials.

The character of the officials who head the departments and agencies of government will also greatly affect the nature of their relations with the President. One official may be a close personal friend of the President and have ready access to the White House, and therefore enjoy a relationship of confidence that gives him a status utterly different from that of any other person in the administrative branch. If the administrative official is an important political figure in the President's party, his relation to the President may be quite different from that of the official who has been brought in from the opposite party to contribute some of the advantages of coalition government. And of course the relationship will differ according to the ability or competence of the administrative official in the discharge of the obligations of his office. If he is wise in judging public demands and adept in getting response from his organization, the President may be glad to give him a free hand; if on the other hand the high administrative official is always in hot water, the President may find it necessary to bail him out from time to time, give advice to the point of nursing, or find some other way of propping him up or covering him over until he can be more satisfactorily disposed of.

The importance of these personal factors in administration can scarcely be overstated. They give to the administrative record of each President its distinctive color and they determine its success. But they introduce so much diversity, uncertainty, and change into the relations between the President and administrative officials that it becomes impossible to make any extended analysis that would have general application. The records left behind by former Presidents and those who have been in a position to observe the relationships between Presidents and administrative officials make it clear that one cannot generalize as to what kinds of questions any one President laid before his cabinet, or the forms of persuasion and pressure he used to induce the administrative action that he desired, or even his willingness to study and his capacity to comprehend the considerations involved in a serious problem confronting his Administration.

This variance in the interest, capacity, and method of Presidents indicates that the institutional arrangements we develop to help the chief executive discharge his functions must allow plenty of room for novel and unexpected forms of communication. It is probable that the less we do to regulate by law the methods he shall pursue in his administrative relations, the better off the nation will be. Because of that probability the discussion which follows deals almost altogether with the authority which the President possesses, scarcely at all with the methods he may pursue to accomplish his purposes.

The provisions of law that create the administrative organization, give it its objectives and duties, and locate it in the general administrative structure have a substantial influence on the relationships that exist between the top officials in that organization and the President. These statutory provisions must be viewed in connection with our great body of presumptions and expectations as to what the relationship between the President and the officials of any particular administrative establishment ought to be. The statute ordinarily represents an effort by Congress and President to confirm and institutionalize the understandings existing at the time the law was passed. And the actual working relations that are developed within the limits of the law reflect at least in part the suppositions of the President and administrative officials as to what the American people will approve of or tolerate.

These presumptions and expectations and the statutory provisions that relate to them involve at least three relationships between the President and the high administrative officials that report to him: his authority to select them, his authority to dismiss them, and his authority to instruct them in the discharge of their duties.

The first two of these powers were discussed in the preceding chapter and need not be further examined here except to comment on their relation to the third. It has been our custom since the foundation of government under the present Constitution to authorize the President to appoint the heads of all administrative departments and agencies. The principal limitations on this authority have been the requirement of Senatorial confirmation and the provision that membership of commissions charged with regulatory activities must not be held entirely by members of any one political party. The purpose of the latter limitation is clearly to keep the President from forcing his policies and those of his party upon the officials who are charged with developing and giving effect to an important body of public policy.

Statutory limitations on the removal power are designed to protect these same officials from Presidential pressure. As stated previously (pp. 290–296), the effect of judicial decisions to date seems to establish that the President cannot by legislation be limited in his authority to remove those officials that are considered by the courts to be "purely executive officers" or to be "restricted to the performance of executive functions." But statutory provisions may limit his authority to remove members of regulatory commissions, at least by naming grounds for removal and requiring the President to charge the objectionable commissioner with having offended on one of these grounds.

The provisions of legislation relating to the President's authority to appoint and remove is perhaps as inconsistent as the constitutional limitations on such legislation are uncertain. Some of the department heads who sit in the cabinet have fixed terms of office; for others the statutes specify no period of service. Some of the regulatory commissions are required to be bi-partisan; others may be made up entirely of members of one party. For three commissions created after the decision in the Myers case and before the decision in the Humphrey case there is no statutory language concerning the power to remove; for other commissions there are several different formulations concerning the conditions which will justify removal. No doubt a good deal of thought went into the wording of some of these statutory provisions; in other cases the particular language may be the result of accident rather than design. A majority of the members of the Hoover Commission thought that in all cases the members of regulatory commissions should be removable "only for cause"; they gave no explanation of why they thought so but one of the two dissenting members seemed to think they were engaged in a "quest for uniformity for uniformity's sake."[1]

The lack of uniformity which characterizes legislation controlling the authority of the President to appoint and remove is even more marked in the case of legislation which governs his authority to review the official acts of administrative officers and issue instructions to them. Not only is there no evidence of a general policy concerning what his authority should be; there is no consistent relation between legislative provisions of that kind and the statutory limitations on his power to appoint and remove. The unsatisfactory state of legislation on this subject is undoubtedly due to failure on the part of Congressmen and Presidents to develop any consistent theory of what the President's reviewing and instructing authority ought to be. But Congressmen and Presidents are not the only ones who have failed in this respect; the professional students of government have not developed any consistent body of theory on this subject either.

[1] *The Independent Regulatory Commissions; A Report to the Congress by the Commission on Organization of the Executive Branch of the Government, March 1949* (Government Printing Office, 1949), p. 7.

There are great areas of public affairs that we consciously and purposely put almost completely beyond the reach of the chief executive. A great deal of our legislation is in the form of civil and criminal law that we entrust to the judicial branch for enforcement. We want the President to have very little indeed to do with this part of our administration. If he thinks the law itself is unsatisfactory, he may properly seek to get it changed. If he thinks the courts are undermanned and ill-equipped or extravagant and wasting money, he may properly try to correct the situation in his recommendations to Congress for appropriations. If he considers the judiciary ineffective in its procedure, he may recommend to Congress that it revise the law regulating the conduct of its proceedings. If he considers a particular judge to be incompetent or guilty of abusing his authority, the President may discuss with members of the House the propriety of an impeachment proceeding. He may use his power to pardon to redress a wrong committed by the judge in a criminal case. But none of these actions by the chief executive involves an intervention in a judicial proceeding while it is in process. We consider it entirely improper for the President to tell the judge what he should find or how he should rule in the case before him.

In contrast to these situations where we want a judicial proceeding free of interference by the President is a vast range of governmental activity where we expect the President to intervene at any time and tell the official in charge what action he would like to see taken. If the enabling legislation and appropriations providing for a public housing program have not removed such questions from the area of executive discretion, the President may properly tell the housing administrator that he thinks houses should first be provided to meet the needs of veterans, or that more money should be put into multi-family dwellings, or that further exploration of prefabricated structures should be made, or that any of a number of other policies should be pursued. We hand over to our administrative departments and agencies for execution innumerable functions with the intention that they shall be carried out in keeping with the general policies of the party in possession of the government. In respect to all or most of these matters we consider it proper for the President to make his wishes known as frequently and as firmly as he chooses.

But we also provide for a wide range of governmental activity which we are not willing to entrust to the courts for execution and which we are not willing to put under the domination of the President either. The regulation of radio broadcasting affords a good example.

The authority given the Federal Communications Commission ranges from the power to establish general policies to the power to make decisions of highly limited application. At the one extreme is the power of the FCC to determine how wide a band of radio frequencies shall be available for broadcast activities and where, within the great range of radio frequencies, broadcast services shall be placed. The competition for command of radio waves is intense and persistent. If the broadcast services (standard or AM broadcasting, FM broadcasting, television broadcasting, etc.) are given more frequencies, there will be fewer for ships at sea, for aviation, for police and fire departments, for connection between moving trains and the land-bound telephone system of the nation, and for any of a thousand other uses already established or as yet unthought of.

Surely it would be proper for Congress to weigh the interests of the American people in one type of radio service as against all others and establish by law a basic allocation of the radio spectrum among types of service. It would be a tough job. But it is also a tough job to allocate between sectors of the American population and the American economy the burden of financing the national government; it is a tough job to arbitrate the conflicting interests of the American people in any of a thousand disputed fields of public policy that are the subject of legislation. Congress exists to make the decisions that are too tough to be made by anyone except a general assembly representing the diverse interests of the nation.

But Congress has not as yet seen fit to take on its own shoulders the painful and distressing job of allocation of the radio spectrum. It wanted the job done by an administrative agency and it vested it in a seven-man Commission. It might have instructed the Commission to prepare a proposed allocation plan and submit it to Congress for approval, modification, or rejection. Or it might have required that the proposal be laid before the President for review. It did neither. It made the judgment of the Commission final save for the reviewing authority of the courts and the possibility of subsequent legislative action to which all administrative bodies are subject.

A later stage in making radio frequencies available for users is the assignment of frequencies within a service. The general allocation plan advises all television broadcasters of the band of frequencies available for their service. But specific frequencies (channels) must be assigned to specific communities. Television stations on Manhattan Island cannot transmit on identical channels with stations in Newark, Hoboken, Jersey City, or anywhere else within the carrying power of the Manhattan stations. The development of a pattern that relates frequency channels to spots on the globe where television transmitters may be located calls for calculations that only radio technicians can make. But the decision as to how many of the channels available for the entire metropolitan area shall go to Manhattan Island and how many to the city of Newark is a question on which the people of the metropolitan area have opinions. If the people are divided in their opinions and feel strongly, politicians get interested in the subject. And if politicians are interested, the matter is likely to come to the attention of Congressmen and other individuals who are close to the President. Is it proper for them to intervene? Would we be satisfied with an arrangement which enabled Congress to review the assignment of frequencies for television among the various municipalities (or some other kind of regional subdivisions) within the metropolitan area extending out from Manhattan Island? Would we count it proper for the President to interpose and order a different assignment than the one worked out by the administrative agency? Or is this the kind of issue that we want settled by some objective procedure that would be disturbed or upset if Congressmen or President injected their preferences into the determinations?

While the regulatory body is engaged in allocation and assignment of frequencies, it is also occupied with a third stage in the licensing of radio stations—laying down the rules to govern the right of individuals to transmit over a specific channel from a specific location. A satisfactory choice among the applicants must rest on many previous determinations of policy. Will a corporation be permitted to operate a radio station? Will a license be given to an individual who is not a citizen of the United States? Must the station be owned and operated by local people or may outsiders invade the city? May one individual or corporation own more than one station? And if so may one individual, corporation, or group get a monopoly on all the broadcast facilities of the community?

These and many others like them are questions that Congress and President might well incorporate into the basic law relating to radio, and some of them are clearly answered by the language of the statutes now in effect. But frequently the question is not foreseen until it arises in a specific instance, the statute is silent on the point, and the case cannot be decided until the question of policy is resolved. In such a situation, are we willing to have the President intervene? Or do we want the regulatory agency to be final on all points not settled by the law, until such time as further legislation may be enacted?

Finally, of course, we encounter the situation where there is no significant issue of policy before the regulatory body. There is only one applicant, and the sole question at issue is a combination of fact and law—is he a citizen of the United States? Or there are a number of applicants who have met every standard that has been established, and a choice between them must be based on a prediction—which one can be depended upon to give the service that will be most acceptable to the community? Is it proper for the President to inject his judgment or his preference into either of these cases? Or do we want these decisions made by a tribunal that is as independent of the political branches as a court?

We have not as yet, in enacting legislation to govern administration, broken the administrative job and the administrative process down in this way and indicated the areas in which the President may and in which he may not intervene. If we create a separate agency to regulate a particular sector of business or industry, we are likely to vest the regulatory authority in a commission, make it bi-partisan, and limit the President's power to remove the commissioners. In that case the commissioners have a basis for contending that they are not accountable to the President and they may resist his effort to influence their action on any question from the broadest formulation of policy (like allocating frequencies to radio services) to the narrowest question of law and fact (like deciding whether the applicant is a citizen of the United States). A good many Congressmen (including many who are prominent in the President's party) can be counted on to support the commissioners in their effort to maintain independence from presidential control. And there is a good chance that the commissioners and Congressmen who offer such resistance will be accorded widespread public approval.

But we do not always vest regulatory authority in a commission. A great deal of federal control over the affairs of the American people is exercised by administrative organizations that are headed by single officers; and perhaps most of this authority is vested in departments that are headed by members of the cabinet. Regardless of where the authority is placed, it frequently involves a range of determinations as comprehensive and as significant as those described above as arising in the regulation of radio broadcasting. The determinations that must be made by the Secretary of Agriculture in fixing and enforcing standards of quality and condition of grain are representative if not typical. He must determine whether, in view of the objectives of the act, it is desirable to extend control to a grain not specified in the statute (broomcorn, buckwheat, millet, etc.); he must fashion standards that will meet the special needs indicated by the usages and necessities of trade in each of the several grains; and he must investigate and make findings in specific instances where there is reason to suspect that the standards which he has promulgated are being violated in interstate or foreign commerce. This is a range of authority that extends from broad declarations of policy eminently suitable for legislative determination to findings of fact and law that differ in no essential from those we customarily entrust to judicial tribunals.

We have engaged in a great deal of loose talk about the "responsibility" of cabinet officers and other top administrative officials to the President, implying when we do not say explicitly that the President may properly tell them what they should do in respect to any part of the activities under their direction. Just as there is a popular expectation that the President will keep his hands off the regulatory commissions altogether, so also there is an opposite popular expectation that he will direct the work of the great executive departments in any way that he pleases. And there is a great deal of support for each of these attitudes in the writings of political scientists.

Neither of these attitudes seems to me to show much appreciation of the facts of administration or the ideals of democratic government. Surely we want the chief executive of the nation to give some direction to the commissions that are charged with making and enforcing regulatory policy. And just as surely we want all political influence removed from certain aspects of the work of the departments that are headed by cabinet members.

If the President is convinced that food is not moving to the seaports of the nation in accordance with the objectives and goals of the European Recovery Plan proposed by him and approved by Congress, should he not feel free to call into conference every arm of the government that possesses authority to advance or hinder that movement? If regulations issued by the Interstate

Commerce Commission affect the availability of freight cars for food shipments, may the President not call the members of the Interstate Commerce Commission into the conference, just as he calls in the Secretary of Agriculture whose grain standards also affect the movement of food? If there is general agreement that the rules of the Commission and the standards of the Secretary are equally responsible for the poor success of the recovery plan, should the President not be as free to say to the one as to the other, "In view of the weight of the evidence and the consensus of opinion, it is clear to me that you ought to restudy your regulations at once with a view to action which will remove the obstacles that you are now imposing to the success of the recovery plan"?

Comparable illustrations can be drawn from almost any area in which cabinet departments and regulatory commissions share authority over the affairs of individuals. If the President is of the opinion that the failure of the FCC to allocate radio frequencies is seriously holding up the effort of the nation to convert its industry from the objectives of war to the objectives of peace, it seems to me he should be as free to urge FCC to action as he is to demand action of the Rural Electrification Administration in the Department of Agriculture. I see no good reason why he should be less free to implore the Federal Reserve Board to use its power over credit in a move against inflation than he is to urge the Secretary of Interior to be on guard against inflationary consequences of his program of land reclamation.

If it be agreed that the President should be in a position to influence the policies and the practices of both regulatory commissions and great executive departments, there still remains the question of how complete and how compelling that influence should be. I think few people will dissent from the proposition that the Interstate Commerce Commission should be drawn into the conference on food shipments, that the FCC should sit in the discussions of conversion of the economy from peace to war, and that the Federal Reserve Board should have a seat at the table when a coordinated drive against inflation is being planned. The members of the three commissions would get their feelings hurt if they were left out. But what is the extent of their obligation to reflect in their official acts the agreements reached at the conference? Putting it conversely, what authority ought the President have to induce the regulatory commission to make its official action accord with the common purposes which he announces for the guidance of all agencies of the government?

As stated above, the statutes setting up the various agencies of the government make no consistent provision for the exercise of direction and control by the President. There is a popular assumption, undoubtedly supported by the general opinion of many Congressmen, that regulatory commissions have no obligation to respond to the suggestions of the President unless there is a specific statutory provision requiring them to do so. This point of view was stated clearly and bluntly by William Hard, a newspaper correspondent with many years of experience in Washington:

We say that Calvin Coolidge should have checked the increase in brokers' loans. We say that he should have checked all the credit inflation of the New Era. No, he should *not* have. It was his duty, certainly, to fill vacancies in the Federal Reserve Board. But it was the duty of the Federal Reserve Board to check credit inflation. And it was and is and always will be improper and vicious, under our form of government, for a President to attempt to sway the decisions of the Federal Reserve Board, which is a body of technicians exercising quasi-judicial functions which should be unspotted by political dictations.

Ditto with regard to the Interstate Commerce Commission. Ditto with regard to the Federal Trade Commission. Ditto with regard to the Federal Communications Commission. Ditto with regard to every other regulatory body of prime importance in Washington. They were all established by the Congress to be independent bodies administering not the wills of Presidents but the laws of the people, and administering them in quasi-judicial fashion. To expect the President to tell those bodies what to do is absolutely next door to expecting him to tell the Supreme Court what to do. It is an expectation which, if continued, and if played upon by Presidents, can end the Republic.[2]

[2] William Hard, "Overburdened Men in the White House," in *Atlantic Monthly*, pp. 533–539 (May, 1936).

If this is sound doctrine for a commission exercising regulatory power, it is surely sound doctrine for an executive department exercising the same kind of power. The Republic will not come to an end because agencies headed by commissions are told what to do by the President. If White House interference is going to end the Republic, it will be because the interference defeats impartial, objective, and highly informed enforcement of laws that are vital to the welfare of the American people. And the shock to the Republic will be just as great where the administrative tribunal is a division of a cabinet department as where it is a commission with nothing but regulatory work to do. The ideals of due process of law and equal protection of the law are not more or less important to us because one or another type of administrative agency has them at its disposal.

The nature of Mr. Hard's language suggests that he understood the action of regulatory commissions to be confined to decisions of a judicial character. If this were the case, perhaps nearly all of us could subscribe to his doctrine of immunity from Presidential direction. For it is at that point—where the administrative action is admittedly of a judicial nature—that it seems to me the authority of the political branches to intervene in administration should stop. Without straining for a definition of a judicial action let us say that when the task before the official is that of applying established law to particular parties involved in a specific set of circumstances, we want the case to be decided by an objective determination of the facts and an impartial application of the law. Political intervention before or during the case does not help to achieve that standard in administration. The men and women who exercise the authority of government in this kind of situation must be subject to control, but the control should be obtained through as clear a statement of the law as can be had before the case arises and through corrective legislation, judicial review, removal from office, or other effective action after the case has been decided.

But a very high proportion of the decisions of regulatory

agencies, as was indicated in the case of radio broadcasting, consists of formulating policy for future application. This is the kind of determination that the political branches of the government regularly engage in—Congress and President through the enactment of legislation, the President alone through the issuance of executive orders. If Congress and President may establish a regulatory policy by statute, it is surely proper for them to provide instead that the policy shall be formulated by an administrative body subject to review by the political branches. If it is sound political theory to give the President a veto over legislation passed by Congress, would it not be sound political theory to give him a veto over the rules, regulations, and other formulations of policy originating with administrative officials?

We have already made some progress toward a systematic differentiation of the methods to be pursued by administrative officials and employees in making decisions of a judicial character on the one hand and decisions of a legislative character on the other. This is evidenced first of all in the statutory requirement that court-like procedures must be followed in making judicial determinations. We took a long step toward the achievement of this standard in the Administrative Procedure Act of 1946, requiring each administrative agency, whether commission or executive department, to segregate its judicial activities to the extent possible and surround them with safeguards characteristic of a proceeding in court.

But these provisions merely protect actions of a judicial character from improper influence regardless of whether that influence originates inside or outside the agency. They do not go to the question of whether the President should have authority to give the agency advice and instructions in respect to those activities that are not of a judicial character. The President's Committee on Administrative Management, reporting in 1937, thought that all non-judicial activities of the government should be brought under the influence of the President and sought to accomplish that end by recommending that the non-judicial activities of regulatory commissions be taken from them and placed in one or another of twelve great executive departments. Under such an arrangement an organization of officials and employees in one of the executive departments would formulate the rules and regulations and make the other determinations of policy necessary to extend or clarify the language of the statute; and a commission attached to the department would have the sole function of applying in specific cases the statutory and other policy which had been given it to apply.

This proposal, as I see it, was based on two principal presumptions—first, that the policy making and the law applying aspects of a regulatory undertaking can be separated and entrusted for administration to different organizations without defeating the ultimate purposes of the regulatory program; and second, that the President cannot get at the men and women who formulate policy with sufficient force to influence their decisions unless those men and women are in an organization headed by a single officer.

Both these presumptions seem to me to be highly questionable. The feasibility of parceling out to different administrative organizations the different aspects of a regulatory program depends on the nature of the particular regulatory job to be done. In every instance we can make some division. Congress can make some policy which it leaves to the courts for application. Doubtless in every area of regulatory activity it would be feasible to vest some policymaking authority in an executive department and to depend for application of its policy on a separate commission. But the very conditions that make it impossible for Congress to formulate a code of law that will provide an answer for every question that arises in an area of affairs that it wants regulated will make it impossible for an administrative organization to extend that policy to its ultimate end by the formulation of rules and regulations. This is so because it so often happens that there is neither recognition of need for the rule nor understanding of the problem sufficient for the formulation of the rule in advance of the examination of the particular case for adjudication. The case must be decided in the absence of previously stated policy; the policy finally appears as the cumulative effect of a volume of individual determinations. It is probably true to say that this is the ordinary rather than the novel situation. It was in large part in this way that the English people developed the common law that we inherited; it is mainly in this way that the meaning of our own national Constitution has been modified and extended to meet the demands of changing times.

If, contrary to the foregoing argument, it is believed feasible to make a workable differentiation between formation of policy and its application and distribute the two parts to different administrative establishments, it remains to be determined whether the policy determination ought to be given to an organization headed by a single officer. There are many reasons why a regulated industry wants the control to which it must submit to be in the hands of an agency that has no other governmental obligations and which possesses authority to act finally on the problems of the industry. And there are many reasons why it prefers that this body of authority be legally vested in a multi-member commission instead of a single officer. For reasons equally persuasive to them, the sectors of the population that are most strongly and most consistently in opposition to the regulated industry appear also generally to prefer that the regulation be administered by a commission with jurisdiction over a limited range of affairs. These considerations need not be examined here.

It is sufficient here to indicate a belief that the central direction and control over regulatory policy which the President's Committee sought to assure to the President by putting the formation of regulatory policy in organizations headed by single officers and located in cabinet departments can be achieved even though the formation of regulatory policy is vested in commissions and dispersed among many of them. Presidential direction and control can be assured by providing in the law that specific categories of acts of the regulatory agency shall be subject to review and corrective action by the chief executive.

This brings us back to the deficiency in our theory and our practice that was pointed out several paragraphs back in this discussion—that we have not fully analyzed the administrative job, differentiated the components of the administrative process, and indicated the points at which the President may and at which he may not intervene. It seems to me that if we do this we will find that it is possible at the same time to avoid tearing into parts a regulatory job that because of its nature needs to be handled as a whole by one administrative organization; to preserve the advantages of a commission for making the crucial legislative and judicial decisions involved in that regulatory job; and to provide for such direction and control as we think the chief executive should exert in respect to that agency.

We have already laid the foundation for such a solution of the problem. Despite our talk about the "independence" of the regulatory commissions, it is well understood that the President may call the members of these commissions into conference as indicated above (pp. 309–311) and declare his own convictions as to their obligations in view of critical public needs. And there is every reason to believe that the ordinary reaction of the commissions has been and will be to find ways and means of lending their authority to the accomplishment of the common cause as stated by the President. For the ordinary situation the President has sufficient assurance of influence if he has an opportunity to state clearly and firmly what he thinks ought to be done. When things come to such a pass that the President of the United States finds it necessary in general practice to issue orders to men and women who are fully cognizant of the great responsibilities of his office, government will be on the verge of breakdown.

For those instances where it is believed that voluntary response of the administrative organization is not sufficient assurance that the wishes of the President will be respected when we want them respected, we can specify by legislative enactment that the President rather than an administrative official shall sign the document which authenticates the governmental action; or that the administrative official shall only put his decision in effect when the President has indicated his approval; or that the President shall have the authority to modify, suspend, or set aside the acts of the administrative official. We have precedent for this in present legislation. The authority to assign radio frequencies to stations owned and operated by the federal government is withdrawn from FCC and given to the President who acts on the advice of an interdepartmental committee; the rules and regulations of FCC may be suspended or amended by the President in time of war; every order of the Securities and Exchange Commission temporarily suspending trading on a national securities exchange must be laid before the President and be approved by the President before going into effect.

We have shown more inclination to give the President specific legal authority over the actions of administrative organizations that are headed by single officers than over the actions of organizations headed by commissions. If we want the President to have authority to substitute his judgment for that of administrative officials (single officers or commissions) in a wider range of situations, we can give it to him.

It is a basic principle of English and American legal and political theory that an executive or administrative officer has no authority except that which is expressly or by reasonable implication given him in the law. This goes for the President of the United States as well as for lesser officials; the President has only such authority as is vested in him by the Constitution expressly or by implication or delegated to him by statute. Since the Constitution makes the President commander-in-chief of the armed forces, he does not need any statutory authorization to issue orders relating to matters that are clearly of a military nature. It is generally supposed that expressions of the Constitution about his relation to foreign affairs also vest extraordinary power in the President to make authoritative decisions on matters which have an international implication. I think, however, that there is a tendency to overstate his authority in this respect. The Federal Communications Commission has been given authority by statute to assign frequencies to radio stations located on American soil and to determine the power that may be put into their emissions; FCC might authorize so many stations to make emissions of such strength that other nations would find radio communication impossible and begin to talk of war. If there were no statute which located authority to regulate radio transmission in an administrative agency, it might be that the President could successfully assert legal authority to order the emissions stopped; in view of the fact that authority in the matter has been vested by statute in a specified administrative agency and no statement is made that the President may intervene in such a case, I think it likely that the courts would deny the President authority to modify or set aside the decisions of the administrative agency authorizing the objectionable emissions.

The character and extent of the President's authority is subject to less dispute where questions of military command and foreign relations are in no way involved. The statement of the Constitution that "the executive power shall be vested in a President" and that the President "shall take care that the laws be faithfully executed" does not give him authority to issue a patent or fix the standards of quality and condition of grain or determine a dam's location. The authority to do any of those things lies in the official that is authorized by statute to do it. The President cannot issue the order for the duly authorized official or modify or revoke it unless a provision of law (expressly or by fair implication) says he may do so. The fact that the authority is vested in a department headed by a single officer—even one headed by a cabinet officer—does not alter the fact as to where the authority lies, though it may be made a ground for interpreting the President's authority broadly and that of the administrative official narrowly. If Congress wants the act of the administrative official to be issued only with the President's approval attested by the President's signature, it must say so in the statute; and if it wants the President to be able to modify or revoke the action of the administrative official against the will of the latter, it must put that in the statute too. And Congress has put such provisions in a substantial number of statutes.[3]

If, as I have argued, it seems desirable to make this formula generally applicable to the President's role in the direction and control of administration—i.e., specify by law his relation to specific actions or categories of actions—the first step will be to determine for any governmental activity whether it ought to be placed in a great department that carries on many different kinds of activity or ought to be placed in a special agency that is set up to administer this particular kind of activity. If the activity is essentially of a business or industrial character, such as building dams or buying and storing surplus commodities, it will probably be thought best to put it in a department headed by a single officer. If it is a regulatory activity, the decision as to where to place it may well turn on its relation to other activities of the government. If it is but one aspect of a bigger undertaking, requiring for intelligent execution a close association with the other phases of a comprehensive program, it may be wise to put the regulatory function in the executive department that has the associated activities. Thus it may be better for the regulation of grain standards (though mainly quasi-legislative and quasi-judicial in character) to be incorporated into

[3] For a list of such statutes, see Edward S. Corwin, *The President: Office and Powers* (1st ed., New York, 1940), pp. 369–373. Harold L. Ickes tells of his refusal, when Secretary of Interior, to comply with the wishes of the President in respect to the sale of helium in "My Twelve Years with F. D. R.," in *Saturday Evening Post* for June 5, 1948. It will be remembered that President Andrew Jackson was not able to order personally the transfer of federal funds between banks and had to go to considerable trouble to get the order signed by the Secretary of the Treasury. For a good account of this incident, see Carl B. Swisher, *Roger B. Taney* (New York, 1935), chs. 9–12; or M. Grace Madeleine, *Monetary and Banking Theories of Jacksonian Democracy* (Philadelphia, 1943), pp. 56–58. For a number of instances in which the President attempted successfully or unsuccessfully to influence the policies and actions of regulatory commissions, see Robert E. Cushman, *The Independent Regulatory Commissions* (New York, 1941), pp. 685 ff.

the whole program of the Department of Agriculture than to be severed from the general agricultural program of the government and administered by an independent commission. In that case the statute providing for the administration of the activity should contain the safeguards thought necessary to make sure that the objective and impartial application of the law that is desired will not be impaired by an undue amount of political interference. If, on the other hand, Congress and President in enacting the law are impressed with the advantages of enforcement by a separate agency headed by a multi-member commission, they may give the regulatory agency an "independent" status carrying with it a general immunity from political interference but make it subject to Presidential direction and control in specific instances. These matters are discussed further in Chapter 21.

A thoughtful attempt to make the President's relations to the conduct of administration consistent with our beliefs as to what that relationship ought to be will require us to consider carefully the part that Congress should play in the direction and control of administration. Perhaps Congress rather than the President should review the proposed act of the administrative agency and determine whether it may become effective. If drastic changes in the general price level are a source of constant terror, and a coordinated effort of many sectors of the administration is necessary to prevent or regulate such changes, it may well be that the President should be authorized to approve or disapprove the orders of the Federal Reserve Board altering the discount rate on loans. But a decision to give the President this power in no sense forces a conclusion that he instead of Congress should be given authority to review and approve the orders of the Federal Communications Commission allocating radio frequencies among the many uses to which they properly may be put. Some of the considerations that should be taken into account in deciding whether Congress should review proposed administrative action and approve or disapprove them were set forth in an earlier chapter (pp. 173–174).

BIBLIOGRAPHIC NOTE

Professor Edward S. Corwin is by a wide margin our best guide on the law and practice as respects the President's power to review the work of administrative officials and give them instructions. See his *The President: Office and Powers* (3rd. ed., New York, 1948), especially chs. 3 and 4. Professor Corwin does not organize his discussion so as to differentiate sharply between what the President may do on his own order and what he may accomplish by influencing the action of administrative officials. See also Frederick F. Blachly and Miriam E. Oatman, *Federal Regulatory Action and Control* (Washington, 1940), ch. 9; essay by John A. Vieg entitled "The Chief Executive," in *Elements of Public Administration*, edited by Fritz Morstein Marx (New York, 1946), pp. 158–183; and C. Dwight Waldo and William Pincus, "The Statutory Obligations of the President: Executive Necessity and Administrative Burden," in *Public Administration Review*, vol. 6, pp. 339–347.

The way in which the President's personal qualities and interests affect his relations with administrative officials is made vivid in Drew Pearson and Robert S. Allen, "How the President Works," in *Harper's Magazine*, pp. 1–14 (June, 1936). A great deal that is relevant to the subject of this chapter can be drawn from books about various Presidents and from the memoirs and other writings of men and women who have been associated closely with Presidents. Illustrative are Frances Perkins, *The Roosevelt I Knew* (New York, 1946); Robert E. Sherwood, *Roosevelt and Hopkins* (New York, 1948); the series of articles by Harold L. Ickes in the *Saturday Evening Post* beginning with the issue for June 5, 1948; and the circular letter of President Jefferson in which he described the nature of President Washington's relations with heads of administrative departments in *The Writings of Thomas Jefferson*, edited by Andrew A. Lipscomb (Washington, 1905), vol. 10, pp. 289–291.

PART IV

THE CENTRAL STAFF AGENCIES

CHAPTER 17

THE BUREAU OF THE BUDGET

Political direction and control of the federal bureaucracy is accomplished through a complicated set of relationships at the top of the government structure. The people elect a President and the members of two houses of Congress. The President and the Congressmen share the job of directing and controlling the men and women who make up the administrative branch. But they share the job not by dividing it neatly among themselves; they share it in a mixture of arrangements for reaching decisions and issuing instructions.

The decisions and instructions of the elected officials are made effective through a complicated organization for communication up and down and across. The President and Congressmen initially learn about some problems and come to a fuller understanding of most problems of government only if information and suggestions come up to them from the men and women who do the work of government. The President and Congressmen can understand one another and work toward common ends only if there are arrangements which move knowledge and ideas to and fro among them. The nature of the relationships which now exist between Congress and the President, and the prospect of creating a more harmonious relationship between them, are the subject of the final chapter of this study.

The arrangements for communicating the decisions of the political branches to the administrative branch are many in number and diverse in character. The simplest case, perhaps, is that of enactment of a statute. Bureaucrats, like you and I, are presumed to know the law; the enactment of a law (the act of declaring a law to be in effect) is notice to administrative officials and employees that they are to shape their conduct so as to comply with the requirements of the law. But many of the decisions of the political branches (including the provisions of law) are not easily comprehended and are subject to different interpretations. Therefore, we resort to many different devices for clarifying the wishes of President, Congress, and Congressmen and for pursuing instructions throughout the administrative branch in order to make sure that the political decisions are understood. In this way the political decision, which may be formulated as a broad or general statement of policy, is defined (extended in this respect, restricted in that respect) and reduced to instructions which men and women can apply in carrying on the day-to-day work of government.

The President and Congress communicate with the administrative branch mainly through five channels: the heads of the several administrative departments and agencies acting as individuals; the heads of certain great departments who act collectively as a cabinet; a small number of specialized bureaucracies that serve as central organizations for advice, service, and control (commonly called central staff agencies); a number of special assistants to the President; and a number of organizations, most of them small in size, which serve as staff for Congress.

Of these five channels for carrying the decisions and instructions of President and Congress to the officials and employees who do the work of government, the first three are by far the most important. The functionaries that are here titled special assistants to the President no doubt render an indispensable service in bringing information and ideas to the President and in helping him reach decisions. They doubtless communicate many of the decisions of the President to the heads of administrative departments and agencies. I doubt, however, that they play an important role in carrying the wishes of the President to lower levels in the administrative hierarchy. (The Liaison Officer for Personnel Management may be an exception. See pp. 265–266.)

Much the same may be said of the staff that serves Congress. The Legislative Reference Service of the Library of Congress, the Legislative Counsel of the two houses, and other organizations which serve the two chambers separately or jointly, help the Congressmen find out what they want to know and help them convert their knowledge and beliefs into decisions and instructions. The small groups of men and women who serve the various committees of Congress are more likely to be charged with communicating the wishes of the committees and committee members to the administrative branch. Their role, however, is mainly that of conveying messages. I do not understand that they have authority which enables them, through decisions of their own, to make significant additions to the decisions and instructions which they convey. For that reason they are not given further attention in this book.

The heads of the great administrative departments who collectively constitute a cabinet participate in the process of defining and augmenting the decisions and instructions of Congress and the President, but they make their impress upon the administrative branch primarily as individual department heads. As a cabinet they advise the President, help him make decisions, and perhaps occasionally make decisions for him. But the cabinet is not primarily an institution to receive the decisions of the President or President and Congress, further define and enlarge them, and pass them on as instructions which administrative officials and employees are expected to follow in carrying on the work of government. The cabinet is, therefore, given no consideration in this book, except as it figures in the highest councils which produce the political decisions that guide the administrative branch.

We have left for examination two primary channels by which the political branches of the government communicate their decisions to the administrative branch: the heads of the several departments and agencies (acting as individuals rather than as a cabinet);

and the central agencies that deal primarily in advice, service, and control. The relation of the head of the department or agency to political direction and control of administration is discussed in the several chapters which constitute Part V of this book. The examination of the role of the central agencies for advice, service, and control begins in this chapter and continues in the two following.

A number of people have argued that we need in the federal government a general manager whose principal or only business would be the day-to-day direction of the administrative branch. Several have suggested that this is the proper job for the Vice President. They presume that the nominee for President will be able to pick his running mate and therefore will have no cause to view the Vice President as a political rival who cannot be trusted with the enormous power which he would acquire in assuming control of the administrative branch. Others think that the choice of a man for this job should wait until the election is over and that the President should then be permitted to pick a man whom he can fire as well as hire. The Hoover Commission seems not to have considered a general manager necessary, for it made no suggestion that such a position be created. It is even more evident that the President's Committee on Administrative Management thought such a position unnecessary, for its 1937 report made clear that the Committee believed the President would have time and energy to manage the administrative branch himself.

For well over a century neither President nor Congress were provided with a substantial staff of assistants to help them direct and control the administrative departments and agencies that carry on the general work of the government. The Treasury Department from the time of its creation in 1789 exercised a great deal of control over the financial transactions of the other departments and agencies. The Civil Service Commission was established in 1883 to assist the President and to assist and regulate the other administrative departments and agencies in respect to matters of employment. The Budget and Accounting Act of 1921 set up a Bureau of the Budget to help the President prepare his annual plan for the financing of government and the General Accounting Office to assist and regulate the administrative branch in respect to the collection and spending of money. The recommendations of the President's Committee on Administrative Management in 1937 stimulated the enlargement of the staff available to help the President, and the study and recommendations of a joint committee of Congress in 1946 led to the enlargement of the staff available to assist the two houses of Congress and their committees.

This brief list does not include all of the special staff available to help President and Congress make their decisions and see that their decisions are respected, but it does indicate the nature of the principal organizations that have been set up for this purpose. The character of these organizations and their position in the general structure of the federal government are determined in large part by the nature of the relations between Congress and President. The Bureau of the Budget, for instance, is regarded as primarily the servant of the President; the General Accounting Office is regarded as primarily the servant of Congress; and the Civil Service Commission may be said to be the servant of both President and Congress.

We cannot undertake in this book to examine all of the provisions for giving assistance to the President and Congress. There are, however, three central organizations—commonly called central staff agencies but more properly called central agencies for advice, service, and control—which play such an important role in direction and control of administration that they must be considered here. They are: the Bureau of the Budget, the General Accounting Office, and the Civil Service Commission. They give advice to the President, to Congress, and to administrative officials. They render service to the various administrative departments and agencies, for they carry on a number of activities that are thought better administered in one place than scattered throughout the administrative branch. They establish and administer controls which are designed to keep administrative officials and employees within the bounds set for them by the President and Congress. The Bureau of the Budget will be examined in this chapter; the General Accounting Office and the Civil Service Commission in the two chapters next following.

The Director of the Bureau of the Budget (hereafter Budget Director and Budget Bureau) heads an organization of approximately five hundred officials and employees located in the Executive Office of the President. The Budget Director and his subordinates have no boss but the President. They are therefore available at all times to advise the President on any matter he chooses to refer to them. Sometimes the President calls for advice from the Bureau on something that another administrative official thinks might more properly have been referred to him. But, since the Budget Bureau is a part of the President's own office, there can hardly be any legal or constitutional objection to his using it in any way he chooses that is not forbidden by law.

The authority and the activities of the Budget Bureau which give it its capacity for direction and control of administration fall mainly under six heads: (1) The Bureau prepares for the President the annual financial program (the budget of the United States) which he submits to Congress and in which he recommends amounts for appropriation to the various administrative establishments. (2) It exercises a limited amount of control over the way in which the administrative establishments spend the money appropriated to them and in respect to the number of people they may employ. (3) It examines the organization, activities, and work-ways of the administrative establishments in order to give the President advice concerning desirable administrative reorganization and to give the administrative official advice concerning matters within his jurisdiction. (4) It has a considerable amount of authority in respect to the communications that administrative officials send to Congress concerning legislation. (5) It prepares executive orders for the signature of the President. And finally (6) the Bureau exercises a considerable amount of control over the efforts of the administrative establishments to obtain information from the public.

Every one of these powers is important, but the preparation of the President's plan for financing the operation of the government greatly overshadows the others in significance. This is bound to be the case; for the appropriations that are finally made by Congress will determine the character and extent of the government's activities during the coming year, and the submission of his requests for appropriations is one of the President's most dramatic appeals to Congress for support of his legislative and administrative program. If the President could not make the initial plan for the allocation of money among different public purposes, he would be deprived of power to supply the kind of leadership in national affairs that we now expect from him.

The preparation of a plan for the year's appropriations has a twofold significance: it is both a request for congressional support of a program of government activity and a way of disciplining the administrative departments. This will be seen from a brief account of the way in which the estimates of financial needs are prepared.

The process starts early in the fiscal year (which begins July 1) with a letter from the Budget Director advising the heads of departments to prepare and submit their own estimates of the money needed for the coming year. Central control starts at this point, for the letter announces the President's attitudes (what he would like and what he will insist on) toward the cost of government for the approaching year.

Each administrative establishment prepares detailed estimates showing how much money its officials think it will need. These estimates involve both tabular presentations of the cost of various activities and statements of the reasons for carrying out the various undertakings on the scale proposed. The preparation of the estimates thus invites each administrative organization to review all of its activities, ask itself again whether everything it does is necessary, and weigh the importance of each activity against other uses to which public money might be put. The estimates-making process provides the head of the administrative establishment opportunity to question every phase of the program administered by his organization and to challenge every subordinate officer to justify his official existence.

The estimates prepared by the departments and agencies are submitted to the Budget Bureau, where they undergo thorough analysis by examiners who make that their principal business. The Bureau is sufficiently staffed with examiners to permit each one to confine his attention to a limited range of governmental activity. Examiners who have been in their jobs for a substantial period of time develop a high degree of familiarity with the activities they study and with the administrative officials who are in charge of those activities. The best of them become competent to challenge the judgment of administrative officials as to what it should cost to perform particular services. Where an operation is common to many parts of the government (the administration of mail and files is a good illustration), standard costs can be developed and the inefficient organization can be forced to acknowledge the deficiencies that it would otherwise be able to conceal. The examiners check with one another, scrutinize the frontiers where the activities of different departments and agencies come together, and induce the heads of the various establishments to straighten out their jurisdictional conflicts.

After the Bureau's examiners have had an opportunity to study the estimates, representatives of the administrative departments and agencies appear before them in hearings. There they supply the kind of emphasis that cannot be set down on paper, give further information that may be required, and generally make an effort to put the examiners in a state of mind favorable to a maximum appropriation.

Ordinarily, the examiners do not fix the amounts of money that are submitted to the President for inclusion in his budget message. Rather, the examiners propose amounts which go to higher officials within the Budget Bureau for review. The reviewing officials, sitting as a committee and handling estimates for many parts of the government, can weigh the needs of one administrative establishment and one set of activities against the needs of other establishments and other activities. We are thus given some degree of assurance that the appropriations for the various parts of the government will be adjusted to the same conception of public welfare and governmental economy.

The recommendations of the reviewing officials are laid before the Budget Director for approval. What he does with them will depend on a number of circumstances. The theory underlying the whole budget-making process supposes that the Budget Director will maintain close contact with the President and high administrative officials and will know the state of their minds as to how the government is to be financed during the upcoming year. If the President and other men who are influential in his Administration make up their minds well in advance of the deadlines for actual decision and take the Budget Director into their confidence, the Director can give his subordinates some indication of the limits within which the estimates for the several departments and agencies must fall. In that case the totals laid before him may require no significant revision and go at once to the President for approval. If, on the other hand, the President and his advisers have not made up their minds as to what they will support before Congress, or if the Budget Director has not been made a party to their decisions, or if their minds are changed at the last moment—in any such case the amounts agreed upon by the Bureau's examiners and reviewing committees may be drastically revised before the Director will submit them to the President.

The preparation of the annual estimates is the coming together of many kinds of consideration (suppositions, hopes, beliefs, decisions) relating to the broadest goals to be achieved, the kinds of governmental activity that will be depended on to achieve these goals, the scope of these activities and the intensity with which they will be carried on, and the amount of money required to accomplish any objective that may be decided upon. The issues that must be decided and the considerations that must enter into their decision range in significance from the highest concern of statesmanship to the most minute detail of administrative routine; and the men and women who participate in weighing the considerations and making the decisions are scattered through all the levels of the administrative hierarchy. The President himself will enter into the discussion of the broadest goals to be achieved, the major areas of governmental activity to be expanded or contracted, and the principal new activities to be undertaken; in sharp contrast, men well down toward the bottom of the administrative hierarchy will estimate the force of employees required to perform a given volume of work of standard character (like operating a mimeograph service) and their decisions are not likely to be reviewed by anyone of political consequence.

In theory the Budget Bureau plays an important role in making decisions or in getting decisions made on all questions involved in financing government, from the most routine to the most politically significant. It is generally agreed that the Bureau does a much better job of estimating the cost of carrying on activities that have been agreed upon than it does of challenging the desirability of carrying on particular activities at all or of carrying them on at the scale proposed. This is a consequence of the President's attitude toward the Bureau and its Director, and of the policy pursued in staffing the Bureau.

Most of the examiners in the Budget Bureau are recruited from the departments and agencies that carry on the work of government and have had practical experience which enables them to judge how much manpower, equipment, and supplies it takes to carry on a particular undertaking. Administrative officials who submit and defend their estimates recognize the competence of the budget examiner in these matters and modify their resistance to his findings and recommendations. But the Bureau's staff includes few men indeed who can win any deference on a question of political significance. The administrative officials who bring in the plans for a program of activities think they know what kind of government the American people want and the political leaders intend to provide. They do not believe that the budget examiner has equally reliable knowledge and they are prepared to resist any downward revision of the estimates which is based on a judgment as to what kind of government the American people and their political leaders want and are willing to pay for.

In theory the Budget Director and his principal subordinates supply the knowledge and influence in respect to political matters which the great body of the Bureau's staff does not have. Actually, there are not enough men in the Bureau who move in high government circles to make the Bureau effective in challenging the desirability of the programs of government that come before it. The few men who can talk to high administrative officials with the expectation that they will be listened to are not able to do the amount of talking that would be necessary to obtain significant revision of the plans that are developed within the administrative departments and agencies. My own inquiry into the relations between the Federal Communications Commission and the Budget Bureau disclosed that in not more than one year out of three has there been any conversation whatever between a member of the Commission and a person of high authority in the Bureau which went to the question of whether FCC ought to do all of the things it proposed to do or do all of them on the scale proposed. And it is perhaps true to say that in none of the few conversations that did take place was there a searching inquiry into why the Commissioners thought their plans were justified.[1]

[1] The following was written, after he had read a preliminary draft of my manuscript, by a man with considerable experience in the preparation of the annual budget, both as an examiner in the Budget Bureau and as an official charged with the preparation of estimates in an administrative agency.

"The steps in the budget-making process within the Budget Bureau are roughly as follows. In the late spring or early summer, the Budget Director confers with the President as to the general policies to be followed in the next budget. By general policies I mean, what is to be assumed in the way of legislation, activity in the business world, taxes, whether there is to be a balanced budget or not, the approximate limit within which the total appropriations should fall, the relative emphasis upon such things as social security and

As best I can learn, only two of the positions in the Budget Bureau have been filled during recent years by men who are well known and highly respected in the highest levels of the administrative branch and who give a major proportion of their time to the preparation of the President's plan for appropriations. These are the positions of Director and the first Assistant Director. And the task force which studied the organization and operations of

---

national defense. In May or June the agencies are asked to make rough estimates of their requirements. Then after the agencies have submitted their rough estimates conferences are held and most agencies are visited to talk to them in order to get an idea of the major developments in the programs that can be expected within the next year.

"Who takes part in the discussions will depend on the size of the agency and the complexity of the program. The President might confer long and hard with the Budget Director and the Secretary of National Defense; the FCC might receive only a telephone call directed to its executive officer from a budget examiner. The preliminary figures are received, the Budget Bureau personnel has group meetings and conferences, and tables are prepared showing the Budget Director what the next year's figures will look like in terms of total dollar amounts. The budget examiners meet with the Director and discuss the agencies' forecasts. The examiners point out where these appear too high, what items appear unavoidable, and where there is a chance of revision. This past year, after the Director had reviewed all the items, summary tables were prepared based upon various assumptions; one set was based upon the minimum assumptions, another set was made with slightly more liberal policy estimates. The Director showed these to the President and upon the basis of their discussion tentative ceilings or target figures were established for the various agencies. All of the big agencies were given their ceilings or target figures. Some of the small ones such as FCC were only given general policy directives in such terms as 'work of high priority' and 'most efficient performance.' The large agencies were given exact figures in their policy letters and were asked to submit their estimates within those figures. The agencies did follow the directions but they also included what has become known as B items. These are items that could not be included in the target figure but which the agency still felt were important.

"The Director will have direct personal contact with the heads of very large agencies and ones that have unusually large problems. He will have contact through his representatives with all other agencies. The Budget Director himself will do a lot of telling to the Secretary of Agriculture; Budget Bureau examiners will do a lot of telling to staff members of the Department of Agriculture. The work of the Budget Bureau examiners is done in such a way that their actions are cloaked with anonymity. Taking decisive actions doesn't require slapping the Secretary of Agriculture in the face—only stabbing him in the back. I say this facetiously, of course, but it gives you the idea."

the Budget Bureau for the Hoover Commission seemed to believe that even the Director enjoys no great influence. The Budget Director, the report stated, "is now little more than a glorified secretary to the President who does not participate in Cabinet meetings. . . . Since the Bureau was transferred to the Executive Office in 1939, the Director of the Budget has become largely an assistant to the President, and ranks about on a par with several other assistants attached to the White House. He has no standing in Cabinet meetings, and is rarely permitted to attend them. He may not decide any budget matters for the major departments of the government which the secretaries cannot appeal directly to the President, and in such cases it is understood that they occasionally get adverse decisions."[2]

This statement is notably lacking in preciseness. It is commonly said that cabinet meetings rarely discuss matters of great importance, or if they discuss such matters rarely carry the discussion to the point of decision; it may be that the cabinet meetings which the director is "rarely permitted to attend" include all of those in which there is any significant discussion of matters affecting appropriations. One wonders what the Director does on the rare occasions when he attends a cabinet meeting, since he "does not participate in Cabinet meetings." The statement that he "ranks about on a par with several other assistants attached to the White House" does not tell us much. If it means that his influence is comparable to that of Harry Hopkins and Judge Samuel Rosenman, then the Budget Director may be of great influence indeed; if it means that he has no greater influence than the fourth or fifth most influential of the Presidential assistants, I do not believe the statement is true. And finally, the statement that "the secretaries" (which does not include the heads of non-cabinet departments) can appeal any of the Director's decisions to the President and "occasionally" get the Director overruled does not tell us much

[2] *Fiscal, Budgeting, and Accounting Systems of Federal Government; A Report with Recommendations, Prepared for The Commission on Organization of the Executive Branch of the Government [Appendix F]* (Government Printing Office, 1949), pp. 31 and 46; see also pp. 66–67.

either. I think it will be a sad day when the heads of the great administrative departments cannot tell the President anything they think he needs to know. And I think it will be a sad day when the President makes no concessions to their demands, even in a good many instances when his own convictions are on the side of the Budget Director.

What we need to know, in order to evaluate the adequacy of our present arrangements for helping the President make up his plans for appropriations, includes such matters as these: Do the Budget Director and his subordinates influence the officials in the departments and agencies to bring in requests for appropriations which are much more nearly in accord with what the President wants than they would otherwise bring in? How often do the Director and his staff cut down these estimates to such a degree that the heads of departments and agencies feel they ought to ask the President to give up the time necessary for an appeal? And what is the evidence that the President, when he decides against the Director, does so because he lacks sympathy with the Director's decision or does so for reasons which the Director could not properly take into account? Until we get a report on these and like matters from investigators who look at the whole budget-making process objectively and who write so precisely that what they believe enters our minds, you and I will have to remain uncertain as to how well the President is served by the present arrangements for giving him help. A careful reading of the report of the task force which advised the Hoover Commission gives me the impression that it did not approach these matters with an open mind and certainly leaves me in doubt as to what actually takes place. My own conclusion, reported above, that the Budget Bureau contains too few men who enjoy political stature to enable it to challenge effectively the desirability of the programs of government which are laid before it, is based on the testimony of men with extended experience in the federal government who speak much more precisely than the task force of the Hoover Commission.

The Budget Bureau's deferential treatment of the big issues in government spending is in sharp contrast to what takes place in the appropriations subcommittees of the two houses of Congress. The Congressmen do not challenge the desirability of every governmental activity which comes before them in an appropriation bill, nor in every case challenge the desirability of carrying on the activity at the scale proposed. Congressmen bow to the President's plans in respect to some things, and they bow to the superior understanding of the administrative official in respect to some things. But it must be agreed that neither the issues nor the men that come before the subcommittee are so big or so important that the Congressmen will not take them on for full examination when they are roused to a fight. The least confident of the Congressmen is likely to view himself as equal in importance to any man who appears before him save an occasional department head, and some of his associates on the subcommittee are pretty certain to be free of even that amount of doubt. What any Congressman lacks in personal confidence is compensated for by the assurance which he derives from his associates on the subcommittee. And the result is that the subcommittee as a whole feels fully competent to inquire critically into the need for the activities and undertakings that are proposed and does not hesitate to make decisions based on its collective judgment.

If the appropriation which finally becomes law differs greatly from the amount which the President recommended, the basis for an important executive control over the administrative establishment is weakened or destroyed. The document which the department or agency submits to the Budget Bureau is a detailed plan of operations for the coming year, with related estimates of the costs that must be incurred to carry out this plan. If the Bureau or the President allows less money than the original estimates called for, the administrative officials will be told what items have been cut out and what amounts have been cut down. The plan of operations for the coming year will then have to be revised in keeping with the changes that have been made in the monetary amounts. The administrative officials who will be responsible for the operations will work out the new statement of the program and will defend it before the subcommittees of Congress. But the plan which they explain and defend will propose a distribution of money among different activities and different parts of the organization which has been at least tacitly agreed to by the Budget Bureau and in theory agreed to by the President.

The plan for the year's operations which the officials of the administrative department or agency defend before the subcommittees is described in two documents—the President's annual budget (which provides a skeleton description) and a "justification" of the plan which is prepared by the administrative officials. The justification shows why the activities are believed necessary and why they should be carried on at the scale indicated, and both the President's budget and the justification indicate how the money will be spent if appropriated. If the amounts which are recommended by the President and explained and defended by administrative officials are actually appropriated, the President's budget and the justification stand as evidence of what is expected in the actual spending of the money. The administrative official has said, "I want this much money for each of these purposes"; if he is given the money requested, he has an obligation to spend it the way he said he would. But if Congress appropriates less money than was asked for, the plan of operations must be revised again and the administrative official is in some measure released from his promises. He cannot carry on the program as promised, because what he promised to do was contingent on his getting an amount of money that he did not get. The appropriation act which makes the money available will limit the range of choice to some degree by indicating particular amounts of money for particular areas of activity or sectors of the administrative organization. But the administrative official will have a greater leeway in applying money to different purposes if his justification has been rendered in part inapplicable than he would have had if he had gotten the exact amount of money he asked for.

If such a relaxation of restraint on spending the money appropriated seems undesirable, there are two principal ways of avoiding or correcting it. We will avoid the relaxation if the President succeeds in making proposals for appropriations which Congress will enact into law without significant change. And we can correct any relaxation which occurs when the appropriations depart significantly from the President's recommendations by giving the President and the Budget Bureau some authority over the reallocations of money which are made after the appropriation act has been passed.

The first of these solutions is the more difficult to achieve, and it may be that we ought not hope to achieve it entirely. We cannot know what the year's activities of an administrative department or agency ought to be; we can only work out agreement as to what it shall be. The administrative officials who will have the job of carrying out the program draw up the original plans within the limits set for them by the legislation which controls their organization and activities. These officials must win the President's approval of their broad objectives or bow to his objections. It is the job of the Budget Bureau to see that the many administrative proposals are viewed in relation to one another and that the President and high administrative officials realize what total cost of government will be incurred if all these proposals are adopted. Congress, finally, must be convinced that the plan for a year of government which is formulated in this way is one of which the American people will approve when they see it in operation and realize what it is costing them.

It seems to me that we are not now achieving the standards of performance that we could achieve at any stage of this agreement-reaching process. It is generally said that the administrative departments and agencies do an inadequate job of reviewing their operations, planning for the coming year, and estimating the costs that will be necessary for a given plan of operations. The President cannot take the time to discuss many of the major issues, even many of high political significance, which arise in preparing

the annual budget. The cabinet does not weld the separate proposals into an Administration program. Most of the departments
and agencies are not even represented in the cabinet, and there is
a great deal of testimony that the cabinet does not undertake jobs
like this anyway. The Budget Bureau does not have enough men
who possess the political stature that is necessary for negotiating
agreement among high administrative officials to bring the heads
of administrative departments and agencies to a common mind
on the most significant features of an Administration program.
And it seems to be a rare occurrence, if indeed it ever happens,
that leaders of the President's party in Congress get an opportunity
to lay a hand on the shaping of the budget until it reaches a stage
of development that compels them to support it as a matter of
party loyalty.

The Hoover Commission noted all of these deficiencies in the
process by which we construct the annual budget and commented
on the significance of most of them. It recommended that the administrative departments and agencies make better provision for
review of their operations, planning future operations, and calculating probable costs; that more intimate working relations between the Budget Bureau and the departments and agencies be
developed; that the Budget Bureau make some changes in its
internal organization; that statements of needs which enter into
the annual budget be "based upon functions, activities, and projects" rather than upon sectors of the administrative organization as at present (the Commission called this a "performance
budget"); and that Congress consider the possibility of adopting
a style for appropriations acts which would make them more
consistent with one another and give the President, the Budget Bureau, and administrative officials more freedom to adjust expenditure to special conditions which arise in the course of administration.[3]

[3] *Budgeting and Accounting; A Report to the Congress by the Commission on Organization of the Executive Branch of the Government, February
1949* (Government Printing Office, 1949).

Nothing that I have learned from other sources causes me to question the soundness of any of these recommendations. But it seems to me that the recommendations of the Hoover Commission do not go to the questions of greatest significance. They do not go to any of these questions: Should the job of Budget Director go to a man who enjoys prestige the equal of that of any man in the cabinet? Should the Budget Bureau contain a number of men who possess a political stature that will enable them to bring high administrative officials to agreement on the most significant issues that arise in planning a year's program for the entire government? If high officials in the Budget Bureau are not to do this job of negotiating agreement, who is to do it? Should leaders of the President's party in Congress be brought into budget making at an early stage, so that the interests and temper of Congress can be taken fully into account in making the original plans for a year of governmental activity?

I have no doubt expressed my own opinions fully enough on each of these points individually. It may be noted here that the key to a satisfactory resolution of all these questions seems to me to be in the establishment of the Central Council which I recommend in the final chapter of this book. Such an arrangement would bring the leaders in the administrative branch and in Congress together for discussion of an Administration program and its implications for the cost of government. High administrative officials and officials in the Budget Bureau could then be informed of the approximate amounts that the President would approve and the leaders of the party in Congress would undertake to enact into law. Having this increased assurance that Congress would not undo its work by making drastic changes in the amounts recommended, officials at all levels in the Budget Bureau could be expected to press more firmly for justification of any feature of the plans of an administrative establishment that seemed to them questionable in view of the goals set for them by the political leaders. And high administrative officials would not be able to escape their commitments to the Budget Bureau on the ground that a major alteration by Congress in the amounts allowed rendered the original plan of operations impracticable.

If we are unwilling to establish the relationships at the top of our government (or being willing, do not get around to it) which result in Congress getting a plan for financing administrative operations that it is willing to approve without significant change, we can still subject the administrative establishment to central control in spending its money by giving the President and the Budget Bureau some authority over the reallocations of money which are made after the appropriation acts have been passed. This is the second item in the listing of authority and activities (on page 330) by which the Budget Bureau exercises direction and control over administration.

A limited amount of this kind of authority has already been granted to the President and the Budget Bureau or assumed by them. Under the terms of successive employee pay acts, the Budget Bureau has been authorized to fix limits to the number of persons who at any time could be employed by an administrative department or agency as a whole or by any particular subdivision of a department or agency. The authority which the Bureau acquires from these statutes is supplemented by further authority (which the Bureau gets by a liberal interpretation of the basic act of 1921) to specify the portion of its appropriation which any department or agency may spend during each quarter of the year. It was pointed out in Chapter 13 (pages 245–246) that the Bureau has frequently used this power to set up reserves within an appropriation, thus inducing the officials in charge of the administrative establishment to proceed more conservatively in incurring costs of administration than they otherwise would.

I have already stated my conviction that the President cannot give personal attention to the application of such controls except in most unusual circumstances. And I have stated my conviction that the Budget Bureau does not have enough personnel of political stature to work out agreement on certain matters that ought to be decided in the process of preparing estimates. It is equally evident that the Bureau is not adequately staffed to bring the administrative departments and agencies to its position on allocations and apportionments of the money which Congress has appropriated in those instances when high administrative officials offer stubborn resistance. This appears to be fully appreciated in the Bureau. The reserves which are set up are nearly always the result of amicable arrangements between the Bureau and the administrative officials concerned.

The remaining powers of the Budget Bureau (listed on p. 330) are so much less important than those relating to the appropriation and expenditure of money that they can be brought into this discussion only at risk of anticlimax. The Budget and Accounting Act of 1921 (which is the basic charter of powers under which the Bureau acts) authorizes the Bureau, when directed by the President, to "make a detailed study of the departments and establishments for the purpose of enabling the President to determine what changes . . . should be made" in the organization, activities, and methods of business pursued. This statutory authorization has been substantially enlarged in actual practice. The Bureau not only makes studies to inform the President of the state of affairs in the administrative branch; it undertakes inquiries at the request of administrative officials and makes recommendations as to how they may improve their operations and overcome their difficulties.

The contribution which the Bureau is able to make toward the improvement of administrative organization and practices is thus directly dependent on the disposition of the President and high administrative officials to turn to it for assistance and advice. As long as the President retains the power to prepare plans for the reorganization of the administrative branch and put them into effect in the absence of Congressional veto (discussed at pp. 110–114), the Bureau will have a great deal of influence on the general structure of the administrative branch. It has become recognized in Washington that the Bureau is the proper agency to identify government-wide needs for change, to make concrete proposals, and to negotiate the compromises that have to be worked out before a proposal can be laid before the President. All the reorganization plans which have been laid before Congress since the President was granted this extraordinary power have been prepared for him by the Budget Bureau.

The studies and recommendations that are inspired by the President himself are likely to be confined to major changes in the general administrative structure. The Bureau will get an opportunity to look into the internal organization and operations of the various administrative establishments only to the extent that the officials in charge of those establishments are willing to accept the Bureau's assistance. The Bureau can and does make some effort to sell its services. Administrative officials are fully aware of the power which the Bureau has over their appropriations. Discussion of the financial needs of an administrative establishment naturally gets around to the way the establishment is organized and how it does its work. This makes it easy for the officials of the Bureau to indicate their willingness to look around and see if they can make any suggestions for improvement. Such a hint is enough to cause some administrative officials to invite the Bureau in for a thoroughgoing study. Other officials may be much more reluctant to disclose their shortcomings or less inclined to suffer the interruption of day-to-day work that results from a study of what is going on; in such a case the Bureau may increase its hints to something approaching insistence that it cannot act on appropriation requests with intelligence unless it is permitted to satisfy itself as to how economically the money which has already been appropriated is being spent.

Whatever be the reason for it, there has been a steady increase in the demand for administrative studies by the Budget Bureau during the past decade. The Bureau now maintains about one hundred employees in a Division of Administrative Management to carry on this kind of work. Academic students of government generally have been effusive in their praise of the work of the Division of Administrative Management.[4] Administrative officials in Washington, on the other hand, appear to be divided in their opinions as to whether the Division has made much of a contribution to the improvement of administration. The task force which examined and evaluated the performance of the Budget Bureau for the Hoover Commission gave an adverse report on the Division of Administrative Management.

"The Division of Administrative Management," said the task force, "has done some good work during the 9 years since it was established. But this work has been done on a casual basis. No comprehensive approach looking toward organizational and management improvement has been planned or utilized by the Division. And there has been no insistence on the part of the Bureau's leadership that such an approach should be made. Indeed, the Division has operated largely on the theory that the work which voluntarily came to it from day to day was the important work for it to do. This seems much too fortuitous for either maximum effectiveness or accomplishment." The task force recommended that the staff of the Division of Administrative Management "be largely merged" with the examiners who analyze and make recommendations concerning the appropriations needed for the administrative departments and agencies, thus creating within the Budget Bureau a number of working groups made up of men who are competent both to evaluate the need of any administrative establishment for money and to help the officials of that establishment improve its organization and practices. The Hoover Commission rejected this recommendation, however, stating that the Division

[4] From a former employee of the Budget Bureau who has contributed fruitfully to the literature of public administration: "It is my opinion that practically all of the writing in recent years about aiding the President has been done by people in the Budget Bureau, people trying to get into the Budget Bureau, or people who get their information from the Budget Bureau. What they have written is decidedly *ex parte*."

of Administrative Management should not only be continued as a distinct organization but "should be expanded and strengthened."[5]

The Budget Bureau is also given authority in respect to the communications between Congress and administrative departments relating to legislation (item 4 in the listing of authority and activities of the Bureau on page 330 above). Congressmen recognize that the President is head of the administrative branch, but this does not keep officials of the two houses, Congressional committees, and individual Congressmen from communicating directly with administrative officials concerning new legislation that is needed and existing law that ought to be changed. Administrative officials are also invited by the nature of their relations with Congress to suggest the advisability of legislative action. There is much to be gained from this direct communication between Congress and administrative officials, but a lot of harm can be done if Congress puts too much trust in a sector of the bureaucracy that may be trying to keep other administrative officials from knowing what it is up to.

To make sure that the left hand of the administrative branch will know what the right hand is doing, an instruction was issued during President Harding's administration requiring all administrative departments and agencies to clear with the Budget Bureau before sending communications to Congress relating to proposed legislation. This directive has since been clarified and supplemented by a number of Budget Bureau circulars which firmly establish the following procedure. When a draft of a letter from an administrative official to Congress comes into the hands of the Bureau, it becomes the job of the Bureau to determine whether other administrative departments and agencies have some relation to or interest in the subject under consideration. If other departments and agencies, and the work which they carry on, will be

[5] The remarks of the task force which are quoted appear on p. 52 of the document cited in note 2. See also p. 40 of that document. The statement of the Hoover Commission appears at p. 28 of the report which is cited in note 3.

affected by the legislation under consideration, the Bureau will discuss the matter with the administrative officials concerned and attempt to formulate a position for the administrative branch as a whole. This will be passed on to the official who submitted the draft of the letter, with appropriate remarks about the relation of the proposed communication "to the program of the President."

The control which is exercised in this way by no means amounts to an absolute veto over communications from administrative officials to Congress. The administrative official may go ahead and say to Congress what he intended to say in the first place, but he is expected to disclose the fact if there is a difference of opinion within the administrative branch. Congress is thus warned that it may be desirable to extend its search for advice to a wider range of administrative experience than it first intended. And other administrative officials are provided with sufficient knowledge of what is going on to enable them to present opposing points of view to Congress.

The considerations that make the Bureau the proper agency for clearing communications between administrative departments and Congress relating to legislation make it also the proper agency to negotiate agreement on the language to be incorporated in executive orders issued by the President (item 5 in the listing on page 330 above). During the past few decades the President has come to be an important source of law, extending and applying much of the legislation enacted by Congress. A great deal of this presidential legislation has an important effect on what the administrative branch must do and how it shall do it. With few exceptions, every proposed executive order comes under the scrutiny of the Budget Bureau. This enables the Bureau to make sure that one administrative official will not put something over on other administrative officials by getting the President (who may have a liking for dispatch and decisive action) to put his signature on an executive enactment that will affect other parts of the federal government adversely.

Finally (item 6 in the listing on page 330 above), the Budget Bureau is given considerable authority over the steps taken by the various administrative establishments to collect information from the public. The act of 1942, which gives the Bureau this authority, contained a number of special provisions for specific situations but provides in general that any administrative establishment which undertakes a general or systematic effort to collect information (statistical or other kind) from any part of the public must submit its forms, letters of inquiry, and other such apparatus to the Budget Bureau for criticism and approval. The Bureau maintains a small force of employees who devote full time to this kind of review. They work directly with administrative officials in planning inquiries and preparing forms for distribution to the public. It is probable that the services which the Bureau has rendered to the public by eliminating nuisances from inquiries is equaled in value by the service it has rendered administrative officials in showing them how they can get information that is more adequate and more reliable in view of the use they intend to make of it.

The things that the Budget Bureau does under these various grants of authority fall, as was indicated above, under the heads of advice, service, and control. In addition to the advice and service that may be rendered, each type of action that has been discussed provides a substantial amount of control over the policies and procedures of the several administrative departments and agencies. As arrangements for control they collectively serve a threefold purpose.

First, they force every administrative organization to bring important aspects of its work before another group of men and either win approval for its plans or change them. Every administrative establishment has within it arrangements for review of plans, inspection of operations, and the checking of one man's judgment against that of another. But the effectiveness of these internal administrative controls often drops to a low point indeed, and practices develop within the administrative organization that no one would attempt to defend. The necessity of revealing these things to outsiders is a stimulus for straightening them out and taking steps to keep them from recurring.

The second purpose that justifies the controls which the Budget Bureau administers is really a particular application of the first. Since every part of the administrative branch brings important aspects of its plans and operations before the Bureau, the officials and employees of the Bureau can provide coordination of administrative activity that could not be provided in any other way. As the Bureau reviews what the administrative establishment is doing and proposes to do in the future, it detects inconsistencies in administrative policy, overlapping and duplication of governmental activity, and the failure of this administrative operation to fit snugly up against that one in the way that Congress and President intended. Only a group of men who have an opportunity to scrutinize the activities of the entire administrative branch can make the suggestions for change in administrative action that effectively coordinate the operations of administrative organizations which are otherwise independent of one another.

Finally, the authority given to the Budget Bureau provides an additional channel by which the President may impress his personal wishes upon administrative policies and practices. He has, of course, other ways of making his wishes known. He may, for instance, tell all administrative officials that he wants economies introduced into administration generally and that he wants fewer automobiles in use around Washington specifically. But the President cannot quiz each department or agency head about the necessity for the automobiles that his organization proposes to keep in use. The President can, however, hear the report of the Budget Director about government-wide practice in the use of automobiles and he can say, "Work it out among the departments any way you think best, but I want the whole number of automobiles cut down at least 25 percent." This illustration can be matched with others from a wide range of public affairs. The President's chances of getting things done the way he wants them done is greatly increased if he can turn to a man in whom he has personal confidence, who commands a staff of competent assistants, and who has a grant of authority that gives him and his associates a license to find out what other administrative officials are doing and tell them how the President wants things done from now on.

If Congress, acting through the entire body or through particular committees, wishes to impress its will on the day-to-day performance of administration, then it also needs a sizable staff to which it can turn for assistance much like that which the Budget Director and his subordinates give to the President. Leaders of Congress have been aware of this for a long time, but not much has been done to provide for the need. The act which established the Budget Bureau expressly provided that the Bureau should furnish aid and information to the revenue and appropriations committees of Congress whenever they might request it. Assistance has been called for and given on a number of occasions, and every once in a while the Budget Director tells Congress that his staff stands ready to render more aid. But in spite of this understanding that the Bureau is available to serve Congress as well as the President, there is a general supposition that its predominant obligation is to the President. This feeling was undoubtedly heightened when the Bureau was made a part of the newly created Executive Office of the President in 1939. More than one Congressman since that time has indicated a doubt that the officials and employees of the Bureau are in a position to talk frankly to Congressmen about any phase of the financial and administrative affairs of the government in respect to which the President has taken a position.

The task force of the Hoover Commission which reported on the Budget Bureau summarized the attitudes of Congressmen toward the Bureau in these words: "One gets the very definite impression, particularly from some members of the appropriations committees, that Congress is not very happy about its relations with the Budget Bureau. While it is generally understood and recognized that the Bureau is a staff agency of the President, many congressmen nevertheless feel that the Bureau's staff should be impartial in its examination and presentation of facts to Congress. But they think that the Bureau, especially in recent years, has often used the facts to argue in support of the President's stand on budget issues, and has been very reluctant to supply information to Congress which might weaken the President's case."[6]

Uncertainty and misunderstanding about the relation of the Budget Bureau to Congress arises, of course, out of the emphasis we have put on separation of powers and the duty of one branch to serve as a check upon the other. If Congress and President were brought into a closer union by the establishment of a Central Council such as is proposed in the final chapter of this book, the role of the central agencies for advice, service, and control would undoubtedly be clarified. If a Central Council, containing the leaders of both the executive and the legislative branch, took on the job of working out the major policies of the government, then the Budget Bureau or its successor would undoubtedly be given unequivocal instructions to lend its services to the preparation and realization of these policies in the legislative and the executive branch alike.

BIBLIOGRAPHIC NOTE

Considering its importance, surprisingly little has been written about what the Bureau of the Budget does and how it does it. The account that helped me most is H. W. Wilkie, "Legal Basis for Increased Activities of the Federal Budget Bureau," in *George Washington Law Review*, vol. 11, pp. 265–301 (1943). Mr. Wilkie was an employee of the Budget Bureau at the time he wrote this article. He examines the different grants of authority to the Bureau, shows what it has done and is trying to do under each grant, discusses the problems that the Bureau encounters in pursuing its objectives, and manages in the course of the article to give a very good picture of how an important central agency for advice, service, and control fits into

[6] Quoted from p. 48 of the document cited in note 2.

the whole structure of the national government. A later article which goes over the same ground, but which seems to me to be much less informative, is F. Morstein Marx, "The Bureau of the Budget: Its Evolution and Present Role," in *American Political Science Review*, vol. 39, pp. 653–684, 869–898 (1945). See also Catheryn Seckler-Hudson, *Budgeting; An Instrument of Planning and Management* (6 mimeographed volumes, Washington, 1944).

The first Director of the Budget, Charles G. Dawes, recorded his experiences in launching the new system in *The First Year of the Budget of the United States* (New York, 1923). Harold D. Smith, who was Director of the Budget from 1939 to 1946, left a less informative record of his experiences and impressions in a limited number of addresses and articles, the best of which are incorporated in a little book entitled *The Management of Your Government* (New York, 1945).

The relation of the Budget Bureau to communications between administrative officials and Congress on proposed legislation is set forth clearly by Carl R. Sapp in "Executive Assistance in the Legislative Process," in *Public Administration Review*, vol. 6, pp. 10–19 (1946). The official who has long been in charge of the Bureau's activities relating to the collection of information from the public by federal administrative departments, Stuart A. Rice, has described this phase of the Bureau's work in "Coordination of Federal Statistical Programs," in *American Journal of Sociology*, vol. 50, pp. 22–28 (1944).

There is a considerable literature on the theory and practice of estimating appropriation needs and on central control of expenditures generally. Among the best of these works are: Frederick A. Cleveland and A. E. Buck, *The Budget and Responsible Government* (New York, 1920); Arthur E. Buck, *The Budget in Governments of Today* (New York, 1934); James W. Sundelson, *Budgetary Methods in National and State Governments* (Albany, 1938); and Daniel T. Selko, *The Federal Financial System* (Washington, 1940).

CHAPTER 18

THE GENERAL ACCOUNTING OFFICE

The General Accounting Office has been in existence exactly as long as the Bureau of the Budget, for the two central agencies were created in the same statute. Like the Budget Bureau, the General Accounting Office (hereafter GAO) is a central agency for advice, service, and control. It helps Congress and the President decide·what they want done, and it shares in the direction and control by which administrative departments and agencies are induced to comply with the decisions which Congress and the President have made. The GAO and the Budget Bureau are not administrative establishments comparable in character to the Department of Agriculture, the Housing and Home Finance Agency, or the Interstate Commerce Commission. Each of these last-named organizations administers a segment of the primary work of government. We maintain government to do such things as promote and regulate agricultural production, make sure that housing will be available, regulate nationwide rail transportation. The GAO and the Budget Bureau engage in no activities of this sort. Their work is entirely secondary. Their job is to assist, advise, and control the other departments and agencies (like the three just mentioned) so as to increase the assurance that they will do what they are expected to do and will do it in a manner acceptable to the political branches of the government.

The GAO and the Budget Bureau are alike in that each is a central agency for advice, service, and control. But there the like-

355

ness ends. The Budget Bureau is a small agency of about 500 officials and employees; GAO is approximately twenty times that big, having more than 10,000 officials and emloyees in 1948. The Budget Bureau is located in the Executive Office of the President and the Budget Director who heads it recognizes no boss but the President. The GAO is generally considered to be an attachment to the legislative branch of the government, and its head, the Comptroller General, recognizes Congress as his principal if not his only boss. The President appoints the Budget Director without the necessity of obtaining the advice and consent of the Senate, and can remove him at pleasure. The President takes the initiative in the selection of the Comptroller General but the Senate must confirm the appointment, and only the two houses of Congress (by concurrent resolution) can remove the Comptroller General from office.

The Budget Bureau and GAO also differ greatly in the nature of the duties assigned to them. The Budget Bureau has a charge which brings all sectors of the administrative branch and virtually all activities and undertakings of the administrative branch within its area of concern, and it exerts an influence on the making of decisions at every stage of government-in-action from the making of highest policy to the establishment and pursuit of routine in the bottom levels of administration. The GAO, in contrast, has a much more restricted charge. Its area of concern is confined to administrative policies and practices relating to financial matters, and its authority in respect to many sectors of the administrative branch has been restricted by legislation.

The business of GAO is what its name implies; it is concerned with the accounts of the federal government as a whole. The Budget and Accounting Act of 1921, which created it and gave it a job to do, is the primary source of its authority and responsibilities today. This act, as subsequently amended and supplemented by óther legislation, makes GAO responsible for a wide range of matters relating to the collection and expenditure of money and the keeping of records that show the nature of financial transactions which take place throughout the federal government.[1]

The specific grants of authority under which GAO acts in giving advice and assistance to administrative officials and exercising control over them are too many in number and too diverse in character to be taken up for separate examination here. The authority of GAO in respect to the collection of money from people outside the government, for instance, is quite different from its authority over the spending of money by administrative departments and agencies. And it exercises much less authority over the borrowing of money through bond issues than it exercises over either the collection of money owed to the government or the paying out of money to defray the costs of government.

The discussion which follows here is concerned only with the authority and influence of GAO over the spending of money by the departments and agencies of the administrative branch. The character and quality of administration is reflected directly in the costs which are incurred by the departments and agencies that carry on administration. As it exercises authority and exerts influence over the spending of money, GAO participates effectively in the direction and control of administration.

In order to understand what GAO does in relation to the spending of money, it is necessary to have some understanding of what takes place in the administrative establishment. A simple illustration will suffice. The Department of Interior has been appropriated money in an act of Congress that clearly authorizes it to construct irrigation systems on Indian reservations. The Department buys motor trucks for use in the construction of irrigation systems; it will need gasoline, oil, and drivers to put the trucks to use. The incurring of obligations starts in the Department of Interior, and there the first record of expenditures must be made. Let us assume that trucks travel distances which make it necessary for the driver to take on gasoline at filling stations along

[1] The law giving GAO its authority can be found in U.S. Code, title 31, secs. 41 ff.

the highway. If the driver pays cash for the gasoline, he will be required to keep a record of the purchases for that will reduce the temptation to collect more from the Department than he pays out to the filling stations and enable officials to check up and see whether he got what he says he paid for. If the Department gives the driver credit cards and the driver signs for the gasoline that he takes on, there must be somebody in the offices of the Department to examine the bills when they come in, to decide whether they are correct, and to certify the amounts to be paid.

There is no workable alternative to an arrangement whereby this bit of record-keeping and this bit of decision-making is done in the Department of Interior. That is where the records are which show who is driving trucks; that is the place where you can find out that a particular driver went on a particular trip at a particular time, which makes it likely or unlikely that he would have issued the orders that have come in; that is where you can check the signature of the driver; and that is where you can find out whether the driver could reasonably have used the amount of gasoline he issued orders for. When the government of the United States has more than two million people at work, in all of the States and most of its possessions, there will be no decent keeping of records concerning financial transactions unless they are kept by the people who do the work and incur the obligations.

This calls, therefore, for elaborate accounting systems in the various administrative departments and agencies of the government. Truck drivers can make a record of their purchases, but they cannot keep the necessary accounts of the obligations they have incurred. It would be too much trouble to teach them how to combine the individual items into a decent financial statement; they would always be careless about it if they were taught how to do it; and someone else ought to be checking up on them anyway. So each administrative establishment sets up a bookkeeping office which receives the incoming claims for payment, checks them against the orders for goods and services that have been issued by the officials and employees of the establishment, makes such further inquiries as it needs to, and certifies the amounts that are to be paid. The number of persons who are engaged principally or full time in this kind of bookkeeping and accounting work in the various administrative establishments of the national government is unknown, but it is probably in excess of 40,000.

At one time or another in the past, each administrative organization paid its own bills and wrote its own checks—for salaries to its employees, for equipment, for supplies, etc. Today, the Treasury Department is paymaster for many of the federal departments and agencies; very few administrative officials have any substantial amount of cash under their control. By centralizing check writing, we get it done more cheaply; and the total amount of bookkeeping for the government is reduced.

It is generally agreed that we need somebody outside of the administrative establishment to impose some limitations on the use to which it puts its appropriations. If no one ever reviewed their acts, administrative officials might spend more than Congress had appropriated; they might spend money for things which the appropriation act had not authorized; and they might, through carelessness or fraud, let public money pass illegally into private pockets. We have never determined to anything like general satisfaction, however, just what that outside control should be. We have tried out a number of different arrangements since the present government was established in 1789.

Our present system, established by the Budget and Accounting Act of 1921, puts the principal authority to review and check the financial activities of the administrative departments and agencies in GAO. The authority of GAO does not apply uniformly to all administrative establishments, however. Speaking generally, the things which GAO can do in relation to the spending of money by an administrative establishment fall under one or more of three heads.

First, GAO has authority to prescribe the forms and procedures relating to finances which shall be installed and maintained in the administrative departments and agencies. The objective in regulating forms and procedures, of course, is to provide documents and records which clearly disclose the character and circumstances of financial tansactions. This in itself is a deterrent to illegal and improper action on the part of administrative officials; it serves also to facilitate the other controls which GAO is authorized to exercise.

Second, GAO has authority to examine specific expenditures and order correction made in case it finds any expenditures not to be in keeping with the law or appropriation acts as interpreted by GAO. This exercise of authority (hereafter called expenditure-review) is control pure and simple. And this is the aspect of relations between GAO and the administrative departments that has excited the most controversy. It arises out of the authority given GAO to "settle" accounts. Under what we may call standard procedure, the administrative establishment can incur obligations and instruct the Treasury Department to pay them. These actions are accomplished by the certification of appropriate documents by an official in the administrative establishment and by the drawing of a check or payment of cash by an official (usually in the Treasury Department) who has been designated disbursing officer. The disbursing officer, according to present law, is personally liable for his own errors and those of the certifying officer who instructed him to make the payment, whether they be wilful misdeeds, careless mistakes, or honest but faulty judgment. The disbursing officer is finally relieved of his worry about what he has done when GAO has examined his records and found his payments properly made and properly accounted for. This is known as "settling the accounts of the disbursing officer."

The examination and settling of accounts goes on day in and day out. If any expenditure in the disbursing officer's record is found not to have been properly accounted for, GAO will order that the error be rectified. The error may be rectified by recovering the money from the person to whom it was wrongfully paid or by collecting the amount in error from the disbursing officer or his bondsman.

Legislation enacted since 1921 has made many exceptions to the above described procedure, particularly for the government corporations and agencies given work to do of a wartime or emergency character. Some of these establishments have authority to settle the accounts of their own disbursing officers and GAO cannot upset the decisions which are made. It may, however, report to Congress any irregularities which it later discovers in the course of auditing the records of the administrative establishment.

Two procedures have been developed to avoid the embarrassment of trying to recover money that has already been paid out of the federal treasury. First, administrative officials may describe expenditures which they contemplate making and call on GAO for advice as to what it will probably do when it later encounters those items in the settlement of the disbursing officer's accounts. These advance opinions are not binding on GAO in its subsequent action but they are carefully prepared and therefore greatly reduce the number of adverse actions which GAO finally takes. Second, the Comptroller General at one time invited all the administrative departments and agencies to route their instructions for payment through the GAO, so that the proposed expenditure could be reviewed in advance of payment. Many departments and agencies did this, and a few of them still do so for all or part of their expenditures. These two procedures—advance advisory opinions and prepayment review—serve a useful purpose, but they have not by any means eliminated adverse action by GAO on accounts that have been paid. Each year a substantial number of cases have to be reopened by one kind of action or another to recover money that administrative officials consider to have been properly paid, but which GAO thinks irregular for one reason or another.

The third type of activity which the law requires GAO to engage in consists of the general examination and criticism of the financial aspects of administration. This for convenience in expression will hereafter be called comprehensive audit. It follows up on the second type of activity (expenditure-review) just as the first type of activity (prescribing forms and procedures) precedes the second.[2] The comprehensive audit gives GAO information which it needs for prescribing forms and procedures, and gives it perspective for its action on specific expenditures as they come before it. Frequently, if not ordinarily, officials of the administrative departments and agencies welcome the criticisms which GAO makes, and put some or all of its recommendations into effect forthwith. And finally, the disclosures which GAO is able to make concerning financial practices and attitudes toward the use of public money are taken into account by Congress and President in subsequent appropriations of money and in the enactment of legislation relating to exenditure of the money which is appropriated.

The authority which GAO exercises under each of these three heads in relation to the administrative branch of the government has been under attack ever since the system was established in 1921. There is general agreement that the third of the above listed activities (comprehensive audit) is necessary, and that it should be carried out by an agency that is as free as an agency of government can be from pressure to protect the administrative branch.

[2] I use the terms "expenditure-review" and "comprehensive audit" to avoid misunderstanding which arises out of different meanings which are given to terms more commonly used. A great deal of confusion arises because of different uses of three terms: "pre-audit," "post-audit," and "independent audit." By pre-audit some people mean examination, by outside officials, before payment is made; others include in their use of the term examination after payment has been made, provided the outside examiners can order recovery or other corrective action in case they find the payment irregular. The last-mentioned examination can be called pre-audit because it is previous to final closure of the transaction. Other persons call the last-mentioned examination post-audit because it is posterior to payment. Some persons use the term independent audit to include any kind of examination by officials who are not under the control of the agency that incurs the obligation; for them pre-payment review of expenditures by GAO is independent audit. Other persons use the term independent audit to refer only to a general examination of financial transactions by an outside agency where the examination results in a report to a superior body which may or may not take corrective action. Thus an examination of the financial affairs of a business corporation by a consulting firm of accountants which reports its findings to the board of directors of the corporation would, in this usage of the term, be considered an independent audit.

There is also general agreement that a central agency staffed with trained accountants should have authority to prescribe accounting forms and procedures for administrative departments (the first of the activities listed above), but there is difference of opinion as to whether that agency should be within the administrative branch and report to the President or should be independent of the President and report to Congress.

The second of the above listed activities of GAO—expenditure-review—is the most controversial of the three types of activity. Some close observers of the way our system works maintain that there should be no control from outside over a department's expenditures; they would let the officials of the administrative department assume the entire responsibility of spending the money which is appropriated, subject to such discipline as might be forthcoming at the hands of President or Congress if a later comprehensive audit discloses an undue laxity in financial matters. Other observers would continue the type of expenditure-review which GAO now provides but would have it carried out by a central agency reporting to the President instead of Congress. Still others thinks the situation is now the way it should be—a check on specific expenditures, exercised by an agency having a maximum of independence from the administrative branch.

The dissatisfaction with our present system of accounting control which prevails among government officials, and the criticisms which have been directed toward it by students on the outside, make it clear that we must subject our present arrangements to a thorough reexamination and reevaluation. The pages which follow attempt to point out the principal questions which must be answered and to indicate some of the major considerations which must be weighed in an effort to answer them. This discussion will be related to the three types of activity now carried on by GAO and will take them up in the order of least difficulty—first, the authority of GAO to make a general examination and criticism of the financial activities of the administrative departments and agencies (comprehensive audit); second, the authority to prescribe accounting forms and procedures; and finally, the authority to approve and disapprove specific expenditures (expenditure-review).

The first of these three matters presents no serious difficulties and requires very little discussion here. As noted above, there is general agreement that the financial actions of every administrative department and agency should be reviewed from time to time by outsiders who possess accounting skills. Furthermore, it is generally agreed that the office which conducts these audits should be directly under the authority of Congress. This would minimize the likelihood that the auditing office would respond to pressure put upon it by administrative officials who fear an adverse report on their conduct. Even more important, it would give Congress assurance that it could get the information that it wants. Our basic theory concerning the relation of the legislative branch of the government to the control of public money makes it highly important that Congress be fully satisfied that it knows what is being done with the money which it appropriates. Congress certainly would not have any assurance that it could find out what is going on in the administrative branch if it had to depend for its information on an agency that takes its orders from the President. Our history is replete with instances where Presidents have ordered administrative officials not to make disclosures concerning their conduct to the houses of Congress. And these denials of information occur when the two branches are in the hands of the same political party, as was demonstrated more than once during the administration of Franklin D. Roosevelt.

The central office which has the job of comprehensive audit should be adequately staffed for continuous inspection of the bookkeeping systems and for critical evaluation of the quality of accounting personnel in the various administrative establishments of the national government. To support its determinations as to the character of record-keeping, it should be able to call up for independent examination blocks of accounts and records which will enable it to determine more certainly the quality of financial

record-keeping that is being maintained. The results of its findings should be reported to Congress and ordinarily, unless Congress instructs otherwise, to the President.

If inquiries of one kind or another are made in sufficient quantity, evidence should turn up which would identify the soft spots
and the sour spots in the adminstrative branch. Congress could
accordingly be advised of the need to direct further inquiry into
particular departments and agencies or into particular kinds of
problems. If convincing reports flowed in sufficient quantity to
the appropriations committees of the House and Senate, there is
every reason to suppose that their examination of administrative
officials in connection with the annual requests for appropriations
would be better directed than at present and would result in
immediate reform in the departments and agencies where irregularity is found. And, of course, reports of this character would
provide a basis for the enactment of legislation that would make
irregular and unlawful occurrences less likely in the future.

The GAO has authority to undertake the kind of critical examination and make the kind of reports that have just been referred to. Its statutory authority appears to be adequate for as
searching analysis as its officials care to make. During the first
several years of its existence, GAO was sharply criticized for
failure to carry out the amount of comprehensive audit that the
Act of 1921 contemplated and that the two houses of Congress
presumably desired. The default of GAO in this respect was
usually charged up against its own officials, who were said to feel
that the first obligation of GAO is to scrutinize and pass judgment
on the legality and propriety of specific items of expenditure as
they arise in the course of administrative operations. Congress and
President did not appropriate enough money to enable GAO to do
everything its officials wanted it to do (including expenditure-
review) and everything that some of its critics thought it ought
to do (comprehensive audit for the whole of the administrative
branch).

There is much less ground for such criticism of the policies of

GAO now than there was during the first decade or so of its existence. Through its officers and committees, Congress regularly calls on the Comptroller General for special studies and reports relating to a wide range of financial matters; the *Annual Report of the Comptroller General for 1947*, for instance, lists more than 200 special reports which were submitted to officers and committees of the two houses. Furthermore, the number of comprehensive audits of administrative operations appears to be on the increase. The *1947 Report of the Comptroller General* states that 23 separate audits were submitted to Congress during the year, most of them relating to a single division of a department or agency. Whether any or all of these examinations and reports represented thorough and adequate examination and criticism according to the highest standards of the accounting profession, I am in no position to say. They range in length from 3 to 147 pages of print in the House and Senate Documents.

The President, as well as Congress, has an interest in knowing what use is made of public money. Like Congress, he may properly insist that the information which he needs be supplied by men with accounting skills who have no personal interest in the activities on which they report. There is every reason to suppose that the accounting office which reports to Congress will usually give the President the information which he needs, if it has that information or can get it readily. This is so even today when President and Congress sometimes find themselves in sharpest conflict over the conduct of the administrative branch; it is much more certain to be the case if President and Congress should be brought into greater harmony by the establishment of the Central Council proposed in my final chapter. But if experience should prove that the President cannot get the information that he wants in any other way, then he too should have at hand or be able to call into existence a force of investigators that can satisfy him as to what is going on.

The second type of central accounting activity to be discussed —actions taken under grants of authority to prescribe accounting systems—cannot be disposed of so easily. The installation of accounting systems cannot be left entirely to the discretion of officials in the various administrative departments and agencies. No matter how aboveboard their intentions may be, some of the smaller establishments of the federal government will need help in devising forms and procedures which safeguard against oversight and error. The occasion will arise when officials in one part or another of the administrative branch will have to be coerced, for the pressure to get work done leads to laxity in making records that adequately reveal the character and circumstances of the financial transactions that take place. And, aside from the necessity of assisting some administrative officials and coercing others, it is important that there be some uniformity in the way records are kept and transactions reported; if the disparity in the accounting systems is too great, comparisons of cost cannot be made and the character of particular transactions may be difficult to interpret.

This is to say that there must be central control over accounting systems, but it leaves open to question where that control should be located. The authority to determine what the forms and procedures will actually be is now divided between departments and agencies that make up the administrative branch and GAO which reports to Congress. The officials of each administrative establishment take the initiative, developing the forms and procedures that they think best suited to their particular administrative operations; GAO reviews the system which is thus developed and has authority to require that the system be changed to meet its standards.

This grant of authority to GAO has been persistently and severely criticized for many years. The President's Committee on Administrative Management, reporting in 1937, was unanimous and unequivocal in the statement that "the authority to prescribe and supervise accounting systems, forms, and procedures in the Federal establishments" should be lodged in the administrative branch where it would be under the authority of the President rather than Congress, except to the extent that legislation might impose standards which the President and administrative officials would be obliged to respect.[3] The position taken by the President's Committee seems to have been accepted as gospel by the academic students of government, hardly a murmur of dissent from its recommendations having appeared in the literature from 1937 until the appearance of the report of the Hoover Commission in 1949.

The Hoover Commission did its own thinking on this question and divided into four groups on the issue. Commissioners James H. Rowe, Jr., and James K. Pollock agreed with the President's Committee that complete authority to determine the character of accounting systems, except as regulated by standards imposed in law, should be vested in administrative officials who answer to the President rather than to Congress, and recommended that legislation be enacted to put their views into effect. Commissioner Dean Acheson agreed with Commissioners Rowe and Pollock on the principle involved, but thought we were working to that end under present legislation and that further legislation at this time might hinder rather than facilitate achievement of that end. Commissioners John L. McClellan and Carter Manasco urged that the authority that is now vested in GAO be continued; but the language of their report makes it uncertain whether they reached their conclusion by weighing the merits of alternative arrangements, or because they thought the Constitution assigned the authority over accounting systems to Congress, or because they thought a proposal to give full control of accounting systems to the President and administrative officials would have an adverse effect on the reception given to the recommendations in general of the Hoover Commission. The remaining members of the Commission avoided discussion of the principle at issue and limited their remarks to little more than the following recommendation: "An Accountant General be established under the Secretary of the

[3] *Report of the President's Committee on Administrative Management* (Government Printing Office, 1937), pp. 21–25.

Treasury [who is generally acknowledged to answer to the President rather than Congress] with authority to prescribe general accounting methods and enforce accounting procedures. These methods and procedures should be subject to the approval of the Comptroller General [who admittedly reports to Congress] within the powers now conferred upon him by the Congress."[4]

The proposition that the character of the accounting systems which are to be installed and administered in the administrative departments and agencies should be determined entirely by administrative officials who answer to the President rather than to Congress is frequently put forward without much explanation or citation of evidence and reasoning to support it. When explanation, evidence, and reasoning are presented, the case for the proposition is usually based on the supposition that the President would favor systems of accounting that would not be preferred by Congress. I find this hard to believe. The interest of Congress and President in this matter seem to me to be identical. Both of them want the work of the government done with dispatch and in accordance with the requirements of law. Both want public money to be conserved rather than wasted. Both want the records relating to financial transactions to reveal what has been done with the money appropriated. And both want the records kept in a way that will facilitate comparative analysis of costs. The force of men with accounting skill that devises a system that fully satisfies either Congress or President, it seems to me, will have devised a system that is highly satisfactory to the other. The controversies that arise as to the character of the arrangements to be set up will be fought out between administrative officials charged with carrying on the work of government and officials in the central agency who oppose their wishes. Congress and President are likely to get into the squabble only as they are dragged in by one side or the other.

I do think it makes a difference, however, whether the central

---

[4] *Budgeting and Accounting; A Report to the Congress by the Commission on Organization of the Executive Branch of the Government, February 1949* (Government Printing Office, 1949), pp. 35–73; quotation at p. 39.

agency which determines what the accounting arrangements will be answers to Congress or answers to the President. And I think that the considerations which make a case for putting the authority over the central agency in one of the political branches just about match those for putting it in the other. The central accounting agency that reports to Congress will have the job of making comprehensive audits, and it will be largely occupied with studies to determine comparative costs. If that agency is given authority also to prescribe accounting systems, it will put a high premium on uniformity in acounting methods throughout the federal service.

But there are limits to the amount of uniformity that officials in the administrative departments and agencies will find tolerable. The paper and figures that make up the accounts of an administrative organization do a great deal more than provide a record of how the organization spent its money. They constitute devices by which the department makes its decisions and issues its instructions in practically every phase of its operations. The leave and attendance records, for instance, may interest the central accounting office only because they show whether men who drew pay were actually at work; but for the officials of the administrative establishments, leave and attendance records constitute a device for making sure that the employees report for work and that the boss is there to see that they work under supervision. We may take it for granted that any central accounting office which is established, even one which reports to the legislative branch, will appreciate the administrative uses of financial accounts and make provision for administrative needs in prescribing an accounting system. But it is likely that a central agency which is responsible for comprehensive audit and study of comparative costs will make fewer concessions to administrative expediency than the officials think necessary. In theory the administrative officials, either directly or through the President, might appeal to Congress to redress the stubbornness of the central accounting agency; in practice such appeals are not likely to afford much relief, for Congressmen are hardly in a position to weigh the merits of such a controversy.

These considerations must be taken into account in evaluating the contention that the President should have authority over the agency which prescribes accounting systems. Administrative officials, particularly those (like cabinet members) who are close to the President, will be able to win concessions from the President that they could never win from Congress. But there is no reason to think that an appeal to the President on such a matter will often, if ever, lead to his weighing the merits of the controversy. The President has no more capacity for choosing intelligently between the considerations supporting the two sides of the controversy than members of a congressional committee; and he has a lot less time to listen to the arguments. If he takes any action, it will ordinarily represent a decision to give one man what he wants instead of the other. When disputes between a major administrative department and a central accounting agency are settled on that basis, the accounting agency is pretty certain to lose. The officials of the accounting agency will know that as well as anybody else, and they can be expected voluntarily to make the concessions to administrative officials which will keep most of the controversies out of the White House. Administrative expediency will undoubtedly triumph over accounting ideals a good deal more often if the central agency which must approve accounting systems reports to the President instead of Congress.

This puts us right back where we started. There is bound to be conflict between two interests in fixing the character of accounting systems. We want the forms and procedures to serve the purposes of administrative officials; but we want them also to lend themselves to interpretation by an outside agency and to facilitate comparative study of costs. We can put the central control over accounting systems in the administrative branch and tilt the decisions in favor of administrative expediency. Or we can put it under Congress and tilt the decisions in favor of comprehensive audit and comparative analysis. The doctors disagree; the patient can make his choice.

This brings us to the third type of activity carried on by GAO and the aspect of financial control over which we have developed our bitterest arguments—central expenditure-review. Ought the officials of the administrative departments and agencies be free to complete their financial transactions according to their own judgment and declare each account closed when they order payment? Or should a central agency review each set of documents while it is fresh in the minds of everyone concerned and make an independent and authoritative determination whether the transaction was proper in every respect and may stand as settled? Without central review the individual who receives a check from the federal government will know that the money is his, unless there is later evidence of fraud on which to reopen the case; and the official who ordered payment will answer to no one for the correctness of his judgment unless subsequent disclosures should present a cause for disciplinary action. If, on the other hand, central expenditure-review is provided, no financial transaction will be closed until the reviewing office says it is. The government employee who is paid for his services, or the business man who is paid for supplies, will not know whether the money is his until the central agency has examined the papers and settled the account. And finally, if there is to be central review of individual expenditures, who should provide it—a central accounting office that answers to the President or a central accounting office that makes comprehensive audits and looks upon Congress as its boss?

We now have three different arrangements in the federal government. The standard procedure, as noted early in this chapter, gives GAO the authority to settle the accounts of the disbursing officers who pay the obligations which are incurred in the various departments and agencies that carry on the work of the government; and GAO will not declare the account of a disbursing officer settled until it has satisfied itself that each financial transaction that enters into his account was legally authorized and was carried out in accordance with the requirements of the controlling legislation and appropriation acts. In this way GAO brings under its scrutiny all of the documents relating to any transaction which it sees cause to question.

There are two classes of exceptions to this procedure. GAO appears to "settle" the accounts of disbursing officers who make payments that are ordered by Veterans' Administration, but in doing so GAO can question the propriety of payments which fall within certain categories only on ground of fraud. The same is true of payments made on order of certain other administrative agencies. And in addition to these exceptions where GAO has only a partial authority to order corrective action, there are a number of administrative agencies whose expenditures do not come to GAO for settlement (i.e., GAO does not settle the accounts of the disbursing officers who make payment for these agencies). In all these cases, however, GAO may later turn up evidences of irregularity in the course of comprehensive audit and report the questionable transactions to Congress.

I have not been able to obtain any estimate of the proportion of total federal expenditures which fall in any one of these three categories. Presumably, we ought to move in one direction or the other until all administrative establishments are on the same basis in respect to comparable expenditures. But experienced public officials and other competent observers are in sharp disagreement as to what direction we should go. Some want no central expenditure-review at all; they would give officials in the administrative establishment the entire responsibility for incurring obligations and ordering payment. Some others would have central expenditure-review, but they would take it away from the agency that makes the comprehensive audit and give it to an office that is answerable to the President rather than Congress. And a third group would extend central review to all administrative establishments and leave its administration right where it is now, in an agency answerable to Congress which is also charged with the general examination and criticism (comprehensive audit) of financial activities throughout the government.

It is noteworthy, and to me most disappointing, that the great controversy which has been waged about central expenditure-review has turned entirely on the questions of whether that review should be carried on by an agency that makes comprehensive audits and reports to Congress and whether the actual examination of documents should be done at a single place (physical location) rather than in the offices of the several departments and agencies where expenditures originate. Prior to either of these questions is another which seems to have missed consideration altogether: Do we need review of expenditures by a central agency of any kind under any circumstances?

The President's Committee on Administrative Management devoted itself so fully to unhorsing the Comptroller General that it found no place in its report for a statement of whether central review of expenditures (i.e., review by a central agency) was necessary, or if necessary, why; and if necessary, in what detail it should be carried on. All one can conclude about the Committee's views on these matters is what he may be able to draw out of the recommendation that "claims and demands by the Government of the United States or against it and accounts in which the Government of the United States is concerned, either as debtor or as creditor, should be settled and adjusted in the Treasury Department."[5]

The task force which reported to the Hoover Commission on fiscal, budgeting, and accounting activities found the question of central expenditure-review worthy of more attention than the President's Committee. It devoted two whole sentences to the subject, stating that the authority which is now vested in GAO "to settle all claims and demands either for or against the Government" should be transferred to the Treasury Department, but giving no indication as to whether the Treasury Department should provide a central review of expenditures comparable to that now provided by GAO. The failure of the task force to make any reference to such review in describing the internal organization

[5] *Report of the President's Committee on Administrative Management*, p. 25.

which would be required to enable the Treasury Department to carry on the activities proposed for it creates a strong presumption that the task force did not contemplate the continuance of central expenditure-review on the scale and with the thoroughness now provided.[6]

The Hoover Commission rejected the recommendations of its task force. It took the position that GAO should continue to settle the accounts of disbursing officers; but it recommended, first, that GAO abandon its effort to examine the documents relating to every expenditure, and second, that it conduct its examination in the offices of the departments and agencies where expenditures originate rather than require the documents to be delivered to the offices of GAO in Washington. According to the Hoover Commission:

> In fulfilling his responsibilities under this section [of the law] the Comptroller General now requires administrative agencies of the executive branch to submit all expenditure vouchers and supporting documents for every individual transaction to the General Accounting Office for examination and "settlement." This is a costly system. It means freight carloads of vouchers from all over the United States hauled to Washington for individual examination in the General Accounting Office . . . this Commission recommends, in view of the fantastic growth of detail, that a spot sampling process at various places where the expenditure vouchers and papers are administratively checked [i.e., in the administrative departments and agencies] might be substituted for much of the present procedure of bringing all these documents to Washington.

Commissioners Rowe and Pollock included in the dissent noted above (page 368) a specific recommendation that "the authority to settle all claims for or against the Government" should be transferred from the central agency that makes comprehensive audits for Congress "to the Executive branch," but they made no state-

---

[6] For the pertinent remarks of the task force, see *Fiscal, Budgeting, and Accounting Systems of Federal Government; A Report with Recommendations Prepared for the Commission on Organization of the Executive Branch of the Government* [*Appendix E*] (Government Printing Office, 1949), at pp. 6, 7, 30, 95–96; quotation at p. 30.

ment concerning the nature of the central review of expenditures which should be provided.[7]

The layman's attitude toward central expenditure-review is likely to be influenced by a glamour that has become attached to the office of the Comptroller General. We have a romantic notion that the Comptroller General is a watch dog of the treasury who scrutinizes the payrolls and other expenditures of the administrative departments and agencies, and makes the decisions that a majority of Congressmen would make if each member of Congress could personally examine the records.

The truth is, of course, that the Comptroller General does not make the decisions himself. He has no business personally looking at any of the paper which comes to his agency, except in the rare instances where a precedent is to be established in a matter of high policy or an issue of first-rate political importance is to be settled. The review of expenditures that takes place in GAO or in any other central agency that may be charged with that task is bound to be, in the main, an examination of documents by clerks whose work is supervised, reviewed, and supplemented by men with training as accountants. There is no reason to believe that the reviewing agency, whether it be one that reports to Congress or one that reports to the President, will have in its employment accountants of any higher skill or integrity than the accountants in the administrative departments and agencies who make the initial determinations concerning the amounts of money that are to be paid out. The same can be said of the clerical and bookkeeping staff that works under the direction of the accountants. The men and women who prepare the documents relating to financial transactions and who maintain the records which show what the administrative departments and agencies have done with the money given them are no more likely, when considered collectively as the bookkeeping and accounting force of the administrative branch as a whole, to treat financial items casually and carelessly or deliber-

[7] The views of the majority members of the Hoover Commission which are quoted appear at pp. 41–43 of *Budgeting and Accounting*, cited *supra*, note 4. For the minority views, see pp. 41–43 and 55–63; quotation at p. 59.

ately to resort to deceit in the preparation and evaluation of records than is the bookkeeping and accounting staff of the reviewing agency.

The issue in deciding whether we need a central agency to examine the expenditures of the administrative departments and agencies and order corrective action in case of irregularity does not turn on the skill and integrity of accountants, bookkeepers, and clerks, however. It turns rather on the state of our confidence that administrative officials who decide how money is to be spent will respect the provisions of legislation and appropriation acts which are intended to control their expenditures, and on the state of our confidence that the accounting officials of the administrative departments and agencies will be permitted to prepare and maintain financial records in accordance with the highest standards of their profession.

The administrative officials of the federal government are almost constantly under pressure from different sectors of the population to do things which Congress and President have not provided for by law; and administrative officials are therefore tempted repeatedly to construe their authority to permit action which persons under less pressure would hold improper. Actions which are based on unwarranted assumption of authority inevitably lead to unauthorized expenditures of money.

The case for review of the expenditures of every administrative establishment by outsiders who can order corrections made when they find irregularities seems therefore to rest on solid ground. Since review is a second examination of documents, errors may be discovered which were innocently made. The administrative official who for any reason would spend his money in a manner not authorized by law may be stopped before too much damage is done. And the accounting official in the administrative establishment who is under pressure from his superiors to make his records cover up a questionable or an unwarranted action receives support in a position that he has not the strength to support by himself.

As I indicated earlier in this chapter, some persons who have given considerable thought to the matter are opposed to central expenditure-review, regardless of where the agency that conducts the review may be located in the structure of the government. No doubt some, if not all of them, agree with everything that was said in the past few paragraphs about the need of a check on the administrative official. But they think that we have sufficient check in a periodic comprehensive audit and the disciplinary action that can be taken if inexcusable irregularities are disclosed by such audit.

I find myself unable to go along with this view. It seems to me that there are situations in which the financial transactions of administrative officials should be subject to immediate scrutiny and correction by a central agency. And I think further that some of this control should be made effective before the money is paid out of the Treasury. We now require by law that all contracts for the purchase of real estate be reviewed in the Department of Justice before the contracts are entered into. This seems to be a sound requirement, even though the administrative establishment proposing the contract has attorneys on its staff who can match in legal knowledge and professional integrity the attorneys employed in the Department of Justice. More is to be gained than lost if attorneys from the two administrative organizations are required to get together and find a common ground on the issue before them. The check which is provided lessens the likelihood that an error of judgment will be made which will cost entirely too much to correct.

It seems to me that there is equal reason for insisting upon a second and independent examination by accountants of certain types of financial transactions in respect to which we cannot afford to make a mistake. This is not to say, however, that every item of cost which is incurred in the administrative branch should go to a central agency for approval before the transaction is closed. The present situation where GAO, either before or after the bill is paid, turns over every piece of paper which moves out of a number of the major departments and agencies of the government seems to me to approach the ridiculous. Surely the public Treasury will be adequately protected if expenditures having certain special characteristics are reviewed by a central agency in advance of payment, and the remaining transactions come under scrutiny in the course of a comprehensive audit of the records and practices of the administrative establishment.

The question of whether the central review of expenditure should be administered by an organization that answers to the President, or by the organization that is charged with the general examination and criticism (comprehensive audit) of financial activities, seems to me to turn on marginal considerations. No matter which of the two political branches of the government has immediate control over the central agency, the review will be made by men with accounting skill who are impressed by the standards and ideals of the accounting profession. Differences of opinion are bound to arise between administrative officials and the accounting office which makes the review; otherwise, there would be no point in providing for the second examination. The weight of merit in a controversy concerning a particular expenditure may lie with the officials who incur the obligation as frequently as with the central agency which makes the review. I think the administrative officials are likely to win very few of the arguments if the reviewing agency takes its instructions from Congress; I think they may win more than their proper share of them if the reviewing agency is under the direction of the President. This is not because Congress and President have different standards concerning the use of public money; it is rather because neither of them is likely to listen to the controversies that arise and resolve them on their merits.

Under the present legislation, which puts review of expenditures in an agency (GAO) subject to Congress, no provision is made for administrative officials to carry appeals to higher authority. If provision were made for Congress to hear appeals, they would doubtless go to a committee on which both parties are represented. In that case the issue might be decided strictly on its merits, on the basis of a party division (if the administrative official making the appeal enjoyed political status), or with a prejudice in favor of the subordinate agency of Congress. The first alternative would be preferable; the second most to be deplored; the third seems to me the more likely. If we escape the second alternative, decision by party vote, I think we may presume that the congressional committee would hear a full presentation of the considerations at issue. The considerations are likely to be evenly matched, for neither administrative official nor central agency is likely to take a weak case to the committee. I would expect the committee ordinarily to uphold the central agency, for Congressmen are likely to find more magic in such phrases as "power of the purse" and "watchdog of the Treasury" on which the central agency will rest its case than in the appeals which the administrative official will make for "authority that is commensurate with the responsibility which Congress has vested in me by law."

If central expenditure-review is placed in an organization within the administrative branch, we may be sure that controversies will be carried to the President, because administrative officials who enjoy prestige in the White House will go to the President with troubles that they would not lay before Congress. In that case we may anticipate that the officials appealing the decisions of the reviewing agency will win a good many of the arguments. As I suggested concerning appeals arising out of disputes over the nature of the accounting systems to be installed, if the President takes any action it is more likely to represent a choice between the personalities involved than a choice between the opposing merits of the controversy. And the officials of the reviewing agency can be counted on to avoid reversal by voluntarily making concessions which are contrary to their best judgment as to what the provisions of law and good accounting practice require.

As I see it, the question of whether to put central expenditure-review under the President or under Congress is another of those matters on which the judgment of the layman is about as good as that of the experts. As one of the laymen, I am inclined to go over to the President's side on this issue. If the administrative officials win too many victories from the central agency because of their superior political prestige, Congress can recapture what has been lost when it considers the report which follows a comprehensive audit of the financial activities of the administrative branch.

BIBLIOGRAPHIC NOTE

For such understanding as I have of the work of the General Accounting Office, I am most indebted to three publications of Mr. Harvey C. Mansfield. His best brief statement is in his report to the President's Committee on Administrative Management in 1937 which appears on pages 169–202 of *The President's Committee on Administrative Management; Report with Special Studies* (Government Printing Office, 1937). The subject is developed at some length in his *The Comptroller General* (New Haven, 1939); and he reviews some of the later development in an essay entitled "Fiscal Responsibility," which appears in *Elements of Public Administration*, edited by Fritz Morstein Marx (New York, 1946), ch. 25.

There is also an excellent brief statement of what GAO does and a concise analysis of what is involved in central control of financial administration in Leonard D. White, *Introduction to the Study of Public Administration* (3rd ed., New York, 1948), ch. 21.

Two publications of the Hoover Commission deal at some length with GAO: *Budgeting and Accounting; A Report to the Congress by the Commission on Organization of the Executive Branch of the Government, February 1949;* and *Fiscal, Budgeting, and Accounting Systems of Federal Government; A Report with Recommendations Prepared for the Commission on Organization of the Executive Branch of the Government [Appendix F].* Both documents were published by the Government Printing Office in 1949.

For information beyond what is found in the foregoing publications, look into the following: *Investigation of Executive Agencies of the Government*: Report to Select Committee to Investigate the Executive Agencies of the Government, prepared by the Brookings Institution, Senate Report No. 1275, 75th Congress, 1st session (Government Printing Office, 1937); *Reorganization of the Executive Departments*, Hearings before the Joint Committee on Government Organization, 75th Congress, 1st session (Government Printing Office, 1937), pp. 45–100, 113–127, 195–414; *Reorganization of the Government Agencies*, Hearing before Select Committee on Government Organization, U.S. Senate, on S. 2700, 75th Congress, 1st session (Government Printing Office, 1937), pp. 281–352, 366–444; *Organization of Congress*, Hearings before Joint Committee on the Organization of Congress, 79th Congress, 1st session on H. Con. Res. 18 (Government Printing Office, 1945), part 3, pp. 525–561; Daniel T. Selko, *The Administration of Federal Finances* (No. 18 of the Brookings Institution Pamphlet Series, Washington, 1937); and Daniel T. Selko, *The Federal Financial System* (Washington, 1940), particularly part 5.

The *Annual Report of the Comptroller General,* published by the Government Printing Office, is not very informative. The rulings of the Comptroller General, principally relating to the validity of proposed expenditures are published by the Government Printing Office under the title of *Decisions of the Comptroller General of the United States.*

CHAPTER 19

THE CIVIL SERVICE COMMISSION

The Civil Service Commission is the oldest of the three great central agencies for advice, service, and control. It was established in 1883 and has continued to date without any significant change in its basic character. It had therefore been in existence nearly forty years when the Bureau of the Budget and the General Accounting Office were created in 1921.

The Civil Service Commission (hereafter CSC) is also the best known of these three agencies to the American people and is undoubtedly the one which they would most strongly defend against serious attack. Any effort to alter the position of CSC in the national government or to reduce substantially its authority is certain to meet widespread opposition as an attempt to destroy one of the most important safeguards of decent and efficient government. And yet, of these three agencies, CSC is the hardest to reconcile with any systematic theory as to how the national government ought to be organized.

The CSC, like the Budget Bureau and GAO, was created to give advice and assistance to the political branches of the government and to share in the central direction and control of the administrative branch of the government. Its area of concern is clearly defined, being limited to matters of employment. But the position of CSC in the general structure of the federal government is peculiar in two respects—CSC does not know who is its boss and it does not know where the boundary lies between its authority and the authority of the departments and agencies which it regulates. This anomalous situation is due to the circumstances under which CSC was created and to the fact that since it was created we have changed our minds as to what we want it to do.

The Budget Bureau is directly accountable to the President. The Director and the Assistant Director are appointed by the President, without the necessity of obtaining the approval of the Senate. The Bureau is a part of the Executive Office of the President, an organization of which the President is himself the executive head. It is located physically as close to the White House as the arrangement of the government buildings permits. The primary obligation of the Bureau is to help the President in any way it can and to do whatever he wants it to do. Congressmen and the heads of the various administrative departments recognize that the Bureau speaks for the President; indeed, they sometimes inquire whether the officials of the Bureau personally believe what they are saying or are only saying what the President prefers to have Congressmen hear.

Such an agency can be readily comprehended; it fits into a scheme of things with which we are familiar. Its form and structure, and the way it is directed and controlled, are consistent with the way it is expected to behave.

The GAO also falls logically in place, for its position in the structure of government is consistent with the service it is expected to perform. Its principal job is to police the administrative departments and agencies in respect to financial matters. We follow the British tradition, which holds that the representative assembly should keep a firm hand on the raising of money for public use and the appropriation of money for public purposes. It follows that Congress should have a high confidence in the agency that studies and reports on the use which administrative officials and employees make of the money given them. Since the administrative departments and agencies which spend the money that Congress appropriates are under the direction of the President, there is good reason to remove from Presidential direction and control the force of officials and employees who study and report upon the legality of those expenditures.

The position which we have given GAO in the structure of the national government is consistent with this reasoning. Its services are primarily for the assistance of Congress; we have made it answerable primarily to Congress. The Comptroller General, who heads GAO, and the Assistant Comptroller General are appointed by the President with the consent of the Senate. But they can be removed only by joint resolution of Congress. Congress, President, administrative officials, and Comptroller General all understand that the primary obligation of GAO is to do what Congress wants it to do.

The officials and employees of the Budget Bureau and GAO know whom they are working for and they know who is their boss. The officials and employees of CSC are not so fortunate. In one sense, it is true, the President has more authority over CSC than he has over the Budget Bureau. The Bureau was created by legislative enactment, and the law clearly contemplates that it will be maintained as an agency of government. The President has an obligation to appoint its principal officials and to see that it performs the duties that the statutes prescribe. The CSC, on the other hand, exists only on the sufferance of the President. At least that is the way the statutes read. The Pendleton Act of 1883, which laid the foundation for a merit system, left it up to the President to decide whether the new law should go into effect. President Arthur was free to appoint the three commissioners, or not appoint them, as he saw fit. Since this feature of the statute has never been changed, it is the law today as it was in 1883 (so far as the plain words of the Act are concerned) that any President may, by refusing to appoint commissioners, put an end to CSC and the authority which it exercises.[1]

The Pendleton Act also gave the President complete authority over the rules and regulations prepared by CSC. Indeed, CSC was

[1] The basic legislation relating to the Civil Service Commission and its work is in U.S. Code, title 5, chs. 12–18.

not empowered to put any rules and regulations of importance into effect on its own authority; it could only lay them before the President, with the recommendation that he sign his name and put them into operation.

Up to this point in the story CSC appears to be a part of the President's management staff, just as the Budget Bureau is. But here the resemblance between the two central agencies ends. The Budget Bureau actually assists the President in carrying out his duties as chief executive. Most of the things it does are directly connected with affairs that the President is personally interested in. This is rarely the case with CSC. The CSC is concerned with federal employment, a matter that requires a good deal of personal attention from the President. The President appoints a number of officials—some on his own authority, some subject to the advice and consent of the Senate. The President also has authority to remove from office a great number of public officials. In respect to both the selection and removal of these officials, he needs advice. But he rarely, if ever, goes to CSC for that advice. The amount of counsel he wants, and where he gets it, varies from President to President. One will lean heavily on his cabinet members and other department heads; another will turn to members of the House and Senate; a third will have more confidence in the party's national chairman. But one thing all Presidents have in common—they do not go to CSC to tell them whom to put in high public office, whom to transfer to a different post, or whom to remove and send back to private life.

There are occasions, to be sure, when the President acquires a personal concern in aspects of federal employment with which CSC has a direct connection. In time of war the distribution of man power among the essential activities of the nation becomes a critical task of the government. At such a time the President becomes concerned about the availability of man power and its effective use in the federal government, just as he is concerned about man power for the military branches and the nation's principal industries. The same thing happens in time of depression. Employment becomes a major problem, and the President cannot escape giving it personal attention. And since the employment of people to work for the federal government is an important factor in the total situation, he will inquire how many people are working for the government, what they are doing, and how this relates to the critical problem that he is trying to solve.

On such occasions man power and employment are phases of public policy which the President studies and struggles with, just as he studies and struggles with the procurement of essential industrial materials or with the availability and adequacy of credit to revive employment in private industry. His effort to solve the problem before him will bring him into contact with CSC, for it is the central employment agency of the federal government. But he is pretty certain to view CSC just as he views the Selective Service Administration, the War Production Board, or the Public Works Administration. His relationship with CSC in respect to these matters will be the kind of relationship that he has with any other administrative establishment which carries on the work that government is set up to do; it will not be the special kind of relationship which the President has with the Budget Bureau when it is helping him direct and control the rest of the administrative branch. It seems necessary to conclude, therefore, that CSC is not an "arm" of the President for direction and control of the administrative branch in the sense that the Budget Bureau serves in such a capacity.

Neither is CSC an arm of Congress in the sense that GAO is. The GAO keeps both ears plastered to the walls of the Capitol to hear the slightest murmur from House or Senate; CSC can spare only one ear for Congress because the other is cocked toward the White House.[2] Whether the President pays any attention to what they do or not, the three commissioners who sit at the top of CSC can hardly escape attaching some significance to the fact that the

[2] I am advised by an accountant in the federal government who has read this chapter that GAO has a convenient deafness which renders it unable to hear many expressions of Congress which would require it to do things that the Comptroller General and other high officials in GAO do not wish to do.

jobs which they hold and the organization which they head exists (so far as the words of the statute are concerned) only as long as the President allows them to exist. They can hardly think of themselves as accountable only to Congress when they are required to obtain the President's approval for the most important regulations they issue.

Nevertheless, a major part of the direction under which CSC does its work comes to it from Congress. It is neither unusual nor illogical for a sector of the government to be required to take instructions from both President and Congress. Most, if not all, administrative departments and agencies are in that position; a great organization of officials and employees can be working on many different things at the same time. The unusual plight of CSC lies in the fact that Congress and the President sometimes ask it to pursue incompatible objectives at one and the same time. At the very moment when the President seeks a relaxation of merit principles in order to find jobs for his political followers, or for some other purpose more or less legitimate, members of the opposing party in Congress put the greatest heat on CSC to hold the line for merit, honesty, and non-partisanship.

A vivid memory of my days on the farm involves two dogs and one cat under a corncrib. The cat was in the middle and there was no escape for it until it lost both an ear and its tail. The CSC has many times been in that same uncomfortable and humiliating predicament. During the period when it is newly come into power, a political party is likely to seek many relaxations of the merit system which CSC was established to make secure. A majority in Congress may support the President in legislation which exempts new administrative services from CSC control or which removes from the jurisdiction of CSC jobs that were formerly under its authority. Legislation of this character is certain to be accompanied by other efforts to divert the attention of CSC or weaken its effort to stand in the path of spoilsmen. The merit system is bitterly denounced as the main support of an incompetent and uncivil bureaucracy, and CSC is pictured as helplessly floundering in its own red tape.

This looks like an opportune moment for CSC to announce its subservience to the President who approves or rejects its principal regulations, who appoints its highest officials, and who may (so the statute says) terminate its existence by a stroke of the pen removing the commissioners from office. But the hope of a quick and easy surrender, if entertained, proves to be a false illusion. Neither President nor the majority of Congress which supports him goes unchallenged in its assertion of authority over federal employment. Members of the party in opposition to the President suddenly reveal their great attachment to the merit system. It is, they claim, for times like these that the merit system was established and CSC created. The CSC, they declare, has only one true boss—the American people; and the American people, it seems, have only one channel through which to express their will—the good men and true in Congress who see through the machinations of the Administration and stand out against the debauchery of the public service.

The President and his party usually win their first objectives and have their way for a time. But the nation as a whole finally comes to the aid of those who have fought against the drive for patronage. It may indeed be correct to say that, if CSC has any boss at all, it is the American people and neither President nor Congress.

The Commissioners who head CSC may speculate as to whether they have a boss, and if so who he is. But the officials who head the administrative departments and agencies in Washington are highly aware that they are in bondage to CSC. The boundary lines between the authority of the administrative establishments which carry on the work of government and the authority of CSC (which advises, serves, and controls them) are obscure at many points, however, and shift with the tides of fortune. The role of CSC in the direction and control of administration today, when

Congress is pleased with its work and generous in financing its activities, is very different from what it was yesterday and may be tomorrow when Congress is skeptical and peevish and cuts down its appropriations. The ups and downs of appropriations determine how much the Budget Bureau and GAO can do, but the character of their activities do not undergo so great a transformation as is the case with CSC.

The big job of the Budget Bureau is to help the President prepare the annual estimate of appropriations needed to carry on the work of government. The size of its appropriation will determine how well the Bureau can do this job but this will be its primary undertaking, regardless of how many men and women the Director is able to employ. The Budget Bureau has other things to do, and some of the things it does this year may have to be cut out next year because there is not enough money to carry them on. But the difference between one year's program of activities and that of the next is essentially a matter of how far the established activities of the Bureau can be extended and how thoroughly they can be carried on; the components that make up the whole program of the Bureau will be essentially the same year after year. The situation is the same with GAO. It does the same things one year after the next; the size of the appropriations determine how extensively and how thoroughly those things can be carried on.

This difference between the Budget Bureau and GAO on the one hand, and CSC on the other, arises primarily out of the way in which their respective activities are divided between advice, service, and control. The main product of the Budget Bureau is advice and assistance to the President. In advising the President as to what he should do and in doing things for him the Bureau exerts control over the administrative departments and agencies. It has, as side-line products, a few services which it provides for the administrative establishments. The GAO deals mainly in two things—control over the admnistrative establishments and advice and assistance to Congress. If it renders any service to the departments and agencies of the administrative branch, it is strictly a by-product of its effort to control them and to give advice and assistance to Congress.

The CSC, in contrast, prefers to maintain a full line of commodities for its clientele. Viewed initially at a time when its appropriation is at a minimum, it appears to be primarily an agency to help Congress and President formulate policies relating to employment, to advise administrative officials as to how they may meet their problems of employment in keeping with the requirements of law, and to review the employment actions of administrative officials so as to modify or nullify them when the legal requirements have been ignored or violated. But this is a hard-times scale of operations. When Congress is generous with appropriations and CSC is prosperous, it greatly expands the line of business that it likes to do best of all—the day-to-day administration of federal employment. The advice which it gave to administrative officials and the control which it exerted over them when its operations were at a minimum become less and less required as the operations of CSC expand, for it now steps in and does for the administrative establishment many of the acts which are necessary to creating, maintaining, and managing a force of men and women who will carry on the work of the administrative establishment.

The original civil service law which authorized the appointment of a Civil Service Commission set forth the authority which the agency (if brought into existence) should exercise and specified certain categories of employees which should come under its authority. The President was authorized to extend the jurisdiction of the agency as he saw fit, and successive Presidents have done so in a long series of executive orders. Positions and employees that are brought under the jurisdiction of CSC by statute or executive order are said to be "within the classified service." The classified service has at no time extended to all officials and employees of the federal government, and the authority of CSC has accordingly never extended to the whole of federal employment. At present, approximately 90 percent of the civilian working force are in the classified service.

Even as respects those sectors of the working force that have been brought within the classified service, the authority of CSC is far from uniform. The most notable distinction is between the officials and employees who constitute the headquarters force (called departmental service) of the departments and agencies and those who are scattered about the country and in foreign places (called the field service). The authority of CSC is in general much greater in the case of the departmental service, which means that, since most of the administrative departments and agencies have their headquarters in Washington, CSC exercises its greatest authority and influence in connection with federal employment in Washington and its immediate environs.

The authority and influence which CSC exercises over officials and employees in the classified service is expressed mainly in four ways: by formulating employment policies (through rules which it issues or asks the President to promulgate); by administering many of the activities involved in creating, maintaining, and managing a force of government employees; by approving or refusing to approve various acts of officials in the administrative departments; and by rendering advice on a wide range of matters relating to employment. The way in which these four types of activity are combined into a system of central employment service and control can best be observed by looking at their application in certain areas of employment policy. While the following by no means embrace the whole range of affairs in which CSC has a hand, the most significant demonstrations of its authority and influence (as expressed in the four ways just enumerated) relate to one or another of four important areas of employment policy: (a) appointments, promotions, and transfers; (b) rating of employees; (c) classification of positions; and (d) discipline and grievances.

The authority of CSC in the appointment, promotion, and transfer of employees is derived from a number of statutes, but primarily from the original Civil Service Act of 1883. In that act, CSC is authorized, subject to the rules which the President may have formulated, to "make regulations for, and have control of" a system of "competitive examinations for testing the fitness of applicants for the public service." Under this authority, CSC prepares and administers examinations for a wide range of positions in the federal service. When the results of an examination have been determined, CSC prepares registers of candidates for employment who have been found qualified for particular positions. As departments and agencies have occasion to fill positions, they are given three names from the top of the appropriate register, and the appointing official may choose any of the three. If none of the three is found satisfactory, the appointing official may be able (and perhaps usually is able) to obtain an additional list of names. But reasons must be given for passing over all persons whose names appear on the first list, and CSC must be satisfied that the reasons are good ones and not a cover for unlawful discrimination. If an administrative official comes back too many times for additional certifications, the suspicion will grow that he is not really acting in accordance with the letter and spirit of civil service legislation, and he may meet resistance from CSC when he has legitimate reasons for passing over all persons who appear on a list of names given him. The CSC has the legal authority to bear down on administrative officials whenever it thinks the time has come to do so.

The CSC does not attempt to administer all the examinations that are set up to determine fitness for federal employment in all the departments and agencies to which its authority extends, even when its appropriation is greatest and it is operating on its largest scale. Some positions are peculiar to a particular administrative establishment and CSC has no special competence for determining who can best discharge the particular duties and responsibilities that are involved. The CSC may take on the job of examination in spite of contrary advice from everybody else who is concerned; if it has no stomach for the job, or not enough staff to do that and all the other things it wants to do, it may turn the job over to the officials of the administrative establishment who will conduct the examinations and select men for employment under the watchful eye of CSC. In this case CSC will have to be satisfied with the men and women who are chosen to prepare and conduct examinations, it may review and require modification of the examinations which the administrative establishment proposes to give, and it may have a good deal to say about the way in which examinations are conducted. If, in spite of such efforts at guidance and assistance, CSC concludes that the administrative establishment will not do the job of examination and selection in accordance with the requirements of civil service laws and regulations, it may recall the special authority which it has given the administrative officials and itself conduct the examinations and certify the names of persons found eligible for appointment.

The examination of men and women who seek federal employment involves a great deal more than determination of their fitness for particular positions. We have standards for admission to federal employment as such. Most in the public mind at this time, no doubt, are the requirements which relate to loyalty to the American people and their system of government. Prospective employees must swear or affirm their loyalty before going on the payroll, and investigations are made to determine the probability that the conduct of the individual will be in keeping with what he swears or affirms. The officials of the department or agency with the job to be filled must be satisfied with the results of the investigation, and CSC must be satisfied too. And any administrative establishment having "sensitive positions" (i.e., positions where possible disloyalty constitutes an extraordinary hazard) may set for these positions requirements for proof of loyalty which are higher than those established for mine-run positions. The CSC, the administrative establishment which is concerned, and special investigating agencies like FBI participate in making the necessary investigations and reaching conclusions as to whether the assurances of loyalty are adequate in the case of any person under consideration for employment.

Once an individual has acquired status as a federal employee, he enjoys certain advantages over outsiders in moving into jobs that suit him better. Even so, there are hurdles to be cleared. If he wishes to transfer to a different kind of work, he may have to take another examination. And if he aspires to a higher level of employment in the kind of work he is doing, someone must pass on his qualifications for the higher job before he can be promoted. The officials of the administrative establishment take the initiative in moving men and women up and down and across in the organization. They are not required to administer objective tests in order to determine which individuals have the best claims for preferred positions. The primary consideration in making these decisions is not fairness to the employee; the primary consideration is the construction of an organization that will do the work of government the way it ought to be done, and administrative officials are given wide latitude in deciding which combinations of personalities and positions will produce the best organization.

But there are, as we shall note later, significant limitations on the right of officials to reduce employees in rank and pay, and CSC must be satisfied that every employee who is moved up the ladder is qualified for the new position into which he goes. If the administrative official making the promotion has a reputation for conservatism in moving people up the line, CSC may approve his recommendations without so much as looking at the employee's record. But civil service legislation vests in CSC the authority to make the final decision as to whether any individual is qualified for the position into which officials propose to put him, and it may prove so hard to convince that the official is obliged to go outside his organization to find a person that CSC will approve for the job he wants to fill.

The authority of CSC over the rating of employees is of more recent origin than its authority over appointments, promotions, and transfers. An act of 1912 required CSC (subject to the approval of the President) to establish a system of efficiency ratings which would measure the quality of service supplied by individual employees. Four years later, responsibility for direction of the rating system was transferred to an independent Bureau of Efficiency, where it remained until 1932 when the responsibility was again lodged in CSC.

It is the job of CSC to prepare for the President's approval and promulgation a system for the rating of employees and to see that it is properly administered. Ratings, of course, can only be made by individuals who have personal knowledge of the employee's performance. This means that the rating system must actually be administered in the various departments and agencies. The CSC gives advice to officials and employees who are concerned in ratings, hears complaints about improper ratings, and provides for the substitution of new ratings when it finds that an employee has suffered an injustice.

Efficiency ratings mean dollars and cents to the federal employee, for there are occasions when his continuance in the federal service or his ability to go into a better job depend on the mark he receives when his services are evaluated. If the rating is too low, the employee may suffer; if it is too high, the employee may obtain an unwarranted advantage over other employees. The CSC performs a useful function in trying to bring order and uniformity into the rating of efficiency. This is, however, a phase of central control that appears not yet to have enjoyed the benefit of intelligent administration. One can search for a long time before finding anyone in Washington who has any praise for the present system of efficiency ratings, and Commissioner Frances M. Perkins seems to have made a new system the first plank in her program for improvement of CSC and its work.

The third area of employment control which was listed above involves the fixing of grade and pay for jobs in the federal service. This is commonly referred to as classification.

The classification of positions is regulated in considerable detail by legislation, the first and most important of the statutes of this character being the Classification Act of 1923. This act established certain categories of service (e.g., professional and scientific positions, custodial positions) and set up in each category a series of grades which shall control the classification of jobs. This is more than a listing of grades; for each grade that is named there is a paragraph which defines the character of the duties and responsibilities that must be involved in a job to entitle it to be assigned to that grade. The range of pay that shall apply to all jobs in each grade is also specified in the statute.

The Act of 1923 has many times been amended to alter the description of work and the rates of compensation, but the determination of the grade and pay to which a particular assignment of work (job or position) is entitled is still controlled by statute. These statutory provisions, however, leave many difficult decisions to be made in assigning jobs to grades, and the final authority in these matters is divided between officials of the administrative establishment and CSC. If the position is not in the departmental service (that is, not in the headquarters organization) of the administrative establishment, administrative officials make the final decisions as to grade and pay for jobs. They are required to adhere to standards laid down by CSC, however, and CSC may study their actions and make recommendations to the proper administrative officials and to Congress if it finds that the standards have not been respected. If, on the other hand, the position is in the departmental service (within the headquarters organization, whether the headquarters be in Washington or elsewhere) of a department or agency that has been brought into the classified service, CSC has final authority. Generally speaking, no position of this character legally exists until CSC certifies that it has examined the job, determined its grade and pay, and allocated it as a position which may now be filled.

The principal decisions in the creation of jobs are made in the administrative establishment, even in the case of those parts of the federal service that fall most completely under the authority of CSC. The administrative official knows what work is to be done and he knows how he wants to divide the work up among employees and officials. He starts the process of creating a job by preparing a statement (called a job sheet) which describes the duties and responsibilities that he proposes to assign to some employee. This job sheet goes to CSC, ordinarily with a recommendation by the administrative official as to what grade (and therefore what pay) he thinks the proposed job is worth. The CSC has no authority to veto the creation of the job or to require that the proposed assignment of duties and responsibilities be changed in any way. Its part in the process is solely that of making the final decision as to what the job is worth in grade and pay, in view of the standards for fixing grades which appear in the law and regulations. If the official is dissatisfied with the grade which CSC fixes, he may decide not to create the job after all or he may work out a new statement of duties and responsibilities (which we hope he intends to live up to when he actually puts some one to work) and see if CSC will give the new proposal a grade which will enable him to pay enough to get the kind of man that he wants for the position.

Jobs which have been classified and allocated and filled with men and women who are at work take on a different character as the nature of the operations of the administrative organization change. If the officials of the administrative establishment do not initiate proposals for reclassification from time to time, CSC may institute its own investigation and take such action as it finds necessary to bring the classification of positions into line with the duties and responsibilities that are actually being discharged.

In carrying out its classification control, CSC has two primary objectives: to make sure that work of equal value commands equal compensation; and to maintain throughout the federal service the relationship of what the employee does to what he is paid that Congress and President had in mind when they enacted the law and regulations relating to grades and pay. These are objectives that no central control agency can ever achieve as fully as we would like. Only the employee and those who observe his work from day to day will ever know what the employee actually does. If supervisors and officials in the administrative establishment assume no responsibility for conformity with service-wide standards of employment they will create more breaches than a central control agency can possibly repair. But the more flagrant violations, certainly those that develop to the point of scandal, become known to CSC and in the course of time it brings the administrative organization back into a more defensible position.

The last of the four major areas of employment control with which CSC is concerned is that of employee discipline and grievances. Differences of opinion are constantly arising between employee, supervisor, and higher officials within the administrative organization. This is bound to be the case in a total employment force as great as that of the federal government—now approximately two million. In order to assure the employee certain minimum standards of fair treatment, we have put into effect (in part by statute but mainly by rules and regulations) a substantial amount of law regulating the conditions under which the employee shall work and the treatment which he shall receive. In order to give this body of law some uniformity of interpretation and application throughout the service, we have placed a considerable amount of responsibility for its enforcement in CSC.

The most noteworthy authority of CSC in this connection is that of accepting complaints of employees, inquiring into the facts and circumstances of their grievances, and taking measures to redress the wrongs which they have suffered. The more serious complaints of employees relate to firing or demotion for improper reasons or to denial of the employee's right to remain in the service or transfer to another job or rise by promotion to a better position. Grievances also arise out of actions relating to sick leave or vacation leave and out of actions which the employee construes as discriminatory treatment because of race, religion, politics, or some other consideration not related to the good of the service. Some grievances of the latter kinds may be very serious but they arise less frequently than those which relate to holding a job or getting a better one.

The authority of CSC in these different matters will vary according to the provisions of particular statutes and regulations. If, for instance, CSC finds that an employee has been fired because of race, religion, or politics, or in violation of his preferred status as a veteran, it may order that he be reinstated in his old job or be given another one which he likes just as well. On the other hand, if the grounds which are given for the firing are proper ones, and the error lies in the fact that the employee appears not to have done whatever it is he is charged with having done—in that case, CSC may be able to do no more than give the injured employee a preferential status for reemployment in another part of the federal service.

The federal employee, like any other American citizen, ought to be given protection in the enjoyment of whatever advantages he is lawfully entitled to. Administrative officials can be, and sometimes are, unnecessarily arbitrary and abusive in the treatment they accord their employees. To redress the wrongs which they inflict, there must be an impartial person or body to whom the employee can appeal. There seems to be general agreement that the authority which CSC exercises is necessary for the proper redress of employee grievances, but as we shall see later there is a widespread conviction that CSC follows some strange procedures in applying its authority to specific cases.

This discussion of four major areas of employment policy has not brought up for examination all of the authority of CSC to advise, assist, and control the administrative departments and agencies in their employment activities. It has, however, indicated what kinds of things the central personnel agency does and it should supply some basis for judging the importance of its work.

The CSC appears to be held in high esteem by the American people at large; it enjoys much less prestige among federal officials and employees in Washington. While those people who know it best have high praise for some of the things which CSC does, they have little but condemnation for many of its activities. Some of the dissatisfaction is no doubt without justification; it may be a rebound from the pain of being told to comply with the law. But a great deal of the dissatisfaction arises out of a conviction that

CSC places excessive and unnecessary handicaps on the effort of the administrative official to carry out the obligations which are imposed upon him. The Hoover Commission, reporting in 1949, brought in a massive indictment of the federal employment system—policies, practices, and organization—which gives a great deal of aid and comfort to the severest critics of CSC. Under the heading, "What is wrong with the career civilian service?" the Hoover Commission presented sixteen numbered paragraphs of "deficiencies of the present personnel practices," and followed this with twenty-nine recommendations for improvement of the system.[3]

Many of the "deficiencies" which the Hoover Commission cited are in no sense chargeable to CSC; perhaps most of them arise mainly if not altogether out of the legislation which CSC is required to enforce. There are, however, at least three complaints of a most serious character against the administration of federal employment which challenge the policies and practices of CSC as well as the legislation which CSC relies upon to support those policies and practices. Two of these complaints are included in the sixteen deficiencies listed by the Hoover Commission; the third, which seems to me more serious than either of the first two, was not included in the Hoover Commission indictment. They are: (1) that the examination of candidates for federal employment and the determination of qualifications of candidates for appointment to positions is unduly centralized in CSC; (2) that it is much too difficult to demote, fire, or otherwise discipline employees; and (3) that the policies and practices that govern the classification of positions excessively and unnecessarily impede the construction and reconstruction of administrative organizations.

Concerning the first of these three complaints, the Hoover Commission stated: "Machinery for recruiting is not adapted to

[3] *Personnel Management; A Report to the Congress by the Commission on Organization of the Executive Branch of the Government, February 1949* (Government Printing Office, 1949). The list of deficiencies appears at pp. 3–6. The twenty-nine recommendations for improvement of employment administration appear at pp. 9–42.

the variety and number of workers required. It has proved to be too slow and cumbersome. As a result, there have been far too many temporary employees in jobs pending the establishment of regular civil-service lists. The Government too often fails to get the right man for the job or the right job for the man." Later remarks in its report make it clear that the Hoover Commission's dissatisfaction extends not only to recruitment of candidates for employment but to examination of candidates, certification for appointment, and completion of the action which puts the employee on the payroll.

Most if not all administrative officials agree that CSC ought to have the job of finding out who is best fitted for the great mass of low-paid positions in the federal service. These jobs, involving like duties and responsibilities, exist in substantial numbers in all parts of the administrative branch. The skills and personal qualities that are desirable for these positions lend themselves to objective testing. It is likely that a central agency can and will do a better job of testing than many of the departments and agencies would do. There is every reason to believe that the central agency can do it more economically. And it is certain that individuals who are seeking federal employment will be relieved of an enormous inconvenience if, by taking one examination, they can establish their eligibility for appointment in any of a great number of administrative establishments.

On the other hand, there are positions at the top of the administrative hierarchy that call for personal characteristics and qualities which cannot be identified and evaluated satisfactorily by a central personnel agency. We fill a number of higher administrative positions by political appointment, for reasons which were discussed in a previous chapter. Immediately under the political appointees are a number of officials whose value to the organization is greatly affected by, if not determined by, their acceptability to their superiors. The head of the administrative establishment has the same ground for wishing a free hand in filling these positions that the President has for wishing to appoint the high officials that report to him. The act which established the Federal Communications Commission provides a good illustration of the provision which can be made for positions of this character. It reads: "Without regard to the civil-service laws . . . (1) the Commission may appoint and prescribe the duties and fix the salaries of a secretary, a director for each division, a chief engineer and not more than three assistants, a chief accountant and not more than three assistants, a general counsel and not more than three assistants, and temporary counsel designated by the Commission for the performance of special services; and (2) each commissioner may appoint and prescribe the duties of a secretary at an annual salary not to exceed $4000."

In between these two extremes—the great mass of employees with routine duties at the bottom and the limited number of officials with unique and highly responsible duties at the top—lies a great number of positions which call for a wide variety of skills and qualities. Civil service laws and regulations require that these positions be filled on the basis of merit, but there is a sharp difference of opinion as to how the relative fitness of applicants for these positions can most satisfactorily be determined.

There is a growing opinion among administrative officials in Washington, including some of the strongest supporters of the merit system, that central examination and certification for positions in these intermediate grades does more harm than good to the federal service. One does not stand in the front yard and ring a dinner bell to bring in applicants for this kind of job. If there is not already someone at work in the organization who can be promoted into a position of this character, somebody has to get busy and hunt up individuals with the required qualifications. Ordinarily, the people who can make this search with the best results are the responsible officials of the organization having the vacancy. The men who direct studies of radio propagation in FCC know better than anyone else where to look for an engineer with the knowledge of mathematics necessary for making such studies because they work the year round with the people who are most concerned with radio propagation. They know whom to ask in order to find out who is available for employment and they know whom and what to ask in order to find out whether a prospective candidate is worthy of fuller investigation.

When the CSC insists on doing this recruitment and selection job itself, it gets its registers clogged up with persons who can make a case for themselves on paper but who look like a mighty big risk to the officials who will be responsible for their work. As a consequence, administrative officials are regularly led to promote into responsible positions men and women they think not fully qualified because someone who is already in the organization looks like a safer proposition than the best prospects that the CSC registers provide. The evidence seems pretty clear that when the department or agency does its own recruitment for jobs in the intermediate levels, the quality of men and women appointed goes up.

Throughout most of the period since it came into existence, CSC has proceeded on the theory that it should do the job of selecting men and women for intermediate positions; and to the extent that its appropriations permitted, it has prepared and administered the examinations. Lack of funds with which to hire a larger staff of examiners from time to time forced CSC to delegate some of the selection to the administrative departments and agencies, but the delegation was usually made with reluctance and regret. The extraordinary demands for personnel during World War II made necessary all manner of departures from the customary ways of recruiting and testing for federal employment and a great deal of the decentralization of employment administration that took place at that time has been continued to date. This includes extensive delegation of authority to the administrative departments and agencies to examine and select men and women for the positions which require unusual skills or involve important responsibilities. There is evidence that CSC intends as a matter of policy for the indefinite future to continue these arrangements, and the Hoover Commission recommended that they not only be continued but that further delegations be made.

But, in my opinion, a proposal to open up to the administrative departments and agencies the opportunity to search for and find men with the special skills and other qualifications that are needed should never include the right to hire without control. The principles underlying our merit system require that all departments of the government adhere to some common standards in the selection of personnel. A central personnel agency can do a great deal to raise the standards of those departments and agencies that let their own selection machinery fall into poor hands. Furthermore, favoritism can become just as offensive in the higher ranks of the federal service as in the lower ranks where the great mass of employment lies. If uncontrolled, some administrative officials would appoint as attorneys only graduates of the law schools in which they did their own work. A Texan at the head of a bureau might get the notion that Texas can supply all the skills and other qualities that his bureau needs. A central personnel agency can put a crimp in such doings as these, just as it can correct the astigmatism that sees merit only in Democrats or only in Republicans.[4]

But to charge an agency with the prevention or correction of abuse in doing a job is not to say that it must do the job itself. We face the necessity of working out a system for selection of federal employees that will combine better than we have to date two desirable features—the superior ability and greater incentive of officials in the administrative establishment to find the kind of men and women they really need, and the restraint of a central agency that has a constant pressure on it to ferret out and expose departures from the standards fixed by law. The proper arrangement, said the Hoover Commission, is for the administrative departments and agencies "to submit their proposed recruiting and examining programs to the Civil Service Commission for approval with the further understanding that the actual conduct of the programs will be subject to inspection by the Commission to enforce adher-

[4] If I correctly interpret his remarks, Mr. James K. Pollock of the Hoover Commission considered this kind of central control over recruitment, examination, and employment to be unnecessary. See his dissent from the recommendations of the Commission at pp. 47–59, *ibid.*

ence to the Civil Service Act and the Veterans Preference Act."[5]

"The separation of inefficient and unnecessary employees has been surrounded with so much red tape as to inhibit action." So the Hoover Commission phrased the second of the three major complaints against present administration of federal employment. The task force which reported to the Commission on matters relating to employment stated that "interviews with several score operating officials, both in Washington and in the field, reveal that almost two out of three share the popular belief that it is extremely difficult to remove employees on grounds of unsatisfactory work performance."[6]

I think it will be denied by no one that it is extremely difficult to get rid of unsatisfactory employees (unsatisfactory because they are unable or unwilling to meet the requirements of their jobs) in a number of administrative establishments. But there is sharp difference of opinion as to the causes of the difficulty. Some persons who have been up against the problem and devoted a good deal of thought to it believe that the statutory provisions which govern removal, demotion, and other disciplinary actions are unduly restrictive. Another group of competent observers have no kick against the law but think that CSC has made it exceedingly difficult to establish in the particular case that an employee is subject to removal. And a third group equally entitled to respect think that neither the law nor CSC presents a serious obstacle to the administrative officials who really want to purge their organizations of unsatisfactory employees and are willing to go about that task in a careful and systematic fashion. Neither the report of the Hoover Commission nor that of its task force offers enough evidence to create a presumption in favor of any of these different views. Lacking a pipe line to a superior source of knowledge, I am

[5] *Ibid.*, p. 17; *cf.* p. 10.
[6] The statement of the Hoover Commission appears at p. 5, *ibid.* The statement of the task force is in *Programs for Strengthening Federal Personnel Management; A Report with Recommendations Prepared for the Commission on Organization of the Executive Branch of the Government [Appendix A]* (Government Printing Office, 1949), p. 62.

unable to say which of the three points of view is nearer to the truth. My observations about the complexity of human affairs in general causes me to suppose that there is some evidence to support the position taken by each of these three groups.

The inevitable effect of the law which governs removal, demotion, and discipline is to limit the authority of the administrative official over the men and women under his direction. We do not need law to give the administrative official authority to remove, demote, and discipline, for that is included in the general authority which he has to run his organization. The purpose of the provisions of civil service legislation which relate to these matters is to protect the employee, as an individual, from unjust treatment and, by assuring individual employees that they will be treated justly, to create a state of mind which results in an effective working force. Legislative provisions which govern removal, demotion, and discipline, therefore, are bound to be a compromise between two considerations. We would like to give the administrative official a wide latitude in dealing with and disposing of his employees so that he will be able to build a good working force and to improve it in keeping with his judgment; but we would like to protect the employee from unwarranted injury and give him confidence that the federal service is a good place to work for a living. Since the law which we enact is a compromise it cannot be fully satisfactory to everybody, and it is likely to be highly unsatisfactory to some people. And it is impossible to know (we can only have opinions) as to which of many possible compromises will prove in the long run to be most satisfactory to most people.

Our present civil service legislation and supplementary regulations make it amply clear that an employee may be transferred from his job, reduced in grade or pay, fired, or otherwise disciplined where that appears to be for the good of the service. The responsible official in the administrative establishment is required to make clear the reasons for the disciplinary action, and the employee is given certain assurances that he will not be punished or subjected to discipline for reasons which have no relation to the good of the service. These assurances include the right of appeal to CSC, but the circumstances under which CSC can stay the disciplinary act or reinstate the employee are definitely restricted. If CSC finds that the grounds for firing, demotion, or other disciplinary act are, as alleged, for the good of the service, it has no choice but to concur in the action. And even when it finds the action not to be justified, CSC ordinarily has no authority to do anything more severe than reprimand the officials who committed the offense and hunt up a position somewhere else in the federal service where it can place the injured employee. There are two notable exceptions to the rule that CSC cannot force administrative officials to keep employees they do not want. Employees who are protected by certain acts relating to persons with military service (veterans, their widows, etc.) may be reinstated in their jobs by CSC if improperly removed. And CSC may, by reinstating employees, force administrative officials to comply with statutory provisions which determine the rights of employees to retain their jobs when a general reduction of the working force of an organization is under way.

A sound legislative base for removal, demotion, and discipline of employees can be rendered ineffective by unsatisfactory administrative procedures. I understand that the greater part by far of the competent observers who are unhappy about the present situation in the federal service put the blame for deficiencies on administrative procedures and not on the statutory requirements. There is less agreement, however, as to whether the procedures that unduly hinder removal, demotion, and discipline are the creation of CSC or of the administrative establishment in which the employee works. It is noteworthy that the procedures which are described in detail in the report of the Hoover Commission's task force, and presented by the task force as models of objectionable practice, are in every case procedures which are pursued within the administrative department or agency. There is no statement in the task force report that such procedures are forced upon the administrative establishment by CSC, and what I have learned from other sources causes me to believe that CSC is not to any significant degree responsible for them. I think the blame for them is properly chargeable to officials within the various departments and agencies, and I think there is ample justification for the statement of an employee-union official (quoted in the task force report) that "more people might be dismissed if administrators had sufficient initiative and gumption to do it."

As I see it, the principal reason why employees who are incompetent or otherwise objectionable stay in the federal service is that administrative officials are not under sufficient compulsion to run them down and get rid of them. The cost of keeping such employees on the payroll is paid out of taxes and therefore is borne by the nation at large. It does not come out of the pockets of officials who might fire them. There is always some discomfort and frequently a great deal of positive unpleasantness connected with the disciplining of individuals within an organization. The discomfort and unpleasantness is increased if Congressmen or other people who have to be listened to come to the support of the employees. The administrative official is always under temptation, therefore, to leave the worthless or troublesome employee on the payroll and to protect his own interests by taking on additional employees to do the necessary work. A great many administrative officials succumb to the temptation; the sin must be charged to them and not to CSC or civil service legislation. We may hope to make the lot of the incompetent and otherwise objectionable employee harder when we give his supervisor and superior officials a sufficient incentive to make his lot hard.

The third of the major complaints against federal employment administration which were referred to above relates to the classification of positions. As stated above, the positions that make up the federal service come into existence ordinarily by an act of CSC. This is accomplished by the approval of job sheets—paper descriptions of the duties and responsibilities of the jobs—which are prepared in the administrative departments and agencies. One job description may cover a number of jobs; all the girls in the stenographic pool, for instance, may be sitting on identical job sheets. But allowing for the use of identical job sheets, the paper work involved in this job-by-job description of the federal service is enormous. The FCC maintains more than 600 different job descriptions for its 1400 employees. The Treasury Department, at one time in 1948, had 16,430 different job descriptions in effect for 77,848 positions.

There is nothing unreasonable in a requirement that administrative officials make up their minds as to what they want a man to do before they hire him. If the work that an administrative department or agency is expected to do remained stable, there would be very little objection to a requirement that it file a description for every job and keep those descriptions up to date. But it is a most unusual administrative organization in the federal government that enjoys a stable program. New services are constantly being thrust upon the administrative departments and agencies by act of Congress. Appropriations are reduced or enlarged and the resulting contraction or expansion of employment makes it necessary to re-assign duties among employees. And changes in congressional policy do not by any means constitute the only compulsions upon the department to reshape its organization and revise its work assignments.

The preparation of job descriptions ought to be a minor consideration in the reorganization of a department. The primary concern of officials should be—what arrangement of duties and responsibilities will give us the greatest assurance that the whole job of this organization will be done the way it ought to be done? The preparation of job sheets should follow the development of the organization and be strictly incidental to it.

No such common-sense relation prevails in the reorganization of a federal department or agency. From the moment he starts to think about changing his organization and reassigning duties, the official is plagued by the question—how can I get enough stuff in this man's job sheet to pay him what he obviously ought to have without taking it from another man who needs it in his job sheet? The official faces this issue at every level of his organization. His working force consists mainly of men and women—good, bad, and indifferent in his evaluation—who have had a hard time getting where they are; they will resist any reorganization that promises to reduce them in rank.

It is no solution for this predicament to say that the official should make up his mind as to what the situation calls for, then announce his decisions and let the chips fall where they may. An administrative organization exists to get work done, and there is great pressure on every organization in the federal government to get work done now, not merely to be in shape to get work done later on. The official who undertakes to improve his organization must keep an eye out for immediate effect on the morale of his working force and the quantity and quality of work that his force will turn out. If a substantial number of the employees, if even a few of the subordinate officials who have important posts, are antagonistic toward the changes that are made, the immediate objectives of the organization will suffer; and likely as not the long-run accomplishments of the organization will suffer too. And a reorganization that cuts men down in grade and pay is certain to produce just such antagonism.

This fact is well understood and respected by businessmen. The businessman recognizes, when he puts through a significant reorganization, that he must give officials and employees assurances about the relation of the reorganization to the status they have already achieved and to their chances of going ahead in the organization. If any man is cut down below his notions as to what he is entitled to, the management must be prepared to accept his resignation. And if he stays on and beefs too much about the rotten judgment that was shown in the reorganization, the management must be prepared either to put him in a spot where he can do no damage or to fire him.

The head of a federal administrative establishment has no such free hand in dealing with the personnel that is adversely affected by reorganization. He may be able to throw some men out of the organization by abolishing their jobs, but many employees will have retention rights that require him to find new jobs for them when old jobs are abolished. If he cuts men down in status, some of them will leave but a number of them will stay on to register their discontent and disrupt the morale of the working force as a whole. Ultimately, he can fire them if he can show that they have injured the program. But he cannot sustain a removal that is supported only by the supposition that an employee will not accept his demotion in good grace; he must wait till the damage is done and then file a statement of the things the employee has done, or not done, that will support a removal for the good of the service. He must operate for a period of time, therefore, with these men festering in the organization.

This is not a situation to be invited, and the administrative official who has been in the federal service long enough to learn the facts of life so far as living and working in the federal government is concerned will carefully survey the prospective effect of his organization changes on the status of employees and officials before he puts them into effect. Every proposed new job sheet, and probably the great proportion of the existing job sheets, must be studied and restudied before the new positions can actually come into existence. Only by means of a great stretching of imagination and straining of conscience can duties and responsibilities be fitted into new patterns that will establish the new positions that are needed yet save grades and pay for individuals who are not to go into positions that, because of the exigencies of moving over to a new organization, must be created first. And the diversion of responsible officials from their proper work as a consequence of this process is something to behold and something to be thoroughly ashamed of.

It is something to be ashamed of, in my opinion, because it seems to me to be totally unnecessary. No doubt there is more than one course of action to which we might turn with certainty of improving on what we have now. I have no wish to urge one alternative above others but in the absence of concrete proposals from people with experience superior to my own, I think it may be useful to set forth the procedure which seems to me to offer greatest promise of satisfaction.[7]

The way to handle the creation of new jobs in the course of expanding or reorganizing an administrative department seems to me to be indicated in the process for handling appropriations. The Budget Bureau does not require administrative officials to write out detailed project sheets showing exactly how they are going to spend every dollar of the money they are given. The Bureau asks for a statement of the nature and scope of the undertaking to be carried on. It wants the best estimates that can be made as to the number of men, at various grades, that will be required to carry on the undertaking. It wants to know the general character of the equipment that will be required, the amount of travel that will be necessary, the amount of money that will be required for supplies and other things incident to doing the job, whatever it is, that Congress has instructed the organization to do. If the undertaking is a new one, the administrative officials are permitted to submit their estimates in less precise form than will be required when they have had the experience of previous operations to guide them in calculating costs.

[7] After reading what I propose, a man who has been for ten years in the federal service with much of it in personnel administration writes: "I agree with your criticism of the classification function but am surprised at the mildness of your attack. However, I do not subscribe to the remedy you propose. I would suggest that first of all we abolish all Services [i.e., such designations as "professional service," "clerical-administrative-fiscal service"] and that the Classification Division of CSC concern itself with grades of pay and developing standards for pay rates; and that the allocation of positions be the responsibility of the agencies, subject to post-audit by CSC. Much of the dissatisfaction with classification has been caused by the refusal of CSC to establish standards through which the agencies would make allocations and by its insistence, instead, that the agencies submit individual positions to CSC for prior approval, with all the delays, etc., incident to such a small-town practice. I am not certain whether you are aware that CSC has established an Inspection Division which makes post-audits of some of the transactions within the agencies. I think this post-audit is excellent and should be expanded to include all relations between the Commission and the agencies. If applied to classification, it would eliminate the sending of a mass of papers to CSC and therefore also eliminate the preparation of additional and superfluous papers."

If administrative officials were required to calculate the costs of their operations in the same detail that is required in the writing of job sheets, they would have to say in advance how many lead pencils and how many typewriter ribbons will be used in each working group in the organization instead of calculating, as they do now, the total cost of all office supplies for the whole establishment on the basis of a unit cost per employee. If project sheets had to be prepared in this detail for the Budget Bureau, it is safe to say that the number of people in the federal service who are engaged in budget preparation would have to be increased at least fourfold; and if Congress appropriated money in the same detail, the number of people engaged in the preparation and audit of accounts would have to be quadrupled also. And the likelihood is that, instead of our saving money in the actual administration of the work of government, the total cost of government would jump up substantially, because administrative officials would no longer be able to effect savings by moving money from project to project as the changing situation demands.

If the process which now obtains in the preparation of appropriation estimates were applied to the creation of new positions, officials in the administrative establishment would prepare a statement of the total number of employees needed for a division of the organization or for the execution of a project that is to be undertaken. The kinds of employees that are needed (typists, lawyers, accountants) would be indicated, with the numbers of employees required at various grades and rates of pay. The estimates of personnel required could then be defended before the representatives of the central control agency, who are in a position to say whether the department or agency is asking for a higher-priced working force than the operations demand, in view of the experience of other sectors of the federal government. As the organization approached stability, the statements of personnel required could become more precise, just as appropriation estimates are prepared in greater detail as experience provides evidence relating to necessary costs.

The Civil Service Commission 415

This is not a proposal to abandon central control of the fixing of grades and pay. Central control is necessary; otherwise, a service-wide standard of equal pay for equal work would be impossible. One organization would hoist its grades and pull choice employees away from other organizations; another organization would yield to pressures from within and pay its employees according to their individual bargaining power rather than according to the character or quality of their work.

The issue is not whether to keep or abandon central control over grade and pay of jobs. The issue is how we can make that control most effectively fulfill its purposes. My belief is that we should abandon a practice of writing job sheets which causes administrative officials to tolerate work assignments and organizational arrangements that have long lost their justification. My proposal is that we substitute arrangements which permit administrative officials to estimate the numbers of employees they will need in different grades, as they now estimate other costs; which will require administrative officials to defend their personnel requests at the time they try to justify their requests for money; and which, having terminated the endless scrutiny of job sheets, will enable the control agency (for the first time in the history of the federal service) to send its employees into administrative departments and agencies with instructions to observe officials and employees at work and arrive at informed judgments as to whether grades and pay bear a proper relation to the duties and responsibilities that are actually being discharged.[8]

[8] The following is from a man who has been employed in personnel administration for at least a decade, a part of his experience including the direction of the personnel program of a major federal agency. "For a man who professes to know nothing about the Civil Service Commission, you do awfully well. In fact I am sure you are on the right track in your critical appraisal. There are two points I would make about the Civil Service Commission. The first is that criticism must be directed at the cumulative effect, the general tone of the administrative environment, which all of these Civil Service regulations create, or, more accurately, have created over a long period of time. In other words, it is the system rather than any single control which produces the frustration and negativism which you describe. Secondly, I would emphasize that the President needs more broad-gauged advice and less technical help in personnel than he is getting from the Civil Service Com-

BIBLIOGRAPHIC NOTE

A great deal has been written about the legislation of the federal government relating to employment and its administration by the Civil Service Commission. What has been written does not give much attention, however, to the relations of CSC to the President and to Congress. While there are many statements that the Commission is responsible to the President or to Congress or to both, I have not found an incisive analysis of its place in the total structure of the national government. It seems to me also that, with the exception of the book by Lewis Meriam which is mentioned below, the literature dealing with the administration of federal employment administration has been written with little or no appreciation of the problems of directing a large administrative organization. I set down my adverse report on classification policies and practices with especial caution, for instance, because the literature relating to the CSC and civil service administration scarcely acknowledges the existence of the problems about which I wrote.

I think by far the most informative single work dealing with employment administration in the federal government is Lewis Meriam, *Public Personnel Problems, from the Standpoint of the Operating Officer* (Washington, 1938). There is also a very sensible analysis of the position of the Civil Service Commission and its relation to administration in an article by John McDiarmid, "The Changing Role of the U.S. Civil Service Commission," in *American Political Science Review*, vol. 40, pp. 1067–1096 (1946). See also the brief but highly suggestive remarks of Wallace S. Sayre in "The Triumph of Techniques over Purpose," in *Public Administration Review*, vol. 8, pp. 134–137 (1948). William E. Mosher and J. Donald Kingsley, *Public Personnel Administration* (New York, 1936), is generally considered the leading treatise on administration of government employment, but this book is too

---

mission. He needs advice at a high level of judgment on where his staff (that is, particularly the executive group in the whole federal government) is superannuated, self-satisfied, irresponsible or mediocre. He needs advice on what he can do about these problems this year, and within his resources of time and within the political environment, rather than advice on split-digit methods of selection or salary administration or efficiency ratings. This advice cannot be given him by the kind of personnel technicians we have developed. I think it can be given him only by a new kind of personnel office which would delegate practically all minutiae of personnel administration to the agencies."

much concerned with the operating practices and problems of personnel administration to be of much use to the lay reader. There is a readable short *History of the Federal Civil Service, 1789 to the Present,* prepared by the Civil Service Commission (Government Printing Office, 1941). I have also had the benefit of two unpublished doctoral dissertations: Paul Van Riper, *The Politics of Office-Holding* (University of Chicago Library, Chicago, 1947); and Ralph S. Fjelstadt, *Congress and Civil Service Legislation, 1933–47* (Northwestern University Library, Evanston, Illinois, 1948).

The President's Committee on Administrative Management, which reported in 1937, gave considerable attention to civil service legislation and its administration, and had for its consideration a substantial study by W. Floyd Reeves and Paul T. David which appears in *President's Committee on Administrative Management; Report with Special Studies* (Government Printing Office, 1937), pp. 55–133. Two documents of the Hoover Commission are relevant: *Personnel Management; A Report to the Congress by the Commission on Organization of the Executive Branch of the Government, February 1949;* and *Programs for Strengthening Federal Personnel Management; A Report with Recommendations Prepared for the Commission on Organization of the Executive Branch of the Government [Appendix A].* Both are published by the Government Printing Office, 1949.

PART V

DIRECTION AND CONTROL WITHIN
THE ADMINISTRATIVE
ORGANIZATION

CHAPTER 20

THE ORGANIZATION AND ITS HEAD

The two million men and women who work for the federal government are not a mass of people who get orders every day from a single person. They are divided up into different organizations variously called departments (Agriculture, Interior), agencies (Federal Security, Federal Works), authorities (Tennessee Valley), corporations (Reconstruction Finance), commissions (Federal Trade, Interstate Commerce), and still other titles not so familiar to the general public. Each of these organizations has its work to do and a force of officials and employees to do that work. What they do and the way they do it determines the character and quality of the government under which you and I live.

The preceding chapters of this book described the setting within which the administrative establishment is placed. Congress and President determine that certain activities of government are to be carried on, create the organization to do that body of work, provide the organization with money to carry on its operations, and give the organization general guidance in the conduct of its affairs. The decisions which are made by Congress and President, and the instructions which they issue, are clarified and extended by the central agencies for advice, service, and control which were discussed in the three chapters immediately preceding this one. The officials and employees of the administrative establishment also have many contacts with people who are affected in one way or another by government. These people indicate what they like and do not like, say what they want and do not want, and through their representations influence the actions of administrative officials and employees. The influence which is exerted in this way supplements the decisions and instructions of Congress and President and the central agencies which help Congress and President direct and control the administrative branch.

It is the purpose of this chapter and the four immediately following to examine the arrangements within the administrative establishment for receiving its instructions and making them effective in the day-to-day work of government. This examination cannot be made in detail, for the direction of a large force of men and women is a complicated undertaking. The arrangements and practices that exist will not be the same in any two organizations, nor in the same organization over a long period of time, for administration necessarily responds to differences in the circumstances that constitute its environment.

The story of direction and control within the administrative organization necessarily begins with its highest official, for he is the central figure who connects the officials and employees of the administrative establishment to the political branches of the government. He is the principal connecting link between the administrative organization and the political branches for two reasons. He has a more intimate association with the President, Congressmen, and other political leaders than any other person within the administrative organization. And he has authority over the officials and employees who make up the administrative organization which is superior to the authority of any other person within the organization. If there is an exception to this rule—if the head of the administrative establishment does not have both the most intimate connection with the political branches and the highest authority over the administrative organization—we have a situation which, it will be generally agreed, is certain to hinder if not defeat the efforts of President and Congress to provide the kind of government they want to provide.

The head of the administrative establishment influences the character and quality of administration by two principal means.

He gets his own preferences incorporated in the more important policies which are formulated and carried out by the officials and employees who are under his direction; and he insists that his judgment be followed in selecting men and women for important posts and in fixing the relationships between officials and employees which shape a group of men and women into an effective organization. The first of these matters, the formation and communication of policies, is the subject of the next chapter. The second, the selection of officials and the construction and reconstruction of the organization, is discussed in the chapter which follows that one.

The ability of the high administrative official to select a staff, build an organization, and determine the policies which will be enforced depends in large part on the character of the administrative establishment which he heads. No two administrative establishments are exactly alike. Some of the characteristics which differentiate them are of no consequence for this study, for they bear no observable relation to the ability of the top official to influence the character and quality of administration which his department or agency provides. Other characteristics, which differentiate one administrative establishment from another, have a direct and important bearing on the ability of the top official to get his wishes put into effect, and they must be appreciated before we begin an examination of the arrangements and practices by which the top official attempts to make his wishes effective. The remainder of this chapter is therefore devoted to an examination of these important distinguishing characteristics. They fall under four heads: (1) the character of the work with which the administrative establishment is charged; (2) the size of the establishment and the location of its personnel; (3) the location of authority within the establishment; and (4) the character of the office in which the highest authority is placed.

1. The Character of the Work to Be Done. The federal government carries on practically every kind of work that business firms engage in and does a lot of other things in addition. As a consequence there is a great variation in the kinds of work that the administrative departments and agencies do. And there is also a great variation in the number of unrelated jobs that may be given to any one of them. The nature of the differences in work assignments and how they relate to direction and control within the administrative establishment can be seen by looking at a few cases.

The Government Printing Office (GPO) has a single job to do. It was set up to do the printing of the federal government and it does nothing else of any consequence. We know how to pick a man who can run the organization, because all we have to do is find a man who can run a big printing business successfully. The head of the organization (he is called the Public Printer) can really direct and control his subordinates, for he can be personally familiar with the major operations involved in printing. He can judge the competence of those under him because he knows what to look for and he can check what they say and do against his own experience. If he is dissatisfied with any part of his operations, he can take effective steps to correct it because he has no other official duties that draw him away from the job of running his printing establishment.

It is much harder for the persons at the top to run the Federal Communications Commission than it is for the Public Printer to run GPO. This would be so even if FCC were headed by a single officer instead of a seven-man commission. The FCC is a regulatory agency, not a business enterprise. There may be no best way to run a printing establishment, but there is agreement within the trade that some ways are better and some ways are worse. This makes it possible to fix standards against which to measure the performance of employees and the product which they turn out. Our present state of mind and purposes will not let us do that for a regulatory undertaking. We do not have a basis for saying what is good and what is bad in government regulation of communications. The FCC can never satisfy the American people because the American people differ in what they want it to do. The regulatory acts of FCC are always the expression of a judgment as to what will satisfy certain interests of the American people without too much damage to other interests. There is never any certainty that the thing which is done will not have to be undone at a later date.

The judgments that enter into regulatory action are never the exclusive product of the men who sit at the top of the organization. The questions that have to be decided by FCC are too numerous and too complicated for the seven commissioners to handle them alone. They do not eat their meat raw; it has to be cooked for them. This is the job of the officials and employees who make up the staff of FCC. They lay before the commissioners what they think the commissioners will wish to see and hear. The process of selection and preparation for submission to the commissioners is a process of choosing between alternatives, and the individual who chooses between alternatives cannot be kept from injecting his own preferences into the choices that he makes. Men are not selected for important positions in a regulatory agency solely on the basis of their knowledge and willingness to work; the "soundness" of their judgment is a prime consideration in the minds of the men who pick them.

The relations between the commissioners and their principal subordinates must be very different, therefore, from the relations between the Public Printer and those below him in authority. The Public Printer can walk about his premises and see what his organization is doing. He can lay down standards of performance and look at work records or the finished product to see whether those standards have been met. The commissioners of FCC can walk about their premises and see that their staff is at work. But they cannot determine by inspection the quality of thought or the soundness of judgment that is going into that work. Neither can they lay down standards that will enable them to determine at once whether a finished piece of work meets the requirements of any one of the seven commissioners. The final determination of an FCC engineer as to the geographic area over which a radio signal will be heard is the best judgment the commissioners can command on that point until more convincing evidence is entered or the actual operation of the radio transmitter has proved that the engineer was wrong. The commissioners can, in time, come to a conclusion as to whether the accountants, engineers, and lawyers are any good but they cannot do so through the kinds of tests that are suitable for a printing establishment.

Furthermore, the commissioners in FCC do not enjoy the luxury of having a single job to do. They are not charged with the regulation of a single industry. They are custodians of the public interest in telephone, telegraph, and radio. And the radio activities of the nation penetrate to dozens if not a hundred different kinds of business enterprises—radio communication for police and fire departments, ship-to-shore communication, broadcasting for the general public, and a number of other services as different from any of these as these are from one another. The commissioners can never direct their staff in the regulation of telegraph as they would like to, because they are too busy with telephone and with radio; and they cannot give as much time to telephone and radio as they would like, for they must give some time to telegraph.

But the task of directing and controlling the 1400 people who constitute FCC must be child's play when compared with the job of running a great organization like the Department of Commerce or the Department of Interior, each with nearly 40,000 people on its payroll, or the Department of Treasury with 90,000. These are multi-purpose departments, and the functions performed by each of them extend to almost every type of governmental undertaking. Merely to list the titles of their principal divisions shows that the Secretary can never hope to acquire a full understanding of the major activities of one of these departments. The Commerce Department embraces the Bureau of the Census, Civil Aeronautics Administration (17,000 employees in this division alone), Coast and Geodetic Survey, Bureau of Foreign and Domestic Commerce, Patent Office, National Bureau of Standards, Weather Bureau, and the Inland Waterways Corporation. The list for the

Department of Interior is equally imposing and the list for the Department of Treasury is half again as long.

The Public Printer may expect to manage GPO. The commissioners in FCC may expect to know what is going on in their organization. The Secretary of Commerce or of Interior or of Treasury can only sit at the head of a great empire, hoping that nothing scandalous occurs in one part of his domain while he makes his presence known in another part.[1].

[1] My discussion, in this chapter and those immediately following, of the relation of the head of a great executive department to the affairs of his organization is based on the presumption that his influence will be limited to broad and general questions of policy. I have supposed that he will not be able to exert a more pervasive influence on the affairs of the organization because of the bigness of the organization and the complexity of its affairs, because he will be so greatly preoccupied with other matters, and because he is not likely to have a long tenure in his position. Two persons, each with more extensive experience in the federal government than my own, who read my discussion disagreed with me. One of them (No. 1 quoted below) asserted that the department head can exert a great deal more influence over his department than I indicated; the other (No. 2 quoted below) stated that he cannot exert as much influence as I indicated. I then formulated my position in a brief statement and sent it, with the comment of reader No. 2, to half a dozen other persons with extensive experience in large administrative departments and found that there was little agreement among them. The following statements received from these critics are worth reading:

No. 1. "It is true that the head of the agency or department exercises a control over the more important basic policy decisions. But a number of problems faced by these agencies are so great and the decisions so complicated that I can't help but feel that any top man in a big department makes little dent on most of the things that go on in that department. I don't think Henry Wallace made the slightest dent on the Department of Commerce. And I don't think Harriman did either. The organization is too large and there is too much inertia in its existing routine to be much affected by a new chief. On the other hand, the chairman of a small regulatory commission can be fairly effective in implementing his policies."

No. 2. "I believe that most heads of agencies do in fact examine all of the major policy questions in some detail and that they give some consideration to what might be called the second order of policy problems. Are you aware of cases in which major departures in policy were undertaken without full consultation with the agency head? I can't think of one. Here is what a competent agency head does while he sits on top of the heap. 1) He budgets his time carefully according to the relative importance of matters requiring his attention; 2) he selects subordinates whom he can trust to faithfully apply his policy decisions and to report facts to him fully; 3) he has set up for his convenience (a) routines for directing his attention to problems in accord-

2. The Size of the Establishment and the Location of Its Personnel. What has just been said about the nature of its work should make it clear that the arrangements for directing and controlling an administrative department or agency will have to take into ac-

ance with relative importance and (b) routines for helping him appraise agency accomplishments and the application of his instructions. If he has, in addition, the courage to make decisions quickly and the judgment to make good ones, he is a 'good administrator'—the rarest of all known commodities. All my experience indicates that department heads routinely see, study, discuss and sign all of the major documents down to a level which is certainly lower than 'broad statements of purpose.' "

No. 3. "In my opinion your reader [No. 2] is right and you are wrong. . . . If your position is a valid one, then civilization is impossible. By analogy, even the universe cannot be conceived of: the sun cannot possibly play its proper role in the solar system, and the solar system cannot possibly be an integrated part duly related to the universe at large. In social terms, no adequate supervision is possible above the level of a squad-leader if one wants to be overwhelmed by a close-up view of the responsibilities of the man who has five squad-leaders to supervise.

"In the first instance, then, the matter is a question of perspective, of seeing the parts of an organization as parts of a whole in relationship to each other and to the whole, and of expectations with respect to performances at different levels. It would actually be criminal to expect the head of a very large organization to do many things you apparently expect him to do; it is criminal to view him in isolation as if there were no organization between him and the 'men who deliver the mail.' Your point of view misses the whole significance of hierarchy, and reveals no understanding of responsibility in successive levels up and down. Everything that you say about the head of a large government department could be said of the department if it were one-tenth as large, or of any non-governmental organization with as many as a couple of thousand employees. Yet successful organizations of size that would be ruled out by such an approach are not only feasible but historical and actual. Civilization *is* possible. . . ."

No. 4 wrote the following: "I think you are right on your main points about the department head and that your reader [No. 2] is an idealist. No present department head, so far as my observation goes, is now equipped to do the job which your reader claims they now do. What they might be equipped to do, if they had all the facilities emphasized in the Hoover Commission Task Force on Departmental Management, is another question. Of course your reader may be working with a different set of semantics than you are. That is, he may be merely contending that general acquaintance with most of the things going on in his department amounts to the kind of scrutiny and understanding and influence you have in mind. I suspect it is true that most despartment heads could utter a sentence or two in explanation of most of the actions taken by their department. This does not mean that they have influenced the decision or that they are masters of the problems which the decision embraces. It all means merely that their information span is broader than the span of their understanding or their influence."

count the number of people who are employed and where they are working. Federal administrative establishments range in size from nearly a dozen that have less than 500 employees each to the National Military Establishment that was credited with nearly 900,000 civilian employees in January, 1949.

The National Archives, with its 400 employees, can be a compact organization if the man at the head of it wants to make it so. It is a single-purpose agency. Its job is primarily one of filing and preserving records. It can do all of its work in one building if it is lucky enough not to be scattered over Washington for the convenience of somebody else. Its problems of directing and controlling a force of employees are as simple as we expect to encounter. The man at the top of the organization can comprehend every part of the operations. His subordinate officials and employees are where he can see them. The way in which individuals under his authority respond to instructions can quickly be found out.

This is in marked contrast to the departments and agencies that carry on most of the work of the federal government. Not only do our great departments have a wide range of business to do, as was pointed out a few paragraphs back; their personnel is scattered all over the continent if it is not in one of the possessions or a foreign country. The Post Office Department has to pick up and deliver mail wherever the people live and do business. Forest fires do not come into Washington to be put out. Smugglers have to be caught along the border where they do their smuggling. As a consequence many of the great departments of government maintain little more than a headquarters in Washington from which they try to direct a scattered empire. The Post Office Department, for instance, depends upon less than 2000 people in the national capital to keep track of approximately 500,000 people who are scattered here and there over the nation doing their work.

It is clear enough that the Post Office Department cannot be run according to a pattern that is satisfactory for the National Archives. The head of the National Archives can shake hands with every one of his employees in the course of a year and can have a chat once a week with every supervisor in the organization that has as many as a dozen employees working under him. The best that the Postmaster General can hope to do is to know some people who know some people who are situated where they can see how the mail is picked up and delivered. If he set out to visit all the post offices in continental United States alone, it would take him eleven years to get around to all of them, even if he called on ten a day and spent 365 days of the year at the job.

Next to the National Military Establishment, the Post Office Department is the largest organization in the federal service in terms of people employed. Its personnel is scattered more widely over the country than those of any other department. Even so, the difficulties of directing the Post Office Department are far less baffling than those of directing at least a half-dozen other departments and agencies. Its operations are largely business operations. Its problems of today are essentially the same as its problems of yesterday and a year ago. The arrangements and practices that are worked out today will be applicable to the situation that is encountered next year. The Veterans' Administration enjoys no such comforting knowledge. Neither does Agriculture or Commerce or Interior or State. For each of these and many other departments and agencies, the problems that are inherent in number and dispersion of employees are many times compounded by the complications that arise from diverse activities and the hazards that accrue from perpetual change in programs of public service.

3. The Location of Authority Within the Administrative Establishment. The job of giving direction and control to one of the big departments of the federal government is tough enough under the best of circumstances. It can be made much more difficult by a peculiar distribution of authority within the organization.

All of the authority of FCC is vested in the commissioners who sit at the top of the organization. If the organization does not operate to suit them, it is because of their failure to make it do so; it is not because they lack authority to give the necessary instructions. They have the power to hire and fire; they can change the organization; they can tell any member of the staff what they want him to do and compel him to do it or get out of the organization; they can call any part of their business up for their personal attention and dispose of it themselves if they wish to do so.

Not every official who heads a department or agency of the federal government has such complete authority over the people who are under his general direction. Several of the bigger departments and agencies are made up, in part, of divisions that once had an independent status. Frequently the statute which attempted to incorporate the independent agency into another establishment did only a partial job of it; in many instances the chief of the division retained, in his own right, a good deal of the authority which he previously possessed as head of an independent agency. There are other cases where the statute which instituted a new governmental activity specified that it should be administered by a new division to be set up in one of the existing departments or agencies, but at the same time definitely located some of the authority for directing the activity in the chief of the division rather than in the head of the entire establishment. Some of the reasons why Congress and President might think it wise to do this were discussed in an earlier chapter (pp. 106–108). Finally there is the extraordinary case of the creation of the National Military Establishment under a Secretary of Defense who was given only limited authority over the three component organizations—the Department of the Air Force, the Department of the Army, and the Department of the Navy.

These are cases where a part of the administrative establishment was given a semi-autonomous status by provision of law. There are a number of other instances where the head of a division is said to have won and maintained a high degree of independence from the head of the establishment without the benefit of a statute which he could quote to support his position. When an organization is transferred against the will of its highest officials from one department or agency to another, the head of the organization that is moved may be allowed more freedom of action than he is legally entitled to, as a sort of peace offering. In other instances, perhaps, the head of the administrative establishment took no interest in a particular sector of his empire and allowed it to acquire a degree of independence that he did not permit for other sectors. Once a degree of autonomy is accorded to or won by a division of the organization, it may be embarrassing if not exceedingly difficult to bring that branch of the service back under full control. This is especially the case if Congressmen who have a special interest in a sector of the federal service insist on dealing directly with the division chief rather than with the official at the top of the establishment. The deference which is thus accorded to one of the subordinate officials may give him a status which the head of the department or agency thinks it not good politics to destroy.

And the President can contribute to such a situation too. President Franklin D. Roosevelt maintained a deep personal interest in many of the activities of government that were inaugurated as a part of the New Deal. Often he developed a personal liking for one of the men most active in formulating a new program and gave that person the job of directing it. In such a case the administrator immediately in charge of the program was likely to report to the White House before he told the head of his department or agency what he was planning to do. If the President had given his approval, or even merely indicated his interest in seeing a proposition tried out, the head of the department or agency had little choice but to acquiesce.

The Hoover Commission found these semi-autonomous situations to constitute a major obstruction to central direction and control of administration. "The line of authority from departmental heads through subordinates," it said, "is often abridged by independent authorities granted to bureau or division heads, sometimes through congressional act or stipulations in appropriations. Department heads, in many instances, do not have authority commensurate with their responsibilities. Such bureau autonomy undermines the authority of both the President and the department head. There is, therefore, a lack of departmental integration in performing the department's major mission." To correct this deficiency, the Commission recommended: "Under the President, the heads of departments must hold full responsibility for the conduct of their departments. There must be a clear line of authority reaching down through every step of the organization and no subordinate should have authority independent from that of his superior. . . . Each department head should receive from the Congress administrative authority to organize his department and to place him in control of its administration."[2]

The undesirable consequences of the semi-autonomous status of divisions of administrative departments and agencies have long been recognized, and we have made considerable progress in reducing the number of such situations. It is said that, until a few years ago, the Secretary of Interior reigned over a loose federation of autonomous provinces and sometimes felt it would be wise to send a diplomatic envoy when he wished to communicate with one of his bureau chiefs. The situation in this department and in some others was cleared up to a considerable extent during the Administration of Franklin D. Roosevelt by the reorganization plans which he laid before Congress and put into effect in the absence of a congressional veto.

I share the widespread conviction that we still have too much bureau and division independence of the heads of administrative departments and agencies, but I am not convinced that the recommendations of the Hoover Commission should be followed without important modifications. As I shall point out in the chapter which follows, I think that many if not all the major departments and agencies of the federal government carry on certain activities which ought to be partially removed from influence by the officials at the head of the administrative establishment.

[2] *General Management of the Executive Branch: A Report to the Congress by the Commission on Organization of the Executive Branch of the Government, February 1949* (Government Printing Office, 1949); quotations at pp. 32, 34, and 37.

4. The Character of the Office at the Top of the Administrative Establishment. The most striking difference in the character of the offices at the top of the departments and agencies of the federal government relates to the number of men who share the highest authority. Departments and agencies are either headed by one man or by more than one man. All of the major administrative establishments are headed by a single officer; the Tennessee Valley Authority, a corporation with less than 14,000 employees, and the Maritime Commission, with less than 7000 employees, are the largest that are headed by a board or commission.

There seems to be a general presumption, at least on the part of people who write on the subject, that a single officer who heads an administrative establishment can effectively direct and control the organization which he heads if he is willing to go to the trouble to do so. This is undoubtedly true in the case of the smaller departments and agencies. I see no reason to doubt that the Archivist and the Public Printer can effectively control what goes on in their respective establishments (400 and 7000 officials and employees). But I think that the influence which they can hope to exert over their respective organizations is utterly different from the influence which the Secretary of Defense can hope to exert over the National Military Establishment (three great military organizations) regardless of how we may define the authority of these three top officials. We must also take note of the fact that one man may head more than one establishment and have to divide his time among them. At one time during World War II, Jesse Jones was said to head more than twenty separate establishments. His connection with most of them must of necessity have been casual. If he gave to the Department of Commerce (one of his holdings) the attention that it ought to get from its head, he had no time left for more than an occasional conversation concerning the affairs of the others.

If an agency of the government is headed by a board or commission we can be certain that the top authority is divided; but we have to look into the particular case to see how it is divided. All of the authority of the agency may be vested in the members of the board or commission collectively, to be exercised by the degree of agreement that is signified in a majority vote. This is the typical situation in the federal government. But there are cases where, in practice if not by statutory provision, the responsibilities which are carried out at the top of the organization are parceled out among the members.

The arrangements and practices within the administrative establishment will also be affected by the nature of the obligations to which the head of the organization must respond. The highest official in any department or agency is only partially occupied in giving directions to his subordinate staff. Since he is the principal connection between his organization and the political branches of the government, a part of his time must be devoted to his relations with President and Congress. He possesses authority which enables him to commit his organization to courses of action; therefore he is sought after by the public that hopes to gain or fears to lose as a consequence of the things which his organization does.

For every head of a government department or agency, therefore, there must be a three-way division of time and energy—between the administrative staff below him, the political branches above him, and the public around him. The prominence which each of these assumes in his official life will depend on the qualities and interests of the individual administrator and the place of his organization in the structure of the national government.

The head of the National Archives may be able to devote himself almost wholly to the direction of his staff. He is likely to be selected for his professional competence; if so his relations with President and Congress may be confined to the annual hearing on his budget unless he manages to get himself involved in a scandal. The nature of the activities of his organization are such that pressures from the public will always be at a minimum and he can transfer most of them to subordinates if he wishes to. This allows the Director to assume the dominant role in both formation of policies and direction of the operations of his organization if he wishes to do so.

The head of an executive department who sits in the Cabinet can have no such relation to the operations of his department as the Archivist may regularly maintain. He will be lucky if he feels that he has a hand in shaping a good share of the basic policies according to which his organization does its work. His department is represented in the cabinet because the affairs with which it is concerned are important in the life of the nation, and the way in which it regulates those affairs is essential to the success of the party which is in control of the government. The cabinet department will therefore be headed by a man whose presence is required in the highest councils of those persons who have been given the job of running the government. I commented on the exceptions to this rule in a previous chapter (pp. 285–287). If he is big enough for his post, he will be preoccupied with issues of public affairs that run far beyond the reach of his own department's authority. And the pressures for his time and energy which originate within the government and among the leaders of his party will be matched in number and insistence by those which originate in the public with which his department is concerned.

The relation of the department head in a major executive department to the direction and control of his department is an extremely important one, but in view of what has just been said it must necessarily be a limited one. He bears the responsibility for the conduct of his department to his political colleagues, to Congress, and to the public; therefore he must have confidence that the operations of the department are managed by men who are eager to know his mind, determined to achieve his objectives, and capable of making the organization respond to their direction. If he is assured on this point, then his personal obligations for the management of the department are discharged when he finds a way to make his mind known to his principal subordinates. If he lacks that assurance, then his first obligation as an administrative official is to acquire that assurance by changing the personnel in the highest subordinate positions.

The professional administrator who heads a business operation like the National Archives or the Government Printing Office, and the political figure who heads a great executive department, stand at two extremes so far as relationship of the highest official to the direction and control of his organization is concerned. At different points between these two extremes are the remainder of the administrative establishments of the government.

There is one further matter to consider which has a most important bearing on the part which the head of the administrative department or agency can play in the direction and control of his organization. Some administrative heads are required by law or public expectation to do personally an important part of the work with which their establishments are charged; other heads have a great deal more freedom as to how they shall use the time and energy they have available for the affairs of the department or agency. The Archivist who directs the National Archives is an illustration of the latter type of administrative head. The law does not require the Archivist personally to read the documents which his agency stores, to wrap them in cellophane with his own hands, or do any of the other time- and energy-consuming work that the National Archives was created to do. Like the manager of a department store, the Archivist can devote his personal attention to that part of his operations that is most desperately in need of it.

But the members of a regulatory commission know no such privilege. They must personally make the determinations that constitute the most important work of their agency. They cannot take time this morning to settle an issue for the staff, because they must sit together like a court and hear evidence concerning a regulatory issue. And they cannot take time for the management of the internal affairs of the agency this afternoon, either, for they must sit like a court to discuss the evidence they have heard and come to agreement concerning the order they shall issue. Their counterpart in the world of business is not the manager of the department store who can devote his attention to the problem that is foremost in need of his attention; their counterpart is the head of a clinic who has too little time for the management of his institution because he must personally see many of the patients and carry an important part of the burden of diagnosis and treatment.

This obligation to do the work of the organization as well as direct it is most common in the regulatory commissions, but it is not wholly confined to them. The Secretary of State suffers from this dual obligation as greatly if not more than the regulatory commissions. He is the nation's Number One diplomat. He must personally attend the major conferences. He must personally discuss the problems of the day with the representatives of foreign countries. He must personally study if he does not draft or revise the documents that may mean peace or war for his country.

The heads of most of the departments and agencies of the federal government fall somewhere between the Archivist on the one hand and the regulatory commissions and the Secretary of State on the other. Statutes require the head of each administrative establishment to sign certain documents; conscience may require him to make some inquiries and do some thinking before he signs his name. The differences which characterize the obligations of high administrative officials in this respect, like other differences noted in this chapter, make it clear that the arrangements for direction and control must be peculiar to each department and agency of the national government. We only delude ourselves if we suppose that the arrangements which have proved successful in one administrative organization can be transplanted in body to another organization. The persistent suggestion in much of the literature relating to public administration, that there is a great body of principles and formulae which have universal application in administrative organizations, seems to me to rest on misapprehension as to the realities in which the administrative official and employee are involved. I suspect that many of the generalizations which abound in the literature reflect a yearning to get back into a Garden of Eden from which we are eternally excluded.

BIBLIOGRAPHIC NOTE

We have an extensive literature which describes administrative organization and a great deal, perhaps most, of this attempts to show how the structure (organizational pattern) affects the ability of high officials to direct and control their respective organizations. I find in print, however, only one effort to point out the prime features of many different administrative establishments and to relate these distinctive features, comparatively, to the problems of providing direction and control for the officials and employees who carry on the work of the government. This analysis, brief in extent and summary in character, was prepared for the Hoover Commission by John D. Millett and is published as *Departmental Management in Federal Administration; A Report with Recommendations Prepared for the Commission on Organization of the Executive Branch of the Government* [*Appendix E*] (Government Printing Office, 1949), pp. 23 ff. See also Frederick F. Blachly and Miriam E. Oatman, *Federal Regulatory Action and Control* (Washington, 1940), ch. 3.

The most convenient place to find a succinct statement of what the different establishments of the federal government do is the *United States Government Manual* published by the Government Printing Office and revised in new editions at frequent intervals. Even briefer descriptive statements are printed in the *Congressional Directory*, also published by the Government Printing Office; each Senator and member of the House of Representatives has a substantial number of copies for distribution free of charge. The Senate Committee on Expenditures in the Executive Departments has several times had printed for wide distribution an excellent chart entitled *Organization of Federal Executive Departments and Agencies*, which shows the principal divisions of the various departments and agencies and indicates the number of persons employed in each division.

The best single place to go for a full statement of what our federal administrative establishments do, how they are organized, and how they go about doing their work is certain issues of the *Federal Register*, a daily publication of the Government Printing Office. The Administrative Procedure Act of 1946 required each administrative establishment to prepare for printing in the *Federal Register* a full statement of information which the public would like to know about it, and to keep this statement up to date by additional disclosures when significant changes occur in its organization, activities, etc. The first printing of this material appeared in the *Register* for September 11, 1946, and issues immediately following. Several of the departments and agencies supplied statements running beyond 50 pages in length.

Attention should also be called to a description of the activities, organization, and procedures of the departments and agencies of the federal government as of about 1937 prepared by the Brookings Institution and published as Senate Report No. 1275, 75th Congress, 1st session, and entitled *Investigation of Executive Agencies of Government* (Government Printing Office, 1937).

Additional references to the literature describing particular administrative establishments of the federal government appear in the note at the end of Chapter 6.

THE FORMATION AND COORDINATION
OF POLICY

The work of government consists of deciding what to do and doing it. Sometimes we decide what we are going to do long before we face the task of actually doing it. Sometimes we make up our minds only when we are confronted with the necessity of acting. Sometimes we hardly decide at all—we are faced by an issue; we cannot make up our minds what to do; circumstances (perhaps what someone else does) finally leave us no choice and we act. There is nothing in this process that is peculiar to government; most human beings behave like this in all manner of situations.

But we recognize that we ought to make up our minds on the basis of inquiry and thought rather than allow ourselves to be forced into a particular action. And we recognize that we ought to take an early and broad view of things and make decisions of a general character that will point to or provide answers for the individual and specific questions that we expect to arise from time to time in the future. When we make a decision as to what we will do in the future, we call it a determination of policy. And if the decision covers a wide range of matters and embraces a number of specific issues which we expect to arise in the future, we say that we have made a major determination of policy.

Whoever dictates the important decisions of policy will have a prime influence on the character and quality of work which is done in the administrative department or agency. If the head of

441

the administrative establishment is resolved to exert a significant influence on the activities and performance of the people who are under him, he must get himself in a position where he controls the major policies relating to the affairs of his establishment. It is not essential that he formulate the policies personally; if others draw up the policies he must be able to review them and require changes before they are put into effect.

The first-level or foundation policies of the administrative establishment are given to it. Some of them are found in general legislation which applies to the administrative branch as a whole. Most of them are found in the statutes which establish the particular department or agency and indicate what it is to do, and in the later enactments which from time to time alter its authority or clarify and make more specific how the administrative establishment is to proceed. In addition, the annual appropriation act restates the scale of administrative operations from year to year. We have said a good deal about the relation of law and appropriations to the activities of the administrative branch earlier in this book and need not go farther into those matters now.

Some of the policies which control the activities of the administrative department or agency originate in the White House. Unless there is specific provisions for it in legislation, the President has no legal authority to tell any of the regulatory commissions what they must do or how they shall proceed. Undoubtedly he has considerably more authority over the other departments and agencies of the government, but there appear to be limits to his authority to give orders to them, as was indicated in an earlier chapter (pp. 317–319). But regardless of what may be his legal authority to give orders to administrative officials, the President can exert influence which effectively limits the choice of the administrator in fixing the policies under which his establishment will operate. The President is the acknowledged head of the government, and even the most independent administrative officials (including the members of regulatory commissions) listen to what he has to say and usually make some concessions in order to give him what he wants.

Congressmen, too, have an influence on the policies of the administrative establishment which extends far beyond the formal provisions of legislation and appropriation acts. Speaking individually or as committees, they indicate their preferences, and administrative officials often find it good politics to pursue policies which fall within the limits indicated by the Congressmen.

And finally, there are public expectations which come to the knowledge of administrative officials through other channels than President and Congressmen. These also the administrative official may feel obliged to comply with, even though he would prefer to follow a different course. As noted earlier, the American people are elaborately organized to make their wishes known and to punish the administrative officials who do not give them what they want.

The policies which come to administrative officials from the outside, and which they feel obliged to respect, fall a long way short of settling all the important questions which have to be decided. There are many specific delegations of authority under which the administrative officials supplement and extend the law which they enforce. If the administrative official has no authority to supplement or extend the provisions of a particular statute, he will still have to use his own judgment as to the order and manner in which he will proceed to do what he is required to do. His choice may even extend to the point of choosing which of his legal obligations he will comply with when he finds two or more of them incompatible. As pointed out earlier, it is sometimes impossible for the administrative department or agency to do everything that the law requires it to do, to the extent and in the manner that the law seems to imply. Sometimes this inability is due to conflict between statutes enacted at different times. More often, no doubt, it arises out of an inconsistency between the language of legislation and the expectations which accompany appropriations.

Congressmen may indicate unmistakably that they expect certain things to be done with the money they make available, but administrative officials may be unable to figure out how they can do everything which the appropriations committee says it wants done and also do everything which the controlling legislation says they must do. This same kind of conflict exists also in the pressures that are directed upon the administrative organization by individuals and organized groups. The administrative official may find himself relatively free (and unhappy in his freedom, perhaps) simply because the pressures upon him to do different things balance out.

This, then, appears to be the setting within which the policies of the administrative establishment are fixed. The individual (or group of individuals) that makes the policies which supplement and extend the policies that come from the outside will effectively direct and control the affairs of the organization. It is of utmost importance, therefore, that the legislation which creates and regulates the administrative establishment make perfectly clear where the authority to make its further policies shall lie.

We may safely say that, as a general rule, the highest official of any administrative organization should be given the authority to make the policies that originate within the organization. This is not to say that the officer, board, or commission that heads the administrative establishment must formulate every major policy that originates within the organization or even sign every such policy to make it authentic. But the authority to determine the major policies (subject to certain exceptions noted below) must lie in the head so that he (or they, in case of a board or commission) can nullify any such policy that he does not like and inaugurate any new policy that he is sure he wants.

There are two reasons why this crucial authority should rest in the head of the administrative department or agency. One of them arises out of the circumstances of evaluating and compromising conflict interests. The other arises out of the position of the head of the administrative department or agency in the structure of the government and political organization of the nation. They will be discussed in that order.

The authority to make the policies of an administrative department or agency ought, as a general rule, to lie in its highest official because the range of his interests and the sweep of his authority is greater than that of any of the officials below him, and this permits him in formulating policies to make allowance for a wider range of interests than any of his subordinates would be able to allow for. This is an application, at the level of the administrative establishment, of the same principle which causes us to create a single lawmaking body and give it authority to establish the highest policies of the nation. Congress and President embrace, in the range of their interest, every concern of the American people which is enough of a problem to become a political question and sufficient in importance to compete successfully for their attention. Congress and President, as the highest lawmaking authority of the nation, constitute the only governmental body we have that is in a position to take into account all of the conflicting interests of the American people, put a value on them, and adopt a policy that effects a compromise between them.

When the lawmaking body creates a number of administrative organizations and gives each responsibility relating to a particular area of affairs, it unavoidably creates a situation which invites conflicting policies of government. The individuals who make decisions in the Department of Agriculture cannot possibly know about and take into account everything relating to the price level of the nation which the individuals in the Federal Trade Commission and the individuals in the Federal Reserve Board know about and take into account. And if there were a way to make sure that influential men in all three of these departments would know about and consider the same things, there would still be conflict in the policies they announced because they would reach different conclusions about the probable consequences of a particular course of action. And so the policies of the Department of

Agriculture concerning the purchase of surplus farm products, and the policies of the Federal Trade Commission concerning agreements among manufacturers, and the policies of the Federal Reserve Board concerning interest rates do not add up to a consistent national policy about prices and inflation. Consequently, Congress and President must always keep a hand in the affairs of the administrative departments and agencies and step in from time to time to straighten out conflicting administrative policies.

Exactly this same situation, applicable to a smaller range of interests, exists within any administrative department or agency. If the policies that originate within the administrative organization are formulated and put into effect by its several divisions, we are bound to end up with conflicting policies. Conflict will arise, in part because the officials in one division cannot know and consider some of the things that are taken into account in another division, and in part because the officials in different divisions would reach different conclusions even if they did consider the same matters. Therefore we need to lift these policies up to the highest level of the organization for decision or final approval, for at that point are the only individuals within the organization whose range of interest and sweep of authority are great enough to make allowance for everything that the officials in the separate divisions bring up for consideration.

If consistency in policies were the only important consideration to be taken into account, we might conclude that it makes no difference who makes and formulates the policies of the organization so long as inconsistencies are avoided. There is, however, another line of reasoning which supports the general rule that the highest official or officials of the department or agency should have full authority in the making of its policies. This line of reasoning, as noted at the beginning of this discussion, arises out of the position of the highest administrative officials in the structure of the government and the political organization of the nation.

The policies of the administrative establishment, as we noted a few paragraphs back, must be related to the policies of other departments and agencies. They must also be related to the new legislation that is being enacted and to the public declarations of the men who have been given the job of running the government as a whole. Only if the public statements of political leaders, new legislation, and administrative policies are consistent with one another will we have government of the day that stands any chance of satisfying the American people.

The head of the administrative establishment is ordinarily the individual who is best able to relate the policies of his organization to the general political and governmental program. The reasons why this is so are easily seen and require only a summary statement here. The top position in the organization is the one of highest authority and honor. It may be the only position in the organization that is filled by action of the President and the Senate. The head of the administrative department or agency, therefore, will ordinarily have the closest relations with the President and the other leaders of the party that is in charge of the government as a whole. If he is a member of the cabinet, he is certain to be a party to many of the discussions in which the broadest policies of the government are agreed upon. And as to matters which fall mainly within the scope of his department, he may well be the individual of greatest influence in the highest political circles. What is true of the department head who sits in the cabinet may be equally true of the heads of other administrative establishments. But whether the head of the establishment moves freely in the highest political circles or not, he may be expected to go higher than any of his subordinates. If there is an individual with higher political prestige below him, we ordinarily suppose that the man who is currently at the top is on the way out.

Enough has been said to make it clear that the head of the department or agency is in a better position than any one else to relate the work of his organization to the plans of political leaders, to the new legislation that is enacted and contemplated, and to the policies of other administrative establishments. He is also a primary channel of communication between the organization he heads and people who are not in political circles but who are interested in what his organization is doing. Because of his prominence in public life, and because he is presumed to have authority to commit his organization to courses of action, people go directly to him on matters relating to every part of the activities of his department or agency.

This, then, is the case for giving the head of each administrative establishment full authority to control all of the policies relating to the affairs of his establishment which have not been made for him by the political branches of the government. As noted more than once in this book, not every department or agency head in the federal government has that authority today. The President's Committee on Administrative Management, reporting in 1937, recommended that all the activities of the federal government be brought together in a dozen departments, but it stated that some of the regulatory activities should not be subjected fully to the authority of the department head under whom they were placed. The Committee's statements on this point were most general in character; apparently it felt that in some instances the head of the department should not be able to control, and perhaps not even be able to exert much influence upon, the policies made by a sector of his department which formerly had had the status of an independent regulatory commission.

The Hoover Commission, reporting twelve years later, had no occasion to express itself on the precise question which the President's Committee spoke about, for the Hoover Commission proposed to leave the major regulatory activities under commissions reporting directly to the President and Congress. I believe the Hoover Commission did not at any point in its many reports express an opinion as to whether, in any instance, subordinate officials of an administrative department or agency should have final authority to determine policies. One or more of its task forces did, however, recommend that authority to make certain decisions of a policy-determining character be put in officials who would not have to answer for their decisions to the head of the administrative establishment.[1]

It is my own opinion that there is a considerable area of policy determination that should be made by subordinate officials who cannot be coerced by the head of the administrative establishment to make decisions that they do not wish to make, and whose decisions cannot be modified or set aside by the head of the establishment in case he does not like them. In order to appreciate what is involved in deciding where to put the authority to make policy in particular instances, it is necessary to have some understanding of what the policies of an administrative department or agency are like and of the problems that are encountered in formulating them and getting them put into effect. We turn now to an examination of these matters.

Some of the policies of the administrative establishment relate to its internal operations. They have to do with getting an organization together and keeping it at work. They are addressed to the officials and employees of the establishment and regulate their relations with one another. The public has no interest in the specific content and application of these policies. If the people who do business with the organization are satisfied with the treatment they get and there is evidence that the organization does its work at reasonable cost, the internal policies of the administrative department or agency meet every standard that you and I set up for them.

Other policies of the administrative establishment are external in their application. They are of immediate interest to the public because they are addressed to the public. The external policies fall

---

[1] For the position of the President's Committee, see *Report of the President's Committee on Administrative Management* (Government Printing Office, 1937), pp. 38-42. The fullest expression of this point by a task force of the Hoover Commission is in *Agricultural Functions and Organization in the United States; A Report with Recommendations Prepared for the Commission on Organization of the Executive Branch of the Government [Appendix M]* (Government Printing Office, 1949), pp. 15-17.

roughly into two classes, procedural and substantive. Procedural policies regulate the relations between the administrative orgainza- tion and the people who do business with it. The rules governing my application to the State Department for a passport are an il- lustration of this type of policy; the regulations of the Patent Of- fice which indicate the kind of documents and models I must submit with my application for a patent are another illustration.

The substantive policies of the various administrative depart- ments and agencies are, in effect, bodies of administrative-made law which supplement and extend the statutory law that regulates our affairs. We have made reference to this kind of administrative policy at various points in this book. The Secretary of Agriculture is authorized to fix standards of quality and condition for a number of grains which are enumerated in the statute and for such other grains as he finds it desirable to regulate in view of the "usages of the trade." The Federal Communications Commission has author- ity to allocate sectors of the radio spectrum to different kinds of communication service and to assign specific frequencies to in- dividual applicants. The acts of the Secretary of Agriculture and the FCC under these statutory grants of authority have the force and effect of law in their impact upon people who ship grain in interstate commerce or communicate by radio transmissions.

The internal policies of the administrative establishment range in character from broad statements of general purpose to definitive instructions. Some statements of policy may be formulated by the head of the establishment and distributed throughout the organiza- tion in his own words. Declarations of this sort are of necessity exceptional. They come at infrequent intervals and they are likely to apply to a specific matter which has come to the attention of the head of the organization. If he has learned that employees are taking home pencils that were bought with taxpayers' money, he can order the practice stopped. The head of a large department or agency of the federal government cannot himself formulate the general body of policies that regulate the people under him, however. These policies consist of a mass of understandings and instructions, many of which have been in existence for years if not ever since the organization was established. If the top official doesn't like the way his organization is operating and proposes to change its ways, he will be wise to say as much to the heads of his principal divisions and tell them to straighten the place out. If he starts issuing edicts himself, he is pretty certain to create a worse mess than the one he is trying to clean up. Changes in policies that improve the routine operations of an organization are best worked out by the people who are responsible for directing those operations. If the head of the establishment is concerned enough to give some time to matters of this sort, he will undoubtedly achieve his greatest gains by encouraging the chiefs of his various divisions to try to institute a new order of things in their respective jurisdictions.

There are also definite limitations on what the head of a large department or agency can do concerning the external policies of his establishment. But the nature and significance of those limitations will vary enormously according to the character of the work with which the department or agency is charged and according to the character of the top authority in the department or agency. The previous chapter pointed out how widely federal administrative establishments differ in these respects; a few illustrations will show how these differences affect the arrangements for formulating and putting into effect the external policies of the administrative establishment.

For some of the administrative establishments, the problem of making policies governing their relations with people on the outside is a simple one. They do business with very few people and they have little authority over the people they do business with. The Government Printing Office and the National Archives are in this position. The GPO prints documents for the President, Congress, the courts, and the administrative branch. It must have policies which advise these people as to how they should submit materials for publication and how the costs of printing will be defrayed. But all these people are within the government; GPO does not do printing for the general public. You and I may purchase government documents from GPO, however; consequently it must adopt some policies governing the price of documents and issue some statements as to how they may be obtained. But the officials of GPO are not faced with the job of formulating policies which govern the way you and I carry on our own businesses. The problems of the National Archives are almost identical with those of GPO. It stores documents which come to it from all parts of the government; people outside the government may go there to look at them. The limited volume and character of the external policies which are required in these two agencies, in each case, permit the head of the agency to review all the policies himself; if he wants to, he may even be able to write out a good many of the policies in his own words.

The regulatory commissions present a second type of situation. They exist primarily to regulate the affairs of the American people. Of necessity, they develop elaborate bodies of policy which govern the American people—policies of a procedural character which tell us how to handle our affairs before the commission and policies of substantive character which tell us what we may and may not do in running our own businesses. The whole purpose in creating the commission and setting up a staff to work under its direction is to get a body of regulatory policy established and to get that policy applied fairly to all persons whose interests and activities come within its scope.

We put a commission at the head of the regulatory agency because we want the regulatory policy to be decided upon and applied by a group of men who deliberate together, who offer some prospect of representing different points of view, and who can draw upon different backgrounds in previous experience and interest. We can realize the advantages of group deliberation and representativeness only if the commissioners personally decide the important questions of policy which they put into effect and if they personally make the decisions which apply the provisions of the controlling legislation and their own policies in the specific situations which arise. The commissioners sit as a subordinate legislature to make policies applicable to a wide range of affairs already existing and expected to come into existence later on; and they sit as a court of first instance to weigh competing considerations and apply the law (acts of Congress and policies of their own creation) when specific questions as to its application arise.

The members of a commission can make personal judgments in these matters only if the range of affairs with which they are concerned is limited and if they are assisted by a staff of people who digest, analyze, and organize for them the evidence and lines of reasoning which they must take into account. If, however, we scatter the regulatory work of the federal government among a large number of commissions, we run the risk that their various policies and practices will conflict with one another. In deciding how wide a range of affairs to bring under the jurisdiction of a single commission, we have to weigh the advantages of personal decision by the commissioners against the advantages of coordinating a comprehensive range of public policy.

The perplexities which confront Congress and the President in deciding how to allocate regulatory work to regulatory commissions will be made apparent by an examination of the over-all problem of regulating transportation and communications. The federal government now provides a good deal of regulation for transportation by rail, highways (motor carriers), pipe lines, air, and water. Most of this regulatory work is carried on in four agencies—the Interstate Commerce Commission, the Civil Aeronautics Board, the Civil Aeronautics Administration in the Department of Commerce, and the Maritime Commission. Each of these great systems of transportation (rail, highway, air, and water) is intimately connected with each of the others; passengers and commodities move for part of their journey by one type of carrier and continue by another. Therefore the regulation of any one of these transportation systems must be coordinated with the regulation of each of the others. Otherwise conflicting regulatory policies would hinder rather than facilitate the movement of people and goods. In the case of rail, highway, pipe line, and inland waterways, the coordination is effected within the Interstate Commerce Commission because it has regulatory authority over all these types of transportation. Coordination of air and ocean transportation policies, and coordination of each of these with the policies of ICC, must be effected through inter-agency relationships.

This complicated problem of regulating transportation is further complicated by the necessity of regulating communications. Communication by telephone and telegraph is essential to the operation of each of the transportation systems we have been talking about. But the regulation of telephone and telegraph is entrusted to still a different agency—the Federal Communications Commission. This introduces an additional problem of inter-agency coordination, though probably not as difficult a one by any means as that of bringing into reasonable agreement the regulatory policies of the four agencies that are primarily concerned with transportation. But the FCC also has authority over radio communication, and that does bring the policies of FCC squarely up alongside the policies of other agencies directly relating to transportation. Railroads, motor carriers, pipe-line companies, and inland water carriers are beginning to make use of radio; transportation by air and ocean commerce as we know them today would certainly not be safe and probably would not be possible without radio communication. In the case of aviation especially, the requirements of FCC concerning radio have to be very carefully related to the other regulations controlling the industry.

There is a good deal of unhappiness about our present arrangements for regulating transportation and communications; no matter what different arrangements we might set up in the future, we can be certain that there will still be a good deal of unhappiness. A lot of people have definite opinions about the way in which they want regulatory policy made and applied; virtually everybody recognizes the necessity of coordinating the different bodies of regulatory policy. But the arrangements which a lot of people insist upon for making and applying policy do not lend themselves to a satisfactory coordination of bodies of policy. Nobody has yet produced a plan for organizing our control over transportation and communications which promises to please people in both these respects.

Most of the men and women who are managing the transportation and communications enterprises of the country want the decisions of the government which control their affairs to be made and applied by a commission instead of a single officer. And they want the members of that commission to be able to give a great deal of time to their problems. This interest leads some of them to argue that we need more commissions than we now have to carry on the regulatory work in which the federal government is already engaged. There is, for instance, some pressure on Congress to divide the present authority of FCC among two or three commissions; the principal demand for this seems to come from people engaged in radio broadcasting who think there should be a commission to give full time to regulation of raido communication, if indeed not a commission to give full time to regulation of that part of radio communication we call broadcasting.

The interest which people have in being assured that their affairs will be regulated by members of a commission who can turn important questions over in their minds and discuss them together has to be balanced against the interest which these same people and others have in being assured that different bodies of regulatory policy are carefully related to one another. Today we have such coordination of these bodies of policy as is effected in the legislation controlling the different regulatory agencies or achieved by means of conferences and other working relations between the various agencies. This does not result in sufficient agreement among the different bodies of regulatory policy relating to transportation and communications to suit some people. In an earlier chapter we discussed the authority and capacity of the President to bring administrative officials, including members of regulatory commissions, together for joint consideration of common problems (pp. 309–311). No matter what authority the President may have to effect coordination by conferences and by issuance of instructions, the country cannot afford to have him give much time and energy to matters of this character; there are too many other things of greater importance to occupy a chief executive of the nation.

In keeping with a recommendation of the President's Committee on Administrative Management in 1937, the President was given a number of assistants to help him direct and coordinate the administrative activities of the federal government. President Franklin Roosevelt decided that one of these assistants should devote himself primarily or altogether to the coordination of the regulatory commissions and appointed one of his sons to do the job. If any actual coordination resulted from this, I have not succeeded in learning what it was. For a while the Chairman of ICC, Joseph B. Eastman, gave up his position on that commission to serve as general coordinator of the activities of the federal government relating to transportation. This arrangement was viewed as a special measure to meet emergency problems of the depression and lasted for only about three years. We did something of the same sort during World War II by means of an Office of Defense Transportation which also was headed by a member of ICC. Neither of these coordinating officials had authority over communications and neither had authority to veto or set aside the regulatory policies and decisions of any of the agencies exercising control over transportation.

The proposal which is most strongly urged at present to bring about a fuller coordination of policies relating to transportation and communications would bring most or all of this regulation within a single department of transportation and communications. The President's Committee on Administrative Management recommended in 1937 that all these transportation and communications activities be brought together in the Department of Commerce, but Congress took no such action. One of the task forces which reported to the Hoover Commission twelve years later advised that the activities relating to transportation be differentiated and divided between two new central administrative establishments—a single commission which would make the regulatory decisions (quasi-legislative and quasi-judicial) relating to all phases of transportation falling under the control of the national government, and a Department of Transportation (to be headed by a single official) which would administer all activities relating to transportation judged not to be of a regulatory character. Since the charge of this task force did not extend to activities relating to communications, it had no occasion to indicate whether it would divide communications activities in the same fashion and place them side by side with the transportation activites in the same two new establishments.

The foregoing recommendation was in part opposed by another task force which was asked to study and report on the present regulatory commissions. This group agreed with the first that regulatory and nonregulatory functions should be differentiated and that the latter should be taken away from the commissions. But the second task force did not favor the single regulatory commission which was proposed by the first task force; it took the position that the regulatory authority which involved decisions of a quasi-legislative and quasi-judicial character should continue as at present in a number of separate commissions having no one between them and the President and Congress.

The Hoover Commission reported unanimous agreement with both of its task forces that the regulatory commissions should be stripped of their nonregulatory authority and that the nonregulatory activities relating to transportation should be brought together in one department headed by a single official. The members of the Hoover Commission disagreed, however, as to how these two kinds of authority should be relocated in the administrative branch. The majority of the members thought that the regulatory authority should continue to be distributed among a number of regulatory commissions, as at present, and that "all major nonregulatory transportation activities of the Federal Government" should be brought together in the Department of Commerce. Commissioners Clarence J. Brown and James K. Pollock dissented on the first of these two points; they thought that the time had come to create a single Transportation Regulatory Commission to make the quasi-legislative and quasi-judicial decisions. Commissioner Brown went on to say that until the single regulatory commission was established, the nonregulatory functions now administered by the several commissions should not be consolidated in a single agency. Commissioner Pollock, however, was willing to see the nonregulatory functions consolidated in the Department of Commerce, even though he lost on his recommendation that the strictly regulatory functions also be brought together under a single commission.

The recommendations which the Hoover Commission made concerning the transportation activities of the national government were not extended to its activities relating to communications. If any members of the Commission thought that FCC now exercises authority of a nonregulatory character, they did not propose that it be taken away from FCC. Commissioners Brown and Pollock did not propose that the regulatory authority relating to communications be combined with the regulatory authority relating to transportation under a single commission which would make the quasi-legislative and quasi-judicial decisions relating to both communications and transportation. It may be that they thought such a combination unnecessary or undesirable; it may be that they would have preferred such an arrangement but saw nothing to be gained by pushing it.[2]

[2] The recommendations of the President's Committee on Administrative Management appear on page 35 of its *Report* cited in note 1. The recommendations of the Hoover Commission appear in two of its reports: *Department of Commerce; A Report to the Congress by the Commission on Organization of the Executive Branch of the Government, March 1949*, pp. 11–25; and *The Independent Regulatory Commissions; A Report to the Congress by the Commission on Organization of the Executive Branch of the Government, March 1949*, pp. 11–22. The report of the Hoover Commission's task force concerned with transportation activities has not been printed. The task force report relating to the independent regulatory commissions is entitled: *Committee on Independent Regulatory Commissions; A Report with*

The meager statements which support the majority and minority recommendations of the Hoover Commission do not fully disclose the grounds for disagreement among the members of that body. It seems safe to conclude, however, that the majority members attached a higher importance than the two dissenters to the advantages that lie in having a wide range of regulatory questions decided by a commission which can give its whole attention to a particular type of transportation (air, rail, water, etc.), and that the two dissenting commissioners attached a higher importance than the others to the gains to be derived from a greater coordination of transportation policies. Congress can be expected to divide on this same issue of values.

What has been said in the past few pages about making and putting into effect the external policies of regulatory commissions is in large part applicable to the major executive departments. Every one of these departments carries on a wide range of activities which have an important impact on the interests of individuals and business enterprises. Some of their activities are of a regulatory character and do not differ in any significant way from the regulatory activities which are now carried on by independent commissions. There is no lack of people to contend that these regulatory activities should be lifted out of the executive departments and entrusted to independent regulatory commissions comparable to those discussed in the preceding paragraphs. But the gains to be derived from such action have to be balanced against the gains now derived from the coordination of a wide range of related activities which the executive department provides. Concede that there are good reasons for creating a separate commission to fix standards of quality and condition for grain; they may be outweighed by closely associating this regulation with other activities relating to agriculture.

Recommendations Prepared for the Commission on Organization of the Executive Branch of the Government [*Appendix N*]. All printed documents of the Hoover Commission were published by the Government Printing Office in 1949.

Where a high value is put upon the coordination of activities, there is a presumption that the head of the department should have authority to control all the external policies of his department; the reasons for this were set forth at some length several pages back (pp. 444–448). It will never be easy for the department head to exercise this control, however; and there are instances where it is at least questionable whether he should have the authority to do so.

The need for changes in policy and for extensions of policy become apparent in the course of applying the policies that are already established. Many policies come into being as the cumulative effect of innumerable individual actions. After a number of interpretations and applications of the initial policies, it becomes apparent that the policies which are actually in effect are not the same as the ones with which the department started. Special effort to be forethoughtful may lessen the extent to which this process takes place; no amount of planning will terminate it altogether, however. Situations develop and move in on the public official too swiftly for imagination and reason to anticipate them.

If the head of the department undertakes to lay a firm hand upon the policies which come about in this way, he must either participate personally in making the day-to-day decisions of his department or he must be content to review and insist upon changes after the policies have been made and have achieved a certain degree of effectiveness. He cannot do the first for all the affairs of his department, for entirely too many things are going on at the same time throughout the realm of government over which he presides. If he undertakes to share in making decisions relating to even a few of the major activities of his department, he may do so at the cost of neglecting other matters that are more deserving of his attention. Perhaps he may be able to examine a digest of the more important policies that have grown up in this fashion in the various parts of his organization and call for a change in respect to the items that offend him most. If he does even this he runs a risk of committing a greater offense than the one he corrects, as we shall see in a moment.

A great many of the policies of an administrative department are codified in the form of rules and regulations. The adoption of rules and regulations is a formal event; the head of the department can know about this when it takes place. If he thinks he has time for it, he can require the provisions which are under consideration to come to his desk and he can say what he wants to be written into them. But rules and regulations, like the policies that grow out of specific decisions, ought to be a reflection of the knowledge and the convictions of men who are intimately acquainted with the particular affairs which the rules and regulations are intended to control. The head of a great administrative department who is busy with the matters that most require his attention will not have time to acquire the kind and amount of knowledge which would permit him to exercise a reliable judgment as to what should go into such a code.

If the reasoning which has just been set down is sound, the definitive work of coordinating the mass of policies according to which an administrative department does its work cannot be provided by the personal decisions of the department head. Other people must do this for him. The department head has a bigger job to do. He knows what the leadership of his party wants in the way of broad programs of action and he interprets those demands to people who run his department for him. He puts a value on praise and complaint which comes to him from people to whom he listens in all parts of the country and he tells his subordinate officials what action he thinks these comments call for. He hears the major issues which the officials immediately below him feel they ought not to resolve themselves and he tells them where his preferences lie when they have told him what they can about the considerations that are relevant to a decision. In setting his department upon a course of action and resolving the major issues upon which his principal subordinates are divided, the head of the department is a coordinator of policy. But the coordination which he provides does not connect directly with the great body of understandings which guide the working force of the department in doing the things that constitute government in contact with citizens. Other people relate his broad statements of purpose to the working policies of the department and effect the kind of co-ordination that brings the activities of one part of the department into some degree of unison with the activities of the other parts.

The ability of the department head to exercise direction and control over the activities in which his department is engaged depends, therefore, upon his ability to obtain the response which he desires from the officials who are immediately under him and upon their ability in turn to obtain the response they desire from people throughout the orgainzation who are engaged in doing the things that constitute government in actual operation. This brings us up against the problem of organization, which is treated in the next chapter. But before going into that, it is necessary to say a few things about limitations upon the authority of the head of the department to insist upon changes in the working policies of his department.

It was said, a few paragraphs back, that there are instances where it is at least questionable whether the department head should have authority to control the external policies of his department. The point of doubt may be restated as follows—are there not certain matters of policy which must be allowed to stand as expressed by the officials within the department who initially formulate and finally apply them?

The granting of patents in the Department of Commerce affords a good illustration of the problem. The provisions of federal legislation relating to the granting of patents leave many questions of a substantive character unsettled. The officials who grant and refuse patents are forced to make presumptions as to what the law requires, permits, and forbids. If these officials achieve consistency in their actions, lines of policy suplementary to the legislation emerge and people who do business with the patent officials develop expectations as to what will be done in future cases. The body of patent law which has been made in this way is now extensive. It is a guide to inventors and other people who control inventions; advised by a specialized profession of patent lawyers, these people depend on certainty in this body of law in deciding what they will do in matters that are of great importance to them.

To the extent that this body of patent law is made by administrative officials rather than judges in our courts, it is administrative-made policy. To the extent that courts allow a range of choice to administrative officials who decide patent matters, there is opportunity for further elaboration of administrative policy in patent affairs. Should the Secretary of Commerce be permitted to control the discretion which the patent officers in his department are permitted by the courts to exercise? If he sets out to control that discretion, he will have to do it by influencing their decisions in the individual cases that come before them; there is no code of substantive patent policy in the form of rules and regulations issued in his department which the Secretary can review and order amended.

We administer our patent law today under a presumption that the Secretary of Commerce should not have this authority. The decisions of the Commissioner of Patents are final, so far as administrative authority in the Department of Commerce is concerned; appeals go directly to a Court of Patent Appeals. The Patent Office is not a completely autonomous division of the Department of Commerce, however. The Commissioner of Patents, according to the controlling statutes, shall superintend or perform his duties relating to the granting and issuing of patents "under the direction of the Secretary of Commerce," and he may establish regulations to govern the proceedings of the Patent Office (procedural rather than substantive policies) "subject to the approval of the Secretary of Commerce." The Patent Office is in the Department of Commerce so that the Secretary of Commerce can see that it is organized and staffed to do its work; it is not there to provide a political control over the substantive policies which are necessary to the granting of patents.

The granting of patents presents an unusual problem, though it is not unique. The substantive policies relating to patents probably have no important bearing on the other policies which are made and put into effect in the Department of Commerce. The Patent Office is in an administrative department to give it some supervision; it is not there for coordination with other policies. The problem of granting patents differs, therefore, from the problems of fixing and applying standards of quality and condition of grain; the policies which are pursued in the inspection and grading of grain need a certain amount of coordination with other policies that are made and applied in the Department of Agriculture. But it does not follow, because policies must be coordinated, that the head of a department must therefore have unlimited authority to say what the policies shall be. When we regulate people in a competitive industry, we have an obligation to maintain a high degree of consistency in the policies which we apply to them. The man whose grain is inspected and graded may properly insist that he be accorded the same treatment as his competitors; otherwise the government is working for his competitors and working against him. Furthermore, he may properly insist that there be consistency in the decisions that are applied to him on successive occasions; if he cannot predict what the government will do when it examines his grain, he cannot exercise a businessman's judgment in buying and selling.

We recognize these interests and make some provision for them in the law governing administrative procedure. If the administrative establishment (executive department, regulatory commission, or other agency) plans to issue rules and regulations having the force and effect of law, individuals and firms whose interests will be affected must be notified of such intention and must be given an opportunity to appear and make a case for the particular provisions which they think desirable. When the administrative organization makes a specific application of the law and its own controlling policies (an action of adjudicatory character), the proceeding must give the interested parties ample opportunity to defend their interests with evidence and argument, and the decision which is made must take this evidence and argument fully into account.

These requirements, incorporated in the Administrative Procedure Act of 1946, are a recognition that the people of this country are entitled to impartial and dependable government at the hands of administrative officials. The effect of these requirements is to curtail the ability of the head of the department or agency to make and alter the policies of his organization where the interests of individuals are involved, as well as to limit the freedom of action of the subordinate officials who put the policies into effect in specific situations. The head of the establishment can no longer order changes at his will in the published rules and regulations of his organization (procedural or substantive) which affect the interests of people outside the government. Interested parties must be given an opportunity to say what they think about the specific changes which he proposes, and what they say must be given consideration. The fair implication of the law, as I read it, is that the head of the department or agency cannot personally make a decision as to what the language of a rule or regulation shall be unless he also personally examines and gives weight to the evidence and argument which the interested parties have presented.

The authority of the high administrative official is similarly curtailed in the review of individual decisions which apply the controlling law and administrative policies in specific situations. He may reserve the right to review individual adjudicatory decisions if he wishes to do so. But if he does personally review and set aside or modify a decision, he must be able to show that he personally examined and weighed the law and the evidence relevant to his decision.[3]

Some students of public administration, and no doubt many administrative officials who have a better basis for judgment, have expressed a conviction that many of the limitations which have just been described will greatly handicap high administrative officials in their efforts to coordinate the activities for which they are responsible and to improve the policies which have been made by their respective organizations.

[3] The Administrative Procedure Act of 1946 is in 60 Statutes at Large 237; *U.S. Code*, title 5, sections 1001–1011.

I do not see why this should be so. The head of an administrative department or agency is not put where he is to make decisions that he does not know enough to make. If the legislation creating his office and fixing his authority presumes that he will personally make decisions relating to policy (as in the case of the regulatory commissions), then the high official (or commission) must find a way to be personally informed before he makes a decision on policy. If he is where he is primarily to give general direction to an organization of officials and employees (as I understand is the case in the great executive departments), then he must either be content to tell other men what general objectives he wants them to achieve in the formulation and enforcement of policy or he must be prepared to make the full study of specific problems which will enable him to apply his purposes intelligently to the interests and affairs of the people who must live under the government which he provides. If the practical result of these limitations is to force the head of the administrative establishment to put the job of coordinating administrative policies that intimately affect the public in the hands of officials or committees who have an opportunity as well as an obligation to be fully informed before they act, I think the nation gains rather than loses. The official at the top of the organization can combat the tendency of his subordinates to overjudicialize their job by making clear the objectives toward which he is working and by removing them if he is not satisfied with their response to his instructions.

BIBLIOGRAPHIC NOTE

We have a substantial literature dealing with the activities and undertakings which government carries on and a substantial literature dealing with the construction and management of administrative organizations to put the activities and undertakings of government into effect. So far as I can learn, no one has brought the two areas of concern together in a comprehensive and incisive analysis of what is concerned in the making and execution of policy by administrative organizations. Paul H. Appleby said a good deal about this in his *Big Democracy* (New York, 1945). Herbert A. Simon treats the subject from a special angle (the processes of decision-making) in his *Administrative Behavior* (New York, 1947). Short essays of a general character include: Avery Leiserson, "The Formulation of Administrative Policy," in *Elements of Public Administration*, edited by Fritz Morstein Marx (New York, 1946), ch. 16; and Ernest Griffith, "The Changing Pattern of Public Policy Formation," in *American Political Science Review*, vol. 38, pp. 445–459 (1944).

A number of books which recount the experience of particular administrative organizations have something to say about how policy is made and executed. I do not have sufficient knowledge of this literature to say which items are best on the subject matter discussed in this chapter; the following are certainly of value: John M. Gaus and Leon O. Wolcott, *Public Administration and the United States Department of Agriculture* (Chicago, 1940), particularly chs. 6 to 13; Arthur W. Macmahon, John D. Millett, and Gladys Ogden, *The Administration of Federal Work Relief* (Chicago, 1941), particularly ch. 4 ff.; and Marshal E. Dimock, *The Executive in Action* (New York, 1945). See also various essays in three volumes bearing the common title *Public Policy* (Cambridge, Mass., 1940–42).

Because of the great public interest in the regulatory activities of government, we have an extensive literature dealing with how the regulatory commissions make policy. I tried my hand at this in three articles dealing with state regulatory bodies: "Administrative Adjudication: An Analysis," in *Political Science Quarterly*, vol. 51, pp. 383–417, 516–537 (1936), partially reprinted in *Selected Essays on Constitutional Law* (Chicago, 1938), vol. 4, pp. 491–517; "The Case Law of the New York Public Service Commission," in *Columbia Law Review*, vol. 34, pp. 67–106 (1934), reprinted in *Selected Essays on Constitutional Law*, vol. 4, pp. 841–879; and "State Administrative Tribunals and 'Fair Play,'" in *Iowa Law Review*, vol. 25, pp. 532–554 (1940). I think the best study yet published of how regulatory policy is made and executed (also an analysis of state authorities) is Edwin W. Patterson, *The Insurance Commissioner in the United States* (Cambridge, Mass., 1927). Among the best items dealing with regulatory commissions of the Federal government are: two books by Frederick F. Blachly and M. E. Oatman, *Administrative Legislation and Adjudication* (Washington, 1934), and *Federal Regulatory Action and Control* (Washington, 1940); Gerard Henderson, *The Federal Trade Commission* (New Haven, 1924); Isaiah L. Sharfman, *The Interstate Com-*

merce Commission (5 vols., New York, 1931–37); *Administrative Procedure in Government Agencies,* Senate Document No. 8, 77th Congress, 1st session (Government Printing Office, 1941); *The Report on Practices and Procedures of Governmental Control,* House Document No. 678, 78th Congress, 2nd session (Government Printing Office, 1944).

On the considerations which are involved in combining separate agencies with a view to facilitating coordination of governmental programs, see: *President's Committee on Administrative Management, Report with Special Studies* (Government Printing Office, 1937), pp. 31–47, 203–243; *The Independent Regulatory Commissions; A Report to the Congress by the Commission on Organization of the Executive Branch of the Government, March 1949* (Government Printing Office, 1949); *Committee on Independent Regulatory Commissions; A Report with Recommendations Prepared for the Commission on Organization of the Executive Branch of the Government [Appendix N]* (Government Printing Office, 1949); *The Report on Practices and Procedures of Governmental Control* (cited above), pp. 135–164; Blachly and Oatman, *Federal Regulatory Action and Control* (cited above), pp. 143–182; Lewis Meriam and L. F. Schmeckebier, *Reorganization of the National Government; What Does It Involve?* (Washington, 1939), ch. 3.

For discussion of efforts to bring into the making and execution of policies representatives of the public who will be effected by those policies, see: Avery Leiserson, *Administrative Regulation* (Chicago, 1942); Avery Leiserson, "Interest Representation in Administrative Regulation," in *Annals of the American Academy of Political and Social Science,* vol. 221 (1942), pp. 78–86; Morris Duane, "Mandatory Hearings in the Rule-Making Process," in same journal, vol. 221, pp. 115–121; Don K. Price, "Democratic Administration," in *Elements of Public Administration,* edited by Fritz Morstein Marx (cited above), pp. 81–91; Ernest S. Griffith, *The Impasse of Democracy* (New York, 1939), ch. 18; John D. Lewis, "Democratic Planning in Agriculture," in *American Political Science Review,* vol. 35, pp. 232–249, 454–469 (1941); and Herman Walker and W. R. Parks, "Soil Conservation Districts: Local Democracy in a National Program," in *Journal of Politics,* vol. 8, pp. 538–549 (1946).

On the Administrative Procedure Act of 1946, see: *Administrative Procedure Act;* Senate Document No. 248, 79th Congress, 2nd session (Government Printing Office, 1946); *The Federal Administrative Procedure Act and the Federal Agencies,* edited by George Warren (New

York, 1947); Nathaniel L. Nathanson, "Some Comments on the Administrative Procedure Act," in *Illinois Law Review*, vol. 41, pp. 368–422 (1946); and two articles by Kenneth C. Davis: "Separation of Functions in Administrative Agencies," in *Harvard Law Review*, vol. 61, pp. 389–418, 612–655 (1948), and "Institutional Administrative Decisions," in *Columbia Law Review*, vol. 48, pp. 173–201 (1948).

CHAPTER 22

ORGANIZATION FOR DIRECTION

AND CONTROL

The administrative establishment (department, agency, commission—whatever its name) is a working force of men and women. These men and women achieve the purposes for which they were brought together only if there is common understanding of what the group as a whole is supposed to do, and if each person understands what part he is expected to play in the common undertaking. The degree to which this understanding prevails will be determined by the relationships that exist among the members of the working force. These relationships, which tell each person where he stands in respect to his fellows, transform a mass of men and women into an organization.

The discussion of the problems involved in making policy and putting it into effect should give some indication of the relation of organization to the character and quality of government which the administrative establishment will provide. The officer (or commission) at the top of one of our smallest administrative agencies can personally formulate many of the policies which his organization will put into effect and can have knowledge of the character of the remaining policies. The head of one of our major departments can have no such intimate connection with the policies which govern the work of his organization. For him the policies of the department fall into two groups. He has personal opinions about some of them, at least in their broadest aspects, and he wants to be assured that his wishes in respect to them will be put into effect; as to the others he wishes only to be assured that he would be satisfied with them if he fully understood what they involved.

The problems of creating, maintaining, and directing an organization are vastly different in the two situations. The head of the small agency is primarily concerned to have an organization that will do things the way he says he wants things done. The head of the large department is concerned primarily to have an organization that will conduct most of its affairs in a satisfactory manner without his knowledge and change its course in respect to the remainder of its affairs when he indicates a wish that it do so. In discussing the problems of organization within an administrative establishment, we have to keep this basic difference in mind. Only a limited number of observations that are worth making will have application to the large and the small establishment alike.

The practical problems of building an organization and maintaining and improving it after it has been built cluster around two components—the quality of the individuals who make up the organization, and their relations with one another. There has been a tendency in the literature relating to administrative organization, during recent years, to extol the importance of relationships and to play down the importance of the quality of the individuals who are to be related to one another in an organization. As a consequence much of the writing has been doctrinaire in character, the generalizations about ideal relationships not having made proper allowance for differences in the qualities of the individuals who share relationships. Surely men and women who possess in high measure any particular combination of qualities that are desired are the rarest and therefore the most precious materials which the man who is responsible for managing an enterprise can command. Surely, when he discovers a rare and valuable talent, he should make the most of it. The ideal arrangement of relationships takes into account the quality of the men and women who are involved and is designed to get the most out of the members of the organization that they are capable of contributing.

The relationships which make an organization out of a group of people must always be adjusted to the qualities of the individuals who are involved. We demonstrate that conviction persistently in business and industry. The pattern of responsibilities in a partnership is usually based on the interests and capacities of the partners. As the sons grow up and claim a place in their father's business, responsibilities are reallocated. The expansion of the small business firm into new activities is frequently no more than a response to the special capacities of certain individuals within the firm.

The bending of organization to the interests and capacities of individuals is doubtless much less common in our largest commercial and industrial corporations than in the small family business or partnership. The men who head these great structures have a more abundant supply of qualified men and women from which to choose in filling important positions. There are many men in the organization who have been tried out and who have proven what they can do. When a key position becomes vacant, there is someone available who can move into it and assume its obligations. But even so the reorganization of major business enterprises to make a fuller utilization of the special capacities of particular individuals is a long way from being a rare occurrence.

There is in the small administrative establishment the same compulsion to reshape the organization to fit the men who are available that we observe in the small business firm. The head of the establishment is not always free, for reasons which we shall soon see, to go outside his organization to fill an important job that has become vacant. He presumably makes the best appointment he can from the limited field of talent that is available to him. And he permits or encourages a reassignment of duties and responsibilities which promises to result in the best performance from the new combination of men who occupy the key positions in the organization. If the constrictions of job classifications and pay scales make it too difficult to formalize the new pattern of duties and responsibilities, the agency often proceeds under an actual organization that is-quite foreign to the printed organization charts and to the statements that are filed with the Civil Service Commission.

The great executive department, like the large-scale business corporation, has a greater reservoir of talent from which to pick in filling important positions, but even here there are factors that greatly limit the availability of men who can fill the requirements of the vacant position. And in the large department, as in the small agency, there is a compulsion to make reassignments of duties and responsibilities in order to obtain a better utilization of the talents of the group of men who hold the important positions.

It is important to understand the extent and character of the limitations upon the ability of the heads of our federal administrative establishments, large or small, to construct an organization and to maintain and improve it after it has been built.

First of all, the administrative official rarely gets an opportunity to create an organization; rather he inherits an organization that is already a going concern. In the rare instances where a new activity of government is instituted and a new organization must be built, the man who has the responsibility for doing so is under pressure to build the organization almost overnight and like as not in the midst of a manpower shortage.

In the second place, the high administrative official is limited in what he can do about the basic structure of his establishment. In many instances the statute which creates the department or agency and sets forth the activities of government it shall carry out also specifies the principal subdivisions which shall be preserved. And if the law does not limit the administrator in moving functions of government from place to place within his establishment, bodies of opinion which he feels obliged to respect may do so. A great many of our governmental activities are of primary concern to various segments of the American people. These groups are likely to identify an activity in which they are interested with a particular bureau or division of an administrative department or agency.

They are likely to raise quite a howl when the administrator does something which suggests that he is tampering with their service, particularly if they get a little encouragement in their protest from someone within the organization who does not like the reorganization either. Congressmen are often effective spokesmen for interest groups in these matters.

Finally, there are the obstructions to reorganization which lie in the requirements for writing job descriptions and which we discussed in Chapter 19 (pp. 409–412). Either because of the requirements of the law or an unimaginative administration of the law by the Civil Service Commission, any reorganization which involves change in duties and responsibilities for a large number of employees causes so much disturbance which has no relation to learning new jobs and getting acquainted with new bosses that one experience in putting through a reorganization is likely to keep the administrator from ever trying another one.

The limitations we have just pointed out handicap the federal administrator in dealing with one component of organization— the relationships that exist between men and women who make up the organization. He is also handicapped in dealing with the other component—the quality of the individuals who make up his organization. The men and women who occupy the positions immediately under the head of the organization—personal assistants and chiefs of major operating bureaus—are of course the ones upon whom he must depend primarily for seeing that the great force of officials and employees carry on the work of the establishment in a manner satisfactory to him. Yet the top official sometimes, if indeed not frequently, has to accept for these posts men and women who are certainly not his first choice and probably not at all to his liking. A tabulation made in 1937 showed that just short of one hundred high officials who were yet subordinate to the heads of administrative departments and agencies were appointed by the President with the advice and consent of the Senate. If this meant only that the head of the department or agency has to recommend for appointment men and women who are acceptable to the President and to the majority of the Senate, there would be little ground for objecting to this method of filling the second row of administrative positions. The fact is, however, as we noted earlier in this book (pp. 287–289), that the high administrative official sometimes finds himself at least partially surrounded by men and women for whom he has no liking and in whom he has little confidence.

Even when the head of the establishment is legally free to make his own appointments and to replace anyone he finds no longer satisfactory, he may still find himself restrained from doing what he would like to do because of pressures from nonofficial sources. He is a part of a political organization and he has to bear his part of the burden of satisfying influential people within the party. Pressures which he calls political may impose no greater restraint on his action in appointing and removing men, or putting men in different positions within the organization, than the pressures which come from the sector of the population that has a special interest in the activities which his department carries on. The head of a department or agency must always weigh the gain in having the man he wants where he wants him against the losses which accrue from antagonizing a sector of the public that has contrary motions about who should be in charge of affairs in which it has an important interest. The length to which an interest group may go in order to influence the selection of men for high administrative positions was demonstrated by a walkout of coal miners in the spring of 1949. Leaders of the union were at the moment opposing the appointment of a certain person to the position of Director of the Bureau of Mines, and the refusal of miners to report for work was declared by union leaders to be a mass protest against the confirmation of the appointment.

Finally, of course, the head of a government department or agency, like the head of any other organization made up of men and women, must consider the effect which his appointments and removals and transfers will have on the attitudes of people in the organization whose attitudes are important to him. Just as clergymen defend their interests on the ground that they are servants of the Lord and college professors bargain for advantage in the name of academic freedom, so men and women in the public service have a moral principle which takes care of their consciences when they promote one action or resist another according to its effect on their personal fortunes—they are acting "for the good of the service." Resistances within the service will not stop a strong administrator from making the changes in personnel which he considers of first-rate importance to his purposes, but even the most forceful administrator is under a strong compulsion to act in keeping with certain expectations of people within the organization when the considerations for and against a particular choice are marginal.

The purpose, in the last few pages, has been to set forth some of the fundamental limitations under which most if not all administrators in the federal government work, regardless of the nature of the administrative establishment involved and regardless of the personality and interests of the particular administrator. These limitations have been discussed as they apply to the head of an administrative establishment; most of them are fully applicable to the chief of a bureau or other major administrative subdivision. Whether they fall with equal insistence upon department head and bureau chief, I do not know. The bureau chief undoubtedly has a far better chance of achieving his purposes in spite of them. He can devote himself more fully to his administrative tasks and he stays much longer in the government service than does the man at the head of the department or agency.

The working out of arrangements which give the head of one of our great executive departments assurance that he is able effectively to direct and control the organization under him must be a major feat of ingenuity and persistence. Those who have gone through the process have not gone to the trouble of telling the rest of us how it was done. As a consequence I am forced to rely mainly on my own experience in smaller organizations for such comments of a general character as I am able to make.

The first objective of the man who attempts to direct one of

our large executive departments must be to get around him men
in whom he has confidence. Other men are going to run the department for him; he must have a basis for confidence that they
will do consistently what he would have them do if he knew
enough to have a judgment concerning what ought to be done.
When a man comes in at the top of the department his first task
must be to find out whom he can trust, if he does not know already. He cannot find out by observation and intuition who runs
the organization and what those individuals are trying to do; someone has to tell him these things. If there is not among the people
who already know these things anyone whose judgment he trusts
and who will be completely frank with him, then the new department head had better bring in someone in whom he has confidence and give him the job of finding these things out.

The immediate purpose of this first inquiry, it seems to me, is
to enable the head of the department to decide whether he wishes
to keep the principal officials that he inherits, including the men
who head the various bureaus. The character and quality of the
government which the department provides is ultimately determined by the men and women in the organization who do
things that constitute government. The character and quality of
government in operation depends on their attitudes, the training
they have received, the instructions that go to them, the supervision and review under which they work. The character and quality of government cannot be changed by issuing an order at the
top; they are a reflection of a mass of relationships that exist within
the organization and will not change until those relationships
change. The positions of authority which men hold within the
organization are a vital part of these relationships. If the men who
hold positions of authority within the organization resist change
in the policies and practices of the department, they can nullify
virtually anything which the head of the department may do to
alter the objectives of the department or change its ways of doing
things. If they respond to the wishes of the department head, he
may look forward to success in achieving his purposes.

Collectively, the bureau chiefs are the most influential of these officials, for each of them is in direct command of a sector of the department's operations. If the bureau chief works at cross-purposes with the department head, then the latter has little prospect of influencing the operations of that sector of the department. If all of the bureau chiefs are loyal to the department head and throw themselves with vigor behind his program of action, the organization as a whole will go forward in keeping with the hopes of the department head.

These are the reasons why the newly appointed department head must at once set about finding out what he needs to know in order to make up his mind whether he is going to keep his bureau chiefs. It is a time-consuming job and requires a lot of talking; snap judgments will not provide an adequate basis for sizing up the men who contribute so greatly to the character and quality of the department's work.

The men who direct the operating bureaus necessarily must be, for the department head, a principal source of knowledge as to what the problems of the department are and a principal source of ideas as to how those problems may be solved. But the department head cannot rely on the bureau chiefs alone. If he did, he would know little about the performance of his department other than what they chose to tell him. The head of the department acquires some capacity for evaluating the work of his department on the basis of praise or complaint which comes to him from the outside. But most of the knowledge which any high official has about the things which his department is actually doing and the way they are being done comes to him from people below him in the organization. Some of the things he wants to know about one sector of his organization will come to the department head from the chiefs of the other bureaus. This may prove to be an undependable source, however, for some men are reluctant to talk frankly to a superior about the work of their associates, and those who talk most readily may be the ones who require the most watching. The department head needs some channels of information from people throughout the department which cannot be cut off by the officials who might profit from limiting his knowledge.

The department head needs some people about him who have an excuse for talking to people throughout the organization and who acknowledge an obligation to pass on to the head what they think he ought to know. There are many ways of providing for this, and the arrangements vary widely from department to department. If the department has an Under Secretary and Assistant Secretaries, they presumably contribute greatly to the Secretary's understanding. Their usefulness in this respect will differ, however, for the Secretary does not have a free hand in choosing them and sometimes he does not get along with one or more of them. Furthermore, the Assistant Secretaries frequently assume responsibility for particular sectors of the department, acquire loyalties to the parts of the organization that report to them, and become protectors rather than critics of the bureau chiefs below them.

The head of the department can always broaden the channels of his information by bringing men into his own office for special assignments. If a man goes about the department with the title of Assistant to the Secretary, other people assume he has a right to get answers to the questions he asks. If he is a happy selection for his job, many people will tell him things that they would not tell anybody else; they have his assurance that he is only finding out what is going on and that he will not use his information in a way that will get his informant into trouble.

The central group of officials who hover about the department head exist for purposes other than giving him information and advice. Some if not all of them assist in the direction and control of the organization as a whole. In some cabinet departments the Under Secretary may be a general executive officer for the department, acting under authorization of the department head as chief of the department's operations. Usually the Assistant Secretaries have substantial delegations of authority to make decisions and give instructions relating to particular parts of the organization or to particular kinds of questions which arise in various parts of the organization. And of course, any person who is known to be in close communication with the head of the department will inevitably exert an influence on the actions of other people in the organization; his remarks, no matter how cautiously given, about the apparent intentions and wishes of the highest officials give other people the guidance they need in making decisions themselves.

In addition to these officials who in practice as well as in theory are eyes and ears for the head of the department, there are other persons whose assignments run across the principal lines of the department's organization. They are the officials whose primary responsibility is giving advice, rendering service, and exercising control. They perform within the department functions equivalent to those that are performed for the government as a whole by such central agencies as the Bureau of the Budget, the General Accounting Office, and the Civil Service Commission. These officials cannot discharge their own responsibilities without giving the head of the department knowledge about the state of affairs in his domain, for the things with which they deal officially are indicators of the policies and practices which prevail throughout the organization. The solicitor, or general counsel, renders legal advice to officials throughout the organization, and his approval may be required before certain kinds of action can be taken. Since 1921 every department of the government has been required by statute to maintain a central budget officer, and since 1938 every department has been required by Presidential order to maintain a central personnel officer. All relations with the Bureau of the Budget and with the Civil Service Commission must be channeled through these offices, which of necessity gives these two officers some authority and a great deal of influence over the actions of the chiefs of operating divisions in respect to monetary matters and employment.

The officials who control the department's money are especially influential in the central direction and control of the department's affairs. The head of the department personally shares the extraordinary influence which the control of money gives. He is the officer who speaks with authority to the Budget Bureau and the President in making up estimates of appropriations needed by his establishment. The examiners in the Budget Bureau who study the department's needs will talk to the bureau chiefs and other people in the department who can answer the questions they raise about the various activities and operations. But they are not likely to allow amounts for the different parts of the departments that are in excess of what the head of the department recommends. The department head may also be an important spokesman for the department before the subcommittees of Congress that consider the appropriation requests. The position that he takes concerning the monetary needs of the department will be an important consideration with the Congressmen in fixing the year's appropriations. His influence, as compared with that of some of his bureau chiefs, may not be as great with the Congressmen as with the Budget Bureau and the President, however, for individual Congressmen develop special concern about particular parts of the department's program and many of them feel no great compulsion to support the superior authority of the department head within his organization.

The influence which the department head enjoys within his organization because of his relation to the appropriations is compounded if the nature of the appropriation act broadens his authority to determine how money shall be spent. In the case of the smaller agencies the appropriation act may make no allocations among the divisions of the agency, leaving the head of the agency a great deal of freedom to distribute the money in accordance with his own judgment. The head of a big executive department is pretty certain to have only a limited amount of such control, however, for the appropriation act will ordinarily designate the amounts which are to be available for each of the major divisions of the department.

The control which the head of the department has over money —by influencing the appropriations or determining the allocation of the money that is appropriated—is frequently the best measure of his power within his department. Some of our agency heads appear to have very little legal authority in respect to the acts of government which the component parts of the agency perform. The Administrator of the Housing and Home Finance Agency is an illustration. In these instances, the influence and authority which he is able to exercise over money may be virtually the only source of power which the administrator has over the different parts of his organization.

In exercising control through his command over the department's money, the department head relies largely upon his budget officer and the official (comptroller) who keeps his financial records. In making up a statement of financial needs, the budget officer takes his instructions from and reports to the head of the department or to some other central officer who has been given a general assignment relating to fiscal matters. It is the budget officer's job to find out not only what the chiefs of operating divisions say they need in the way of money; it is his job to make critical inquiries about the uses that have been made of money in the past and the uses that are contemplated for the future. It is not his job to tell the bureau chiefs and their subordinate officers that the amounts which they wish will not be presented to the Budget Bureau and Congress; but it is his job to convince them, when he is sure of his position, that the head of the agency is not of a mind to support the amounts which they request and not likely to come around to their support if operating officials choose to press the matter before him. If the budget officer has personal qualities which other men respect, if he has knowledge of the affairs of the department which enables him to discuss specific activities and operations on their merits, and if he exercises good judgment in putting a valuation on the various representations which are made to him—if he combines these merits, his recommendations are pretty certain to be highly persuasive with the head of the department and the men upon whom the department head leans in making up his mind on appropriation matters.

The comptroller, or other officer who keeps the department's financial records, is not likely to exercise any great influence on the development of the department's plans for carrying on its work, but he does play an important role in controlling the use of money. If he is in complete mastery of his accounts, he keeps the operating officials of the department informed of the state of their funds and sees to it that the allocations of money which were made by the top officials of the department are respected in practice. He is supposed to know the law and the lore of government finance—the proper interpretation of the language in the appropriations acts, the regulations and the interpretations of the General Accounting Office, and the attitudes which Congressmen are most likely to take concerning different ways of using money.

In addition to this battery of central officers who provide advice, service, and control, many departments have set up various kinds of organization to carry on central study and evaluation of the activities and operations of the department, to make specific recommendations for coordination and improvement of the department's work, and to develop plans for future courses of action. Some of these central functionaries specialize in problems of organization and operating procedures; other (frequently labeled program analysts) may specialize in making studies, offering recommmendations, and preparing plans which relate to the character and quality of the government which the department is providing for the American people. If the individuals who do this kind of work have the qualities that are needed and work hard at their jobs, they can be a rich source of information and ideas to the top officials of the department and they can exert a great deal of influence on the operating officials of the department.

Recent writing about administrative organization in this country has had as a major objective to increase the use of and enlarge the authority of agencies for advice, service, and control. This tendency in the literature was given a marked stimulus by the President's Committee on Administrative Management in 1937. The Committee announced its mission as that of investigating and reporting upon "administrative management"; its recommendations in respect to administrative organization were concerned largely if not primarily with what it called "managerial and staff agencies"; its concept of managerial and staff agencies embraced the kind of functions that I have called advice, service, and control.

There should be developed in each department, the Committee said, "managerial agencies under the secretary dealing with such matters as finance, personnel, and planning, and centralized institutional services for legal advice, supplies, records, correspondence, and information. . . . These managerial and institutional agencies should be under the direction of a single executive officer, who should be a career official. . . . In the executive officer would be centered the authority and responsibility under the secretary for the development of administrative management within the department. This position would correspond to the manager of a great corporation. It would be the highest managerial position in the career service of the Government. . . . The operation of the department would be carried on through bureaus and semi-autonomous agencies, manned throughout by civil servants, and under the administrative supervision of a career executive officer."[1]

The statement that the proposed executive officer would exercise "administrative supervision" over the bureaus, and the comparison of this officer to the manager of a corporation, seems to make it clear that the Committee envisaged him as a director of operations. Subject only to the Secretary and such other political appointees as might assist the Secretary in the general direction and control of the department, the executive officer, drawn from the ranks of the civil service, would actually direct (be the boss over) all of the activities of the administrative department. The Committee did not say what it thought ought to be the respective

---

[1] The quotation is from the *Report of the President's Committee on Administrative Management* (Government Printing Office, 1937), pp. 39 and 46. In order to arrive at an understanding of what the Committee intended to be the authority of the proposed executive officer, and of what it intended to be the relative position of bureau chiefs and "managerial and staff agencies," one must read carefully pages 31–47 of the *Report*.

roles of bureau chiefs and of officials who head special agencies for advice, service, and control in helping the executive officer (director of operations) decide what ought to be done and make plans for putting his decisions into effect. It is noteworthy, however, that the Committee stressed at various points in its report the importance of utilizing and relying upon what it called managerial and staff aides, and that its only reference to the authority and influence of the officials (bureau chiefs and their subordinates) who actually direct the segments of the working force was pointed to the special case of regulatory activities that ought to be insulated against political control and new governmental activities whose proper place in the structure of the department has not been found. It would be too much to say that the recommendations of the Committee and the commentary which supported those recommendations urged that the officials who deal primarily in advice, service, and control be given a greater voice than the bureau chiefs in deciding how the work of the department ought to be carried on; I think it is not too much to say, however, that there is a good deal of evidence in the report that the Committee viewed such a result as desirable.

The Hoover Commission and the task force which advised it on the organization and direction of administrative departments recognized that the officials who deal primarily in advice, service, and control can make important contributions to the solution of the problems that confront the officers at the top of the department. I think it is clear, however, that they had no wish to build them up to the pre-eminence in the department which I think the President's Committee on Administrative Management may have had in mind. Neither did the Hoover Commission nor its task force propose that there should be a single official under the Secretary who would possess authority and exercise influence comparable to that of the general manager of a corporation.

The task force which advised the Hoover Commission on these matters felt that there should be one man in each department and agency of the federal government whose assignment would be "to direct the preparation of departmental budgets, supervise personnel operations, review administrative operations in order to achieve improvements in work organization and methods, and perform such central services as may be desirable." The task force was of the opinion that this position should be filled "by a career employee" and thought that if he did his job well, he would be able to "exercise an important influence upon all departmental matters—upon the substance of policy and program as well as upon the practical procedures essential to execute any work." The Hoover Commission appears to have agreed with its task force, for it said that "there should generally be an administrative assistant secretary who might be appointed solely for administrative duties of a housekeeping and management nature and who would give continuity in top management," and who, in order to assure continuity, should come out of the "career service." But the Hoover Commission did not attach enough value to this proposition to include it in the formal recommendations which it submitted to Congress.[2]

The recommendations and apparent convictions of the two great study groups which have just been reviewed go to three points of prime significance in the internal organization of the administrative department: the respective roles, in making the policies and plans of the department, of bureau chiefs and of the officials who deal primarily in advice, service, and control; the provision for continuity of experience at the top level of authority in the department; and the desirability of centering direction of all the department's activities in a general manager or chief or operations. They will be considered in the order given.

[2] For the position of the task force, see *Departmental Management in Federal Administration; A Report with Recommendations Prepared for the Commission on Organization of the Executive Branch of the Government* [*Appendix E*], particularly pp. 14–18, 33–34, 44–59; quotations at p. 14. For the recommendations and comment of the Hoover Commission, see *General Management of the Executive Branch; A Report to the Congress by the Commission on Organization of the Executive Branch of the Government, February 1949*, pp. 36–39; quotation at p. 37. Both documents were published by the Government Printing Office in 1949.

If the President's Committee intended, as I suspect it did, to build up the officials who head the special agencies for advice, service, and control to a position of authority and influence equal to that of the bureau chiefs, it must have had a concept of how men and women communicate with and influence one another in big organizations which is significantly different from my own. In a paragraph that is a model of succinct, lucid, and challenging expression the Committee pointed out that government is a human institution. "It is human throughout," the Committee said; "it rests not only on formal arrangement, skill, and numbers, but even more upon attitudes, enthusiasms, and loyalty. It is certainly not a machine, which can be taken apart, redesigned, and put together again on the basis of mechanical laws. It is more akin to a living organism. The reorganization of the Government is not a mechanical task. It is a human task and must be approached as a problem of morale and personnel fully as much as a task of logic and management."[3]

Surely this is simple truth as well as lucid, graphic English. It describes government which is the doing of men and women joined together in the administrative organization just as truthfully and accurately as it describes government in its more comprehensive form of Congress, courts, and executive-administrative branch. Because government by the administrative organization is men and women doing things and influencing people, the fundamental character of the organization must conform to the ways in which men and women habitually and traditionally behave.

The officials who are at the top of the administrative department are there for the purpose of keeping the behavior of the administrative force in harmony with the policies of the political branches. They can fulfill our expectations only if they have full and certain information as to what the men and women below them are doing and if they have assurance that the men and women below them receive their instructions, understand them, and re-

[3] *Report of the President's Committee on Administrative Management* (Government Printing Office, 1937), p. 38.

spond to them. The establishment and maintenance of these channels of communication between the top, bottom, and all the in-between levels of the administrative department constitute the first objective of the organization into which the entire force of officials and employees is molded.

The men and women who do the things that the administrative department was created to do constitute the primary source of information about what the department is actually doing in its contacts with the American people. They are by far the richest source of ideas as to how the department could do more expeditiously and more economically whatever it is doing. They are one of the most dependable sources of knowledge and opinion as to what the American people like and dislike about the activities of the department and what the American people would like to see in the way of change in the department's activities. The work which these people do is reviewed by other individuals (most of whom have done the work themselves at one time) who also give them their instructions.

From the bottom floor of the department where the work of government is actually being carried on to the official who heads the bureau there is a natural chain of communication. By chain of communication I mean that there are men and women with differing positions of authority who see one another and talk to one another. I call it a natural chain of communication because it is in the nature of men and women who are associated in a common undertaking to talk together about the affairs in which they have a common interest. Each of these individuals talks with people who are below him in rank, with people above him, and with other people who are on the same level. And the things they talk most about are what the department does and how it does it—what the department is doing now, what it used to do, and what it will do or may do in the future; how well certain things are being done and how they might be done differently from now on; who likes what is being done, who doesn't, and how things might be done to please people better. Men and women talk most about the things which preoccupy their time and attention, and for all of us in and out of the government the greatest preoccupation during working hours is the job through which we make our living.

This natural chain of communication must not be permitted to come to an end with the bureau chief; it must continue right on up to (connect directly with) the official at the top of the department who is expected to relate the work of the department to the decisions and instructions of the political branches of the government. I do not believe that the head of the department, or any other official who attempts to relieve him of his highest responsibility, can effectively direct an administrative organization except as he sits at the pivotal point in this natural chain of communication; he must be the peak to which information flows from all parts of the organization and he must be the source from which many of the most fundamental and most comprehensive instructions flow out to all parts of the organization. This means that the head of the department must make his decisions in close consultation with the bureau chiefs, for in the bureau chiefs converge the upflowing streams (which supply top officials with information, ideas, and proposals for action) and through them spread out the downflowing streams (which approve and disapprove proposals and supply subordinate officials and workers with instructions). If the head of the department (or any other official or group of officials who try to run the department for him) turns his back on the bureau chiefs, he cuts himself out of his richest source of information and advice; and if he offends the bureau chiefs by denying them the place in his counsels to which they feel entitled, he invites their indifference, if not sabotage, in putting his proposals into effect.

It may be said that the chain of communication which I have described is ideal and rarely found working smoothly. That is to be expected, people in the government service being human like the rest of us. But the thing to do when these channels are broken or clogged up is to get them repaired and open, not to ignore them and try to skip messages from place to place by special couriers.

The only occasion I can see for trying to run a department without this full utilization of and reliance on the bureau chiefs is when the man at the top of the department has decided he cannot do business with one or more of them and has not yet been able to replace them. Even under these circumstances, and even for a limited time, it is risky business to cut them out or go around them. When any man in the customary line of communication is flagrantly ignored, other people are thrown into doubt as to where authority lies (they do not know to whom they should go for what) and disorder sets in because men and women are forced to rely on their own imagination in establishing new relationships.

What I have said in the past few paragraphs does not deny an important place in the highest councils of the administrative department to the officials who head the special agencies for advice, service, and control. They supply information and ideas to the officials at the top of the department and to the bureau chiefs which supplement the information and ideas that flow upward through the main streams of communication which I have described. The men and women whom they direct and who report to them have specialized interests and concerns. These men and women travel over the entire range of the department's organization and penetrate into all of its affairs. Because of their special preoccupations and special opportunities for observation, they discover significances that are not apparent to other people. By putting observations together in new patterns, they generate ideas and produce proposals that would otherwise not come into being.

The officials who head the special agencies for advice, service, and control make a contribution of equal value in getting the decisions of the department head put into effect. Because the men and women under their direction have special concerns and have a license to work with people in all parts of the departmental organization, they can establish a common understanding in all parts of the organization as to how the highest officials want certain things done; by working with the people in all parts of the organization who have to put the new policies and practices into operation, they increase the likelihood that the department as a whole will move forward in harmony when it changes its course of action.

But these contributions of the men and women who deal primarily in advice, service, and control only supplement the contributions of the men who head the sectors of the departmental organization that actually carry on the activities for which the department was created. Their knowledge and understanding is not superior to and I doubt that it is anyway near equal to the knowledge and understanding which the bureau chiefs collectively bring into the highest councils of the department. Their capacity to get the decisions which are made at the top put into effect at the bottom of the organization is negligible when compared to that of the bureau chiefs.

It seems to me indisputable, therefore, that the department head can hope to make policies that offer any prospect of accomplishing his objectives and can hope to get the policies which he does adopt put into operation only if those policies are arrived at by putting his judgment together with that of the bureau chiefs. This may be done in part by general conferences among all the highest officials of the department (staff meetings); it will have to be done in part in special conferences between the head of the department (or other high officials who assumes his responsibility) and the particular bureau chief or bureau chiefs who are concerned with a particular matter.

The President's Committee on Administrative Management and the Hoover Commission agreed that is is desirable to have the special agencies for advice, service, and control under the direction of a single officer. I have not heard any person with experience in a large administrative department question the wisdom of such an arrangement. Much of the information and advice which these agencies supply is required for the officials at the top of the department; much of the control which they exercise is for the fulfillment of policies made at the top of the department. The head of the department cannot be the immediate boss over these activities because he cannot give the time and attention which so many organizations would require. If all of these special agencies are joined together under one superior officer who reports directly to the department head, the man who occupies that top position can be sure that he holds a position with potentialities of great influence. Such a position will be accepted by men who have the qualities which the department head values most highly and therefore can be filled by a man in whose judgment the department head has greatest confidence.

Both the Committee on Administrative Management and the Hoover Commission saw a need for more continuity of service among the officials next to the Secretary than we ordinarily get in our great executive departments. Both were of the opinion that one of the highest officials should be drawn from the career service (but not necessarily from the service of that department), and that this official should be given the direction of the special agencies for advice, service, and control. A careful reading of the language used by each of the two bodies leads to the conclusion that each used the phrase "career service" advisedly; each of the two study commissions seems to have intended to say that this position should be filled by a man who has acquired civil service status, who expects to continue indefinitely in the federal service, and who is willing to move from place to place in the federal service according to the challenges and rewards offered him by different jobs. A person who had acquired extensive experience in a position filled by Presidential appointment with Senate consent (one of the department's Assistant Secretaries, for instance) might fill the position as capably as any person with civil service status; I presume the two study commissions felt that such a person could not give sufficient evidence of intention to stay in the job indefinitely. Such a person might easily acquire civil service status; I do not know whether either or both of the study commissions would have considered that sufficient to convert a political appointee into a career official.

The men and women who hold important positions in the

special agencies for advice, service, and control can do what is expected of them only if they have a high familiarity with the laws and regulations governing the federal service and know how business is carried on throughout the federal government. There is a great deal to be gained if the high official to whom they report also has the same kind of knowledge. But an understanding of the laws, regulations, and ways of the federal government is not the first consideration to be taken into account in filling this office; it is of much greater importance that the person who goes into this position enjoy the fullest confidence of the department head and the other officials at the top of the department. The men and women who deal primarily in advice, service, and control can make the greatest contribution of which they are capable only if the officer who connects them with the highest officials in the department enjoys high prestige among those officials. It may be that every department head can always find in the career service some person upon whom he is willing to place great reliance. It would surely be a great mistake to set up a requirement for this office which would cause the head of a department in any instance to fill it with a man in whom he has less than the fullest confidence.

The agreement between the President's Committee on Administrative Management and the Hoover Commission concerning the place of a career official near the top of the department extended only to the point that he should have authority over the special agencies for advice, service, and control. The President's Committee recommended that his authority be enlarged to include the operating divisions of the department also, so that he would become the general manager or chief of operations for the department. The Hoover Commission made no such recommendation and said nothing which indicates that it would favor such a concentration of authority in one man other than the department head.

I can see the usefulness of a general manager or chief of operations under certain circumstances. If the Postmaster General is going to be also chairman of the national committee of his party and devote 99.44 percent of his time to affairs that have no relation to the conduct of the Post Office Department, he cannot personally run the Post Office Department with the remaining .56 percent of his time. In that case he may well need a general manager or chief of operations to run it for him. If any other department head is so preoccupied with affairs that are external to his department (fulfilling his obligations as a member of the cabinet and advising on matters of general policy, for instance) that he cannot personally become acquainted with the major problems confronting his subordinates and advise them as to what he wants done, then he too may need to turn his authority over to one man who will run the department for him. But if the department head intends to participate actively in the affairs of his department, discussing problems with the heads of his principal divisions, then he had better ponder his situation carefully before setting up one man as general manager or chief of operations. If he tells the chiefs of his principal divisions (bureaus) that another man is their boss and has full authority to give them instructions, then the chiefs of divisions become limited in what they can say to the head of the department and the head of the department becomes limited in what he can say to them. A man is not general manager or chief of operations unless he is authorized to tell the chief officials under him what they are expected to do. If the Secretary starts telling these principal officers what they are expected to do, it will soon become apparent either that the man who was told that he is general manager is not the general manager at all or that the department has two general managers who frequently give conflicting instructions.

I think it may be possible for the Secretary to participate actively in making policy for his department and criticizing the things which his department is doing and yet let one other man direct the operations of the department for him. But in that case the Secretary will have to be most circumspect in what he says to the chiefs of the principal divisions and most circumspect in what he permits them to say to him. In that case, furthermore, he must put into the office of general manager or chief of operations a person in whom he has highest confidence, and the inquiries which he makes concerning the way the department does its work must always be made with a view to reconsidering (continuously or intermittently) whether his confidence is justified.

Where the head of the department must repose so great a confidence in one man, and in a man whose decisions will so greatly affect the character and quality of administration, I think it would be the height of folly to tell the department head that he must find that person within the career service of the federal government as the Committee on Administrative Management would have required him to do. It seems to me that the department head should be free to look where he pleases for a man in whom he has highest confidence and that he should be forced to find a man in whom the President and Congress have confidence too. This suggests that if there is to be a general manager or chief of operations for a great executive department, the title of that official should be Under Secretary and the appointment should be made by the President with the advice and consent of the Senate.

BIBLIOGRAPHIC NOTE

A good place to begin in the study of the relationships which constitute organization is Chester I. Barnard, *The Functions of the Executive* (Cambridge, Mass., 1938). Mr. Barnard's experience has been mainly in private industry but what he says in this book is fully applicable to administrative departments and agencies of government. Two other books written mainly with industrial and commercial experience in mind but having application to government departments are James D. Mooney and Alan C. Reiley, *The Principles of Organization* (New York, 1939); and Paul E. Holden, L. S. Fish, and H. L. Smith, *Top-Management Organization and Control* (Stanford University, California, 1941). Much of the recent writing in the United States and England relating to organization has been greatly influenced by Mary Parker Follett. The best of her essays are in *Dynamic Administration;*

The Collected Papers of Mary Parker Follett, edited by Henry C. Metcalf and L. Urwick (New York, 1942). See also *Papers on the Science of Administration,* edited by Luther H. Gulick and L. Urwick (New York, 1937); Lyndall Urwick, *The Elements of Administration* (New York, 1943); and Richard Warner, *The Principles of Public Administration* (London, 1947).

Organization must be based on knowledge, beliefs, and suppositions about the way men and women tend to behave. For a report and analysis of the findings resulting from a recent study of the behavior of men and women in a larger industrial organization, see Fritz J. Roethlisberger, *Management and Morale* (Cambridge, Mass., 1941); Fritz J. Roethlisberger and William J. Dickson, *Management and the Worker* (Cambridge, Mass., 1940); and Elton Mayo, *The Social Problems of an Industrial Civilization* (Boston, 1945).

A number of the reports of the Hoover Commission and studies prepared for it by its task forces deal with organization for direction and control of the administrative departments of the federal government. Of these, see: *Departmental Management in Federal Administration* [*Appendix E*]; *The Organization of the Government for the Conduct of Foreign Affairs* [*Appendix H*]; and *Agricultural Functions and Organization in the United States* [*Appendix M*]. Each of these bears the subtitle, *A Report with Recommendations Prepared for the Commission on Organization of the Executive Branch of the Government;* and each was published by the Government Printing Office in 1949. The special report relating to organization within the administrative departments which was prepared for the President's Committee on Administrative Management in 1937 is in its *Report with Special Studies* (Government Printing Office, 1937), pp. 245–270.

We now have a number of books that deal especially with organization of the administrative departments of the federal government, the following being among the most useful: Arthur W. Macmahon and John D. Millett, *Federal Administrators; a Biographical Approach to the Problem of Departmental Management* (New York, 1939); Schuyler Wallace, *Federal Departmentalization* (New York, 1941); John M. Gaus and Leon O. Wolcott, *Public Administration and the United States Department of Agriculture* (Chicago, 1940); C. Herman Pritchett, *The Tennessee Valley Authority* (Chapel Hill, N.C., 1943); and Marshall E. Dimock, *The Executive in Action* (New York, 1945).

There are several short essays, written by men with experience in federal administration, which provide a careful analysis of what we are up against in organizing our big federal departments and which comment thoughtfully on how these problems may be met. Of these, I found the following most helpful: Arnold Brecht, "Smaller Departments," in *Public Administration Review*, vol. 1, pp. 363–373 (1941); Donald C. Stone, "Notes on the Governmental Executive: His Role and His Methods," in the same journal, vol. 5, pp. 210–225 (1945); Paul H. Appleby, "Organizing Around the Head of a Large Department," in the same journal, vol. 6, pp. 205–212 (1946); and John D. Millett, "Working Concepts of Organization," in *Elements of Public Administration*, edited by Fritz Morstein Marx (New York, 1946), pp. 140–157.

CHAPTER 23

THE REGULATORY COMMISSION

The preceding chapter was concerned primarily with organization for direction and control within the great executive department. This chapter is concerned with the arrangements for direction and control of the working force of the regulatory commission.

The agency which we call a regulatory commission differs from the executive department in three important respects: the organization is headed by a group of men instead of one man; the agency exists primarily to make policy rather than to administer governmental programs, and therefore requires a small working force; and the acts of the agency which constitute government for you and me are for the most part the acts of the officers at the top of the organization rather than the acts of the employees at the bottom of the organization.

The first of these three distinguishing features—the multiple rather than the one-man head—requires no explanation. It should be noted, however, that the regulatory agencies are not the only ones that have a group of men at the top of the organization. There are at least sixteen federal agencies which are headed by boards or commissions, and nine of them at the most can be said to be engaged primarily in regulatory activity.

The other two features which distinguish the regulatory commissions do require some explanation. Their significance can be brought out most clearly by a few comparisons with the executive departments.

The principal job of the Post Office Department is to pick up letters and parcels at one place and deliver them at another. The men and women who do this are in the lower ranks of the organization and are scattered all over the United States and its possessions. These employees, along with other employees who write out and cash postal orders and do other things that the Post Office Department was set up to do, provide the service which you and I get out of this segment of our government. The acts of these employees (nearly 500,000) at the bottom of the organization are government in operation. The high-paid officials who sit in Washington do some things that you and I recognize as government in operation; they decide, for instance, whether a particular book or magazine may be sent through the mails. But for the most part the officials at the top of the organization are occupied in telling other people in the organization what to do and how to do it. Ordinarily their decisions are not addressed to the public; rather, they speak to men and women below them in the organization and the men and women at the bottom speak to the public. The number of higher officials that are needed is determined, therefore, by the number of employees that must be supervised; the number of employees at the bottom is in no sense determined by the need of higher officials for assistance in doing the few acts of government which they perform.

The Treasury Department's Bureau of Internal Revenue carries on government in essentially the same manner as the Post Office Department. So do the Bureau of Reclamation in the Interior Department and the Forest Service in the Department of Agriculture. The Bureau of Internal Revenue cannot accomplish its purposes simply by announcing policies which tell you and me how to calculate the amount of taxes we should pay to the federal government. The Bureau must mail out tax forms, receive the tax returns and the payments of money that accompany them, examine the tax returns, tell people whether they owe more money and how much, and follow up in one way or another to collect the money that people do not pay willingly. To do this work, the Bureau employs about 50,000 people. The Bureau of Reclamation employs nearly 15,000 people. The job of this Bureau, speaking roughly, is to make land more productive. It does not do that simply by announcing policies which require people to improve their land; rather, the Bureau plans the dams and irrigation systems that it thinks are needed and gets them built. The primary task of the Forest Service is not to announce rules and regulations which you and I must obey in order to make sure that the nation will have a supply of timber. Instead the Forest Service is actually managing nearly 200 million acres of public lands and is helping the owners of timberland keep their forests productive. To do this, it employs more than 10,000 people.

Government by the regulatory commission follows a very different pattern. Most of the things it does which people outside the agency know about and call government in operation are the acts of the commissioners at the top of the organization, not of the employees at the bottom. The principal job of the regulatory commission is to tell one or another sector of the American people what they may and may not do, not to carry on a great service enterprise. The Federal Communications Commission, for instance, does not operate the telephone and telegraph service of the nation, or provide the nation with radio broadcasts as the British government does through its BBC. The basic job of FCC is to set standards for the telephone and telegraph service which business corporations supply and to make such inquiries as are necessary to find out whether these standards are complied with; to allocate radio frequencies among different kinds of radio service (broadcasting, aviation communication, etc.) and assign specific frequencies to individual users; and to maintain enough surveillance over the radio transmission that goes on in the country to see that the federal statutes and its own regulations are complied with. The commissioners themselves consider the important problems of telephone and telegraph service and decide how the order shall read which tells a telephone or telegraph company whether and in what way it may alter its rates. It is the seven members of the commission who, after personally listening to argument and looking at the charts and tables, decide which sector of the radio spectrum shall be set aside for television. And it is the seven commissioners who evaluate the competing considerations and decide that the license for a radio station in Bogalusa shall go to Havrylak and not to Adams or Weeks or Holl, who also applied for it.

If the acts of the regulatory commission affecting the public were confined solely to things which the commissioners personally decide, the size of the agency would be determined entirely by the number of people needed to help the commissioners make their decisions and to see that their decisions are made known to the people who are affected by them. This appears not to be the case in many instances, if indeed in any instance. In each of the executive departments, some of the acts which constitute government for you and me are preformed by high officials in the department. So also in most if not all the regulatory agencies headed by commissions, some of the acts which constitute government for the American people are performed by men and women in the lower levels of the organization. The regulation of radio presents an example. There are a number of applications for radio licenses (e.g., most applications for radio on aircraft) which involve only questions that have already been decided; the commissioners have announced their policies and issued instructions which determine what is to be done in each case. Men and women in the lower ranks of FCC receive these applications, examine them, decide whether the applicant has met all the requirements for a license, and make out a license and send it to him if he has. There are other people in FCC who inspect certain kinds of radio equipment (installations on seagoing vessels, for instance) and check the transmissions that go out on the air to make sure that everybody stays on the channel that was assigned to him. The employees of FCC who do these kinds of work represent government to people who make use of radio in their business operations, just as the postman who carries my letters represents government in action to me. But the employees in FCC who actually perform acts of government in this sense are few in number, and the statement can stand that most of the men and women who make up the organization are there to help the seven commissioners make their decisions and to see that the people outside the government who are affected by those decisions know what has been decided.

What has just been said about FCC is true generally of the regulatory agencies that are headed by commissions. The consequence is that all these agencies are small in size. The biggest of them, the Interstate Commerce Commission, has less than 2500 officials and employees. Only two have as many as 1000 employees. Collectively, the eight regulatory commissions (I exclude the Maritime Commission as not primarily engaged in regulation) have a payroll of less than 10,000 men and women, which is a small item indeed in a total federal civilian employment of more than two million.

The three distinctive features of the regulatory commissions which have been discussed—the multiple head, the fact that they exist to make policy rather than to administer governmental programs, and the fact that they act through the top rather than the bottom—have two consequences of primary significance for the internal organization of these agencies. First, the principal objective in organizing the working force must be to make sure that information and ideas will flow up from the staff to the commissioners; second, the organization which is developed must allow the flow of ideas and information to spread out at the top to as many points as there are commissioners who wish to talk to members of the staff.

Before entering upon an examination of these two considerations, it must be noted that they are not found in the regulatory commissions only. The State Department, for instance, must be organized with a primary concern for the flow of information and ideas to the top of the structure so that the Secretary of State and others can make the decisions which constitute some of the most important acts of our government. And there are a number of agencies not primarily concerned with regulation which are headed by a group of men and which may maintain as many channels for communication as there are men who share the top authority.

The problems of organization which are peculiar to the regulatory commissions center at the point where the commissioners connect with the officials and employees who make up the working force of the agency. The relationships which tie officials and employees together in the lower ranks are not essentially different from the relationships at the same level in any other type of agency. An organization must be created which will move information, ideas, and questions up the line and move information, ideas, and instructions down the line. But the arrangements for the connection of the working force of officials and employees to the commissioners is pretty certain to be different from that which connects the working force of another type of agency to the official or officials at the top.

The commissioners at the top of a regulatory agency want information and ideas to come to them from the staff and they want to decide for themselves what the nature of that body of information and ideas shall be. They do not want any single officer below them to be in a position to determine for them what they shall see and hear. They want that flow of information and ideas to come to them as a group and they want it also to come to them as individuals. Their first concern in arranging the organization of the staff at the level immediately under them is to give themselves assurance that they, and not somebody else, shall control that flow.

It is because of this basic concern of the commissioners at the top that several if not most of the regulatory commissions of the federal government are organized on a basis of specialized knowledge and skill rather than on the basis of sectors or segments of the industry (or area of affairs) to be regulated. This can be illustrated readily by the organization of FCC. Four principal officers report directly to the commissioners, and a fifth reports directly to the chairman of the commission. Three of these principal officers head divisions of the staff that are concerned with the whole range of affairs over which FCC has regulatory authority, each division being concerned with an aspect of those affairs which calls for a particular kind of knowledge. A chief accountant heads a division that deals with accounting problems; a chief engineer heads a division that deals with engineering problems; and a general counsel heads a division that deals with legal problems. A fourth officer called the secretary heads a force of clerical employees who do routine work relating to all phases of regulation. And finally, an executive officer, who reports to the chairman, has authority relating to the internal affairs of FCC, including the kinds of activities that I have referred to in earlier chapters as advice, service, and control.

The commissioners regulate the telephone, telegraph, and radio activities of the nation by deciding specific issues which come before them. Shall the range of frequencies available for television be expanded? Shall the rules be amended to permit a particular type of radio license to be held by a corporation? Is there reason to believe that Voskuil, who has applied for a radio station in Garretstown, will provide better service for his listeners than Erickson, who has also applied? And so on.

The commissioners decide these questions as a group. They sit together and have in their hands an analysis of the problem before them and recommendations for action to be taken. The document which they look at may have been put together by one man but it is based on studies made in the three divisions (accounting, engineering, law) and it may contain three different recommendations. The commissioners consider the issue with members of the staff before them to tell them facts and give them opinions concerning the consequence of alternative actions. Since most of the questions involve accounting, engineering, and legal problems, there are at least three men in the presence of the commissioners who are familiar with the case. The accountant speaks primarily to the accounting aspects of the question but if he has been on the job a substantial period of time, his judgment extends to the general questions of public policy which are involved in the issue. The same can be said of the engineer and the lawyer. If one of the three seeks to limit the commission's understanding of what is involved in the case, there are two other men present who ordinarily have enough understanding of the matter to upset his plans. If one of the commissioners is skeptical about what he is being told, he can check his doubts with two other men.

The alternative organization that occurs to one is to arrange the staff in terms of the industry to be regulated—perhaps a division for telephone, one for telegraph, and one for radio. If this were done, the full study (analysis of accounting, engineering, and legal aspects) of a case arising from any industry would be carried out under the direction of one official; the chief of the telephone division, for instance, would have under him accountants, engineers, and lawyers who would study the problems relating to telephone regulation and prepare their reports under his direction. If this style of organization were in effect, the commissioners (sitting to hear facts, consider alternatives, make a decision) would be confronted by only one man or by one man supported by other men who work under his direction. If this official brought before the commissioners only subordinates who agreed with him as to the issues and proper disposition of the particular case, the commissioners would be limited in the range of choice available to them. If the official in charge of one area of regulation (telephone, telegraph, radio) were too far to the left or too far to the right to suit some or all of the commissioners, they would get little help in deciding how much correction to make for the bias which consciously or unconsciously entered into his statements of fact and recommendations for action.

Under the organization which now obtains in FCC, there is not much likelihood that one man will prejudice the commissioners to a decision which they would not otherwise willingly make. The view of the facts and the evaluation of alternatives which are laid before the commissioners are not dictated by one man. Only if at least three men happen to be of common mind will the commissioners be at the mercy of a single attitude or point of view.

The likelihood that the commissioners may be restricted in their freedom of choice must be weighed against certain advantages that may be expected to accrue from a reorganization which arranges the staff according to the sectors or segments of the industry which is regulated. If one man were head of a telephone division in FCC, having full control of the work relating to the telephone industry, he could estimate the size and character of his job and make plans to move work forward according to his understanding of when and how particular things should be done. He could direct that matters of less importance be given summary treatment so that men would be available to do carefully the things of greatest importance. He could relate the work of one man to that of another so that a job could be finished when it ought to be finished.

No man below the seven commissioners is in a position to coordinate and direct the work of FCC in that fashion today. Accountant, engineer, and lawyer negotiate in order to decide what questions shall be taken up next and how much work shall be done on the particular case. If agreement is reached (and it usually is) as to how men in the three divisions shall relate their work on a particular case, the individuals who actually do the work get their instructions from different superior officers and the original agreement is readily upset because someone forgets his part of the agreement or neglects to tell somebody else that a more pressing matter has arisen and he has reassigned his man to another task. The practical consequence of this situation is that the work which men in three different divisions do on a specific case is not well timed. Sometimes the case which should have gotten up before the commission last month, and which is scheduled to get there this month, does not actually get there until month after next. And it is not because men who analyze the cases lack competence or loaf on the job; it is because there is no one (short of the commissioners themselves) who has authority extending over all three divisions and is able to coordinate the work.

The situation is even more complicated than the above paragraphs make it appear. When an agency is organized according to specialized knowledge or skill, there is a good chance that the men who head the divisions will not do a very good job of directing the men under them; and there is a good chance that everybody will choke to death on paper. The members of a commission, like the head of any other agency, like to promote to a high position the individual who impresses them as having the best qualities for the job. The job, as the commissioners see it, is to make careful and penetrating analyses of the factors involved in complicated problems and to give the commissioners imaginative and thoughtful counsel on the probable consequences of alternative solutions for those problems. Therefore they tend to promote to the top position in each division the man whom they consider to be the most competent and the most dependable accountant or engineer or lawyer, as the case may be. And the man who excels in the qualities which the commissioners value most is likely not to be effective in directing the work of other people. This is the case in part because, in developing his high competence in his profession, he devoted himself to analytical work and got little practice in laying out work for other people and directing them in doing it; in part because, knowing that the commissioners value him for his insight and judgment, he feels obliged still to devote himself mainly to personal study of the most important problems that come before the commission rather than to the job of seeing that other men make careful studies and use sound judgment.

The strangling effect of paper is equally an inevitable consequence of a style of organization which arranges work on a basis of specialized knowledge or skill. All large organizations leave a trail of paper to mark what they have done. A regulatory agency lives in a world of paper. People who want permission to do something apply on paper. Complaints about something that someone else has done come in on paper. When the agency acts, it puts its decision on paper. The whole performance of the agency is therefore regulated by a movement of paper. The officials above can tell whether the officials and employees below are dead or alive only by observing whether paper which used to be at one place has moved to another place.

In order to achieve dispatch and economy in handling paper and to make somebody responsible for keeping each piece of paper where it can be found, FCC maintains a number of employees who have nothing to worry about except the location of pieces of paper. Men and women, working under the direction of the secretary, receive the paper when it comes in, make the necessary records about it, file it, take it out of the files when other people want it, put it in shape to be sent about the agency and keep a record of where it went to, and file it again when it comes back. And they do the same sort of thing with paper that originates in the agency and goes out to the people who have to be notified of what FCC has decided.

It is clear enough that the people who maneuver this paper about do it as a service to other people—the accountants, the engineers, the lawyers. What they do to the paper, and where they send it, is a matter of no importance to the people who are in this paper-moving division. They work under a boss, the secretary, who has no personal interest in what is done to the paper or where it goes, for the paper exists for the use of other people, not for him. The secretary gets complaints from the accountants that the paper which should have come to them is not there, and the secretary runs furiously about his little domain to find why things are not done according to his orders, only to learn that the engineers or the lawyers have impounded the paper and appear totally unaware that accountants exist. Engineers tell the secretary that the paper which comes to them no longer contains the annotations which they once found so useful, and the secretary learns that the girls who used to digest the documents are now preparing annotations which the lawyers and the accountants say they cannot do without. The secretary has authority to tell the people who work for him exactly what they are to do; but he does not know what they ought to do until the accountants and the engineers and the lawyers get together and negotiate agreement as to what they ought to have. We will see a bit more about this problem of paper in the chapter which follows.

It would appear from the foregoing remarks that the commissioners who head a regulatory agency have to choose between two sets of values. They can organize the staff according to specialized knowledge or skill, suffer delays, and incur excessive costs in getting matters brought before them for attention, but have the assurance that the commissioners will get a full disclosure of the important considerations which they ought to take into account in making their decisions. Or the commissioners can organize the staff according to the industry (or area of affairs) to be regulated, have the assurance that there are men below them with ample authority to coordinate and direct all of the work on each and every problem that comes before the commissioners, and take a chance that these men will not, consciously or unconsciously, prejudice the decisions of the commissioners by failure to make available to them the information and points of view which they ought to consider. These two alternatives present the primary choice which must be made in organizing the agency's staff, I am sure, but there are some additional considerations which will complicate the decision.

Let us assume that FCC organized its staff into a telephone division, a telegraph division, and a radio division. In that case the commissioners would indeed have three men under them, each with ample authority to coordinate and direct all of the work relating to all of the cases which arise in his particular area of affairs. Each of these men could give the secretary definitive and authoritative instructions as to what he wanted done with the paper relating to his affairs—indeed, each of these three divisions might be given custody of its own paper. It does not follow, however, that the commissioners would ordinarily appoint to these three positions men who are effective in coordinating and directing work. The main consideration in the minds of the commissioners must not be forgotten. They value men first for their insight into and judgment upon regulatory matters; they are likely to choose as heads of the three divisions the men who impress them as having these qualities in highest degree, not the men who have revealed the greatest competence in directing the work of other men. And, regardless of his competence in administration and desire to direct his staff effectively, the head of any of these divisions will be under a great compulsion to devote his time largely to personal study of the more important and more difficult problems, with a consequent drain on the time and energy that should be available for the direction of other men.[1]

There is one further point to be considered. It was mentioned above that the commissioners want information and ideas to come to them individually as well as collectively. They do not do all of their thinking while they are sitting together. They work on the tough problems as individuals and they do a lot of work before the case gets to the point of decision. The business of working on a problem is, in large part, a matter of talking, of laying one man's thoughts beside another man's so that alternatives can be clearly seen and fully considered. Most of the talk in which the commissioner engages is with the members of the staff. The commissioner does not understand the significance of this set of figures about land formation and propagation of radio waves in a coaxial cable. So he has not one conference but many conferences with an engineer who is working on the case. The commissioner may be a lawyer and have confidence in his ability as a lawyer, but he has not

---

[1] An attorney employed for several years in a regulatory commission (not FCC) organized in the way I have just described (i.e., all technical skills were brought together in a division having responsibility for all aspects of a particular area of affairs) writes: "The director under whom I worked was prone to do intensively the very kind of work which you talk about, that is, the substantive job of analysis and decision. With the mass of cases which the Division had to process, however, the individual attention which the director insisted on bestowing on each case necessarily served as a roadblock and resulted in a substantial slowing down of the work of the Division. The Commission insisted, in selecting a successor, that the Division be reorganized at the top and that an associate director be provided so that the director could spend more of his time in actual administration as distinguished from analysis and synthesis."

gone into the most recent cases. And so he must talk with a lawyer who has studied them and then see him again after he has thought more about the problem.

It is not always, and perhaps not usually, the head of the division of accounting or engineering or law that the commissioner wants to talk to. He wants to talk to the man who has the facts that he needs; therefore he wants to talk to the man who has already been at work on the case, who understands fully what the issues are, and who has already figured out some ideas of his own as to what the consequences of different actions would be. It is natural for the commissioner, as he works on a case with members of the staff, to forget that they are working under the direction of other men. He tells them what he wants them to do and he tells them he wants it done in a hurry; he does not call up the chief of the division and say, "Can you detail so-and-so to me for three or four days, and if you can't give me him, can you give me somebody else?" Furthermore, there will be conferences in the commissioner's office which are attended by the chief of a division and by one or more men who are under him. The commissioner ought, no doubt, to remember that one man is boss and that the other men work under his direction, and defer to the chief of the division on any matter which affects his prestige as a superior officer. The commissioners do not always remember.

What has just been said about the relations between the individual commissioners and members of the staff is, in large part, descriptive of what happens when the commissioners sit collectively. They hear the chief of the division but they want to hear other people too. In the FCC, if the chiefs of the divisions came alone to a sitting of the commission, the commissioners would tell them to "get the people in here who actually worked on these cases." If the chief of the division disagrees with his subordinate on the recommendation to be laid before the commission, the commissioners will respect his right, as a superior officer, to say what the formal recommendation shall be. But they will ask the subordinate what he initially proposed and how he arrived at his conclusion. The commissioners will talk out loud to one another and to the members of the staff about the merits of the two propositions, and the things they say and the decisions which they reach are not likely to make much allowance for relationships of prestige between the chief of the division and his subordinates.

Certainly these relationships between the commissioners and the staff are not conducive to the development of what one calls firm administrative relationships. I doubt that a change in organization to fit the main divisions to the industries or areas of affairs that are regulated would make much difference in these relations. The commissioners, individually and collectively, would continue to talk to the individuals most likely to give them the information and ideas that they want. And it is unlikely that, in regulating these contacts, they would make a greater allowance for considerations of prestige that support firmness on the part of superiors in directing the work of those who are below them in the organization.

The considerations which have just been discussed in their relation to the organization of FCC undoubtedly complicate the construction of a satisfactory organization in every other regulatory commission. And I have no doubt that many of the obstacles to orderly relationships which I have described obtrude in other types of administrative agency as well. I suspect, however, that the regulatory commission (because it is a commission and because its primary job is regulation) is most perplexed by these considerations and witnesses in greatest concentration the frustrations which they inevitably entail.

Both the President's Committee on Administrative Management of 1937 and the Hoover Commission of 1949 took a look at the regulatory commissions and made recommendations for their improvement. The President's Committee sought to solve the problems of organization by scattering them. It recommended that the regulatory process be split down the middle. Under its proposal, all decisions "essentially judicial in nature" were to be made by a commission; all other decisions involved in regulation (including the making of rules and regulations which extend the statutory law) were to be turned over to a bureau in an administrative department. The bureau chief, confronted with the necessity of formulating a policy (let us say the designation of frequencies to be available for television), would face the same problem in organization which the commission now has, that of fixing a style of organization which gets work done but also gives him assurance that no one subordinate can control his understanding of an issue or prejudice his choice between alternatives. The commission, under the arrangement proposed by the President's Committee, would have the same concern that it now has for a full and fair presentation of the facts and issues of a case but it would be greatly limited in what it could do about it. If the proposals of the President's Committee were put into effect, the commission would lose all control over the facts and ideas presented to it by officials and employees of the government, for the latter would be under the direction of a bureau chief instead of the commission. Only in a formal proceeding where parties other than the government appear to testify and argue could the commission be confident of getting at the facts that it needs and of hearing the arguments that it wants to weigh.

The President's Committee stated that the division of work which it proposed between judicial and nonjudicial aspects "would be relatively simple." It also stated that the plan which it proposed "meets squarely the problems presented by the independent commissions." I find it much easier to believe that the members of the Committee and the persons on whom they relied for advice did not know what the problems were.[2]

The Hoover Commission and the members of the task force which advised it seems to me to have brought a great deal more

[2] For the recommendations of the President's Committee and the report on regulatory commissions which was prepared for the Committee's use, see *President's Committee on Administrative Management, Report with Special Studies* (Government Printing Office, 1937), pp. 39–42, 203–243.

understanding to the study of what is involved in regulation than did the President's Committee. And they made their recommendations in a spirit of greater humility.

The task force which made a study of the regulatory commissions for the Hoover Commission rejected the recommendation of the President's Committee that the regulatory activity of each of these agencies be split into two parts and divided between a bureau in an administrative department and a commission which would serve as a judicial section for the same administrative department. "We have concluded," the task force said, "that the independent commission is a useful type of agency for regulation under certain conditions and should be continued for such specialized tasks."

Having concluded that a number of regulatory agencies, each headed by a commission, should be continued, the task force went on to inquire into the nature of the internal organization most likely to enable the commission to do its work with dispatch and with results most satisfactory to the American people. Its statement of the relation of internal organization to the ability of the commissioners to understand what issues confront them and what choices they have in making decisions is the best that I have seen in print. With some hesitancy, because it could see advantages both ways, the task force recommended that those commissions which had organized the staff on a professional basis (e.g., with divisions of accounting, engineering, and law) reorganize on what it called a functional basis (e.g., according to the sectors of the industry or areas of affairs to be regulated). With much more assurance, it recommended that the chairman of each commission be given enough authority to enable him to become boss of the officials and employees who make up the staff. And in order to enable the chairman to give effective direction to the staff, the task force recommended that each regulatory commission set up an executive officer who would do for the chairman what the chairman might not have time to do himself.

The Hoover Commission agreed with its task force at least in part. It stated that "the independent regulatory commissions have a proper place in the machinery of our Government," and it recommended that "all administrative responsibility be vested in the chairman of the commission." It did not offer any advice to Congress as to how the staff below the commission and the chairman should be organized, however; and it did not say anything about the need for an executive officer to help the chairman out.[3]

In considering these recommendations for reorganization of the regulatory commissions it is important to keep in mind the conditions which characterize life in those agencies, and which I tried to set forth above. It must always be kept clearly in mind that the agency exists primarily, if not altogether, to make decisions which constitute important determinations of public policy, and that these decisions will be made by the commissioners themselves. Therefore, no organization can be tolerated which hinders the free flow of information and ideas from the staff to the commissioners.

These considerations make it highly questionable whether the chairman of a regulatory commission can actually function as its executive officer, giving direction to the principal officials who in turn direct the activities of the working force of lesser officials and employees. The chairman is (and according to my preferences, ought to be) given his position because of his understanding of regulatory problems and his judgment in dealing with them. It is more important, in my opinion, that he be a leader of the commissioners than that he be a director of the officials and employees below the commission. It is more important, it seems to me, that he be known as a vigorous spokesman for policies which balance competing interests and produce a regulatory program

[3] The task force report is entitled *Committee on Independent Regulatory Commissions; A Report with Recommendations Prepared for the Commission on Organization of the Executive Branch of the Government* [*Appendix N*]; quotation at p. 18. The report of the Commission is entitled *The Independent Regulatory Commissions; A Report to the Congress by the Commission on Organization of the Executive Branch of the Government, March 1949;* quotations at pp. 3, 5. Each document was published by the Government Printing Office in 1949.

under which the nation can go forward with confidence than that he establish a record for competent management of the internal affairs of the agency.

If the chairman is to play the role in regulatory policy which I have suggested, he will need all the time he can find for the regulatory problems which come before the commission for decision. Actually, he will usually if not always have less time for these matters than other members of the commission, even though he has no special responsibilities for directing the work of the staff. Because he is the most prominent member of the commission, he will be more sought after than the other commissioners by people outside the organization who have an interest in questions which are before the commission. Congressmen, for instance, who are concerned about general policies of regulation or acting as Washington agent for a constituent are most likely to take their questions and suggestions to the chairman. If the chairman of a regulatory commission charged with advancing the public interest in matters of great importance to the American people attempted to do the job of direction and control that is needed within his agency, I think we should soon either have to bury him as the consequence of overwork or have to acknowledge that he has no prospect of playing the part intended for him in supplying leadership and making decisions on regulatory policy.

It was doubtless these considerations which caused the Hoover Commission's task force to avoid precise language in describing the relationship which it would have the chairman (and his alter ego, the executive officer) bear to the officials and employees who work in the agency. The special duties of the chairman as head of internal administration, it is clear, would include the direction of the activities which I have throughout this book referred to as advice, service, and control. The budget officer, the personnel officer, the comptroller, the officer in charge of supplies—these and other officials who deal primarily in advice, service, and control would be arranged in a hierarchy and report to the executive officer who acts for the chairman. But it is not clear what the task

force thought the relation of the chairman and his executive officer should be to the divisions that work on regulatory matters.
The duties of the chairman, said the task force, should include
"supervision of the various bureaus and divisions from the administrative point of view, such as their work load, back log, progress,
and programs." But "the executive officer would not be concerned
with the policy decisions of the commission. The staff bureaus
would still remain responsible to the whole commission for advice
and recommendations on policy questions."[4]

The most reasonable interpretation of the language of the task
force seems to be that it wished the chairman, acting through his
executive officer, to be the day-to-day boss of the divisions that
study regulatory matters and make reports and recommendations
that guide the commissioners in their decisions, but that the instructions of the chairman and executive officer should not extend
to the content of specific reports or to the character of particular
recommendations. The chairman, through the executive officer,
could tell the officials and employees who work on regulatory
matters how they can do more quickly and more economically
what the commissioners want them to do. The chairman and the
executive officer could hire, promote, and fire men, assign and re-
assign duties, schedule work to be done, and take steps to see that
a force of men and women set to work in time to meet the sched-
ules. But whether the end product of the work which the staff carried out was satisfactory or not would be for the commissioners to
say; it would be no concern of the executive officer whatever, and
it would be the concern of the chairman only when he expressed
his feelings as one of the commissioners.

My experience in one such agency convinces me that the staff
of a regulatory commission can profit from a great deal more boss-
ing than it gets. And I think that the line of command by which
instructions are issued to the staff should come to a peak in the
chairman rather than the commission as a whole. The executive
officer cannot establish his right to confidence with five or seven

[4] Task force report, *supra*, pp. 46 and 48.

or a greater number of commissioners as he can with one of them (the chairman). The executive officer will be reluctant to make proposals for change if he knows that all the commissioners must take time out to consider them; he will be less reluctant if he must request time from the chairman only. There will be inconsistency in decisions relating to administration if the decisions are made by the commission as a whole, for those commissioners who are most indifferent to administrative matters will be moved by different considerations at different times. And finally, questions of administration that go before the whole commission will meet with vacillation. The primary concern of the commissioners is with issues of regulatory policy. They strive for an atmosphere of mutual good feeling so that they may stand together on issues of regulatory policy. When the agency is under attack from any sector of the public, the commissioners will go to great lengths to avoid an issue that might divide them. When they are divided on important issues of policy, they will go to great lengths to avoid the widening of the breach. Under such circumstances, the particular commissioner who wishes to do nothing about a matter of internal administration is likely to win. He may be offended if action is taken; the other commissioners can tolerate for a while longer what they are already tolerating.

Even if the chairman is acknowledged to be the head of the administrative affairs of the regulatory commission, there is a good chance that the other commissioners will not allow him and his executive officer to exercise enough influence to give the staff the coordination that it needs. No matter what authority is given one man to direct the activities of the staff, I suspect that he will never have anything approaching a monopoly on that direction, even if he is chairman and has an executive officer to work at it all of the time. The commissioners can be expected, as individuals and as a group, to persist in consulting with members of the staff. And consultation will lead to instructions that nullify the instructions which the chairman or the executive officer has given. A commissioner will decide that Burt and Hollis and Davis should work on this matter, right when the chairman or the executive officer has decided that they should work on something else; and the executive officer will be lucky if he hears about the change in plans from the commissioner or the chairman before he hears about it from Burt and Hollis and Davis. The commissioners will tell the chairman and the executive officer who ought to be kept when men threaten to leave and they will tell them who ought to be promoted when there are vacancies to be filled. If the chairman and the executive officer yield to the wishes of particular commissioners in particular instances, they may undermine the respect for their own authority which they have painfully attempted to build up among the staff. But if they do not yield to the wishes of the commissioners in such matters, they run the risk of defeating the major end toward which they are working—a relationship between the commissioners and staff which gives the commissioners (not the executive officer) confidence in the information and ideas which the staff brings to them.

BIBLIOGRAPHIC NOTE

There is an admirable general statement of the nature of the regulatory commissions and the problems which they present in an essay by James W. Fesler, in *Elements of Public Administration,* edited by Fritz Morstein Marx (New York, 1946), ch. 10. The most comprehensive general treatment of all the regulatory commissions of the federal government is by Robert E. Cushman, *The Independent Regulatory Commissions* (New York, 1941). The book is primarily descriptive in character, though it does offer comment on a number of important problems which are involved in relating these agencies to the remainder of the administrative system and the bodies of public policy with which they are concerned. Wilson K. Doyle, *Independent Commissions in the Federal Government* (Chapel Hill, N.C., 1939) is much less comprehensive in scope.

For the recommendations of the President's Committee on Administrative Management relating to the regulatory commissions and the study prepared for it on that subject, see: *President's Committee on*

Administrative Management; Report with Special Studies (Government Printing Office, 1937), pp. 39–42, 203–243. For critique of the presumptions and argument in the report of the President's Committee and the special study prepared for it, see: Frederick F. Blachly and M. E. Oatman, *Federal Regulatory Action and Control* (Washington, 1940), pp. 143–182.

Two documents of the Hoover Commission of 1949 deal with the regulatory commissions: *The Independent Regulatory Commissions; A Report to the Congress on Organization of the Executive Branch of the Government, March 1949;* and *Committee on Independent Regulatory Commissions; A Report with Recommendations Prepared for the Commission on Organization of the Executive Branch of the Government [Appendix N].* Both were published by the Government Printing Office in 1949.

There is an extensive literature dealing with particular regulatory commissions of the federal government but these works throw little light on the problems of internal organization which I discuss in this chapter.

CHAPTER 24

THE PROBLEM OF INEFFICIENCY

AND RED TAPE

To the popular mind, the two besetting sins of the federal bureaucracy are inefficiency and red tape. This analysis of the problems of direction and control within the administrative department may well close with an examination of what it is that we object to and denounce as inefficiency and red tape; how those objectionable aspects of administration come into existence and why they persist; and what the head of the administrative department might do to minimize or eliminate them.

A discussion of inefficiency must necessarily start with some consideration of efficiency. We decide whether a man or a machine or a process is inefficient by first deciding what kind of performance is entitled to be considered efficient. Efficiency, as a precise term, refers to ability to do something according to specifications with a minimum expenditure of energy and materials. The engineer measures the efficiency of a machine with great precision. He knows how much energy he puts into the machine; he measures the product which comes out of it; and he calculates the ratio of what goes in to what comes out. If the ratio, in the case of one machine, is the same as that in the case of another, the two machines have equal efficiency. How efficient they are in an absolute sense will depend on what he sets up as a standard. If he decides that the average efficiency of all his machines will be fixed as the standard and equal 100, then the particular machines that do better than the average will be given a rating in excess of 100.

It is not feasible, if indeed it is possible, to measure the efficiency of human beings in this precise way. The worker controls the amount of energy that goes into his efforts and he has no way of measuring his input. When we speak of efficiency on the part of employees, we are likely to think of output only. We say that typist A is more efficient than typist B because, while their work is judged to be of equal quality, A turns out more pages of manuscript per hour. This is not enough to establish the relative worth of the two girls to the organization, however; the faster typist may wear out more typewriters than the other, or work herself into a frenzy and have to take off more days in sick leave, or make so much noise that no one else in the office can do any work.

When you and I charge people in the public service with inefficiency, we have no sharp definition of efficiency in mind. Inefficiency is an emotional word in which we wrap up a wide range of things we don't like. We call government inefficient if it is doing something we think it ought not to be doing (buying surplus potatoes, for instance); we call it inefficient if we don't like the way in which it does something (buys potatoes direct from farmers instead of through brokers, or vice versa); we call it inefficient if we don't like the performance of the officials and employees who do the work of government (they can't tell an Irish potato from a sweet potato).

Red tape is a special term for a special dislike. Unlike efficiency, it has not acquired a precise meaning in any context. Its origin seems to lie far back in the history of British bureaucracy. Papers which went out of the active files and into archives were tied up in bundles with red ribbon. If a matter once thought settled were reopened, the papers relating to the case were said to be "in red tape," and it took a long time to get them. Red tape consequently came to signify delay in getting action. Anything which the government takes more time in doing than you or I think necessary we call red tape. Delay is likely to go hand in hand with indirect, rather than direct, ways of doing things. Therefore if we run into something that seems an unnecessarily long-way-round process, we call that red tape too. If a government employee is insolent, we have other words to describe his conduct. But if it takes too long to do something, or we have to fill out too many forms, or we have to see too many people—in any of these instances, we say that the bureaucrats are all tangled up in their red tape.

The analysis of inefficiency and red tape involves two stages of inquiry. We must look (first) into the nature of the deficiencies that exist, see how they come to be, and observe who may be responsible for them. When we have done that, we will be in a position to consider (second) what administrative officials can do to correct them.

The simplest case with which we have to deal is the personal shortcomings of the individual employee. These are matters of capacity and of attitude. They do not require much comment, for we are all familiar with what is involved. The government secretary who cannot read her own shorthand is just like the secretary in a business firm who cannot read her own shorthand. The government clerk who is not interested in his work and makes mistakes in his figures is just like the clerk in a business house who makes foolish mistakes because he is not interested in what he is doing. The loafer and the dead beat pursue the same techniques for avoiding work under a public employer that they pursue under a private employer. The thing that calls for comment in the case of incompetent and indifferent employees is what the administrative official can do to deal with them, and that will be taken up at a later point.

Most of the shortcomings of government which we denounce as inefficiency and red tape cannot be charged entirely to the qualities and conduct of individual employees. They are the joint product of many different people, working in different parts of the organization, and occupying positions at various levels in the hierarchy of the government. And the factors or considerations that lead to the appearance and persistence of the things we object to are just as mixed up as the people who are involved in them. Some of them are practices we were proud of at one time when they served a useful purpose; the practices hang on after the need for them has passed and they are only a nuisance today. Some of them are due to ignorance and indifference; the practice is a poor way of doing a thing, but the employee who worked it out did not know any better way to do it, and more experienced employees and officials gave him no help. Some of the things we object to serve a useful purpose for one individual or a group of individuals in the organization; if the purpose is not legitimate, we call them a private racket. But many other things that we find most objectionable and denounce most roundly are simply good things carried too far. Too much precaution to avoid an error and too much pains to do a thing well can run up costs, delay action, and create annoyance for the general public comparable if not equal to that which results from incompetence, indifference, and dishonesty.

If the foregoing is a fair generalization of how these deficiencies of administration come to exist and why they persist, it follows that the administrative official really has a job on his hands in trying to run them down, size them up, and correct them. We had better make sure, therefore, whether these things we denounce as inefficiency and red tape are really so complicated. That can best be done by examining a few specific cases, all of which are drawn from my own observation in the Federal Communications Commission and consequently represent situations in which I am sure we know the essential facts.

The simplest problem is represented by *The Case of the Missing I*. In the spring of 1946, Mr. Jesse I. Miller, attorney-at-law in Washington, D.C., and recently retired from his position as Colonel in the Army, called the executive officer of FCC to complain that he had not had any return on his petition for admission to practice before FCC. One of his clients wanted the Colonel to represent him in a case involving a license for a radio station, and the Colonel could not appear in the case until he obtained permission to practice before FCC. He had filed his petition for admission to practice weeks before, he had not had any return on his petition, the date for hearing on his case was getting close, and the Colonel thought it was time for FCC to do something.

The executive officer's inquiry into the status of the Colonel's petition brought forth the information that "Colonel Miller's papers are going back to him today." The Colonel's papers got back to him promptly, and the Colonel just as promptly got back on the phone for further complaint to the executive officer. He would like to be told what was wrong with his signature. He had typed out his petition for admission to practice on the proper form— "I, Jesse I. Miller, hereby apply, etc."—and he had signed his name in the proper place. "They have returned my application," said the Colonel, "because they say they cannot find an *I* in my signature. If they will lift up the last *e* in Jesse, and look under it on top of the *M* in Miller, they will find an *I* in between."

The Colonel might have asked what business it was of FCC whether he had an *I* in his signature anyway. He had fixed his bona fide signature—the signature on which he got married, on which he got to be a colonel in the army, and on which he bought and sold property. Why should FCC not accept it, even if it were only Jesse Miller or for that matter only J. Miller, so long as he had attached the signature by which he customarily authenticated his acts?

An inquiry into the reasons for returning the Colonel's application yielded the reply that "the rules laid down for handling these petitions say that 'the signature shall be in conformity with the name of the petitioner.' If Jesse I. Miller is typed at the top of the petition, then Jesse I. Miller must appear in the signature at the bottom."

The rule is no doubt a good one. Henry Wells ought not sign Leon Crutcher's petition. A rule which was designed to make sure that each attorney would sign his own application became in practice a requirement that every applicant must write his name in such a way that every letter can be identified. The fault was in the administration, not in the rule. It is easy to set this case down as the fault of a dumb girl clerk and to suppose that it will be remedied by firing the girl who returned the application. That is too easy a diagnosis. If that kind of error represents dumbness, then dumbness characterizes a very large proportion of the American people and the government will have to be staffed in large part with dumb people. The fault was in the girl's supervisor rather than in the girl. She had never been told what the rule meant and how it should be applied in close situations.

The Case of the Beautiful Dreamer is also a simple one and illustrates the point that a waste of time and money can be nothing more than the overextension of a virtue. Andy Morrison came into FCC fresh out of law school, eager to get ahead and imbued with the idea that the best way to get ahead is to do a good job at what you are doing. His first assignment was to examine the records of certain individuals who had applied for licenses to operate radio transmitters. Each of the applicants had acknowledged, or had been found guilty of, some infraction of the law, and their files had come to the general counsel for advice as to whether the nature of the offense in each case constituted a disqualification for a license. From the general counsel's office the files bounced downstairs, past the assistant general counsel and past the chief of the section, to land on Andy Morrison's desk. Andy knew he liked to work for FCC the minute he examined his assignment. These were real legal problems. Wife-beating, fighting at a football game, breaking out windows at the age of fourteen—these offenses had no relation to a man's qualifications for sending messages over the air, on land or at sea, in voice or in code. He could justify a license in every one of these cases and support it with law. He fell to work with enthusiasm, and as he moved from the law of California to the law of Missouri to the law of Tennessee he caught beautiful glimpses of future events. . . . "This is really a nice point in conflict of laws, and the general counsel will appreciate it when he sees how I handle the cases." "Nice brief, this," he says to the assistant general counsel. "Who is this man Morrison? New here, I guess." "Oh! You mean Andy Morrison," says the assistant general counsel. "Yes, he's new and he's doing excellent work. I don't think he missed a point on these radio-operator cases. . . ."

These were the dreams of Andy Morrison, and they were, no doubt, proper dreams for a young man buried in his work and looking forward to the future. How was he to know that no one ever reads a memorandum if the recommendation is that the license be granted? You can get in trouble if you refuse to give a man a license. In that case the memorandum is read carefully, maybe by two or three people, before the word goes out that the license is rejected. But if the recommendation is that the license be issued, all anybody wants to know is that you looked into the case and are sure of your position. You don't need any memorandum for that. They call you up on the telephone and you tell them what you conclude.

The case of Andy Morrison is no fantasy. All over Washington lawyers and men and women who are not lawyers are preparing memoranda which no one will ever read. They go into files. Some people find out that they are never read and quit preparing them; they attach a note to the documents saying that the matter was looked into and that everything is in order. Perhaps some people find out that their memoranda are never read and go on preparing them anyway; preparing memoranda has become a way of life for them. Until they learn better, the conscientious and ambitious Morrisons put a lot of time, and therefore a substantial amount of the taxpayer's money, into the preparation of documents that are admirable in every respect but one—they are never used.

The Case of the Beautiful Dreamer is different only in details from *The Case of the Two Men in the Glass House*. Call the principals Beckett (the superior officer) and Owen (the subordinate). And witness their relations as told to the executive officer of FCC by Owen.

"Sure, I am behind in my work," said Owen. "I'll get further behind. All I do is read memoranda and write memoranda. I never go into

Beckett's office and he never comes in here. He puts everything he has to say on paper, and he makes me put everything I have to say on paper."

"I've heard it's pretty bad," was the executive officer's reply. "Someone told me the other day that you and Beckett sat for eight years in an office with nothing between you but a glass partition, and passed memos back and forth, day after day."

"That isn't the half of it," said Owen. "We used the same secretary. Beckett would call her in and I would hear him dictate a memo to me. Then she would go to her desk to type it out, and if she couldn't read her shorthand, she would come to me instead of him to ask what he had dictated."

Was Beckett a fool and a fit candidate to be fired? A further bit of evidence is essential. A few years back, the chairman of the commission went on a rampage and roasted Beckett on all sides in the presence of a bunch of his associates. The chairman had examined the file in a case and had told someone, let us say a Senator, that he was under a misapprehension, and that the facts in the case were not as the Senator understood. But it later turned out that the chairman, and not the Senator, was in error. There were considerations in the case which the file did not show. The chairman was out on a limb and he was mad; and Beckett was blistered in the presence of his colleagues because his files were not complete. Thereafter there was nothing missing from the record in any case that came under Beckett's jurisdiction, if he could devise a memorandum that would cover it.

Beckett's memoranda, and the memoranda he forced Owen to write, were too much of a good thing, just as the careful legal opinions of Andy Morrison represented virtue carried too far. The chairman wanted memoranda; so he got memoranda.

These are simple cases. It is easy to see what is going on and why it is going on. There are public officials close enough to these practices to understand them who also have ample authority to correct them. But many if not most of the things we complain about in federal administration are not so simple. They are not the result of idiosyncrasies and shortcomings of particular individuals.

Usually what we call inefficiency and red tape is a compound of the activities of many officials and employees. The administrative official who has authority over all these activities is likely to be so far removed from most of them that he neither knows exactly what is going on nor appreciates that the final result of all these activities is a governmental operation that costs more than it needs to and gives you and me less satisfactory government than he wants to provide. And the officials below him, who do know exactly what is going on at different points in the operation, neither have a good view of the operation as a whole nor possess sufficient authority to order changes in the process which would correct the deficiencies of the operation as a whole. Furthermore, in many instances, there is no official up the line who could correct the deficiencies of the operation either, for some of the things that are being done may be specifically required by law.

The licensing of land-mobile radio systems provides a representative instance of a governmental operation that for several years was both unnecessarily costly in time and effort and unduly annoying to the part of the public that was affected by it. It reveals how complex the considerations are which combine to create an objectionable administrative operation. And it also provides an illustration of what administrative officials can do to terminate or reduce objectionable features of an administrative operation if they apply ingenuity and determination to the job.

A land-mobile radio system consists of one or more radio transmitters located in a fixed position (the land station) and a number of associated receivers and transmitters located on mobile vehicles (e.g., in automobiles or on boats). The communication system of a city police department, with its central transmitter and radio-equipped squad cars, is a familiar example; an electric utility company may direct its repair crews by radio communication operating between its fixed transmitter at headquarters and receivers and transmitters located on its repair trucks.

All persons who maintain such communication systems (individuals, business firms, government agencies) are required by act of Congress to obtain first a permit to construct (so as to avoid building a station that will not qualify for a license) and second a license to operate the radio stations involved. Now observe the actual process of obtaining permits and licenses for land-mobile radio systems before and after a systematic effort of FCC to make its operations as economical and as convenient to the public as the controlling law will permit.

First, *The Case of Irvin N. Bondage.* Bondage filed his first application with FCC in 1940. Bondage's initial plans called for the erection of a fixed station at his central plant and mobile transmitters on each of five trucks. He wrote FCC to inquire what he should do to get permission for the operations which he planned. FCC mailed him two forms to be filled out and returned, one an application for permission to construct his fixed transmitter, and the other an application to construct his five mobile transmitters. A mimeograped document was also enclosed which told Bondage what frequencies were available to him, indicated how much power he could utilize, and gave him other relevant information about the requirements he would have to meet in order to get a license. Bondage returned his application with necessary information about his equipment and plan of operations, including the make and style of the mobile transmitters he expected to purchase ready for use from a leading manufacturer of radio equipment. FCC found his application in order, mailed him his two construction permits (one for the fixed transmitter and one for the five mobiles), and enclosed a single application form on which he could apply for his license to operate his system. Bondage returned this form, filled out to show that he had constructed his transmitters in accordance with expectations, and in due time received his license—a single document authorizing him to operate all six transmitters, accompanied by five small certificates which he was advised to post on or in proximity to each of the five mobile transmitters.

All of this was in compliance with the law, and in respect to all this Bondage could have little objection. He filled out only three forms; he had assurance that his plans for construction of a fixed transmitter were acceptable before he spent any money on it; he knew that the mobile transmitters which he intended to buy were satisfactory before he contracted for them; and he saw no reason why he should not post certificates of authorization in connection with each transmitter which he used.

Bondage's complaints against the procedures of FCC began when he smashed a truck and had to replace a mobile transmitter, and they continued when he decided to put transmitters on additional trucks in his fleet. By 1940, mobile transmitters were factory-made and factory-adjusted to the frequency which the purchaser was licensed to use. Bondage had installed standard transmitters when he started his operation with five trucks; when he smashed up a transmitter, he proposed to replace it with another one identically like the first; when he decided to put two-way radio on additional trucks, he proposed to add transmitters of the same make and style that he already had in use. Yet each time he replaced or added a transmitter, he had to apply first for a construction permit and later for a license. In the eyes of FCC each transmitter (whether fixed or mobile) was a separate radio station and required by law to be covered first by a permit to construct, and second by a license to operate. Therefore Bondage was required to file an application for permission to construct each new mobile transmitter, even though construction (so far as he was concerned) involved nothing more than bolting the transmitter to the truck and plugging its cord into the electric circuit. As a consequence Bondage was required repeatedly to participate in the following ritual:

Bondage to FCC: Please send form for construction permit. I want to install another mobile.
FCC to Bondage: Here is your application form. Please fill out carefully.
Bondage to FCC: Here is my application form. Please send construction permit.
FCC to Bondage: We hereby return your application for construction

permit. Please correct it. You forgot to have it notarized (or wrongly stated what frequency you planned to use or did something else wrong).

Bondage to FCC: (after finally getting his construction permit, and also getting an application form for the license without asking for it) Here is my application for a license. I have completed construction as required (four bolts and two screws put firmly in place, and cord plugged neatly in socket).

FCC to Bondage: Application for license returned for correction. You say you have completed construction but you do not give the date when construction was completed. Furthermore, you have not indicated the manufacturer's serial number for the transmitter; we cannot license a transmitter unless we know what transmitter it is. Furthermore, there appear to be errors in your application, to wit . . .

Bondage to FCC: Here is the application for license again. I have put in the serial number for the transmitter; I have corrected my typist's error to show that I wish to operate on the frequency which you have already assigned me; I have corrected another error in typing to show that this new transmitter will use exactly the amount of power that you already know it will use anyhow; and I have had my signature notarized.

FCC to Bondage: Everything is in order and here is your new license (the old one typed over to include the new as well as all the old transmitters).

The foregoing account is not descriptive of what happened to every person who operated a land-mobile communication system in 1940; on the other hand, it is by no means untrue of what happened to many of them. The statute said that anyone proposing to operate a radio station must apply for a construction permit (unless he fell in one of five excepted groups, and land-mobile systems were not among them) and, after completing construction, apply for a license. The statute specified that each of the two applications must set forth the frequency and power to be used and bear the notarized signature of the applicant.

To the individuals who determined the procedures in use in FCC in 1940, this specific statutory language meant that there must be a personal application for a construction permit for each transmitter, even though the transmitter was already constructed; that there must be a report that construction was completed in accordance with the permit before a license could be issued; and that the applicant must state over his signature, and under oath or affirmation, what frequency he wished to use, what amount of power he intended to pour into his transmitter, and certain other kinds of information which the statute referred to. If the applicant applied for a frequency which FCC had not assigned to that kind of radio use, FCC would not alter his application so as to indicate a frequency which it would authorize; nor would it ignore the applicant's misunderstanding or error and grant him a license, even though only one frequency was available for him. Instead, the application was returned and the applicant was required to request the proper frequency over his notarized signature. Similarly, if the applicant specified the make and style of transmitter which he intended to install, but wrongly stated its input of power, employees and officials of FCC would not correct the application, though they knew much better than the applicant what power that particular transmitter was built to utilize.

The consequence of this rigid adherence to the letter of the law, as respects nuisance for the public, is shown in the experience of Irvin N. Bondage. Another consequence was excessive cost in carrying on operations within FCC. Since each mobile transmitter was viewed as a separate licensed radio station, FCC maintained a record (make, style, and serial number) of every mobile transmitter in use in the United States and its possessions, including those in the five classes of radio stations that were not required to obtain construction permits. Experience seemed to show that the best way to keep the records accurate, both for FCC and the owner of a land-mobile system, was to list all the transmitters in a single license document, and rewrite the document every time a transmitter was replaced or added or taken out of use. This was not much of a job in the case of a small operator like Irvin N. Bondage. But if the city of Detroit had 250 transmitters on its police squad cars, it became several hours' work for FCC to retype the license and proofread all the transmitter serial numbers; and that is what was done just as often as the city of Detroit filed an application to replace or add or take a transmitter out of use.

So much for the tribulations of Irvin N. Bondage, and so much for the paper work in FCC in 1940. Note the difference in procedure in *The Case of Wofford Orr-White* in 1948. Orr-White, like Bondage, decided to build a land station for communication with two-way radio on his trucks. Like Bondage, he wrote FCC, asking what he should do to get his radio license; and like Bondage, he learned that he had to apply first for a construction permit and then, after completion of construction of his fixed station, he would have to apply for a license. But once Orr-White had been issued his original license to operate a land-mobile system, his business with FCC virtually came to an end. In response to Orr-White's initial request for information, FCC advised him that he might install any standard make of mobile transmitter that had been found acceptable for the kind of radio use he contemplated; and told him that he should specify in his application for a construction permit the maximum number of mobile transmitters he expected to put into use within the near future. When Orr-White finally got his license, it carried an authorization to put into service any number of mobile transmitters of the type or types he proposed to use, up to a maximum number which was specified in the license.

Under the terms of this license, Wofford Orr-White could replace, add, and retire from use mobile transmitters as he pleased without any notification to FCC or further authorization from it, so long as he installed only the type or types of transmitter named in the license and so long as he did not exceed the maximum number of transmitters specified in the license. And neither did Orr-White have his one application for a construction permit and his one application for a license bounce back on him; by 1948, FCC had adopted a policy of ignoring omissions in applications and correcting errors in applications, if from the application as a whole the officials and employees of FCC could tell what the applicant wanted and ought to have. Naturally, Wofford Orr-White never became a personality to the clerical staff of FCC as Irvin N. Bondage had been; he was but a passing incident in their lives, whereas Bondage, for many years, had virtually lived with them.

The new procedures for licensing land-mobile communication systems which FCC had adopted by 1948 were part of a general house cleaning which the commissioners ordered at the close of the war. New ways of doing things, just as significant as those relating to land-mobile systems, were instituted throughout the operations of FCC. Many of the changes in procedures had to be approved by the commissioners themselves; no one below them in the organization could authorize the changes to be made. This was true for two reasons.

In the first place, all of the crucial procedures involved men and women who worked in different divisions of the agency. The licensing of land-mobile systems was a joint activity of clerical staff in the secretary's division, of engineers under the chief engineer, and of lawyers under the general counsel. There was no single officer below the commissioners who had authority over all the men and women involved in this licensing process. Conceivably, the secretary, the chief engineer, and the general counsel might by process of negotiation have worked out new procedures; it was the responsibility of no one of them, and collectively they did not see their responsibility.

In the second place, only the commissioners could order some of the changes in procedures because, basic to the changes, was a new attitude concerning the interpretation of controlling statutes. The commissioners want to decide for themselves what their obligations are under the law. It was a decision of the commissioners sitting together, for instance, which established the new rule that a license could authorize an indeterminate number of mobile transmitters in a land-mobile system, so long as they were all of an approved type and did not exceed a maximum number specified in the license. Only the commissioners, sitting as a commission, could rule that a single document—a combined permit to construct and license to operate—would, in the case of mobile transmitters, satisfy the statutory requirement that "no license shall be issued . . . for the operation of any station . . . unless a permit for its construction has been granted by the Commission upon written application therefor."

The work-review program by which FCC accomplished the reforms which have just been mentioned seems to me of enough significance to be worth describing here. But before entering upon a specific case study, some general observations should be made about the circumstances and conditions which facilitate and hinder the efforts of administrative officials to improve efficiency and eliminate red tape.

The ideal way of dealing with inefficiency and red tape is to run the administrative establishment in such a way that these deficiencies never appear. The ability of administrative officials to approach that ideal is a product of three factors. They must have a clear understanding of what their objectives are; they must be determined to make the maximum use of their resources in achieving these objectives; and they must have a high degree of understanding as to how they can direct a force of men toward the achievement of the objectives they have in view. Putting it more succinctly, they must know what they are trying to do; they must be determined to do it; and they must know how to do it.

Rarely, if ever, do the head of the establishment and the officials under him have complete command of these three factors. As we saw in an earlier chapter the principal objectives of the administrative department or agency are usually given to it by the controlling statutes and by the expressions of political leaders. Frequently these statements of purpose are in some measure inconsistent with one another; even when they are entirely consistent, they are subject to change. Some of the features of administration which you and I dislike and denounce as inefficiency and red tape are the unavoidable consequence of conflict in objectives or change in objectives, and they occur in spite of the most conscientious, determined, and intelligent effort on the part of the officials who are directing the department or agency.

Furthermore, we have seen that even when the administrative official is clear as to what his objectives are he may be unable to proceed according to his best judgment in his efforts to achieve them, because of legislation which regulates the way he must proceed or because of demands of political leaders and sectors of the population to which he feels obliged to yield.

The responsible officials of the administrative establishment are, therefore, under substantial handicaps in their efforts to get work done economically, with dispatch, and with concern for its consequences to people who are affected by it. The success which they enjoy within these limitations, as I see it, will depend on the quality of the men and women who make up the department or agency, the way they are organized, and the incentives which are present to cause men and women to respond to their opportunities and meet their obligations. The possibilities of improving the quality of personnel by more careful selection, by training, and by other measures seem to me to be mainly a by-product of organization and incentives. If the organization of the administrative establishment is what it ought to be and incentives which stir men to conscientious and thoughtful effort are present, then we have our greatest assurance that officials and employees will approach their capacity for useful service.

The problems of organizing the administrative establishment for direction and control have also been discussed at some length (Chapters 22 and 23). Something further should be said, however, about organization as it relates to incentives and as it relates to special efforts to identify and eliminate what we popularly call inefficiency and red tape.

Incentives and organization cannot be sharply differentiated for consideration here. There must be incentives for creating good organization; and one of the objectives of organization is to provide incentives. Incentive may be defined as anything which induces an individual to do something. Whatever contributes to his desire to do something, spurs him on, heightens his interest, makes him feel uncomfortable if he does not do it—these things are incentives. Incentives may therefore be positive or negative; I may be stimulated to do something because it is pleasant to do it or stimulated to do something because it is unpleasant not to do it. Incentives may be direct or indirect; I may get deep satisfaction out of my own conviction that I have done something neatly and accurately or my satisfaction may come from what I can get with the extra money which I am paid for doing a job neatly and accurately. And incentives can be either immediate or long run; I may work hard because my pay is determined in proportion to what I produce or I may work hard because I am confident I will get a promotion later on.

There appears to be a popular belief in this country (at least a widely held supposition) that incentives cannot be provided for the public service which will result generally in the kind of effort that we expect in the well-managed business establishment. In order to see whether there is justification for this belief, we must see what appears to be the situation in respect to incentives at two points in the administrative establishment—the employees at the bottom and the principal officials at the top. What we find to be effective at these two levels of the organization may be presumed to be effective for supervisors and officials at various points in between.

First, the employees at the bottom of the administrative establishment who do the great volume of work and whose efforts, in most cases, represent the government which the administrative organization provides. I do not see why these people cannot have the same incentives for maximum productiveness (in quantity and quality) that are available for employees of business establishments who occupy like positions and do similar work. In either case, the employee is paid a wage or salary. To the extent that quantity and quality of work can be measured, compensation can be adjusted to output in government as it is in industry. In either case, records of performance can be maintained, employees can be rated, and advancement in compensation and responsibility can be promised and given in keeping with performance. As for non-monetary incentives—praise, honors, invitation to participate in making decisions, special consideration, and special treatment of any sort—I do not see why we cannot make them available in government equally with private business and industry. The federal government can be as good an employer as the nation's business and industry if the people who make the highest policies of the government are determined that it shall be. President and Congress must acknowledge this as a goal, however; for statutes must be changed to remove some limitations in respect to the compensation and rewarding of public employees, and the language of appropriation acts must not impose on the administrative departments and agencies restrictions which defeat this end.

The foregoing paragraph makes no mention of the profit system which we generally suppose to provide incentive for people employed in private business and industry, but which is absent from government. The fact is, of course, that expectation of personally sharing in profits is not an incentive for the great mass of employees in business and industry. They are not owners of the enterprise for which they work; if profits are the fruit of their efforts, the profits go to someone else. Indeed, there is a good deal of reason to believe that the view which the American working-man takes of profits causes him to diminish rather than increase his efforts on the job. Certainly there is more institutionalized feather-bedding and a greater readiness to strike in private employment than there is in the public service; and there is probably a much greater willingness to put in overtime without compensation on the part of public employees than one finds among the same classes of employees in business and industry. We can undoubtedly say that if the prospect of making a profit has influence on the quantity and quality of work done by the employees at the bottom of the business organization, the influence is exerted indirectly. Those individuals who hope to reap profits from the efforts of the mass of workers may indeed go to a lot of trouble to make sure that the workers have reason for maximizing their effort.

The second point at which we must look, in making a comparison of incentives in private enterprise and in government, is the top of the organization. Expectation of obtaining profits is likely to be a most important incentive for the individuals charged with the top management of a business undertaking; profit-making is not an incentive for the men who direct a department or agency of the government, for there are no profits to be made. It is frequently said that the necessity of making profits causes the businessman to maintain records of costs and income which tell him how efficient he is, whether he is making profits, and therefore whether he can stay in business; but that the head of the government establishment, because he is not concerned with making a profit, has no way of relating the costs of his organization to the value of its services and therefore has no way of knowing whether it is being efficient. This kind of statement invites us to reach false conclusions because it mixes up a lot of considerations that ought to be kept separate in analysis.

I think it is better to say that a major part of business activity consists of a multitude of transactions which are carried on among a great number of different firms and individuals. Out of the volume of transactions, a body of common experience leads to common evaluation of commodities and services. Prices are fixed as a way of expressing these common valuations. Any person or organization, be it private or governmental, that deals only in things for which prices are established can record income and outgo in terms of money. A government experiment station that operates a test farm, buying everything on the open market and selling everything on the open market, can calculate its costs and determine profit and loss just as accurately as a businessman. Most government establishments, however, do not market commodities or services for which the open market has fixed a price. The nation's price system fixes only one side of their accounts. The government department or agency may be able to determine its costs just as accurately as the businessman; it hires men and women to work for it and it buys equipment and supplies, and for each of these it must pay a price that is in keeping with the prices which the businessman must pay. But the service which the government renders, and for which it incurs its costs, may be a monopoly product. Nobody else is offering the services of an army or is engaged in regulating railroads or is holding forth to fight forest fires by the day or on contract. Therefore, there is no market which fixes a proper price for these services. Since there is no market to establish a price for its service, the government has no way of knowing whether the service it offers is worth in money what it costs to render the service.

It should be remembered, however, that many business firms do not have a market to tell them what constitutes a proper price either. If a corporation owns all of the copper ore in the world, which it acquired years ago without any true knowledge of how much ore it was getting, it will have to make an administrative determination as to the figure to enter on the books as the cost of its ore. The physician who serves an isolated community and has no competitors is also in much the same situation as a department or agency of the government; he knows what it costs him to live and keep on rendering service, but he does not know what his services are worth in terms of money. If he is a generous person he may ask for small fees, work himself to death, and barely make a living; if he is less generous he may set his prices high, see more people continue in sickness without his help, and still become one of the richest men in the community.

The administrative establishment, as I see it, has no excuse for not knowing its costs, and the fact seems to be that most of the departments and agencies of the federal government do. That is the result of accounting systems which they are required by law to maintain and which are subject to audit by the General Accounting Office. They can also keep detailed records of the commodities which they produce and the services which they render. Some of them do that too. The Post Office Department can keep as accurate a record of the pieces of mail it handles and the number of pound-miles of mail it handles as the Railway Express Company can keep for the things that it carries about the country. And if

Congress authorized them to do so, the officials of the Post Office Department could fix prices for mail service which would represent the value of that service to you and me just as accurately as the prices of the Railway Express Company represent the value of its service.

A number of the federal administrative departments and agencies sell some or all of their commodities or services for a price —the Post Office Department and the Tennessee Valley Authority are illustrations. Most of them, however, make no charge for their services, and their costs are paid for out of taxes. I do not think the absence of a price for governmental services imposes any serious limitations on the ability of high administrative officials to measure the performance of individual employees or the performance of the organization as a whole. The work of the government establishment, like that of the business firm, breaks up into parts. Administrative officials can if they wish (and many of them do) break the work of employees down into standard units and keep records which, in time, will reveal what a resourceful and hard-working employee ought to do. And the same methods can be used for setting standard performance for a section or division of the establishment or for the establishment as a whole. Many employees will be doing things which are not subject to measurement and application of performance standards, but that is equally true of many employees in private business and industry.

The foregoing paragraphs, if they are convincing, support a conclusion that the absence of a profit objective on the part of government does not prevent and need not deter the top officials of an administrative establishment from keeping records of performance by which they can determine the quantity and quality of work which is being done by their organization. The absence of opportunity to share in profits does, however, deprive them of an incentive, which the businessman may have, to keep records and insist upon performance. But there is a good deal of misunderstanding on this point, just as there is popular misunderstanding of the relation of the presence and absence of profits to ability to devise standards and measures of performance.

The man who owns and manages his business gets his income out of the earnings of the business. He may pay himself a salary and enter his salary on the books as a cost, but there will not be any money to pay his salary if his business does not have income in excess of the other costs which are incurred and paid. If the business yields more income than is required to meet its costs, including his salary, the owner-manager can take profits or increase his salary or put money back into the business with expectation of a greater income later on. In any case the incentive to work hard, to plan carefully, and to put pressure on his employees is clear enough.

If the manager of the business enterprise owns no part of it and personally collects none of the profits, he is nevertheless keenly aware that his own prosperity depends on the company's earnings. He may be paid a bonus which is measured by the net profits for the year. If he gets no bonus, his prospects for holding his position or getting a higher salary or moving on to another firm will be affected by his success in running this one. Even if he has no ambitions and wishes to take it easy, he may find it difficult to do so because of the attitudes of other businessmen with whom he is associated. The influence of profit-making on the behavior of American businessmen extends far beyond the individuals who personally hope to make a profit. Regardless of how it came about, the dominant concern of American business is to make money; the ways of doing things that lead to making money have become the established ways of running a business.

The ways of American business carry over into the government service, just as any other dominant feature of our culture affects the way public officials and employees go about doing things. Officials who are at the top of our government departments and agencies set standards for the performance of those below them which are based on experience in business. There is a great deal in the environment of public administration which supports or reinforces the presumption of the administrative official that he ought to get as good a day's work out of his minor officials and employees as the businessman gets out of his. The government establishment is frequently if not usually behind in its work, and the pressures from the public that expects it to act create a powerful compulsion to speed up work, especially when the pressures are channeled through Congressmen. Pressure may also come from officials in other departments and agencies when the activities of one organization are dependent in some way on what another organization does. There are always ambitious men within any organization whose efforts to get ahead constantly challenge other men to special effort in order to maintain or improve their own position. And finally, every high official is influenced by considerations which are personal to him—his desire for a reputation as an official who knows how to get things done; his great interest in the service which his organization provides and his wish to see that service as effective as possible; his determination to contribute his share to the success of the Administration so that the voters may be induced to continue it in power; and so on.

In spite of the effectiveness of these incentives, I am sure they do not provide the compulsion for high standards of performance which the hope of making money provides for the businessman. If the businessman allows any part of his operations to snarl up —fail to produce or produce at unreasonably high cost—he is challenged, both by personal interest and by the mores of his profession, to straighten it out. The situation is quite different for the official in charge of an administrative establishment. He does not want his operations to snarl up and he will straighten them out if he can get around to it. But the loss which results from a shortcoming in administration does not come out of his pocket as it does in the case of the man who manages his own business. And the men with whom he is most closely associated, and whose approval he wants, do not judge him primarily on his ability to hold down costs in relation to production. They judge him primarily on the character of the policies which he puts into effect and on the adequacy of the service which his organization provides, without much concern for how much the service costs. This is true of the Congressmen who have legislative authority over the area of affairs with which his organization is concerned and who fix his appropriations; they are much more likely to make a searching inquiry into the nature of the service which his establishment provides and the consequence of the policies which guide its activities than to explore carefully the dispatch and economy with which the job is done. It is also true (perhaps more true) of the individuals and groups of people who are affected by the government which the administrative establishment provides; their great concern is to get the service which they want, and their pressure to get what they want and get it quick is not modified by sympathy for the wish of the administrator to keep his costs of operation low.

The consequence of this situation is that the administrative official is always reluctant to interrupt or slow down any part of his operations, even temporarily, in order to straighten things out and get them to working on a more satisfactory basis. He is tempted, instead, to ask Congress to bail him out with an increase in appropriation which will enable him to meet the demands that are placed upon him without the necessity of putting his house in order. Most administrative officials succumb to the temptation a good deal of the time, and Congressmen let them get away with it, for they, too, are subject to pressures from the public to keep government going without even a temporary letdown.

This is the situation, as I see it, in respect to incentives for running a department or agency of the government in accordance with our highest standards for administrative performance—that is, for running it in such a manner as will give us the kind of service we want, with dispatch, at minimum cost, and with a minimum of inconvenience and annoyance to the public. It may be that we can provide additional and more effective incentives for providing this kind of public administration; I leave that question for exploration by others.

It is important to bear in mind that the things which keep what we call inefficiency and red tape at a minimum are essential to any hope of success in rooting them out once they have crept in. The officials who have important authority in the department or agency must be determined to run it in the best way they know how and they must provide incentives which will enlist the best efforts of others in the organization. High officials must clearly understand what their objectives are and they must see to it that those objectives are also understood by everyone who needs to know what they are. They must build the best organization they know how to construct and they must staff it with the best men and women they can get. If, in spite of all this, the performance of the organization falls below expectation, what special steps can be taken to identify specific deficiencies and correct them? Two measures have been tried with great success in many if not in all departments and agencies of the federal government; the evidence is that too little emphasis is placed on them. These measures are: the development and application of standards of performance, and the systematic review of operations and accomplishments.

The first of these measures, the development and application of standards of performance, must of necessity be peculiar to the different kinds of operation that are involved. Some types of operation are common to many if not all departments and agencies, and standards for measurement of this kind of work can be developed and made applicable throughout the government service. No administrative official need be in doubt about the quantity and quality of service which he gets out of the section of his organization that duplicates material by mimeograph; he can measure its product against dependable standards of quantity and quality. He does not even have to develop the standards; he can borrow them ready made from other branches of the service that have already worked them out. The Post Office Department, on the other hand, will have to work out its own standards (as I presume has been done) for measuring the volume of mail which is sorted by clerks and for judging the accuracy with which they sort it. Other departments can do the same for the operations peculiar to them.

As noted earlier in this chapter, not everything that goes on in the administrative establishment will lend itself to objective measurement. Enough of it can be tested against standards based on past experience, however, to give the responsible officials warning when important parts of their activities are not coming along at the rate they should.

The development and application of standards of performance can be supplemented by systematic review of the operations and accomplishments of the organization (henceforth referred to as work-review). The officials and supervisors in the lower levels of the organization know exactly what is going on, but frequently (perhaps ordinarily) they are not in a position to judge the necessity of doing the things that are being done. If lower officials are sure that certain things ought not to be done, or ought to be done differently, they usually lack authority to correct the situation themselves; they may lack the initiative or courage to bring them to the attention of someone who does have the authority to correct them; and they may not get a hearing if they do bring them up with the proper officials. That this is a true statement of what actually happens in large organizations ought to be clear from some of the illustrative cases of red tape which were described at an earlier point in this chapter.

A program of systematic work-review can locate these shortcomings in administration and point to ways of clearing them up. Officials who are higher up in the organization will have to conduct the review, for the scrutiny of what is being done and how it is being done will have to be extended to the related activities of many parts of the organization. The radical change in the licensing of land-mobile communication systems which was described earlier in this chapter (pp. 529–534) was one of the many improvements which resulted from a program of work-review carried out by the Federal Communications Commission over a period of months after the close of World War II.

The work-review program of FCC owed its success primarily to the chairman of the commission, who insisted that the organization should not travel by a circuitous route to reach an objective which it could arrive at by a more direct course. Whatever natural inclination the chairman had to get things done in the most simple and most economical way possible was reinforced by demands from the public (people interested in radio, telephone, and telegraph) that the agency act on business they had before it, and by the refusal of Congress to appropriate money which would enable the agency to meet these pressures without changing its ways.

The chairman of FCC could supply a large proportion of the motive force which made work-review a success; he could not carry out the review by himself. Other officials who commanded some prestige in the organization had to give time to it. This became the primary responsibility of the executive officer, who also bore the title of assistant to the chairman. It was the job of the executive officer first to find out where improvements were needed and how improvements could be effected; and second to induce the officials who had authority to do so to make the changes in practice which would result in improvement.

If experience in FCC is representative, the minimum equipment for the officer who directs a house-cleaning job in a government establishment is a good set of ears and a larynx that will stand up under hard usage. Legs and eyes will help, for they enable him to walk about the organization and see what is being done and how things are being done. But primarily he talks to people and listens to what they say in return. The executive officer who directed the work-review program in FCC did not discover anything which no one else knew; he only assembled the knowledge which other people had. The organization was replete with people who thought they were doing things that did not need to be done; with people who thought there was a better way of doing the things they were doing; with people who thought their own work was hampered by the failure of someone else to do something that he ought to be doing. It was the job of the executive officer to assemble the ideas and knowledge relevant to any one problem or complex of problems. He did it mainly by talking and listening.

There prevails among academic students of public administration a supposition that the officials and employees who have special responsibility for preparing the annual budget (i.e., estimate of appropriation needs) possess a comprehensive body of knowledge as to the way work is done in the organization and are a rich repository of ideas as to how organization and operations can be improved. I found little to support this supposition in my experience as executive officer in FCC. The people who have this responsibility were kept so busy the year round assembling and reassembling figures that they had little time for observing or talking about how work was being done. By the time one compilation of estimates was prepared and pursued through the Bureau of the Budget and the congressional appropriations committees, it was time to start work preparing the next annual compilation. And the time that was not given to the preparation of estimates and communication with Budget Bureau and appropriations committees was largely taken up in preparing statements which would govern the allocation of money among the different parts of the organization.

Just the opposite was true, however, of a small group of men and women who constituted a unit bearing the title Organization and Procedures Section. They had little to do with organization, for not many officials in FCC wanted anybody else's advice as to how they could improve their organization. But the way one part of FCC does its work is of great concern to several other parts (see pp. 506–509) and the special group that worked on procedures was constantly on the move throughout FCC, doing what it could to make paper move readily and smoothly from one part of the organization to other parts. As a consequence, they knew what was going on, they knew who were the protectors of established ways of doing things, and they had judgments as to the interests and qualities of men who could advance or retard improvements. They were an indispensable aid to the executive officer. They told him which channels of communication were most clogged up by willows along the banks and log jams in the stream; they told him whom to see to get knowledge of actualities and suggestions for improvements; they informed him of vested interests and helped him to find the men whose interests counter-balanced the interests of other men; they collected supplementary information which the executive officer found that he needed; and they devised solutions for problems when solutions were not obvious.

The officer in charge of the group regularly concerned with organization and procedures in no sense controlled or managed the work-review program. The executive officer spent much more of his time talking to other people scattered throughout FCC than he spent in conference with the organization and procedures group. When he found the persons who had the most accurate knowledge of what was being done, he relied on their statements as to what was actually going on. And usually the persons with the most accurate knowledge as to what was going on had the strongest convictions that improvements could be made and sup-plied the most convincing recommendations as to what changes should be made. It was the job of the executive officer to decide which problems (complexes of problems) were of sufficient im-portance to justify a real effort for solution, and it was his job to make a preliminary selection among alternative solutions.

The little talks of the executive officer were preliminary to a big talk. The big talk was a conference at which three classes of persons were present—the supervisors and minor officials who could say with finality what was actually being done (they also had good judgment as to what could and could not be done); higher officials who could authorize changes in policies and in-structions for their respective divisions; and someone high enough in authority or prestige to resolve issues between the higher officials. The executive officer could do the resolving if the issue was a minor one; but if higher officials were expected to hold strongly to different judgments as to what ought to be done, the conference was in the office of the chairman and several or all the commissioners might be present.

The purpose of the conference was to take the measure of convictions and to create agreement. The executive officer might, by extending his conversations with individuals, have made up his mind as to what should be done in respect to problems, formulated his recommendations in statements of policy, and put them before the chairman or the commission for adoption. And the chairman or commission (assuming a high degree of confidence in the executive officer) might have ordered his proposed policies put into effect. But the success of any innovation in policy depends on the response with which it is greeted by the men and women at various levels of the organization who are expected to change their ways of doing things. By calling together the men and women who were most concerned in the problem under consideration, the convictions of one man were laid down beside those of other men. Different suppositions as to facts, which stubbornly support different judgments concerning alternative courses of action, were dissipated when the people who collectively knew all the relevant facts were enabled to put their facts together. Attitudes which had been held on to most stubbornly were weakened and might crumble when they were put up against the attitudes of other men recognized to be worthy of respect. And the course of action agreed to in conference could be accepted as the only feasible course of action by the men and women who were most skeptical that it represented an improvement over what was already going on. The conference provided a maximum of assurance that people would understand what was expected of them and it extended to everyone a challenge to make the new arrangements work in practice.

In FCC, the program of work-review was a special effort to identify activities that could be terminated, to find quicker and more economical ways of doing things, and to find out how things could be done with less annoyance and inconvenience to the public. The success of the program was heightened by the fact that everyone concerned knew that the agency could not continue to do everything that was being done and do everything the way it had been done in the past. At the end of the war, FCC had a volume of work confronting it that was at least twice as great as it had ever been confronted with before. People with business before FCC were clamoring for action. There was no reason to believe that the President would recommend or that Congress would appropriate enough money to enable the agency to meet the demands upon it without changing its ways. The resistance to improvement which the chairman might otherwise have encountered was therefore largely dissipated by the force of circumstances.

The need of any department or agency for a special effort to clean house, such as the effort made in FCC at the close of World War II, will depend on the degree to which its affairs are kept in good order or allowed to get in a mess. Many departments and agencies of the federal government employ a number of men and women who make work-review their principal preoccupation; they are commonly known as organization, program, and procedures analysts. They have time, since that is their business, to look carefully into operations that higher officials (who are responsible for those operations) are too busy to examine. They have authority, if they are attached at a high level of the organization, to pursue relationships into many parts of the agency. They have, therefore, an invitation to examine and a license to recommend. If they are sophisticated in the ways of the organization, acquiring their sophistication perhaps by many years of service in the operations which they study; if as individuals they have personalities which invite communication and confidence; if they acquire prestige through the good sense of their recommendations —in that case their study and suggestions may become a major bulwark against the development of the conditions which invite public condemnation in charges of inefficiency and red tape.

BIBLIOGRAPHIC NOTE

In view of the widespread complaint about red tape in the federal government, it is surprising that no one has provided a thorough explanation of what it is, how it comes about, and how it can be gotten rid of. Mr. J. M. Juran devoted the major part of a very small book, *Bureaucracy; A Challenge to Better Management* (New York, 1944) to this subject. Marshall E. Dimock also presents some helpful observations in "Bureaucracy Self-Examined," in *Public Administration Review*, vol. 4, pp. 197–207 (1944).

Most of the literature which deals with economy in operations, avoidance and elimination of red tape, and other matters which I have discussed in this chapter is directed to the situation in business establishments. Much of it, nevertheless, is highly relevant to public administration. Because it is so voluminous I do not undertake to cite it here. There is a steady increment of writing, however, which is based on experience in the federal government. The following seem to me to be of greatest usefulness: J. M. Juran, work cited above; Marshall E. Dimock, *The Executive in Action* (New York, 1945); three essays by Fritz Morstein Marx, Henry Reining, Jr., and Donald C. Stone in *Elements of Public Administration*, edited by Fritz Morstein Marx (New York, 1946), chs. 18 to 20; Mary C. H. Niles, *Middle Management* (New York, 1941); *Administrative Management; Principles and Techniques* (The Graduate School of the U.S. Department of Agriculture, Washington, 1938); and six articles dealing with management in the Army Service Forces during World War II in *Public Administration Review*, vol. 4, pp. 257–308 (1944).

A special literature is now growing up about procedures (fixed ways of carrying on particular activities). See Comstock Glaser, *Administrative Procedure* (Washington, 1941); and Dwight Waldo, "Government by Procedure," in *Elements of Public Administration* (cited above), ch. 17. On possibilities of establishing standards by which the work of public employees can be measured, see Public Administration Service, *The Work Unit in Federal Administration* (Chicago, 1937); and Joel Gordon, "Operating Statistics as a Tool of Management," in *Public Administration Review*, vol. 4, pp. 189–196 (1944). For a systematic, incisive analysis of incentives in administrative organizations of the government, see Wallace S. Sayre, "Morale and Discipline," in *Elements of Public Administration* (cited above), ch. 21.

PART VI

THE UNIFICATION OF POLITICAL
DIRECTION AND CONTROL

CHAPTER 25

CONGRESS, PRESIDENT, AND CENTRAL COUNCIL

The purposes for which government is established are achieved primarily through administration. Administration, in modern government, is the product of a great working force of officials and employees. They are the bureaucracy. Bureaucracy has its place in modern government. It is in its proper place if it receives its instructions from the elected officials of the government and responds with alacrity, with vigor, and with faithfulness to those instructions. That is the whole argument of this book. If I have chosen my evidence wisely and reasoned as soundly as I hope, everything I have said is related to the prospect that our federal bureaucracy will give us the kind of government Congress and President decide we are to have.

The administrative officials and employees of the federal government can meet our expectations in this respect only if the instructions which they receive from Congress and President are consistent with one another. If the President tells administrative officials not to do what Congress has told them to do, or vice versa, government in operation will not meet the standards of a democratic nation. I think there is evidence throughout this book that we have not achieved the consistency in instructions from the two political branches that the nation has a right to demand. It seems to me that the American people are confronted by a compelling need to make the political and governmental changes which promise to reduce conflict between Congress and President and give us decisions which are the result of agreement between the two political branches of our government.

A consideration of the relationships between President and Congress brings us up against a basic question of political theory that has plagued us ever since we set up our present system of government. Authority in our national government comes to a head at three points—President, Congress, and Supreme Court. The men who established this system of government spoke of the three branches as equal and coordinate, and they described the relationships between the three branches as predominantly those of separation of powers and checks and balances. A study of experience under this system of government reveals that we have indeed put great emphasis on the idea of separation so far as relations between President and Congress are concerned. During much of the brief period under the Constitution, President and Congress have moved in unison to accomplish agreed-upon purposes. During as much or even more of the time, however, their relations have been those of driving toward different goals or driving toward the same goals by different routes. Frequently, and sometimes for substantial periods, relations between President and Congress have approximated stalemate or deadlock so far as the issues of greatest current significance were concerned.

The basic question of political theory which confronts us, as respects relations between President and Congress, is therefore one of balance between separateness and unity. We do not want separation carried to the point of stalemate and deadlock, for if that happens we get little or no decision by the political branches and the bureaucracy will become its own boss. Neither do we want union carried to the point where President or Congress is completely subject to the other. We do not want Congress to be completely subject to the President because we do not like what has happened in various parts of the world where authority is centered in one man instead of many men. And we do not want the President to be completely subject to Congress because we have developed political organization and states of mind (bodies of understanding) which presuppose that the President will have important authority in governmental affairs. We seek, therefore, what we can never know how to get until we find that we have it —a satisfactory balance between separation and union in the relationships between President and Congress. What we do in respect to this fundamental problem will vitally affect the arrangements we set up to subject administrative officials and employees to the will of the men and women who are chosen by the people to run the government.

If we are to continue essentially the same arrangements which we have maintained to date, putting a substantial emphasis on separation of powers and the checking of one branch by the other, it is imperative that we reconsider and at least clarify the allocation of authority between President and Congress. The testimony of those who have observed most closely the operation of our national government is increasingly to the effect that the present division of authority between Congress and President (whether expressed in deliberate contradiction or unintended confusion) puts obstacles in the path of the administrative official who has respect for the wishes of his political superiors and provides opportunities for the official who hopes to play one of the political branches off against the other. Some clarification of the relationships between President and Congress will be needed, therefore, even if we are to continue essentially what we have at present, emphasizing separation of powers and checks and balances.

If, on the other hand, we decide that Congress and President ought to be more closely united for vigorous and persistent attack on the greatest problems that confront the nation, we must prepare ourselves for a major revision of the working relations between these two centers of power. It will take both planning and experimentation to eliminate the conflicts that characterize their present teamwork. And it will take both political ingenuity and wise leadership of the whole nation to change over from one system of relationships to another without doing violence to the established understandings and expectations of the American people.

Furthermore, if having brought Congress and President more closely together we expect them to provide agreed-upon and consistent rather than conflicting and inconsistent direction and control for the administrative branch, we will have to reshape some of the institutional arrangements by which their decisions are put into effect. It is possible, for instance, that instead of having central agencies for advice, service, and control that report to the President (like the Bureau of the Budget) or to Congress (like the General Accounting Office), we will want some agencies that report to the President and the leaders of his party in Congress and others that report to the leaders of the opposite party in Congress.

The leaders of the new American nation who drew up the Constitution considered the desirability of a close union between the chief executive and the legislative assembly and voted down a proposal (persuasively supported by prominent members of the convention) to unite them by giving the Congress power to choose the President. An arrangement which put emphasis on separation of powers and checks and balances seemed to them a better risk than one which put emphasis on union of powers and agreement in common council. To depart at this stage of our national existence from their theory as to how our government should be organized at the top level is not to imply that the framers of the Constitution were unwise in organizing it as they did at that time. The framers of the Constitution presumed first that the new national government would exercise only a minimum of authority over the people (the major authority of government was thought to rest in the states); second that both legislature and executive would be capable of and might resort to treachery and oppression; and third that there was no way of holding one branch within the limits that the nation as a whole would find acceptable except by setting the other two branches up in opposition to it.

There was, at the time the Constitution was drawn up, ample

ground to support each of these presumptions. With such presumptions prevailing, the establishment of a system of separation of powers and checks and balances was an act of common sense. The case for a significant modification or for abandonment of that system of division and counteraction must rest on a conviction that one or more of the basic presumptions is no longer tenable.

The basis for the first presumption, that the national government will not frequently exercise powers of great significance to the individual, is now completely vanished. If there was, as late as 1932, any supposition by informed and thoughtful people that the national government was to be one of restricted power, that supposition must surely have been destroyed by subsequent events. The legal and constitutional theories that once barred the national government from the areas of affairs that present our most persistent and aggravating problems have now been drastically modified if not entirely abandoned. There is every reason to believe that the conditions of life in the United States which caused us to turn to the national government to undertake new programs of action during the past few decades will induce us to increase its authority over our affairs in the future.

The second and third of the three presumptions on which the system of separation of powers and checks and balances was founded are intimately related and must be treated together. The presumption that our highest elected officials are likely to abuse their power must be examined in connection with the companion presumption that there is only one dependable device for keeping abuse of power at a minimum.

The likelihood that men who are trusted with authority in the legislative and executive branches will be inclined to abuse it will depend upon the personal qualities of the individuals whom we elevate to those high places, their suppositions as to whether an attempt to go beyond the bounds of public acceptability will be observed and countered, and their estimate of the chances that any act which is popularly condemned will in some way react upon them adversely. If there are any guarantees that men who hold our highest elective offices will not be inclined to abuse their power, or being inclined will not risk it, those guarantees are most likely to be found in the political system by which men rise to high places in the government. By matching one elective branch of the government against the other we may make abuse of power difficult and provide a measure of assurance that abuse of power will be exposed. But the importance of such an arrangement is lessened if we succeed in developing a political system which reduces temptation to abuse authority or discourages men from succumbing to temptation.

The men who instituted our system of separation of powers and checks and balances had no comprehension of the political system under which the nation conducts its public affairs today. They could not comprehend it because it did not exist. The origins of our present political system were present in theirs, but there was no way of telling in which of many possible directions the later development would go. The framers of the Constitution had no experience with highly organized political parties and no basis for supposing that nationwide party organization as we know it would someday dominate the nation's political life. They expected the President to be the actual choice of electoral colleges made up of distinguished men and could not foresee that the chief executive would come to be chosen by popular vote in a political campaign that would be universally regarded as our most important political event. They could at best only speculate about the developments—in press, advertising and distribution of goods, education, sports, travel, and other things—that would ultimately unite us into a nation and provide the foundation for a system of government resting upon the will of the people.

Having before them no prospect of a political system such as we have developed, the founders of our government could not devise a system that would depend for the discipline of high officials upon checks within a party organization and fear of repudiation by voters at the polls. They were obliged to rest their hopes for a commendable behavior on the sense of honor possessed by the men who might come into positions of authority and on the expectation that the men who constitute one political institution (branch of the government) would be a brake on the ambitions of men who constitute another. It is quite possible that if they had anticipated a political system containing within itself the assurances of discipline that (as I will try to show) have now been realized, they would have voted finally, as they did on at least five preliminary motions, for a joining of legislature and executive under a common leadership.

What the framers would have written into the Constitution if they had foreseen the character of national life and affairs that has come to exist today is not of sufficient relevance to merit further discussion. But what the framers actually did establish in respect to forms and methods of government, even though designed for a situation that no longer exists, is not only highly relevant but of greatest importance to us. This is so because our political past is an essential part of our political present. The things that the American people can do under any set of political institutions depend in large part on what they have already had experience in doing. In government and politics, as in family relations and in making a living, what we do today grows out of what we were doing yesterday.

For this reason it seems to me unwise if not futile to urge the American people to make radical departures from their present political system and venture into relationships and ways of doing things that are completely foreign to their experience. This is not to urge conservatism in governmental reform on the ground that fundamental changes cannot be made to appear attractive and be sold to the people. It is rather to say that a nation that is devoted to democratic government should, to the extent possible, forego revolutionary change in favor of gradual adaptation; that a quick installation of fundamental changes, even when we are caught flat-footed by the deficiencies of existing arrangements, is likely to defeat the very purposes which cause it to be advocated. The people, who must ultimately indicate their satisfaction or discontent with the way things are going, can only do so with confidence if they feel at home among the institutions available to them for exerting influence. If fundamental understandings about the form and methods of government are upset, the people will flounder in their efforts to participate in political life. Only the man who makes politics his principal business can be expected to fully comprehend and consistently bear in mind a set of relationships fundamentally different from what he has been living under; the average citizen, if he does not altogether withdraw from political participation, will lose his sense of sureness and fall more than ever the victim of other men who have no intention of using the authority of government in accordance with his wishes. This is as true of college professors, newspapermen, and others who call themselves the intelligentsia and vote a mixed ticket as it is of the man who mixes plaster for a living and votes his own convictions only in hard times.

If the foregoing paragraphs have accomplished their purpose it will now be clear that a judgment as to the desirability of bringing Congress and President into closer union depends on the answers one gives to each of three questions: (1) Are the problems ahead of us more likely to be solved to our satisfaction if President and Congressmen find it easier in the future than at present to meet in conference and work out agreement? (2) What risks are involved in substituting a closer union of powers for the present emphasis on separation of powers? Does our political system now provide the safeguards against abuse of power that the framers of the Constitution sought to provide by setting one branch up to check the other? And (3) how far may we push in the direction of uniting more closely the executive and legislative branches without doing too great a violence to the firmly held understandings and expectations of the American people?

My own answer to these three questions is in each case favorable to a closer union of President and Congress. The reasons why I reach such a conclusion are the subject of the next several paragraphs. That discussion will be followed by a statement of the changes in relationships at the top of our government that seem to me to be called for at this time. All of this analysis is undertaken, of course, because it has an important bearing on the effectiveness of political direction and control of bureaucracy. The discussion must of necessity be posed in broader terms, however, because the Congress and President that we depend upon to give administrative officials and employees their instructions have other things to do, and the arrangements that we establish to enable them to do one part of their work must contribute to a satisfactory discharge of all their other duties.

It is evident that the American people have come to expect the national government to play a role in affairs which calls for legislative and administrative programs penetrating into nearly every sector of American life. It is imperative, as I see it, that the President take a lead in suggesting and formulating proposals which, when found acceptable by a majority in each house of Congress, will provide the legislative base for these programs of government. It is equally important that Congress participate with the President in directing and controlling the bureaucracy that puts those programs into operation.

There is every reason to believe that we will get effective legislative solutions for our toughest problems only if the President supplies vigorous leadership in legislation. This conclusion seems to me to be dictated by the very nature of our political system. We have advanced so far in democratic theory and practice that the men who are running the national government will go forward on important departures in government only when they have a pretty clear indication of public approval. Congressmen, President, and administrative officials all have ears to the ground that pick up evidences of public demands and public approval and disapproval. But the development of consensus among groups of the public as to what will be acceptable solutions for a problem lags far behind public recognition that the problem exists and public demand that a solution be found. The men and women who are active in politics cannot wait until the people have indicated a choice among alternative solutions; it is their job to point out possible solutions and to help people relate alternatives to their personal interests. Leaders and workers in the party out of power contribute to the public education equally with leaders and workers in the party that has control of the government, for they decry the inactivity and the mistakes of those who are running the government and, when they think it is good politics, tell how they would do it themselves.

This process comes to a head in the political campaign. And the political campaign in the United States centers in the race for the Presidency. Each party stands for what the Presidential candidate says it stands for. It is in the nature of things that, when one of the two candidates is endorsed by the people and inducted into the highest office of the land, he will call upon the Congress that goes into power with him to lay a base in law and appropriations for the program that he has sponsored. Since he was the authoritative spokesman for the program when the people had it under consideration, he is the logical formulator of it now that it has received public endorsement. The nation would not understand what is going on if, after the candidate for president made his promises and supported them by argument, he lapsed into silence when the time came to put his program into effect.

To the force of the reasoning just offered may be added the evidence of history. Our political system has not yet produced any dependable substitute for the President as leader in legislation. Each house of Congress can organize for its own orderly proceedings, but it can rarely if ever provide a leadership that the nation will listen to as the authoritative voice concerning the plans of the party that has been elevated to power. And neither can Congressmen, when the party in control of the government is badly divided on issues of policy, provide a leadership that will show the members of the party where they should stand on the issues that have divided it. The President can do this because of the high prestige of his office and because of the popular understanding that he is the one who can speak authoritatively about the problems that confront his government. If government does not always come to a standstill when the President refuses to play this role of leadership, there is nevertheless always enough confusion and inaction to make the foregoing statements essentially true.

The gains that we expect to derive from vigorous Presidential leadership must be matched against the dangers of too great a concentration of power in the chief executive. No matter how certain we may be that the earlier presumptions in favor of sharp separation between the two branches ought to be abandoned, we must still depend on the legislative branch to keep the President from abusing his authority. The power of the President to tell Congress emphatically what he wants it to do and to put pressure on individual Congressmen to support his program must never be allowed to become power to force Congress to do his bidding or power to ignore Congress altgether and put his purposes into effect by executive decree. We must always depend upon the collective good judgment of Congressmen for the best determination of what the people want. We must always depend upon the integrity, courage, and independence of the individual Congressmen for protection when chance or a weakness in our political system gives us a President who needs to be curbed instead of followed.

The explanation of the power of the representative assembly is as simple as it appears at first glance. Barring an act of God, there is nothing to control the action of men except the action of other men. The representative assembly we have established for our national government is chosen by separate constituencies scattered from one end of the country to the other. The voters in these constituencies can be just as independent as their interests and their courage incline them to be, and the representatives they send to Congress can and do defy the President when conscience or local interest disposes them to do so.

It is a great honor to serve in Congress, and men of ambition and capacity for achievement seek that honor. Most of the constituencies are populous (entire states in the case of Senators) and generally it takes tough men to win seats and hold them. Congressmen are pretty stout politicians in their own right, and there are a lot of them in the two chambers. No President has ever succeeded in lining them all up, even in time of war; and rarely, if ever, does a President have a firm hold on the loyalty of all of them who belong to his own party.

The conclusion to be drawn from what has just been said is that Congress provides, and must continue to provide, the brake on the President and the administrative branch which keeps the policies of the national government within limits that are acceptable to the American people. Any departures that we make in the relations between Congress and President must not be allowed to impair the understanding that Congress is never under a legal or constitutional obligation to make effective the wishes of the President. Our political system must be so regulated that the man who is chosen by the people for the nation's highest office can lay his program before the representative assembly in a way that permits no doubt as to what he wants and can make a dramatic appeal to the people for support in his demand that Congress adopt his program. But the individual Congressmen, even those who are in the President's own party, must at all times feel free to weigh the evidences of public demand which the President can produce against the evidence which comes to them that the people of their respective constituencies will or will not go along with the President. A system of government that is entitled to be called democratic will let the final decision lie in the judgment of the elected representative assembly.

There are many political scientists who refuse to go along with this line of reasoning. During a campaign, they argue, the candidates for President draw the issues and dominate the debate. Only the candidates for President (and Vice President) appeal to the whole nation. Only the successful candidate for President (and Vice President) has been given a popular endorsement by people living in all parts of the country. The promises which the newly elected President made in the campaign are the only promises which the whole nation has asked to have fulfilled. Particular

Senators and Representatives have a mandate to oppose the President. But the Senators play second fiddle and the Representatives are hidden in the back row of the orchestra which the President conducts. And, the argument closes, even those voters who live in the smallest of our congressional districts know less about their Representative in Congress than they know about the man who lives in the White House.

Every one of the foregoing statements can be accepted as true. They do not, however, force us to the conclusion they are intended to support. The supposition that a single official, even though occupying the most exalted position in the land, can be trusted with the dominant political authority overlooks the importance of spreading power among a number of individuals and the importance of dividing the power to select those men among different sectors of the nation. A particular President may at a given moment enjoy a greater measure of popular confidence among the people than any majority that could possibly be created out of the membership of the two houses of Congress. But a nation cannot build its institutions on a presumption that a monopoly of authority will always be wisely exercised. There is no evidence that mankind in any generation and in any country has ever been able to devise an electoral system that will always turn up men of honor who will conscientiously seek to carry out the public will. No matter what devices we provide to enable an official to determine what the people want, we cannot be sure that he will make use of them or conform to what they reveal. We are thrown back, therefore, in our hope for accountability to the people, upon an assembly made up of a large number of men.

The adequacy of the representative assembly for popular government necessarily depends upon the quality of the men elected to it and on the power they can exert in making and enforcing the nation's policies. The quality of the men is determined by the health and vigor of the entire political system of the country. If the people are concerned about public affairs, if the people are reasonably in control of the party organization at the bottom, if the national organization of parties is firmly based on the local party organizations—then it may be taken for granted that the quality of the men who are sent to the national assembly will correspond to the authority which that body possesses in national affairs and the prestige which it commands in the public mind.

It is our problem then to develop arrangements for Presidential leadership and congressional consideration which will give us assurance that vigorous and carefully formulated policies will be submitted to the representative assembly and approved by it unless the individual members are convinced that the people in their respective constituencies will support them in disapproval. It has frequently been argued that we can develop such a balance between Presidential leadership and congressional consideration only by establishing a system which calls for the dissolution of Congress when it refuses to support the President. Only if the President can immediately dismiss Congress and force the issue back to the people in a national election, it is argued, will there be any assurance that the Congressmen will honestly weigh the merits of the President's program against the other pressures to which they are subjected.

This seems to me to indicate far too little confidence in the political system we have developed. It assumes a condition of mind among the American people which makes the whole will of the people something very different from the will of the people living in the several Congressional districts. It assumes a shortness of memory on the part of the American people that will enable them to punish their Congressmen by defeat for re-election only if the issue is forced at once by an act of dissolution. I do not think our experience to date justifies any such pessimism.

Proposals for Presidential power to dissolve Congress also attach too little weight, in my opinion, to the values involved in a widespread familiarity with the way the government works. It took this nation several generations to develop the organization and method of politics that give us such popular control over our government as we now have. Our present political understanding is adjusted to fixed terms of office and a national campaign that we prepare for over a period of years. The political organization and the political activity which give us such popular control as we have over our state and local government are geared into the national political organization and the national campaign. I do not see any ground for certainty that we would readily adjust ourselves to a new set of arrangements based on dissolution and forced elections. And I think it is possible that an unsuccessful effort to make such an adjustment might result in the loss of some of the most essential features of democratic government which we have won.

The parliamentary system developed in Great Britain has many and notably great advantages, and if we are sufficiently impressed by its merits there is no compelling reason why we should not work toward it as an ideal. Some steps in that direction will be harder to take and more difficult to retract than others, for they will require constitutional amendment. But there are undoubtedly many things we can do without constitutional change that will be an improvement upon our present arrangements and give us a better basis for deciding whether we wish to move still farther in a direction that requires the President and Congress to get along together or get out.

It seems to me that the time is now ripe for one innovation in the relationships at the top of our government that promises to give the President a firmer hold on the loyalty of his party in Congress and at the same time give Congress a better opportunity to tell the President in advance what it will and will not tolerate. Some persons may see in the proposed arrangement a first step toward a parliamentary system. It certainly will not erect an obstacle to later moves in that direction. The proposal is made, however, without concern for its relation to the parliamentary style of government; I put it forward because it promises to improve working relationships at the top of our government that seem to me badly in need of improvement.

The time has come, it seems to me, for the creation of a Central Council made up of leaders of the party that has been given the job of running the government. The Central Council would be given responsibility for formulating the program of the government-of-the-day and for directing its execution. The President, as the party's acknowledged leader and the man elected by the people to head the government, would select from among the members of his party who are to serve in Congress a small group that he recognizes to be essential to the success of his Administration. This group, with the President always taking the lead, would enlarge its own membership until it is agreed that the group includes those individuals who, collectively, can command the support of the party as a whole and give the country a program of legislation and administration that promises to return the party to power at the next election. Some members of the group of leaders thus brought together (the Central Council) presumably would occupy official positions in the two houses of Congress; others would head important administrative establishments; some persons who hold no public office in the ordinary sense of the term might be included because they can bring to the Council advice and public support which are essential to the success of the party.

Such an arrangement, it seems to me, would greatly reduce the likelihood that the President by his personal declarations and actions will overtly commit his party to programs which he cannot actually induce his party to put into effect. The leaders of the party in Congress would be given a sure means of finding out what policies they are to try to enact into legislation—surely a great improvement over our present situation in which a smile or a nod of the President often gets blown up into a supposed White House demand for legislation. And such a Council should make it difficult for individual Congressmen, administrative officials, and others to put the whole party out on a limb by making public announcements that they never could have sold to the party leadership as a whole.

If the decisions of such a Central Council are to be converted into legislation, the members of Congress who are included in it must be in a position to find out what the rank and file of the party membership in the two houses will accept. And they must also be in a position to give the Council's decisions the status in legislative proceedings that will afford the greatest possible assurance of passage. The Congressmen who are members of the Council must, therefore, hold most or all the important positions in the two legislative chambers. Committee chairmanships could no longer be filled in accordance with the seniority rule; instead, these and other key positions in the two houses would be filled by nominees of the Central Council. If the majority party in either house of Congress refuses to elect the persons nominated by the Council for key positions, its rejection of the Council's recommendations will prove beyond question that the members of the Council were not wisely selected. If the President cannot recruit for the Council a group of men who are both acceptable to him and influential with the whole party membership in Congress, then the party is too badly divided to give the nation a satisfactory government under any kind of arrangement.

I have no intention of suggesting that the Central Council described above would bring harmony into the relations between the executive and the legislative branches at a time when one party has the President and the other party has control of one or both houses of Congress. A Central Council made up of leaders of the President's party certainly would not create a worse situation than we get under present arrangements when neither party has the power to carry through a program of government. Our present constitutional provisions regulating terms of office, which seem to be the prime contributors to divided or two-party control, ought to be reconsidered regardless of whether we do or do not establish such a Council as I have recommended. The same thing can be said of the malrepresentative character of the Senate and of the awkwardness involved in dividing authority between two chambers of the legislative assembly. The root question which we must face is this: Do we want one political party (the one lately successful at the polls) so fully endowed with authority that it can put over a program of government and cannot escape public censure for failure to do so? If the answer to that question is yes, then no matter what arrangements we set up for achieving that result (Central Council or no Central Council), we will have to decide whether we can tolerate a Senate that gives Nevada a vote equal to that of New York and whether we can afford (on a weighing of advantages and disadvantages) a bicameral legislature which requires the party in power to prove twice for every legislative issue that it is still the majority party. These features of our constitutional system will put obstacles in the path of a Central Council and limit its accomplishments as long as they remain in effect. They must be taken fully into account in making up our minds whether a Central Council, such as I have proposed, would prove in practice to be a substantial step in a direction that we want to go. But we must not conclude that there is no gain to be derived from a Central Council, simply because it cannot overcome all obstacles that we have set up in our Constitution.

A Central Council constructed as I have indicated would contribute to a party program in administration as well as legislation. The present cabinet, consisting of the President and the heads of the principal administrative departments, has rarely proven satisfactory, either as an advisory body for the President or as a coordinating device for administration. Its inadequacy for these purposes undoubtedly is due mainly to the fact that many of the cabinet posts go to men who are not influential members of the President's party (see pp. 285–287). It is important to keep in mind that the problems of administration which are worthy of the President's attention are problems having significant political implications and frequently are problems that can be solved satisfactorily only by enactment of legislation. The President can hardly commit himself to solutions on the advice of cabinet members who are neither in a position to tell him what are the political consequences of a proposal nor in a position to guarantee the legislative support that he needs. The Council that I have proposed could confidently take a firm position on any major issue of administrative policy, because the individuals who are in the best position both to give advice and to guarantee action are present when alternatives are considered and decisions reached.

I have argued at some length in previous chapters that the President can supply only a small part of the direction and control that the administrative branch ought to receive from elected officials. This will be the case even when the President is unusually successful in his choice of high administrative officials. Congressmen must always be well informed about what the administrative branch is doing and feel free to express their pleasure and displeasure with what is going on, for they are a vital part of the organization we have set up to determine what the character and quality of administration shall be. A Central Council that brings into close association the President, leaders of Congress, and the heads of the principal administrative departments should make it virtually impossible for government in operation (government as it is administered) to get very far beyond the boundaries set for it in legislation without the full knowledge of the leaders of Congress.

If, as so many students of government have argued, the country has suffered from meddling in administration by individual Congressmen and small groups of Congressmen pursuing special interests, the proposed Central Council should go far to correct that abuse also. As I have said earlier in this book, I think free-lancing Congressmen (whether working singly or in groups) rarely obstruct orderly administration in respect to matters in which respected leaders of the dominant political party take a personal interest. Congressmen butt into administration largely because they think the administrator is calling his own signals. If the President states what he wants an administrative department or agency to do or not to do, Congressmen who do not have the authority of one or both houses behind them are not likely to coerce the administrator to do otherwise. If the head of the administrative establishment is prominent in the affairs of the party in power he can usually protect himself from unwarranted interference. It is the administrative official who lacks sufficient prestige to protect himself and who cannot get the President (because the President is occupied with other things) to protect him that suffers from interference which obstructs or defeats the objective and impartial administration he has undertaken to provide. A Central Council made up of party leaders should give him a place for appeal, for in it would be men who are not too busy to listen to his troubles and who are competent to say whether the pressures put upon him represent the wishes of the men who have been given the responsibility for running the government.

The proper relationship between Congress and President has been a persistent problem of concern to the American people ever since we drew up the present Constitution of the United States. It has been the subject of a great deal of theoretical writing, much if not most of which is centered on two phrases: separation of powers, and checks and balances. In addition to what we may call a systematic literature, we have produced almost a constant stream of proposals to alter the existing relationships, most of which leave us with great uncertainty as to what the consequences of the recommended reform would be.

Separation of powers, and checks and balances, as matters of political theory or political principles, are discussed in *The Federalist*, most fully in Nos. 47 and 48. Recent careful re-examinations of the subject are by Carl J. Friedrich, *Constitutional Government and Democracy* (Boston, 1946), ch. 10; Herman Finer, *Theory and Practice of Modern Government* (London, 1932), vol. I, ch. 6; Charles Aiken, "The Nature and Exercise of Legislative Power: A Phase of the American Doctrine of the Separation of Powers," in *Georgetown Law Journal*, vol. 26, pp. 606–636 (1938); and Jacob Finkelman, "Separation of Powers: A Study in Administrative Law," in *University of Toronto Law Journal*, vol. 1, pp. 313–342 (1936).

On the specific question of relationships between President and Congress, Woodrow Wilson's *Congressional Government* (Boston, 1885) is now a classic. Of later works that deal generally with this subject, I am most impressed by Wilfred E. Binkley, *President and Congress* (New York, 1947), which traces historically the issues of policy and power that have predominated and the solutions that have been worked out. Harold J. Laski's *The American Presidency* (New York, 1940) seems to me to be verbose, cocksure, and lacking in appreciation of the attitudes and ways of the American people. E. Pendleton Herring has a little book called *Presidential Leadership* (New York, 1940), but it does not evidence the quality of thoughtfulness that has characterized most of Herring's writing. A later article by Herring which deals more incisively with the problem is "Executive-Legislative Responsibilities," in *American Political Science Review*, vol. 38, pp. 1153–1165 (1944). Another recent effort to deal objectively with the general subject of Presidential-congressional relationships is Edward S. Corwin, *The President: Office and Powers* (3rd ed., New York, 1948), ch. 7. Lawrence H. Chamberlain, *The President, Congress and Legislation* (New York, 1946), is a most useful study showing the relative contributions of Congress and President in the enactment of legislation during recent years.

A number of people have tried their minds at devising a new set of arrangements which would bring about a closer coordination of the President and Congress. Some of the proposals involve only a few minor reforms; others involve drastic reorganization. Of the more significant changes that are recommended, two turn up persistently. One type of proposal would admit the President's top executive staff (cabinet members and other department heads, and sometimes the President too) to debate and questioning in one or both houses of Congress. The other type of proposal would establish a council or cabinet headed by the President and including leaders of the two houses of Congress, with or without provision for dissolution of Congress and a general election whenever President and Congress cannot agree on issues that are crucial to the legislative program.

A good illustration of the first type of proposal was authored by Estes Kefauver, member of Congress from Tennessee. Mr. Kefauver introduced a resolution in the House of Representatives (H. R. 237, October 19, 1943) to accomplish a change of this character and fully explained his reasons for doing so in an article, "The Need for Better Executive-Legislative Teamwork in the National Government," in the *American Political Science Review*, vol. 38, pp. 317–325 (1944).

My proposal for a Central Council did not originate with me; it has been put forward in conversation if not in writing by many people for many years. Professor Corwin suggested such an arrangement at pp. 303–306 of the first edition (New York, 1940) of his book on the Presidency cited above. He elaborated on this proposal in an article in *New York Times Magazine* for October 10, 1948, at p. 14; and at pp. 361–364 of the third edition of his book cited above. My argument for such an arrangement was written before Professor Corwin's fuller elaboration of his views appeared, but his later justification of the proposal comes in time to strengthen my conviction that the proposal is a sound one.

Proposals to introduce a system of dissolution and forced elections range from sober and carefully thought out analyses of our present situation and needs to what seem to me to be utterly fantastic recommendations that we turn our backs on all our experience. Of these analyses and arguments, I find most persuasive by far Thomas K. Finletter, *Can Representative Government Do the Job?* (New York, 1945). Mr. Finletter recommends the establishment of a Central Council such as Professor Corwin and I have proposed but, whereas Professor Corwin and I think that we should see how things work out under that arrangement before deciding what major step to take next, Mr. Finletter says he would proceed now "to amend the Constitution so as, first, to give to the President the right to dissolve Congress and the Presidency and to call a general election of all three whenever a deadlock arises between Congress and the Joint Cabinet, and, second, to make the terms of the Senate, House, and Presidency of the same length—say six years from the date of each election . . ." (p. 110).

In striking contrast to the restraint and reasonableness with which Mr. Finletter writes is a recent book by Mr. Henry Hazlitt, *A New Constitution Now* (New York, 1942). Mr. Hazlitt would throw out of the window practically everything the nation has become used to in the structure and procedures of its government. He states that he has tried to recommend arrangements which would be ideal "if we could start with a clean slate—i.e., if we could start without the accumulated prejudices, the timid conservatism, and the powerful vested interests in the existing political system that we actually have." (p. 200). I think that, when the slate is cleaned of those ugly aspects of a nation's character, it is also inescapably cleaned of all other cumulations of knowledge, conviction, and interest; and the population that survived such a purge would not be able to govern itself through any set of institutions. Another recent book which seems to me to deal with an imaginary world and which proposes drastic changes in the relationships between President and Congress is Caleb Perry Patterson, *Presidential Government in the United States: The Unwritten Constitution* (Chapel Hill, N.C., 1947).

Further reading on the subject of Presidential-congressional relations that may be pursued with profit includes: an essay by James Hart entitled, "The President and Federal Administration," in *Essays on Law and Practice of Governmental Administration*, edited by Charles G. Haines and M. E. Dimock (Baltimore, 1935), pp. 47–93; Don K. Price, "The Parliamentary and Presidential Systems," in *Public Administration Review*, vol. 3, pp. 317–334 (1943); an exchange of views by Mr. Price and Mr. Harold J. Laski growing out of the foregoing article, in *Public Administration Review*, vol. 4, pp. 347–363 (1944); and the testimony of Walton H. Hamilton in *Organization of Congress*, Hearings before Joint Committee on the Organization of Congress, 79th Congress, 1st Session, pursuant to H. Con. Res. 18, part 3, pp. 699–719 (Government Printing Office, 1945).

Accounting, *see* General Accounting Office; Monetary transactions; Property, public

Acheson, Dean, 368

Administration, objectivity and impartiality, 48–51, 82–83, 464–465; range of activities, 62–63; relations with public, 64, 150–153, 260–263; subject to law, 31–32; subject to political direction and control, 47–48, 56–57, 63–64

Administrative authority, nature and extent of, 30–32, 86–89, 294–295, 306–315; insulation from political influence, 191–192, 284–285, 311–315, 448–449, 462–466; over external policies, 448–450, 451–466; over internal policies, 449, 450–451

Administrative officials, role as leaders, 32–34, 63–64, 90, 95, 279–288
  See also Assistant Secretary; Bureau chief; Head of establishment; Under Secretary

Administrative organization, characterized and described, 22–23, 220–222, 421–439; roles of Congress, President, and head of establishment in creating, 94–114, 219–232, 470–476; status of bureaus, 97, 105–108, 226–227

Administrative Procedure Act, 35, 152–153, 156–157, 261, 313, 464–466

Administrative working force, loyalty, 20; political activity, 143–145; quality, 26–28, 44–45
  See also Administrative officials; Bureaucracy; Employment

Advice, service, and control, by central agencies, 57, 140, 155, 326, 328–330, 355, 560; within administrative establishments, 479–486, 490–491, 549–550, 552

See also Budget, Bureau of; Civil Service Commission; General Accounting Office

Agriculture, Department of, 87–88, 126, 127, 149, 156, 311, 320, 430, 450, 464; Secretary of, 87–88, 311, 450

Ann Arbor RR. Co. v. U.S., 173 (n.)

Appointment to office, by head of administrative establishment, 284, 287–289, 474–476; by President, 176, 179–183, 187, 190, 281–289, 302–303; senatorial confirmation, 182–197

Appropriations, significance of, 119–120, 234–236; action by Congress, 120–123, 125–130, 237–238, 245–247, 250–251, 343–344; action by congressional committees, 123–124, 132–133, 339; apportionment and allocation, 244–250, 341–342, 344–345, 481–482; interpretation and enforcement of, 129–135, 339–340; part played by President, 236–251, 335 (n.), 336 (n.), 338, 341–344; preparation of estimates, 238–244, 331–338, 341–344, 480–481
  See also, Budget, Bureau of; General Accounting Office

Archivist, 434, 435, 436, 437

Arthur, President Chester A., 263, 385

Assistant Secretary, 283, 287–288, 479

Attorney General, 167 (n.), 173–174

Attorney General's Committee on Administrative Procedure, 36, 151–152, 156–157

Audit, *see* General Accounting Office

Barnard, Chester I., 495

Belknap, William F., 177

Brookings Institution, 35

Brown, Clarence J., 458

Budget, *see* Appropriations; Budget, Bureau of

Budget, Bureau of, 57, 61, 140, 155, 261–262, 329–330, 355–356, 383, 390; and administration, 223–224, 230, 345–348; and apportionment of money, 244–247, 343–344; and communications to Congress, 348–349; and inquiries, 350; and preparation of estimates, 239–244, 331–339, 413–414, 480–481; and preparation of executive orders, 349; competence for its work, 335–338, 343, 344–345, 347; functions summarized, 330–331, 350–352; relation to Congress and President, 330, 351–352, 356, 384, 386

Budget and Accounting Act, 238–239, 244, 246, 261, 328–329, 345, 356, 359

Bureau chief, 283, 431–433, 476, 477–479, 484–485, 486–487, 489, 490, 491, 494

Bureaucracy, defined and characterized, 3–4, 22–23, 558; power of, 9–10, 20–35; size and cost, 6–9; subordinate to political branches, 15–16, 23–25, 47–48

See also Administration; Administrative working force

Cabinet, 326, 327, 337, 342, 574

Cardozo, Benjamin N., 212

Case of the Beautiful Dreamer, 526–527

Case of Irvin N. Bondage, 530–534

Case of the Missing I., 524–526

Case of the Two Men in the Glass House, 527–528

Case of Wofford Orr-White, 534–535

Central Council, 343, 353, 366, 571–576

Checks and balances, 558–564

Civil Aeronautics Administration, 453

Civil Aeronautics Board, 22, 453

Civil Service Commission, 57, 140, 155, 192, 269, 271, 328, 329, 383–384,

473; classification of positions, 396–399, 409–415, 474; discipline, grievances, and separation, 399–400, 406–409; employee ratings, 395–396; examination, appointments, promotions, and transfers, 392–395, 402–406; functions summarized, 389–392; performance criticized, 400–402, 413; relation to Congress, 387–389; relation to President, 264–266, 274–275, 276–278, 385–389

See also Employment

Classification Act of 1923, 396–397

Commerce, Department of, 22, 295, 426, 427 (n.), 430, 434, 456, 457, 462, 463, 464; Secretary of, 295, 427, 463

Commission, *see* Regulatory commissions

Commission on Organization of the Executive Branch of the Government, 107–108, 232, 261, 328, 347–348, 352–353, 428 (n.); on authority to determine organization, 98–99, 101, 102, 106, 112, 227, 229; on authority within organizations, 432–433, 448–449, 485–486, 491–492, 493; on central control of employment, 269–273, 275–277, 401–402, 405–406, 408–409; on control of accounts and expenditures, 148, 368–369, 374–376; on estimates and appropriations, 128–129, 247, 337, 338, 342, 343; on property administration, 145, 146, 258; on regulatory commissions, 456–459, 513–515; on relation of President to administration, 254–257, 303; on senatorial confirmation, 190–191, 283; publications of, 116–117

Comptroller General, 178, 238, 356, 361, 366, 369, 374, 375, 376, 385; publications of, 382

See also General Accounting Office

Congress, 30, 58–60; action and influence of committees, 59, 120–121, 123–125, 165–167, 172, 339; and determining activities of government, 77–91, 213–214, 305–306; and deter-

mining administrative organization, 94–114, 220–222, 224–227; and discipline and removal of officials and employees, 198–201; and fixing standards of administrative conduct, 139–155; and political direction and control, 24–25, 50–51, 56–58, 61, 62–72, 325–329; and review of administrative acts, 158–174, 351; attitude toward appropriation reserves, 245–247; authority over appropriations, 119–135, 339–340; how informed re administration, 64–65, 348–349; relation to President, 61–62, 68–69, 557–578
  See also Congressmen; Removal
Congressional Directory, 35, 439
Congressmen, personal relations with administration, 60, 70, 159–165, 169–170, 172, 572
Control, *see* Advice, service, and control; Direction and control
Corwin, Edward S., 297–298, 321, 577–578
Court of Patent Appeals, 295, 463

Dawes, Charles G., 354
Defense, Secretary of, 431, 434
Delegation of powers, *see* Administrative authority
Democracy and democratic government, defined and explained, 10–12, 16–17; essential institutions, 12–16
Direction and control, 5–6, 9–10, 15, 23–25, 94; by judiciary, 57–58; defined and explained, 38–40; issue in political theory, 66–71; methods of providing, 40–53; political direction and control discussed, 56–72
Director of Budget, 188, 239, 240, 242, 243, 244, 330, 331, 333, 334, 335, 336, 337, 338, 343, 351, 352, 354
Dodd, William E., Jr., 199, 200

Eastman, Joseph B., 456
Efficiency and inefficiency, 7–8, 34–35, 141–142, 262, 521–522, 523–535, 544–546
Efficiency, Bureau of, 264

Elections, 12–13, 14–15, 26–28, 280–281
Employment, legislation regulating federal, 140–145, 263–264, 391, 392; authority of President, 263–270, 273–278, 386–387, 388–389, 391; classification of positions, 396–399, 409–415; discipline, grievances, and separation, 399–400, 406–409; employee ratings, 395–396; recruitment, examination, and appointment, 393–395, 401–406
  See also Civil Service Commission
Executive Office of President, 223–224, 265, 352, 356

Federal Communications Commission, 128, 310, 311, 317, 318, 320, 335, 336 (n.), 403, 410; extent and nature of authority, 305–307, 450, 454, 455, 458, 500–501; organization and internal relationships, 424–427, 430–431, 501–502, 503–512; red tape and its elimination, 524–536, 547–552
Federal Personnel Manual, 155
Federal Register, 35, 439–440
Federal Reserve Board, 310, 311, 445, 446
Federal Trade Commission, 22, 291, 292, 293, 294, 311, 445, 446
Federalist, The, 72
Finletter, Thomas K., 578
Follett, Mary Parker, 495
Forest Service, 499, 500

General Accounting Office, 57, 130, 134–135, 140, 147–148, 149, 178, 238, 259, 260, 329; and accounting systems, 359–360, 363, 366–377; and audits, 361–362, 364–366; and expenditures, 360–361, 362 (n.), 363, 372–381; functions summarized, 356–357; performance criticized, 362–363, 365–366, 374–375; relation to Congress and President, 355–356, 364–366, 367–371, 379–381
  See also Comptroller General
Glass v. Sloop Betsey, 211 (n.)

Goodnow, Frank J., 73
Government Printing Office, 424, 451–452
Grain standards, 87–88, 319–320, 450, 464

Hard, William, 111, 112
Harriman, William A., 427 (n.)
Hart, James, 297–298
Hatch Acts, 27, 144–145
Hazlitt, Henry, 578
Head of establishment, character of office, 104–105, 434–439; and control of organization, 99, 105–107, 225–232, 430–433, 470–475, 476–495; and policies, 89–91, 99, 441–466; and selection of subordinates, 287–289, 475–476; appointment and removal, 180–187, 190–191, 279–281; authority and influence (general), 32–33, 68–70, 282, 422–439; monetary powers, 331–332, 480–483; political role, 63–64, 279–280, 283–288
Herson, Lawrence, 115
Hoch-Smith Resolution, 172 (n.), 173 (n.)
Hoover, Herbert, 110, 111
Hoover Commission, *see* Commission on Organization of Executive Branch of Government
Hopkins, Harry, 337
Housing and Home Finance Agency, 112, 482
Humphrey's Executor v. U.S., 290, 291–293, 295, 303

Ickes, Harold L., 319
Impeachment, *see* Removal from office
Incentives, 537–546
Indian Affairs, Bureau of, 128
Inefficiency, *see* Efficiency and inefficiency
Institute for Government Research, 116
Interior, Department of, 22, 128, 357–358, 426, 430, 499; Secretary of, 310, 319, 427, 433
Internal Revenue, Bureau of, 167, 499–500; Commissioner of, 167

Interstate Commerce Commission, 128, 172, 310, 311, 453, 454, 456, 502

Jackson, Andrew, 280, 319 (n.)
Johnson, Andrew, 177
Joint Chiefs of Staff, 215
Joint Committee on Internal Revenue Taxation, 167
Jones, Jesse, 434
Judiciary, relation to administration, 57–58, 137–139
Justice, Department of, 378

Key, V. O., 174

Lane, Franklin K., 183
Law, equal protection of, 48–51, 82–83
Legislative Counsel (Congress), 327
Legislative Reorganization Act of 1946, 122, 135
Liaison Officer for Personnel Management, 265–266, 327
Library of Congress, Legislative Reference Service, 327
Lovett, Robert Morss, 199, 200

McClellan, John L., 368
McKellar, Senator Kenneth, 162 (n.), 163 (n.), 195, 196, 197
Macmahon, Arthur W., 136, 202
Majority rule, 10 (n.)
Manasco, Carter, 368
Mansfield, Harvey C., 381
Maritime Commission, 434, 453, 502
Merit system, *see* Employment
Miller, Jesse I., 524, 525
Mines, Bureau of, 475
Monetary transactions, regulation of, 147–150, 259–260
    See also Appropriations; Budget, Bureau of; General Accounting Office
Myers v. U.S., 290–291, 295, 303

National Archives, 429, 435, 437, 451, 452
National Defense, Secretary of, 336 (n.)

National Industrial Recovery Act, 211–212
National Military Establishment, 7, 429, 430, 431, 434

Office of Defense Transportation, 456
Office of Price Administration, 104
Overman Act, 108, 109

Patent Office, 295, 450, 463
Patents, Commissioner of, 295, 463
Patronage, 193–195
Pendleton Act, 140–141, 142, 143, 263–264, 266, 385, 392–393
Performance standards, 542–543, 546–547
Perkins, Frances, 396
Personnel Classification Board, 264
Pollock, James K., 271–272, 275, 276, 277, 368, 375–376, 405 (n.), 458
Postmaster General, 42, 290, 291, 294, 430, 493–494
Post Office Department, 7, 149, 295, 429, 430, 494, 499, 541–542, 546
President, relation to administration (general), 89–91, 384–385; and apportionment of money, 244–250, 344–345; and contingent fund, 250–251; and determination of activities of government, 207–217; and political direction and control, 24–25, 47–48, 52, 53, 56–58, 62–71, 252–257, 299–302, 325–329, 421–422; and review of administrative acts, 303–320; appointing power, 176, 179–184, 281–289, 302; capacity for task, 60–61, 170–171, 239–243; concern with public-administrative relations, 260–263; executive power, 30–31, 83; relation to administrative organization, 95–106, 108–114, 115, 173, 219–232, 345–346; relation to appropriations, 234–244, 333–334, 335 (n.), 336 (n.), 337–338, 341–344; relation to Congress, 58, 61–62, 77, 84, 95, 207–209, 557–576, 577–578; relation to employment, 141, 263–278, 385–389, 392; relation to financial administration, 258, 259–260, 366, 367–371; relation to property administration, 258; removal power, 178, 290–297, 303; wartime power, 108–109, 214–217
President's Committee on Administrative Management, 256 (n.), 261, 328, 456; on authority to determine administrative organization, 97–98, 101, 102; on authority within organizations, 107, 449, 484–485, 487, 491, 492, 493, 495; on central control of employment, 267–269, 272–273, 275, 276; on control of accounts and expenditures, 367–368, 374; on regulatory commissions, 313–314, 512–514; on relation of President to administration, 254–256; Report and Studies, 116, 232
Pressures, by individuals and groups, 45–47, 64, 109, 164–165
Property, public, 145–146, 258
Public Printer, 424, 425, 427, 434
Public works, 79–81, 85–86, 144
Public Works Administration, 80

Randolph, Edmund, 209
Reclamation, Bureau of, 499, 500
Red tape, 521, 522–536
   See also Efficiency and inefficiency; Work-review
Regulatory commissions, authority of, 452–459, 512–514; distinctive characteristics, 498–502; internal organization and relationships, 502–512, 514–519; relation to Congress and President, 285, 291–295, 302–303, 308, 309–316; role of chairman and commissioners, 437–438, 500–501, 514–519
Removal from office, authority of Congress, 198–201; by head of administrative establishment, 282; by impeachment, 176–178; by President, 178, 289–297, 302–303
Reorganization, *see* Administrative organization
Reorganization Act of 1932, 110–111; of 1933, 111; of 1945, 111–112, 228; of 1949, 112–114, 227

Reporting, by administrative officials, 29–30
Representative assemblies, relation to democratic government, 30–31, 567; relation to provision of money, 119–120
Roosevelt, Franklin D., 103, 109, 111, 208, 239, 256 (n.), 300, 432, 433, 456
Rosenman, Samuel, 337
Rowe, James H., Jr., 368, 375–376
Rule of law, 50, 137–139, 317
Rural Electrification Administration, 310

Schechter Poultry Corp. v. U.S., 212
Senatorial confirmation, *see* Appointment to office
Separation of powers, 558–564
Service, *see* Advice, service, and control
Smith, Harold D., 354
Soil Conservation Service, 149–150
Staff, *see* Advice, service, and control
State, Department of, 115, 430, 450, 502; Secretary of, 438, 502
Stewart, Senator Tom, 162 (n.), 163 (n.)
Supreme Court, 177, 211, 212, 290–292, 295, 296

Taft, William Howard, 238
Tariff Commission, 172 (n.)

Tennessee Valley Authority, 434, 542
Treasury, Department of, 7, 115, 147, 149, 239, 259, 328, 359, 360, 374, 375, 410, 426, 499; Secretary of, 239, 368–369, 427
Truman, Harry S., 111

Under Secretary, 283, 479, 495
United States Government Manual, 35, 439
United States v. Lovett, 200

Vandenberg, Senator Arthur H., 79 (n.)
Veterans' Administration, 7, 128, 373, 430
Veterans' Preference Act, 406
Vice President, 328

Wallace, Henry A., 427 (n.)
War, Department of, 115
War Manpower Commission, 104, 215
War Production Board, 104, 215
Washington, George, 209
Watson, Goodwin, 199, 200
Weber, Max, 18
Wilmerding, Lucius, Jr., 135–136, 174
Wilson, Woodrow, 73, 108, 109, 183, 300
Work measurement, *see* Performance standards
Work-review, 547–552